understanding movies

LOUIS D. GIANNETTI
Case Western Reserve University

SECOND EDITION

understanding movies

PRENTICE-HALL, INC., *Englewood Cliffs, New Jersey*

Library of Congress Cataloging in Publication Data

GIANNETTI, LOUIS D.
  Understanding movies.

  Includes bibliographies and index.
  1. Moving-pictures. I. Title.
PN1994.G47 1976   791.43   75-31563
ISBN 0-13-936302-5
ISBN 0-13-936294-0 pbk.

© 1976, 1972 by PRENTICE-HALL, INC.,
Englewood Cliffs, New Jersey

Printed in the United States of America

10 9 8 7 6 5 4 3

PRENTICE-HALL INTERNATIONAL, INC., *London*
PRENTICE-HALL OF AUSTRALIA, PTY. LTD., *Sydney*
PRENTICE-HALL OF CANADA, LTD., *Toronto*
PRENTICE-HALL OF INDIA PRIVATE LIMITED, *New Delhi*
PRENTICE-HALL OF JAPAN, INC., *Tokyo*
PRENTICE-HALL OF SOUTHEAST ASIA (PTE.) LTD., *Singapore*

In Memoriam
Lynn R. Jones

Take him and cut him out in little stars,
And he will make the face of heav'n so fine
That all the world will be in love with Night
And pay no worship to the garish Sun.
—WILLIAM SHAKESPEARE

contents

The motion-picture medium has an extraordinary range of expression. It has in common with the plastic arts the fact that it is a visual composition projected on a two-dimensional surface; with dance, that it can deal in the arrangement of movement; with theatre, that it can create a dramatic intensity of events; with music, that it can compose in the rhythms and phrases of time and can be attended by song and instrument; with poetry, that it can juxtapose images; with literature generally, that it can encompass in its sound track the abstractions available only to language.
—MAYA DEREN

preface

As Maya Deren's observation suggests, analyzing a good movie is no easy task. Because film can express so many ideas and emotions simultaneously, the viewer is sometimes overwhelmed by the sheer density of information he's bombarded with. Hopefully, the following chapters can be of use in helping the moviegoer understand some of these complex elements. I entertain no grand pretense at teaching viewers how they "ought" to respond to movies, only in suggesting some of the reasons they respond as they do: there are very few "musts" and "shoulds" in the following pages.

The rewriting of this text has been strongly influenced by the many comments I have received, especially from teachers who have used the book in their classrooms. The following pages reflect, I hope, the high value I place on their advice and criticism. The same principle of organization has been retained from the first edition. Each chapter isolates a basic technique film directors have used in conveying meaning. Naturally, the chapters don't pretend to be exhaustive: they're essentially starting points. They progress from the most specific and narrow aspect of cinema ("Photography") to the most abstract and comprehensive ("Theory"). But the ten chapters aren't tightly interdependent. Indeed, even the subsections within each chapter were written with the idea that they might form relatively discrete teaching units. The first five chapters are oriented towards technique, while the last five tend to have a more theoretical thrust. Those wishing to concentrate only on feature length fiction films might wish to skip the chapters on "Documentary" and "Avant-garde" entirely, though both types of film have influenced the techniques and attitudes of fiction filmmakers considerably. A reader coming from a background of theatre might prefer to begin with Chapter 7, "Drama." Similarly, the reader who is oriented more towards literature might prefer to begin with the subsections on language in Chapter 5, "Sound," and Chapter 7, "Drama," and then go on to Chapter 8, "Literature." All of the chapters are approximately the same length except for "Literature," which is longer because of the inclusion of the two script versions of *North by Northwest*. However, there's no reason why this subsection can't also be read out of sequence—in a unit on editing, for example. Inevitably, such looseness of organization involves a certain amount of overlapping, but I have tried to keep this to a minimum. Technical terms are generally defined when they're first used in the text, but for those who read the chapters out of sequence, the glossary at the end of the book should provide adequate temporary clarifications. Glossed items appear in boldface the first time they're mentioned in each chapter.

A word about the illustrations. Most of the stills used in this book were released by the film's producing studio or distributing company for publicity purposes. Though a photo may closely resemble a shot from a movie, in most cases the publicity stills were actually photographed with a 35 mm still camera during rehearsal periods. In short, some of the illustrations aren't scrupulously accurate, though for the most part they are sufficiently similar to warrant inclusion here. The photos from *Nanook of the North, Persona, Potemkin,* and *The Seven Samurai* are actual frame enlargements taken from 16 mm prints of the movies. The photographic quality of these stills is thus inevitably inferior to that of most publicity photos, but frame enlargements allow for a more precise form of visual quotation. Most publicity photos are in black and white, though the movie itself may be in color. Even in those rare instances in which color photos are available, the complexities of reproduction almost invariably distort the original color, and hence, I have reluctantly decided against including such photos in this revised edition. Furthermore, most publicity stills are cropped to a conventional aspect ratio, even though the film itself might have been photographed in some kind of widescreen process. Whenever possible, I have tried to locate uncropped photos, but faced with the alternatives of using cropped stills or no stills at all, I generally opted for the former. I have, however, avoided the inclusion of vertically cropped photos, for though illustrations of this type are common in even the best books on film, such drastically mutilated visuals couldn't be aesthetically justified in a volume which takes such pains to stress the film artist's visual precision.

A number of people have helped in the writing of this book: James Monaco, Floyd C. Watkins, Gerald Barrett, William Bell, Jack Ellis, Jameson Goldner, and Arthur Knight were all generous with their advice and assistance on the first edition. For assistance on the revised edition, I'm indebted to James Monaco, my toughest and best critic; Jonathan Benair of the Larry Edmunds Bookshop, who helped me tirelessly in locating many of the stills; Ferenc Hrabak worked on the frame enlargements; Ray Kowalski designed the covers: the front cover photo is from *Singin' in the Rain* (M-G-M), directed by Stanley Donen and Gene Kelly; the rear cover is from *The Kid* (rbc films), directed by Charles Chaplin. I'm especially grateful to Ingmar Bergman, who was kind enough to allow me to use the frame enlargements from *Persona,* and Akira Kurosawa, who graciously consented to my using enlargements from *The Seven Samurai.* In addition, I would like to thank Herbert Marshall, who helped me with some of the intellectual background to Eisenstein's aesthetic, and Stefan Czapsky, my great friend-in-need, who seems to be making a career of extricating me from difficult situations.

As usual, I owe a debt of gratitude to my students at Case Western Reserve University, who patiently allowed me to test this material on them beforehand, and in particular, Rick Whitbeck, Evelyn Hayes, Pam Roberts, and Bill Montanary. Finally, I've plundered some of my own previous writings, especially *Godard and Others: Essays in Film Form* (Fairleigh Dickinson University Press, 1975). If some of these ideas now seem altered, one hopes the discrepancy is due not to inconsistency but to my intellectual growth since the Godard volume went to press.

I would also like to acknowledge and thank the following individuals and institutions for their assistance in allowing me to use materials under their copyright: Andrew Sarris, for permission to quote from "The Fall and Rise of the Film Director," in *Interviews with Film Directors* (New York: Avon Books, 1967); Svensk Filmindustri, United Artists, and William Pinzler for the use of the frame enlargements from *Persona;* Jonas Mekas, Stan Brakhage, and the New American Cinema Group for permission to quote from *The Film Culture Reader,* edited by P. Adams Sitney (New York: Praeger Publishers, 1970); Kurosawa Productions, Toho International Co., Ltd., and Audio Brandon Films for permission to use the frame enlargements from *The Seven Samurai;* from *North by Northwest,* The MGM Library of Film Scripts, written by Ernest Lehman. Copyright © 1959 by Loews Incorporated. Reprinted by permission of The Viking Press, Inc.; Albert J. LaValley, *Focus on Hitchcock* © 1972, reprinted by permission of Prentice-Hall, Inc., Englewood Cliffs, New Jersey; Albert Maysles, *Documentary Explorations,* edited by G. Roy Levin (Garden City: Doubleday & Company, Inc., 1971); Vladimir Nilsen, *The Cinema as a Graphic Art* (New York: Hill and Wang); Maya Deren, "Cinematography: The Creative Use of Reality," in *The Visual Arts Today,* edited by Gyorgy Kepes (Middletown, Conn.: Wesleyan University Press, 1960); Marcel Carné, from *The French Cinema,* by Roy Armes (New York: A.S. Barnes & Co., 1966); Richard Dyer MacCann, "Introduction," *Film: A Montage of Theories* (New York: E.P. Dutton & Co., Inc.), copyright © 1966 by Richard Dyer MacCann, reprinted with permission; V.I. Pudovkin, *Film Technique* (London: Vision, 1954); "The Pusher," by Steppenwolf, Columbia Pictures and Dunhill (ABC Records); André Bazin, *What is Cinema?* (Berkeley: University of California Press, 1967); Michelangelo Antonioni, "Two Statements," in *Film Makers on Film Making*, edited by Harry M. Geduld (Bloomington: Indiana University Press, 1969); Alexandre Astruc, from *The New Wave*, edited by Peter Graham (London: Secker & Warburg; New York: Doubleday & Co., 1968); Akira Kurosawa, from *The Movies as Medium*, edited by Lewis Jacobs (New York: Farrar, Straus and Giroux, 1970); Jean Cocteau, from *Jean Cocteau*, by René Gilson (New York: Crown Publishers, Inc., 1969); Pauline Kael, *I Lost It at the Movies* (New York: Bantam Books, 1966); John Grierson, *Grierson on Documentary*, edited by Forsyth Hardy (New York: Harcourt, Brace and Co., 1947).

Cleveland, Ohio   LOUIS D. GIANNETTI

understanding movies

*A photograph is by no means a complete and whole
reflection of reality: the photographic picture
represents only one or another selection from the
sum of physical attributes of the object photographed.*
—VLADIMIR NILSEN

1 photography

REALISM AND EXPRESSIONISM

Even before the turn of the last century, movies began to develop in two
major directions: the **realist** and the **expressionist.** In the mid-1890s in
France, the Lumière brothers delighted audiences with their short movies
dealing with everyday occurrences. Such films as *The Arrival of a Train*
fascinated viewers precisely because they seemed to capture the flux and
spontaneity of events as they were viewed in real life. At about the same
time, Georges Méliès was producing a number of fantasy films which emphasized purely imagined events. Such movies as *A Trip to the Moon* were

1

typical mixtures of whimsical narrative and trick photography. In many respects, the Lumierès can be regarded as the founders of the realistic tradition of cinema, and Méliès of the expressionistic tradition (1-1).

"Realism" and "expressionism" are general rather than absolute terms. When used to suggest a *tendency* towards either polarity, such labels can be helpful, but seldom are they completely definitive. Few films are exclusively expressionistic in style, and fewer yet are completely realistic. There is also an important difference between "realism" and "reality," though this distinction is often forgotten. Realism is a particular *style,* whereas physical reality is the source of all the raw materials of film, both realistic and ex-

(a)

(Museum of Modern Art)

1-1a. *A Trip to the Moon.*
Directed by Georges Méliès.
1-1b. *The Arrival of a Train.*
*Directed by Auguste and
Louis Lumière.*
Many film historians regard the Lumière brothers and Georges Méliès as the godfathers of the two main stylistic trends in movies. The fantasy films of Méliès launched the expressionistic cinema, which emphasizes magical, imagined events or highly distorted and subjective interpretations of the real world. The realistic *"actualités"* of the Lumière brothers, on the other hand, are primitive documentaries, stressing the charm of ordinary events as they can be seen in everyday life.

(b)

1-2. The Godfather.
Directed by Francis Ford Coppola, cinematography by Gordon Willis.
Though all realists manipulate the materials of reality to some extent, these distortions seldom call attention to themselves. Generally such filmmakers prefer an "invisible" style, in which conspicuous or self-conscious technical flourishes are avoided. The primary concern of most realists is that their pictorial reality gives the *illusion* of being a mirror of the actual observable world.

pressionistic. Virtually all movie directors go to the photographable world for their subject matter, but what they do with this material—how they shape and manipulate it—is what determines their stylistic emphasis.

Generally speaking, realistic films attempt to reproduce the surface of concrete reality with a minimum of distortion. In photographing objects and events, the filmmaker tries to suggest the same richness of detail and the copiousness of life itself (1-2). Both realist and expressionist film directors must select (and hence, emphasize) certain details from the chaotic sprawl of reality, but the element of selectivity in realistic films is less obvious. The realist, in short, tries to preserve the *illusion* that the "world" of his film is an unmanipulated and objective mirror of the actual world. The expressionist, on the other hand, makes no such pretense. He deliberately stylizes and distorts his raw materials so that only the very naive would mistake an expressionistic image of an object or event for the real thing. Details are more rigorously selected, and often they're wrenched from their spatial and temporal contexts. The "world" of an expressionistic film, then, is conspicuously different from the material world as it's ordinarily perceived.

Style in a realistic film is generally unobtrusive. The artist tends to be self-effacing before his materials, and is more concerned with *what* is being shown rather than how it's manipulated. The camera is used rather conservatively: it's essentially a recording mechanism that reproduces the surfaces of tangible objects with as little "commentary" as possible. Realistic filmmakers often aim for an "invisible" style, one that doesn't call attention to itself. A high premium is placed on simplicity, spontaneity, and directness. This is not to suggest that these movies lack artistry, however, for at its best, the realistic cinema specializes in an art that conceals art. In the hands of a master of this style—a Jean Renoir or a Vittorio De Sica—realism can be profoundly subtle.

Expressionistic movies are stylistically flamboyant. The director is concerned with expressing his unabashedly subjective and personal "vision" of reality (1-3). Expressionists are often concerned with inner spiritual and psychological truths, which they feel can be conveyed best by distorting the external surface of the material world. The camera is used as a tool to comment on the subject matter, as a method of emphasizing its *essential* rather than its physical nature. There's a high degree of manipulation, of "interference" with nature, in expressionistic movies, but it's precisely this "deformed" reality that can be so artistically striking in such films.

Realistic films tend to encourage audience participation. The director presents his materials so that considerable leeway is allowed in interpretation. Characters and events are often deliberately ambiguous—as they are in life—and the viewer is sometimes given only the barest hints concerning the significance of certain scenes and sequences. Expressionistic films tend to be more explicit in these matters. The viewer is generally more passive, for the director provides him with most of the necessary clarifications and value judgments.

Most realists would claim that their major concern is with content rather than form or technique. The subject matter is always supreme, and anything that distracts from the content is viewed with suspicion. Indeed, in its most extreme form, the realistic cinema tends towards documentary, with its emphasis upon photographing actual people and events. The expressionistic cinema, on the other hand, tends to emphasize form and technique. The most extreme example of expressionism in film is found in the **avant-garde** cinema. Some of these movies are totally abstract so that pure forms (that is, non-representational colors, lines, and shapes) constitute the only content.

But these are generalizations only, and in the eclectic world of the cinema, there are many exceptions and hybrids. For example, a good many documentaries are expressionistic stylistically, and there are some instances of realistic avant-garde films. Most fiction movies fall somewhere between these two extremes. Furthermore, some directors have worked in both styles. For instance, the early works of Federico Fellini—movies like *I Vitelloni, La Strada,* and *The Nights of Cabiria*—all fall within the realistic end of the stylistic spectrum. *La Dolce Vita* has elements of both styles. *8½* and most of Fellini's subsequent movies are predominantly expressionistic in emphasis.

1-3. The Scarlet Empress.
Directed by Josef von Sternberg, cinematography by Bert Glennon and von Sternberg.
Expressionist film directors are seldom concerned with literal truth. Just as a poet often distorts reality in order to capture the underlying essence of certain experiences, so does the expressionist filmmaker distort the external world in order to convey **symbolic** rather than literal truths. Expressionists are primarily concerned with presenting us with a subjective, personal "vision" of reality, one that has no counterpart in the actual world. When asked why he preferred to work with studio sets rather than authentic historical locations, von Sternberg replied simply, "Because I am a poet." This film deals with the life of Catherine the Great, but the costumes, décor, and even the statuary (all closely supervised by von Sternberg) owe little to what literally existed in 18th century Russia.

Even the terms "form" and "content" aren't so distinct and clear-cut as they may sometimes seem. Indeed, in many respects, the terms are synonymous, though to be sure, they can be useful in suggesting a degree of emphasis. The form of a shot—the way in which a subject is photographed —is its true content, not necessarily what the subject matter is perceived to be in reality. The communications theorist Marshall McLuhan has pointed out that the content of one medium is actually another medium. For example, a photograph (visual image) depicting a man eating an apple (taste) involves two different mediums: each medium communicates information— "content"—in a different way. A verbal description of the photograph of the man eating an apple would involve yet another medium (language), which communicates information in yet another manner. In each case, our information is determined by the medium, though superficially all three have the same "content."

1-4. *Intolerance*.
Directed by D. W. Griffith, cinematography by G. W. "Billy" Bitzer.
Extreme long shots are almost always exterior shots, showing a vast portion of the locale. They are especially common in **epic** films, in which the dramatic values are sweeping and larger than life. Griffith's monumental exterior set for the Babylonian sequence of this film was the largest and most costly ever constructed in its time.

In literature, the naive separation of form and content is sometimes called "the heresy of paraphrase." For example, the "content" of *Hamlet* can be found in a college outline, yet no one would seriously suggest that the play and the outline are the same "except in form." The differences in other mediums are even more obvious. What is the "content" of a taste? Or a sound? A mathematical formula? All of these communicate information, each in a different way. To paraphrase any of this information—in words, for example—is inevitably to change the true content as well as the form. An argument could be made that the "forms" of *Oedipus Rex* and many hack mystery plays are the same; similarly, the "content" of a Raphael madonna and a cheap holy card can also be said to be the same. In literature and painting—which have older critical traditions than cinema—only the most insensitive critics would make such observations without going on to subtler (and more basic) issues. Unfortunately, most film criticism is almost exclusively devoted to discussions of "content" in this naive sense.

One reason why the overwhelming bulk of movie criticism is misleading is that most critics never get beyond the gross subject matter of a film, which they postulate as its content. Such criticism might just as easily be about a novel or a play as a movie. Shallow commentaries of this sort don't tell us specifically why and how a film succeeds or fails—they merely give us a general notion of what a film is "about." Herman G. Weinberg, in his excellent study, *Josef von Sternberg,* puts it succinctly:

> The way a story is told is part of that story. You can tell the same story badly or well; you can also tell it well enough or magnificently. It depends on who is telling the story. That is why form is, in the last analysis, . . . of more decisive importance than content, though under ideal conditions the latter dictates the style of the former.

No intelligent critic of literature or painting would value a work of art because of the "thematic importance" of its subject matter. To do so would put one in the dubious position of preferring a post-office mural to a portrait of an ancient hag by Rembrandt, or of preferring a mediocre epic novel like *Gone With the Wind* to a "domestic love story" like *Pride and Prejudice.* As obvious as this may seem, in the area of film criticism, such superficial judgments are being made all the time—by otherwise cultivated and intelligent people. A film by Alfred Hitchcock is dismissed as a "mere thriller," despite the fact that *Hamlet*—on this level of criticism—could be similarly dismissed. A discussion of Hitchcock's *Psycho* without an appreciation of its subtle and complex images is just as irresponsible as a discussion of *King Lear* without an appreciation of its language. On the other hand, critics often praise a didactic potboiler like Stanley Kramer's *Ship of Fools* because of its "important" theme, yet in terms of form it's a dull and uninspired movie.

"Form" and "content" are best used as relative terms, useful for temporarily isolating specific aspects of art for the purposes of closer examination. Such an unnatural isolation is artificial, of course, yet frequently this technique yields more detailed insights into the work of art as a whole. By beginning with an understanding of the basic components of the film medium, its various "languages," as it were, we will eventually understand how form and content in the cinema, as in the other arts, are ultimately the same.

THE SHOTS AND ANGLES

The different cinematic **shots** are defined by the amount of subject matter that's included within the **frame** of the screen. In actual practice though, shot designations vary considerably: a **"medium shot"** for one director might be considered a **"close-up"** for another. Furthermore, the longer the shot, the less precise are the designations. In general, however, shots tend to be determined on the basis of how much of the human figure is in view. The shot is not necessarily defined by the distance between the camera and the object photographed, for in some instances, certain **lenses** distort distances. For example, a **telephoto lens** can produce a close-up on the screen, yet the camera itself in such shots is generally quite distant from the subject matter.

The more area a shot covers, the less detailed it is. The less area it covers, the more disorienting is the image in terms of its wider context.

(a)

1-5a. *The Gold Rush.*
Directed by Charles Chaplin.
1-5b. *Little Caesar.*
Directed by Mervyn LeRoy.
The long shot is one of the vaguest of cinematic terms. The full shot (a) represents its closest range. At its most distant ranges, the long shot can include as much space as a large stage in the legitimate theatre (b). Long shots tend to be preferred ranges of most realist directors, for they preserve the important interrelationships between characters and their physical context.

(b)

Realist directors generally wish to preserve the spatial continuity of a scene—our sense of where details fit in a larger given space—and hence, such filmmakers tend to favor the longer shots, for they preserve the relationships between people and their surroundings. Expressionist directors, on the other hand, tend to favor the closer shots, which fragment real space into a series of detailed pieces of the whole. In actual practice, however, the choice of shots is generally a matter of emphasis rather than exclusion, for few directors can totally dispense with either long or close shots without confusing the audience. Though there are actually many different kinds of shots in the cinema, most of them are subsumed under seven basic categories: the **extreme long shot**, the **long shot**, the **full shot**, the medium shot, the close-up, the **extreme close-up**, and the **deep-focus shot**.

The extreme long shot is taken from a great distance, sometimes as far as a quarter of a mile away: it's almost always an exterior shot, and shows much of the locale (1-4). Extreme long shots also serve as spatial frames of reference for the closer shots, and for this reason are sometimes called "establishing shots." If people are included in extreme long shots they usually appear as mere specks on the screen. The most effective use of these shots is often found in epic films, where locale plays an important role: westerns, war films, samurai films, and historical movies, for example. Not surprisingly, the greatest masters of the extreme long shot are those directors associated with the epic genres: D. W. Griffith, Sergei Eisenstein, John Ford, and Akira Kurosawa.

The long shot is perhaps the most complex in the cinema, and the term itself is also one of the most imprecise (1-5). In general, however, long shot ranges correspond approximately to the distances between the audience and the stage in the legitimate theatre. The closest range within this category is the full shot, which just barely includes the human body in full. Charles Chaplin favored the full shot because it was best suited to the art of pantomime, yet was close enough to capture at least gross facial expressions. Long shots are favored by most realist directors, since they include a considerable portion of the locale as well as the human body in full. These ranges are ideally suited to those filmmakers who communicate their ideas primarily through their **mise-en-scène**, or the arrangement of objects and figures in a unified space. Expressionist directors tend to favor photographing these objects and figures in separate shots, thus destroying the unity of actual space.

The medium shot contains a figure from the knees or waist up. A functional shot, it's useful for shooting exposition scenes, for transitions between close-ups and long shots, and for **re-establishing** after a long or close shot. There are several variations of the medium shot. The **two-shot** contains two figures, from the waist up (1-6). The **three-shot** contains three figures; beyond three, the shot tends to become a long shot, unless the other figures are in the background. The **over-the-shoulder shot** usually contains two figures, one with his back to the camera, partly seen, the other facing the camera. This shot is useful as a variation of the standard two-shot, and as a way of emphasizing one person's dominance over another.

The close-up shows very little if any locale, and concentrates on a relatively small object—the human face, for example. Since the close-up magnifies the size of an object hundreds of times, it tends to elevate the importance of things, often suggesting a symbolic significance (1-7). In Hitchcock's *Notorious,* for example, the heroine suddenly realizes that she's gradually being poisoned by her evening coffee. Suddenly, a close shot of the coffee cup appears on the screen—a huge distortion of its real size. The image of the delicate demitasse captures not only the heroine's sudden realization, but also the veneer of elegance that protects her corrupt poisoners from being detected. In short, the image becomes a symbol for the particular life style of "respectable" Nazis at the end of World War II. The extreme close-up is a variation of this shot. Thus, instead of a face, the extreme close-up might show only a person's eyes, for example, or his mouth.

The deep-focus shot is usually a variation of the long shot, consisting of a number of focal distances, and photographed in depth. This technique captures objects at close, medium, and long ranges simultaneously (1-8). The shot is especially useful for preserving the unity of space. The objects in a deep-focus shot are carefully arranged in a succession of planes. By using this layering technique, the director can guide the viewer's eye from one distance to another and another. Generally, the eye travels from a

(United Artists)

1-6. Bananas.
Directed by Woody Allen.
The medium shot is often used in dialogue sequences and those scenes in which physical movement is restricted—voluntarily or otherwise. In this shot, a "friendly F.B.I. agent" occupies the same shower stall as the perpetually bemused Woody Allen, who adjusts himself to life's little annoyances with resigned stoicism.

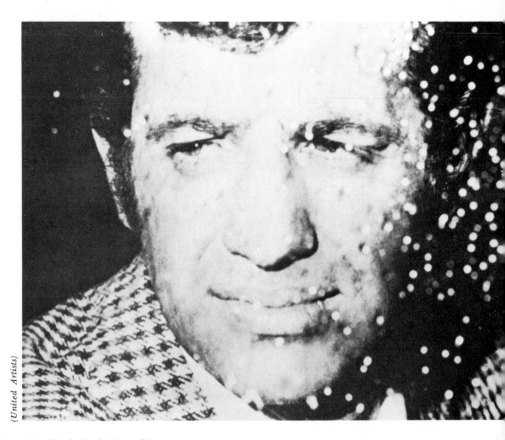

(United Artists)

1-7. Mississippi Mermaid
Directed by François Truffaut, cinematography by Denys Clerval.
Because the close-up wrenches objects from their spatial contexts and expands them
many times on the huge screen, this type of shot can be used to suggest a symbolic
expansion: in a sense, the close-up represents a "big" moment within the dramatic
context. Often close-ups are reserved for moments of high emotional intensity. When
this shot is overused in a movie, the viewer instinctively feels that the subject matter
is being milked dry, that the emotional effects are dramatically unearned. Realists are
particularly sparing in their use of close-ups.

close range to a medium to a long. A famous scene from Orson Welles'
Citizen Kane employs the deep-focus shot effectively. Kane's wife has un-
successfully attempted suicide, and is resting in bed. At the bottom of the
screen, in close-up range, stands the bottle of poison; in the middle of the
screen, in medium range, lies Mrs. Kane in bed; in the upper portion of
the screen, in long range, Kane enters through a door. The shot also suggests
a kind of cause-effect relationship: 1) the poison was taken by 2) Mrs. Kane
because of 3) Kane's inhumanity.

The angle from which an object is photographed can often serve as an

1-8. The Grapes of Wrath.
Directed by John Ford, cinematography by Gregg Toland.
The deep-focus shot can include objects from close-up range to infinity with acceptable visual clarity. Deep-focus shots tend to use a layered effect in the mise-en-scène: the eye tends to travel in succession from the foreground ranges to the mid-ground to the background. Toland was particularly famous for his deep-focus cinematography in the late thirties and early forties. *Citizen Kane* is perhaps the most dazzling example of his use of this technique, but his photography in the works of Ford and Wyler, while less flamboyant, is often equally brilliant.

authorial "commentary" on the subject matter (1-9). In a sense, angles can be likened to a writer's use of adjectives: they often reflect his attitude towards his subject. If the angle is slight, it can serve as a kind of subtle emotional coloring. If the angle is extreme, it can represent the major meaning of an image. The form-content division is particularly meaningless in this context. A picture of a man photographed from a high angle actually suggests opposite meanings from an image of the very same man photographed from a low angle. The subject matter is absolutely identical in each image, yet in terms of the information we derive from the pictures, it's clear that the form *is* the content, and the content the form.

Realist directors tend to avoid extreme angles. Most of their scenes are photographed from eye level, roughly five to six feet off the ground—approximately the height of an actual observer. Usually, these directors attempt to capture the clearest view of an object. Eye-level shots are seldom intrinsically dramatic, since they tend to be the norm. Virtually all directors use some eye-level shots, particularly in routine expository scenes. Even realist directors use a variety of different angles, however, especially in **point-of-view shots**—when the camera records what (and how) a character sees. Thus, an image of a man looking from a ladder might be followed by a high-angle point-of-view shot, showing both the subject and the manner of the man's observation.

Expressionist directors are not always concerned with the clearest image of an object, but with the image that best captures an object's essence. Extreme angles almost always involve distortions. Yet many directors feel that by distorting the surface realism of an object, a greater truth is achieved —an inner psychological reality. Both realist and expressionist directors know that the viewer tends to identify with the camera's lens. The realist wishes to make the audience forget that there's a camera at all; the expressionist is constantly calling attention to it. The realist's use of angles tends to be guided by physical probability; the expressionist's by psychological and dramatic appropriateness.

There are five basic angles in the cinema: the **bird's-eye view**, the high angle, the eye-level shot, the low angle, and the **oblique angle.** As in the case of shot designations, there are many intermediate kinds of angles (1-10). For example, there can be a considerable difference between a low and extreme low angle shot, though usually, of course, such differences tend to be matters of degree. Generally speaking, the more extreme the angle, the more distracting and conspicuous it is in terms of the subject matter being photographed. Indeed, in many cases, the "commentary" of the angle is more significant than the object itself.

The bird's-eye view is perhaps the most disorienting angle of all, for it involves photographing a scene from directly overhead (1-11). Since we seldom view events from this perspective, the subject matter of such shots might initially seem unrecognizable, and for this reason, directors tend to avoid this type of camera **set-up.** But in certain contexts, this angle can be highly expressive. In effect, bird's-eye shots permit us to hover above a scene like all-powerful Gods. Indeed, the angle strongly implies destiny and fatality. The people photographed seem ant-like and insignificant, completely in our control. Directors whose themes revolve around the idea of fate—Hitchcock and Fritz Lang, for example—tend to favor high angles, and occasionally these filmmakers will use a bird's-eye shot at the moment of Destiny's greatest impact—as in the famous stairs murder in Hitchcock's *Psycho,* for instance.

Ordinary high angle shots are not so extreme, and hence not quite so disorienting (1-12). The camera is placed on a crane, or some natural high promontory, but the sense of audience omnipotence is not so overwhelming. Somewhat akin to the **omniscient point of view** in literature, high angles give a viewer a sense of a general overview, but not necessarily one implying destiny or fate. In terms of the object photographed, high angles reduce the height of objects. Movement is slowed down: this angle tends to be ineffective for conveying a sense of speed, useful for suggesting tediousness. The importance of setting or environment is increased: the locale often seems to swallow people. John Ford's high angle long shots are particularly

(a)

(b)

(c)

1-9a, b, c.
Photos by Barry Perlus.
The angle from which a subject is photographed determines much of its meaning. Here the same subject is captured from eye-level (a), and from high (b) and low (c) angles. Although the subject matter is the same, the shots suggest different meanings. Eye-level shots put us on an equal footing with the subject, implying a sense of parity. High angles tend to reduce a subject to insignificance, suggesting vulnerability; we are superior to the subject. Low angles, on the other hand, increase a subject's importance, creating a sense of dominance over the viewer.

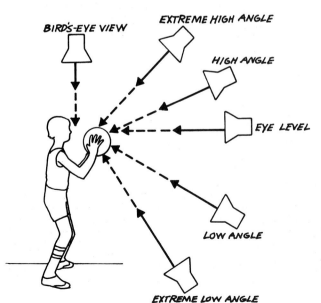

1-10.
The Angles
The designation of each angle is determined on the basis of where the camera is placed in relationship to the subject photographed.

1-11. *Psycho.*
Directed by Alfred Hitchcock.
When the subject is photographed from directly overhead, the angle is disorienting, which perhaps explains its infrequent use. "Bird's-eye shots" are sometimes employed in films dealing with the theme of fate and destiny, for this angle provides us with a kind of Godlike omniscience, in which the characters below can seem insignificant.

effective in conveying this sensation. High angles reduce the importance of a subject. A man seems harmless and insignificant photographed from above.

There are some directors who avoid angles because they are too "presumptuous," too loaded morally. In the subtle works of the Japanese director Yasujiro Ozu, the camera is usually placed four feet from the floor —exactly where an actual observer would view the events if he were seated Japanese style. Ozu always treats his characters as equals, and he discourages us from viewing them either condescendingly or sentimentally. For the most part, they are ordinary people, neither very virtuous nor very corrupt, but Ozu lets them reveal *themselves.* He dislikes the value judgments that are implied through the use of angles. His camera is neutral, dispassionate, sometimes even clinical. It permits viewers to make up their *own* minds about what kind of people are being presented.

Low angles have the opposite effect of high: they increase height, and thus are useful for suggesting verticality (1-13). More practically, they can increase a short actor's height. Motion is speeded up, and in scenes of violence especially, low angles can capture a sense of confusion. The battle scenes of Kurosawa's *Seven Samurai* are magnificently effective, in part because many of them are photographed from low positions. Environment is usually minimized in low angle, and often the sky or a ceiling is the only background. There are exceptions, however. In *Citizen Kane,* the overhead

(a)

(b)

1-12a. *Bonnie and Clyde*.
Directed by Arthur Penn.
1-12b. *The Burglers*.
Directed by Henri Verneuil.
The difference between a high angle shot (a) and an extreme high angle (b) is generally a matter of degree. High angles tend to suggest powerlessness, vulnerability, and in some cases, inferiority. The higher the angle, the more it tends to imply fatality and entrapment.

photography   **17**

(a)

(b)

1-13a. Cheyenne Autumn.
Directed by John Ford.
1-13b. The Stone Killer.
Directed by Michael Winner.
Low angle shots (a) can make a character seem heroic and larger than life. When an extreme low angle (b) is combined with a perspective-distorting wide angle lens, characters can seem threatening, for they loom above us like towering giants.

ceiling is a constant reminder of how Kane is confined by his own possessions, especially his mansion. Lighting for interior low angle shots can't be from above (its usual position), since the lights would appear in the picture (1-14). In this case, they are placed in front, on the sides, or behind. Psychologically, low angles heighten the importance of a subject. The figure looms threateningly over the spectator, who is made to feel insecure and dominated. A man photographed from below inspires fear, awe, and respect. For this reason, low angles are often used in propaganda films, or scenes depicting heroism.

An oblique angle involves a lateral tilt of the camera. When the image is projected, the horizon appears tilted (1-15). A man photographed at an oblique angle will look as though he's about to fall to one side. Psycho-

(M-G-M)

(a)

(RKO)

(b)

1-14a. *A studio set with lighting set-ups at Metro-Goldwyn-Mayer Studios.*
1-14b. *Citizen Kane.*
Directed by Orson Welles.
The lights for most movies are hung primarily from above (a). When extreme low angle shots are used in interior settings, however (b), the cinematographer must light the scene from other positions, for the ceiling will be included within the shot.

(Continental 16)

1-15. *The Third Man.*
Directed by Carol Reed.
Sometimes called a "tilt shot," the oblique angle is taken with the camera tilted to one side. The stable horizontal and vertical lines of a set are thus converted into tense diagonals, which can produce a sense of irresolution, imbalance, or impending disaster.

logically, oblique angles suggest tension, transition, and impending movement: the natural horizontals and verticals are forced into diagonals. Oblique angles aren't often used, for they can disorient a viewer. In scenes of violence and confusion, however, they can be effective in capturing precisely this sense of violent disorientation. More prosaically, oblique angles are sometimes used for point-of-view shots—to suggest the imbalance of a drunk, for example.

LIGHTING AND COLOR

Generally speaking, the cinematographer is responsible for arranging and controlling the lighting in a film, usually at the specific or general instructions of the director. The illumination of most movies is seldom a casual matter, for lights can be used with pinpoint accuracy. Through the use of spotlights, which are highly selective in their focus and intensity, a director can guide the viewer's eyes to any area of the photographed image. But motion picture lighting is seldom static, and with even the slightest movement of the camera or the subject photographed, the lighting shifts. Movies take so long to complete in part because of the enormous complexities involved in lighting each new shot. The cinematographer must make allowances for every movement within a continuous **take.** Each different color, shape, and texture reflects or absorbs differing amounts of light. If an image is photographed in deep focus, an even greater complication is in-

1-16. *The Nights of Cabiria.*

Directed by Federico Fellini, cinematography by Otello Martelli.

Light-dark symbolism is almost inevitable in a film shot in black and white. As Fellini's title suggests, darkness is associated with sexuality, romance, mystery, and fantasy in this movie. Light tends to be associated with clarity, truth, and reality. In this scene, Fellini's symbolism is more complex. The central character (Giulietta Masina, pictured) is an absurdly comical prostitute, who fancies herself as tough, worldly, and self-sufficient. In a seedy side-street theatre she is hypnotized by a magician, and under the glare of a spotlight, she re-enacts her innocent, tender girlhood. The symbolism of the light suggests that what we are seeing is a true picture of Cabiria's essential nature. But this is an "artificial" light, one associated with the magician (a common symbol of the artist figure in Fellini's works), and hence the light suggests an underlying *spiritual* truth rather than a literal one. In Fellini's films, the Italian Catholic Church is often associated with show business. Conversely, show business—even in its tackiest, most degraded form—is often associated with spirituality and salvation. In this movie, it is the artist-magician who reveals Cabiria's poetic spirituality, not the priests at a religious shrine, who seem more concerned with showmanship and theatricality.

volved, for the lighting must also be in depth. Gregg Toland, the cinematographer who popularized many in-depth techniques, was largely responsible for the expressive layered lighting effects in *Citizen Kane*. Unlike the still photographer, then, the cinematographer must account for shifting temporal and spatial variables in his lighting. Furthermore, the filmmaker doesn't have at his disposal most of the darkroom techniques of a still photographer: variable paper, dodging, airbrushing, choice of development, enlarger filters, etc. In a color film, the subtle effects of lights and darks are often obscured, for color tends to obliterate shadings and flatten images. Color is also a distracting element, and often an object that dominates a black-and-white image will recede in importance when photographed in color.

There are a number of different styles of lighting. Usually the style is geared closely to the theme and mood of the film. Comedies and musicals, for example, tend to be lit in a **"high key,"** with bright, even illumination, and few conspicuous shadows. Tragedies and melodramas are often lit in **"high contrast,"** with harsh shafts of lights and dramatic streaks of blackness. Mysteries and thrillers are generally **"low key,"** with diffused shadows and atmospheric pools of light. Films shot in studios are generally more stylized and theatrical, whereas location photography tends to use **available lighting,** hence a more natural style of lighting.

Lights and darks have had symbolic connotations since the dawn of man. The Bible is filled with light-dark symbolism; Rembrandt and Caravaggio used light-dark contrasts for psychological purposes as well. In general, artists have used darkness to suggest fear, evil, the unknown, and misery. Light usually suggests security, virtue, truth, and joy. Some movies are thematically organized around lighting motifs. Fellini's *Nights of Cabiria,* for example, uses night to suggest romance, mystery, and self-deception. The bright glare of day suggests harsh reality, disillusionment, clarity (1-16). The central character, a rather impractically romantic prostitute, vacillates between the two extremes, ending finally in her natural milieu—the evening.

Because of this time-honored tradition of symbolism, some directors— especially "perverse" directors like Hitchcock—will deliberately reverse light-dark expectations, to puncture our smug sense of security. By using many subjective techniques—devices forcing the viewer to identify strongly with the protagonist—Hitchcock strips away our complacencies, often in the most terrifying manner. In *North by Northwest,* for example, the hero is stranded in Chicago, where sinister, lurking shadows seem to threaten him at every turn—yet nothing happens. We laugh at ourselves for our paranoia. Later, the protagonist finds himself in an isolated rural area. There is total visibility for miles, for the sun glows radiantly over the vast flat terrain. Nothing could seem more secure or more boring—yet suddenly a shocking outrage is committed against the hero in broad daylight. In Hitchcock's universe, as in Kafka's, paranoia turns out to be the most appropriate attitude to life.

Lighting can be used realistically or expressionistically. The realist tends to favor available lighting, at least in exterior shots (1-17). Even out of doors, however, most directors use some lamps and reflectors, either to augment the natural light, or, on bright days, to soften the harsh contrasts

(a)

(b)

1-17a. The Garden of the Finzi-Continis.
Directed by Vittorio De Sica,
cinematography by Ennio Guarnieri.
1-17b. The Last Picture Show.
Directed by Peter Bogdanovich,
cinematography by Robert Surtees.
Realist filmmakers tend to avoid light-dark symbolism unless it's contextually probable. That is, the symbolism is generally integrated within the realistic texture of the dramatic situation. A face half plunged in darkness can symbolize self-division (a), but on a literal level, the lighting can be justified by showing an actual source of illumination at one side of the set. In *The Last Picture Show,* a character (Ben Johnson) speaks of a love affair he had as a younger man. As he recalls the extraordinary joy his loved one inspired, the sun comes out from behind a cloud (b), showering the landscape with a symbolic radiance that's totally appropriate to the dramatic context. Since the sudden outburst of brightness occurs within an uninterrupted take, we accept the phenomenon as a happy coincidence, though in fact, Bogdanovich probably set up the shot to allow for the sun's appearance at just the right dramatic moment in the dialogue.

produced by the sun. With the aid of special lenses and more light-sensitive film **stocks,** some directors have managed to dispense with artificial lighting completely. Most of the movies of Jean-Luc Godard, for example, are shot completely with available lighting. Available lighting tends to produce a "documentary look" in the film image, a hard-edged quality and an absence of smooth modeling. Boris Kaufman's cinematography in *On the Waterfront* and *The Pawnbroker* is deliberately antiromantic in its harshness, largely because of his reliance on available light. Not all exterior shooting is necessarily hard-edged, however. Through the use of special lenses and additional lighting, John Ford and Akira Kurosawa have both been able to evoke a nostalgic romantic past while still using actual locations. For interior shots, realists tend to prefer images with an obvious light source—a window, for example, or a lamp—or they often use a diffused kind of lighting with no artificial, harsh contrasts. In short, the realist director

(a)

(b)

(c)

1-18a, b, c, d. (top to bottom)
Photos by Barry Perlus.
The lighting of a subject can be of greater importance than the subject itself. Here are several examples of how form (light) can determine content. Lighting in most movies is from above and in front (a). Lighting from below generally makes the subject appear sinister (b). Lighting from directly above can suggest spirituality (c). When the subject blocks out the source of light, viewers can be made to feel insecure and trapped, for we tend to associate light with safety (d).

(d)

doesn't use "theatrical" lighting unless the source of the light is contextually probable.

The expressionist director uses light less literally. He's guided by its symbolic implications, and will often stress these qualities by deliberately distorting natural light patterns. A face lighted from below, for example, almost always appears sinister, even if the actor assumes a totally neutral expression. Similarly, anything placed in front of a major light source tends to assume frightening implications, for the audience associates light with security, and any blockage of light is therefore a threat to this sense of safety (1-18). On the other hand, in some contexts, especially in exterior shots, a silhouette effect can be soft and romantic, perhaps because the open space acts as a counter to the sense of entrapment suggested by a confined interior.

When a face is obviously lighted from above, a certain angelic effect is the result, perhaps because such lighting implies God's grace descending. "Spiritual" lighting of this type tends to border on the cliché, however, and only the best lighting technicians—Raoul Coutard, Godard's favorite cinematographer, for example—have handled this technique with subtlety. When a face is lighted only from the front, its sculptural contours tend to be flattened out. Such flat images are seldom found in professionally photographed films, for they tend to be associated with amateur movie making. Back lighting, which is a kind of semi-silhouetting, is soft and ethereal, producing a feminine, romantic effect. It's especially evocative when used to highlight a woman's hair. In the thirties in Hollywood, this technique became nearly universal, having been popularized by the films of Ernst Lubitsch and Josef von Sternberg.

Through the use of spotlights, an image can be composed of violent contrasts of lights and darks (1-19). The surface of such images seems disfigured, torn up. The expressionist director uses such severe contrasts for psychological and thematic purposes. In *Citizen Kane,* the mixture of decency and corruption in Kane is suggested often by the harshly contrasting lights: sometimes his face seems split in half, with one side brightly illuminated, the other plunged into darkness. In Ingmar Bergman's *Wild Strawberries,* the joy and innocence of childhood is suggested by brightly lit sets and light costumes; the enervating joylessness of adulthood is conveyed by somberly lit sets and dark costumes. One of D. W. Griffith's most powerful images in *Birth of a Nation* shows the mangled corpses of "war's peace": the grotesquely strewn bodies are lighted in such harsh contrasts that we barely recognize what's being photographed, until in horror we realize that these are human bodies.

By deliberately permitting too much light to enter the aperture of his camera, a director can **"overexpose"** an image—producing a blanching flood of light over the entire surface of the picture. Overexposure has been most effectively used in nightmare and fantasy sequences. In Fellini's *8½,* for example, the hero's recollections of a traumatic childhood experience are shown in deliberately overexposed images. Sometimes this technique can suggest a kind of horrible glaring publicity: a sense of emotional exaggeration. One sequence in Bergman's *Sawdust and Tinsel,* for example, uses overexposure to emphasize a character's anguish over a public humiliation.

1-19. *The Seventh Seal.*
Directed by Ingmar Bergman, cinematography by Gunnar Fischer. In most black and white movies, light areas tend to come forward, while dark areas tend to recede. The harshly contrasting lighting in this shot produces a "torn up" surface, a sense of violence and disfigurement which is psychologically appropriate to the dramatic context.

(Janus Films)

Although color in film didn't become commercially widespread until the forties, there were many experiments in color before this period. Some of Méliès' movies, for example, were painted by hand in assembly line fashion, with each painter responsible for coloring one minute area of the film strip. The original version of *Birth of a Nation* (1915) was printed on various tinted stocks to suggest different moods: the burning of Atlanta was tinted red, the night scenes blue, the exterior love scenes pale yellow. Relatively acceptable film color was developed in the thirties, but for many years a major problem was its tendency to prettify everything. If color enhanced a sense of beauty—in a musical, for example, or a western or historical extravaganza—the effects were often appropriate. Thus, the best feature films of the early years of color were usually those with "artificial" or remote settings. The earliest color processes tended also to emphasize garishness, and often special consultants had to be called in to harmonize the color schemes of costumes, make-up, and décor. Furthermore, each color process tended to "specialize" in a certain base hue—red, blue, or yellow, for example—while the other colors of the spectrum were somewhat distorted.

It was well into the sixties before these problems were resolved. Compared to the subtle color perceptions of the human eye, however, and despite the apparent precision of most present-day color processing, cinematic color is still a relatively crude approximation. After the late sixties, virtually all feature fiction films were automatically photographed in color. Exceptions to this rule, like Peter Bogdanovich's *Last Picture Show* and *Paper Moon*, were shot in black and white for nostalgic reasons, to suggest the milieux of the fifties and thirties respectively—or, more accurately, the milieux of the *films* of the fifties and thirties, for Bogdanovich was a film critic as well as a director, and these two movies are in part homages to the American cinema of these periods.

There are some brilliant cinematographers who have produced relatively realistic color in film, among them Lucien Ballard (*The Wild Bunch*), Sven Nykvist (*Scenes from a Marriage*), Raoul Coutard (*Weekend*), and Vilmos Zsigmond (*McCabe and Mrs. Miller*), but in general, the most famous color films tend to be expressionistic in emphasis. Michelangelo Antonioni's attitude is fairly typical: "It is necessary to intervene in a color film, to take away the usual reality and replace it with the reality of the moment." In *Red Desert* (photographed by Carlo Di Palma), Antonioni spray-painted natural locales to emphasize internal, psychological states. Industrial wastes, river pollution, marshes, and large stretches of terrain were painted gray to suggest the ugliness of contemporary industrial society, and the heroine's drab, wasted existence. Whenever red appears in the film, it suggests sexual passion, yet the red—like the loveless sexuality— is a pitifully ineffectual cover-up of the pervasive gray.

Psychologically, color tends to be a subconscious element in film: it's strongly emotional in its appeal, expressive and atmospheric rather than conscious or intellectual. Psychologists have discovered that while most people actively attempt to "interpret" the *lines* of a composition, they tend to accept its *color* passively, permitting it to suggest moods rather than concrete objects. Lines are associated with nouns, colors with adjectives. Line is sometimes thought to be masculine, colors feminine. Both lines and colors suggest meanings, then, but in somewhat different ways.

Since earliest times, artists have used color for symbolic purposes. Color symbolism is probably culturally acquired, though its symbolic implications are surprisingly similar in otherwise differing cultures. In general, cool colors (blue, green, violet) tend to suggest tranquility, aloofness, and serenity. Cool colors also have a tendency to recede in an image. Warm colors (red, yellow, orange) suggest aggressiveness, violence, and stimulation. They tend to come forward in most images. Many film directors have exploited these symbolic and psychological implications. In *A Clockwork Orange,* for example, Stanley Kubrick used orange and blue as thematic motifs. The first "ultra-violent" half of the film deals with the sexual and social aggressions of the protagonist (Malcolm McDowell), and appropriately favors hot colors—oranges, reds, and pinks. The second "weepy-tragic" half shows the protagonist as victim, and most of these sequences feature cool colors, especially blues and grays. Humanity is symbolized by orange, mechanization by its complement, blue. This weird fusion of the human with the mechanical is the theme of Kubrick's film, and is suggested by the title, which was taken from Anthony Burgess' novel, the original source of the movie.

Many films are organized around such symbolic color polarities. Bergman's *The Passion of Anna,* for example, deals with the theme of sterility versus passion, or isolation versus personal commitment to others. These thematic polarities are symbolized by white versus red. Throughout the movie, snow and blank walls are used to suggest the (essentially masculine) world of egotism and self-isolation. Fire and blood are associated with the (essentially feminine) world of emotion, love, and possible violence. Bergman's *Cries and Whispers* is somewhat similar in its structure: red suggests passion, violence, and adulthood; white symbolizes innocence, childhood, and in some contexts, sterility.

Some directors deliberately exploit film color's natural tendency to garishness. Fellini's *Juliet of the Spirits* features many bizarre costumes and settings to suggest the tawdry but fascinating glamor of the world of show business. Similarly, the flashy color in Godard's *Weekend* perfectly captures the vulgar materialism of bourgeois life. Bob Fosse's *Cabaret* is set in Germany and shows the early rise of the Nazi party. The colors are appropriately "neurotic," with emphasis on such thirties favorites as plum, acid green, purple, and florid combinations, like gold, black and pink.

Directors often complain of how colors have a tendency to "run away," to dominate images in a way that was never intended. Hitchcock solves this problem by simply suppressing color as much as possible. Indeed, in some films, he uses *lack* of color as an appropriate symbolic comment on the drabness of Communist life. *Topaz,* for instance, features a credit sequence showing a Soviet military parade in which everything (including people) is photographed in a pervasive blue-gray. Only the red stars of the huge banners and soldiers' caps "enliven" these images—a typical instance of Hitchcockian wit. In *Torn Curtain,* a refugee ex-countess wears a gay splashy scarf which is conspicuously out of keeping with her lacklustre environment, an Eastern European People's Republic. "I am not Communistical," she announces haughtily, yet not without that touch of pathos which seems to characterize most people who feel out of tune with the times.

Black and white photography in a color film is often employed for symbolic purposes. Some directors alternate whole episodes in black and white with entire sequences in color. The problem with this technique is its facile symbolism: the bleached black and white sequences are too jolting, too obviously "Symbolic" in the most corny sense. A more effective variation of this technique is simply not to use too much color, to let black and white predominate. In Tony Richardson's *Tom Jones,* the luxuriant greens of the countryside are dramatically contrasted with our first glimpse of an eighteenth-century London slum—drained of color, except for a few washed out browns, gray-blues, and yellowish whites. Color drainage can also be used to suggest time differences. In Vittorio De Sica's *The Garden of the Finzi-Continis,* which is set in Fascist Italy, the early portions of the film are richly resplendent in shimmering golds, reds, and almost every shade of green. As Fascist repression becomes progressively more brutal, these colors almost imperceptibly begin to wash out, until near the end of the film, the images are dominated by whites, blacks, blue-grays, and dull browns.

LENSES, FILTERS, STOCKS, AND OPTICALS

Because the camera's lens is a crude mechanism when compared to the human eye, some of the most striking effects in a film image can be achieved through the distortions of the photographic process itself. Particularly with regard to size and distance, the camera lens doesn't make psychological adjustments, but records things literally (1-20). For example, objects placed

1-20. The Emigrants.
Directed and photographed by Jan Troell.
In perceiving this scene in real life, we would probably concentrate most of our attention on the people in the wagon. But there are considerable differences between reality and realism, which is an artistic style. In selecting his materials from the chaotic sprawl of reality, the realist filmmaker necessarily eliminates some details and emphasizes others into a structured hierarchy of visual significance. For example, the stone wall in the foreground in this shot occupies more space than the humans. Visually, this dominance suggests that the inert rocks are more important than the people. The unyielding stone wall symbolizes divisiveness and exclusion—ideas that are appropriate to the dramatic context. If the wall were irrelevant to the theme, Troell would have eliminated it and selected other details from the copiousness of reality—details which would be more pertinent to the dramatic context.

closer to the camera's lens tend to appear larger than objects at a greater distance. In the deep-focus shot of *Citizen Kane* alluded to earlier, the bottle of poison appears to be larger than Kane himself, for it stands just in front of the lens, and Kane is quite distant from it. The context of the scene tells us this size difference is not literally "true," of course, but Welles is able to convey a precise symbolic relationship through the distortion the lens creates.

Realist directors tend to use "normal" lenses in order to produce a minimum of distortion. Such lenses photograph subjects more-or-less as they're perceived by the human eye. Expressionist directors often prefer lenses and **filters** that alter the surface of reality. These optical modifiers

(a)

(b)

(c)

1-21a, b, c.
Photos by Barry Perlus.
The same subject matter, photographed with a normal lens (a), a wide angle lens (b), and a telephoto lens (c). The camera is at the same distance from the subject in each of these shots.

intensify given qualities and suppress others. Cloud formations, for example, can be exaggerated threateningly, or softly diffused, by using different kinds of filters. Different shapes, colors, and lighting intensities can be achieved through the use of specific optical modifiers. There are literally dozens of different lenses, but most of them are subsumed under three major categories: those in the non-distorting "normal" range, the telephoto lenses, and the wide angles (1-21).

The telephoto lens is often used to get close-ups of objects from extreme distances. For example, no cameraman is likely to want to get near enough to a wild lion in order to photograph an ordinary close shot, and in cases such as these, the telephoto is used, thus guaranteeing the safety of the cameraman while still producing the necessary close-up. Telephotos also permit a cameraman to work discreetly. In crowded urban locations, for example, passersby are likely to stare at a movie camera. The telephoto permits the cameraman to remain hidden—in a truck, for example—while he shoots as many close shots as he needs through the windshield or back window of the truck. In effect, the lens works like a telescope, and because of its long focal length, it's sometimes called a **"long" lens.**

Telephoto lenses produce a number of side effects that are sometimes

1-22. *The Seventh Seal.*
Directed by Ingmar Bergman, cinematography by Gunnar Fischer.
The telephoto lens is sometimes used when a director wishes to blur out the background of a scene. The tree to the left, in soft focus, suggests the brush strokes of a painter rather than the recording of a camera. Indeed, the entire image suggests the abstract patterns of lights and darks of a nonrepresentational painting.

exploited by directors for psychological purposes. Most long lenses are in sharp **focus** on one distance plane only (1-22). Objects placed before or beyond that distance, blur, go out of focus. The longer the lens, the more sensitive it is to distances, and in the case of extremely long lenses, even objects placed a mere few inches away from the selected focal plane can be out of focus. This deliberate blurring of planes in the background, foreground, or both, can produce some striking photographic and atmospheric effects. In *The Garden of the Finzi-Continis,* for example, the wealthy and rather short-sighted Jewish family of the title are often photographed in this manner, especially when they are in their garden, which symbolically suggests an innocent, lush Garden of Eden. The photographic blurring becomes a metaphor for the family's innocence and lack of political "vision." They see only what is immediately before them, while everything outside—in this case, Fascist Italy—remains "out of focus" for them.

The focus of long lenses can usually be adjusted while actually shooting, and thus the director is able to neutralize planes and guide the viewer's eye to various distances in a sequence—a technique sometimes called **"rack focusing,"** or **"selective focusing"** (1-23). In *The Graduate,* Mike Nichols used a slight focus shift instead of a cut when he wanted the viewer to look first at the young heroine, who then blurs out of focus, then at her mother, who is standing a few feet off in a doorway. The focus-shifting technique suggests a cause-effect relationship, and parallels the heroine's sudden realization that her boyfriend's mistress is her mother.

Long lenses also "flatten" images, decreasing the sense of distance between depth planes. Two people standing yards apart might look as though they're inches away when photographed with a telephoto lens. Indeed, with very long lenses, distance planes can be so compressed that the image can resemble a flat surface of abstract patterns. When anything moves towards or away from the camera in such shots, our sense of its movement is slight at best. In *The Graduate,* the protagonist (Dustin Hoffman) runs desperately towards the camera, but due to the flattening of the long lens, he seems to be running "in place" rather than moving towards his destination.

The wide angle or so-called **"short" lenses** have short focal lengths and wide angles of view. These are the lenses used in deep-focus shots, for they preserve a sharpness of focus on virtually all distance planes. The distor-

1-23. *The Godfather.*
Directed by Francis Ford Coppola.
When some objects or figures are in soft focus yet still occupy a position of prominence within the image, the director generally wishes to remind the viewer of the presence of the blurred figure without necessarily giving him primary visual stress. In effect, selective focus is a kind of holding action. Rather than cutting to separate shots of different characters, some directors prefer the technique of rack focusing, whereby one distance plane is blurred while simultaneously another comes into sharp focus. Rack focusing is a method of preserving the unity of space while forcing our attention to a *succession* of different areas within the frame.

(Paramount Pictures)

(a)

1-24a. A Clockwork Orange.
Directed by Stanley Kubrick.
1-24b. Magnum Force.
Directed by Ted Post.
Wide angle lenses are often employed precisely because of their
distorting tendencies. A close-up of
a human face photographed with an
extreme wide angle lens (a) can
make even handsome features seem
grotesque and hideous. Symbolism in
the cinema is often related to size
and volume, particularly when exaggerated by the wide angle lens (b).

(b)

tions involved in short lenses are both linear and spatial. The wider the
angle, the more lines and shapes tend to warp, especially at the edges of
the image. Distances between various depth planes are also exaggerated
with these lenses: two people standing a foot away from each other can
appear yards apart in a wide angle image. *Citizen Kane* is filled with such
shots. Welles' *The Trial,* based on Kafka's novel, uses such lenses to emphasize the vast, vacuuous distances between people. In close-up ranges, wide
angle lenses tend to make huge bulbs out of people's noses, and slanting,
sinister slits of their eyes (1-24). Welles used several such shots in *Touch
of Evil.* Movement towards or away from the camera is exaggerated when
photographed with a short lens: two or three ordinary steps can seem like
inhumanly lengthy strides—an effective technique when a director wants

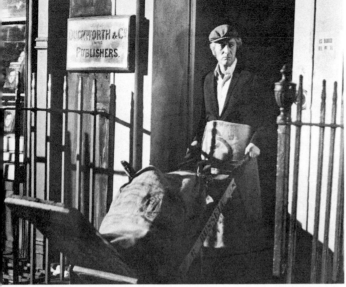

(a)

(Universal Studio)

1-25a. Frenzy.
Directed by Alfred Hitchcock.
1-25b. The Emigrants.
Directed by Jan Troell.
1-25c. Blonde Venus.
Directed by Josef von Sternberg.
There are many types of filters in the cinema: some make minor modifications in the subject matter, others can totally transform it. Day-for-night filters permit a director to photograph a scene in sunlight; because certain types of light are filtered out, the scene looks as though it is taking place at night (a). Other filters can soften the harshness of a photographic image, producing a hazy, romantic effect (b). Sparkle filters trap and refract certain types of light and produce a diamond-like glitter in the image (c).

(b)

(Warner Brothers)
(Paramount Pictures)

(c)

to emphasize a character's strength, dominance, or ruthlessness. The **fish-eye lens** is the most extreme wide angle lens, and it creates such severe distortions that the edges of the screen seem reflected in a sphere, as though we were looking through a crystal ball. John Frankenheimer, in his science-fiction film *Seconds,* used the fish-eye to suggest the protagonist's eerie semi-conscious state.

In *Long Day's Journey Into Night,* Sidney Lumet used specific lenses for each of the four main characters, and these lenses changed as the characters developed during the course of the film. Lumet referred to this technique as a "lens plot." For the morphine-addicted mother (Katharine Hepburn), Lumet used a series of progressively longer lenses, which blurred the background into a fuzzy remoteness: a metaphor of how drugs are helping her to forget or at least blur her problems. For the weary father (Ralph Richardson) and the cynical older son (Jason Robards), Lumet used progressively wider angled lenses. The distortions produced by these lenses suggest how Mary Tyrone's addiction has deformed their own lives. Only Edmund (Dean Stockwell), the naive younger son is photographed with a nondistorting lens, suggesting his relative normality. But he too is characterized through a wide angle lens later in the film, after he realizes (as his father and brother had much earlier) that their situation is without hope, that Mary will always be an addict.

Lenses and filters can be used for purely cosmetic purposes—to make an actor or actress taller, slimmer, younger, or older. Josef von Sternberg sometimes covered his lens with a transluscent silk stocking to give his images a gauzy, romantic patina. A few glamor actresses beyond a certain age even had clauses in their contracts stipulating that only certain beautifying "soft-focus" lenses could be used for their close-ups. These optical modifiers tend to eliminate small facial wrinkles and skin blemishes. In *The Magnificent Ambersons,* Welles coated the edges of his lens with vaseline in some shots, which blurred the edges of the images and gave them a nostalgic, faded picture-album look—a technique sometimes called **"vignetting."**

There are even more kinds of filters than there are lenses (1-25). Some trap light and refract it in such a way as to produce a diamond-like sparkle in the image—a technique especially favored in the thirties, usually to emphasize opulence or glamor. Many filters are used to supress or heighten certain colors. Color filters can be especially lovely in exterior scenes. The romantic, ethereal images of Jack Clayton's *The Great Gatsby* were largely the result of Douglas Slocombe's expert filtered photography. *McCabe and Mrs. Miller,* directed by Robert Altman, used green and blue filters for many of the exterior scenes, and yellow and orange for interiors. These filters emphasized the bitter cold of the winter setting, and the communal warmth of the rooms inside the primitive buildings.

Though there are a number of different kinds of film stocks, most of them fall within two basic categories, **"fast"** and **"slow"** (1-26). Fast stock is highly sensitive to light, and in some cases can register images with no illumination except what is available on location, even in night-time sequences. Slow stock is relatively insensitive to light, and requires as much as ten times more illumination than some fast stocks.

(Janus Films)

(United Artists)

(b)

1-26a. *The Seventh Seal.*
Directed by Ingmar Bergman, photographed with slow stock by Gunnar Fischer.
1-26b. *The Passion of Anna.*
Directed by Ingmar Bergman, photographed with fast stock by Sven Nykvist.
Through the use of slow film stocks, the director is able to achieve some striking theatrical effects, for these stocks are capable of capturing a high degree of linear definition as well as a broad spectrum of blacks, grays, and whites (a). Fast stocks are highly sensitive to light, and can record images with no additional illumination except that which is available on a set or location (b). Fast stocks tend to produce somewhat fuzzy, grainy images.

1-27. *The Battle of Algiers.*
Directed by Gillo Pontecorvo.
Fast film is generally used by documentarists since it permits the cameraman to photograph events while they're actually occurring, without the necessity of having to set up cumbersome lights. Fiction filmmakers like Pontecorvo sometimes use fast stock to dedramatize and deglamorize their images, to lend them a gritty, documentary-like authenticity.

Traditionally, slow stocks have been used in fiction movies, for this type of film stock produces images of great crispness and sharpness of detail. Lines are reproduced with razor-sharp clarity, and variations in gray (in a black-and-white movie) can be extraordinarily subtle. Slow color stocks are capable of capturing colors with great precision, without washing them out.

Fast stocks have traditionally been associated with documentary movies, for with their great sensitivity to light, these stocks can reproduce images of events while they're actually occurring. The documentarist is able to photograph people and places without having to set up cumbersome lights. Because of this light sensitivity, fast stocks often produce a grainy image, in which lines tend to be fuzzy, and colors tend to wash out. In a black-and-white film, lights and darks contrast sharply, and the many variations of gray are generally lost.

Ordinarily, technical considerations such as these would have no place in a book of this sort, but the choice of stock can produce considerable psychological and aesthetic differences in a movie. Since the early sixties, many fiction filmmakers have switched to fast stocks in order to give their images a documentary sense of realism and urgency. Godard has particularly favored the use of fast film, and his cinematographer, Raoul Coutard, has created some extraordinarily striking effects, notwithstanding the presumed visual limitations of these stocks. Gillo Pontecorvo's *The Battle of Algiers* is so harshly contrasting in its blacks and whites, so deliberately grainy, and fuzzy in its image resolution, many viewers assume the movie is a documentary (1-27). The very visual "blemishes" of fast stock turn out

(Warner Brothers)

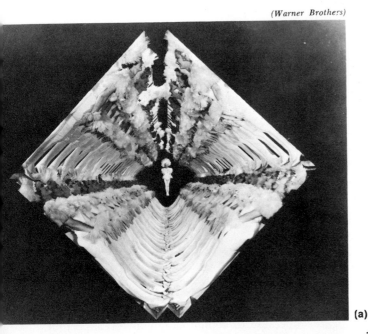

(a)

(Museum of Modern Art)

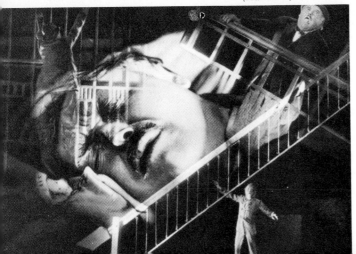

(b)

1-28a. *Dames.*
Directed by Busby Berkeley.
1-28b. *Secrets of a Soul.*
Directed by G. W. Pabst.
The optical printer is an invaluable piece of equipment, particularly to the expressionist filmmaker, for among other things, it permits the superimposition of two or more realities within a unified space. Berkeley's celebrated abstract dance sequences owed much to the optical printer (a), and dream and fantasy sequences (b) are frequently produced with the aid of this complex piece of machinery.

1-29. Darby O'Gill and the Little People.
Produced by Walt Disney.
Although negative images are seldom used in motion pictures, they can be highly effective in sequences dealing with the supernatural. Negative images suggest a sense of looking beneath the surface of things, and are particularly evocative in portraying ideas of death and dying.

to be aesthetic virtues in this film, for its sense of immediacy and realism is largely due to these technical characteristics.

The **optical printer** is an elaborate machine that produces many special effects in the cinema (1-28). It includes a camera and projector precisely aligned, permitting the operator to rephotograph all or a portion of an existing frame of a film. **Double exposure** or the superimposition of two images, is one of the most important of these effects, for it permits the director to portray two separate realities simultaneously. For this reason, the technique is often used in fantasy and dream sequences, as well as in scenes dealing with the supernatural. The optical printer can also produce **multiple exposures**, or the superimposition of many images simultaneously. Multiple exposures are useful for suggesting mood, time lapses, and any sense of mixture—of time, places, objects, events.

Multiple exposure techniques are often used in **montage** sequences—transitional bridges of rapidly edited images which are used to suggest the lapse of time or the passing of events. (In Europe, *"montage"* usually refers to the whole complex art of editing.) In *Citizen Kane*, Welles uses a *montage* sequence to compress Susan Alexander's lengthy operatic tour:

shots of Susan singing her heart out are superimposed and **dissolved** with shots of **newspaper** headlines, flickering stage lights, rising curtains, etc.

Negative image—the reversing of lights and darks of the positive, or finished print—has not been much used in the cinema except by avant-garde experimentalists (1-29). Movie-makers apparently find this technique too flamboyant and obscure for conventional fiction films: the viewer's light-dark expectations are reversed, which is disorienting. Godard has used the technique with considerable effect in *Weekend* and *Alphaville,* where it suggests an x-ray effect, looking beneath the surface of things. Jean Cocteau has used negative images to suggest dehumanization, the pervasiveness of death and dying.

THE CINEMATOGRAPHER

The cinema is a collaborative enterprise, the result of the combined efforts of many different artists, technicians, and businessmen. Because the contributions of these individuals vary from film to film, it's very difficult to determine who's responsible for what in a movie (1-30). Most sophisticated viewers agree that the director is generally the dominant artist in the best films, and his principal artistic collaborators—actors, writers, cinematographers—perform according to the director's instructions. But the dominance of the director is far from universal. Many movies seem to be stamped by the personalities of others—a prestigious **star,** for example, or a skillful editor who manages to make sense out of a director's botched **footage.** A great many American films made between 1930 and 1950 seem to be dominated by the aesthetic and social sensibilities of the studios that produced the movies. For example, there's a "Warner Brothers look" in most of the works produced by this studio, especially during the thirties and forties. Virtually all film historians and critics recognize this style immediately, though they might be hard pressed to guess the name of the director who presumably "stamped his personality" on the film. Some movies are dominated by their producers. This is certainly the case with many of the films produced by Stanley Kramer, for example, for most of them are predictably literary and politically liberal in emphasis.

Cinematographers have been known to chuckle sardonically when a director's "visual style" is praised by critics (1-31). Some directors don't even bother looking through the viewfinder, and leave such "details" as shot choice, composition, angles, and lenses to the cinematographer. To be sure, in most cases the cinematographer is at least consulted in such matters, but when the director ignores these important formal elements, he virtually throws away his most expressive pictorial opportunities, and functions much like a stage director, who is more concerned with dramatic rather than visual values. That is, with the script and the acting rather than the quality of the image itself.

On the other hand, a few cinematographers have been highly praised for their artistry when in fact the effectiveness of their images is largely due to the director's pictorial skills. Hitchcock, for example, often provides individual frame drawings for the shots of his films. His cinematographers merely line up their shots according to these sketches. Hence, when the

1-30. *Scarface*.
Directed by Howard Hawks.
Most knowledgable film enthusiasts consider the cinema a director's medium. Too often, however, the collaborative nature of the filmmaking process is grossly minimized and in some cases totally forgotten. *Scarface,* for example, reflects important artistic contributions from a number of different sources. Hawks' direction is characteristically fast-paced and energetic; the preponderance of eye-level medium shots and the lean economical editing style are also typical of this director's work. But the movie owes much to its writer, Ben Hecht, a former journalist who specialized in terse cynical scripts which often featured tough guys, tarts, and off-beat characters. The main character of this film was loosely based on the personality of the gangster Al Capone, and Hecht conceived of his protagonist as a contemporary Cesare Borgia in a gangland Chicago setting. Scarface was acted with gleeful flamboyance by Paul Muni (pictured), one of the biggest stars of the thirties. Indeed, in the mind of the public, *Scarface* was "a Paul Muni picture." The film's visual style, with its rich textures and atmospheric use of shadows, is typical of the work of Lee Garmes, whose low-key "northern light" technique was a photographic signature, derived from Rembrandt's paintings. In short, the collaborative nature of the moviemaking enterprise presents the film critic with many frustrating dilemmas, since he can never be completely certain who was responsible for what in a movie.

director claims that he never looks through the viewfinder, Hitchcock means that he assumes his cinematographer has followed instructions. This is not to denigrate the considerable skills of these technicians—particularly Robert Burks, who photographed most of Hitchcock's greatest works. But like many cinematographers, Burks' excellence as a craftsman was based mostly on his ability to execute Hitchcock's precise requirements.

Sweeping statements about the role of the cinematographer are impossible to make, for it varies widely from film to film, and from director to director. Some cinematographers specialize in realistic photography: James Wong Howe, for example, insists that all his best work is "naturalistic," and Arthur C. Miller was impatient with any images that distorted reality. Stanley Cortez and Lee Garmes, on the other hand, were at their best in off-beat expressionistic styles, with richly textured surfaces, and

1-31. *Fellini Satyricon.*
Directed by Federico Fellini, cinematography by Giuseppe Rotunno.
In referring to the "texture" of a film image, one necessarily speaks metaphorically, for texture is a tactile term, referring to the feel of a surface. But the camera can photograph the surface of objects, and some of the most striking cinematographic effects are captured by contrasting different textural qualities. The works of Fellini are rich in textural effects. Here, befitting a Roman orgy, the textures seem to run riot. Note the sweating bodies of the slaves, the smokey atmosphere, the grease-stained table, the squishy mud floor, and the garish costumes and hair designs.

(United Artists)

1-32. *Juliet of the Spirits.*
Directed by Federico Fellini, cinematography by Gianni Di Venanzo.
Although some cameramen are best known for a certain style of photography, each new movie requires a fresh attitude, and most cameramen willingly discard their stylistic preferences in favor of a more appropriate method of lighting. The brilliant Italian cinematographer, Gianni Di Venanzo, for example, photographed many of the austere films of Antonioni as well as two of Fellini's most extravagantly romantic movies.

(Rizzoli Films)

subtle chiaroscuro effects in their use of shadows. In actual practice, however, virtually all cinematographers agree that the style of the photography should be geared to the story, theme, and mood of the film. William Daniels, for example, had acquired a prestigious reputation as a "glamor" photographer at MGM, and for some years, he was known as "Greta Garbo's cameraman." Yet Daniels also helped to shoot Erich von Stroheim's harshly realistic *Greed,* and the cinematographer won an Academy Award for his work in Jules Dassin's *Naked City,* which is virtually a semi-documentary. In the films of Antonioni (*La Notte, Il Grido, Eclipse*), the cinematography of Gianni Di Venanzo is crisply realistic, but in the works of Fellini (*8½* and *Juliet of the Spirits*), it's extravagantly expressionistic (1-32). Similarly, Coutard's work for Godard is relatively realistic, but when working for François Truffaut, Coutard's camerawork is noticeably more romantic and lyrical.

Generally speaking, the greatest directors tend to prefer working with the greatest cinematographers. Indeed, the names of some cameramen are inextricably linked with specific directors: Billy Bitzer with D. W. Griffith, Edouard Tisse with Sergei Eisenstein, Sven Nykvist with Ingmar Bergman, Gabriel Figueroa with Luis Buñuel, Freddie Young with David Lean, Gregg Toland with William Wyler, and many others. Some cinematographers eventually became distinguished directors, most notably Jan Troell, George Stevens, Nicholas Roeg, Jack Cardiff, and Haskell Wexler. Lee Garmes and Raoul Coutard both tried their hand at directing, and Josef von Sternberg was a card-holding member of the American Society of Cinematographers.

During the halcyon years of the American studio system, some of the greatest cinematographers were associated with a specific studio, and indeed helped to establish the semi-official style of that studio. MGM—the most prosperous studio during this period—was justly proud of an impressive roster of cinematographers, including Hal Rosson, William Daniels, and Ray June. Independent producer Sam Goldwyn gave Gregg Toland virtual *carte blanche* to carry on his elaborate experiments in lighting. At Paramount, Lee Garmes, Karl Struss, Charles B. Lang, and John F. Seitz were the big names. Warner Brothers specialized in moody low-key styles, popularized by Tony Gaudio and Sol Polito, who was generally regarded as Hollywood's most gifted cinematographer in mobile camera work. For many years, Twentieth Century-Fox was the employer of Arthur C. Miller and Leon Shamroy, who was the first to explore Fox's new **widescreen** process, CinemaScope. Even the poorer studios could boast a few great cameramen, like Columbia's Joseph L. Walker, for example. Lowly Universal had under contract two of the greatest cinematographers of the American cinema: Russell Metty and Stanley Cortez.

Some directors, like Bergman, understand the technology of cinematography very well indeed, but others are totally ignorant of such matters, and require impossible results from their cameramen. Astonishingly, these artists often manage to produce such results. Cinematographers have to be extraordinarily hearty, flexible, and resourceful. Daniels, for example, was required to work in 132° heat for the Death Valley sequences of *Greed*. Cortez had to perform near-miracles for Welles in *The Magnificent Ambersons* (1-33). Often cameramen must work under water, in deep dark narrow pits, high overhead on precarious ledges, and in almost every kind of dangerous situation (1-34).

(*Janus Films*)

1-33. *The Magnificent Ambersons.*
Directed by Orson Welles, cinematography by Stanley Cortez.
Although there is a certain thematic consistency in most of Welles' movies, the visual style of each is unique. Cortez's lushly romantic lighting for *Ambersons* is totally appropriate to the nostalgic, elegaic tone of this film. The high-contrast lighting and razor sharp deep focus in *Citizen Kane,* on the other hand, are more in keeping with that film's more intellectual tone, its overt theatricality, and flamboyance.

1-34. On the set of *Deliverance*.
Directed by John Boorman, cinematography by Vilmos Zsigmond.
Cinematographers are expected to work under the most dangerous conditions, often with heavy, cumbersome equipment. In this film, Zsigmond and his crew had to work from a rubber raft which often swirled precariously in the currents of the wild Chattooga River in Georgia.

There are some great films that are photographed competently but not necessarily with great distinction. Realist directors are especially likely to prefer an unobtrusive, functional style. Many of the earlier works of Buñuel and De Sica, for example, can only be described as "professional" in their cinematography. Rollie Totheroh, who photographed most of Chaplin's films, merely set up his camera and let Chaplin the actor take over. Photographically speaking, there are few "memorable" shots in his movies: what makes his images forceful is the genius of Chaplin's acting. This photographic austerity—some would consider it poverty—is particularly conspicuous in those rare scenes when Chaplin is off-camera.

But there are far more films in which the *only* interesting or artistic quality is the cinematography. Hollywood has a particularly dismal record of cheapening the talents of some of its most brilliant cinematographers. For every great work like Fritz Lang's *You Only Live Once*, Leon Shamroy had to photograph four or five bombs of the ilk of *Snow White and the Three Stooges;* Lee Garmes photographed several of von Sternberg's visually opulent films, but he also was required to shoot *My Friend Irma Goes West;* some of James Wong Howe's most brilliant techniques—including deep-focus interior photography and ceilinged sets—were wasted on a mediocre potboiler entitled *Transatlantic,* which was made ten years before *Citizen Kane,* the film often cited as the first movie to use interior deep-focus and ceilinged sets.

In this chapter, we've been concerned with visual images largely as they relate to the art and technology of cinematography. But the camera must have something to photograph—people, objects, locations. Through the manipulation of these physical materials, the director is able to convey a multitude of ideas and emotions visually. This manipulation or arrangement of objects in space is referred to as a director's mise-en-scène, the subject of the following chapter.

FURTHER READING

ALTON, JOHN. *Painting with Light*. New York: Macmillan Company, 1949. A study of the art of cinematography, with particular emphasis on lighting techniques.

BAZIN, ANDRÉ. "The Ontology of the Photographic Image," in *What is Cinema?* Berkeley: University of California Press, 1967. (Paper) A brief theoretical exploration of the essentially realistic nature of photography and cinematography.

CLARKE, CHARLES G. *Professional Cinematography*. Hollywood: American Society of Cinematographers, 1964. A standard reference work of the techniques of cinematography.

FIELDING, RAYMOND. *The Techniques of Special Effects Cinematography*. New York: Hastings House, 1965. A detailed explanation of how special effects are achieved in film, with particular emphasis on the optical printer.

HIGHAM, CHARLES, ed. *Hollywood Cameramen*. Bloomington: Indiana University Press, 1970. (Paper) Interviews with famous American cinematographers, including Shamroy, Garmes, Daniels, Howe, Cortez, Miller, and Karl Struss.

JOHNSON, WILLIAM. "Coming to Terms with Color," *Film Quarterly*, vol. XX, no. 1, 1966. Reprinted in *The Movies as Medium*, ed. Lewis Jacobs. New York: Farrar, Straus & Giroux, 1970. (Paper) A brief historical survey of the technical and aesthetic problems of film color.

MALTIN, LEONARD, ed. *Behind the Camera: The Cinematographer's Art*. New York: New American Library, 1971. (Paper) Interviews with famous American cinematographers, including Miller, Ballard, Hal Mohr, Hal Rosson, and Conrad Hall.

McLUHAN, MARSHALL. *Understanding Media*. New York: Signet Books, 1964. (Paper) A philosophical exploration of how film and other mediums convey information and hence alter our everyday lives.

SPOTTISWOODE, RAYMOND. *Film and Its Techniques*. Berkeley: University of California Press, 1951. (Paper) Essentially a handbook; though somewhat out of date, it defines most of the technical terms used in the cinema.

VON STERNBERG, JOSEF. "Film as a Visual Art," in *Film and the Liberal Arts*, ed. T. J. Ross. New York: Holt, Rinehart and Winston, Inc., 1970. (Paper) A witty and urbane discussion of the importance of the cinematographer's art.

2 mise-en-scène

Mise-en-scène (from the French, meaning literally "placing on stage") is a
term borrowed from the legitimate theatre. The phrase refers to the arrangement of all the visual elements of a theatrical production within a given
space—the stage. This playing area can be defined by the proscenium arch,
which encloses the stage in a kind of picture frame; or the acting area can
be more fluid, extending even into the auditorium. No matter what the
confines of the stage may be, its mise-en-scène is always in three dimensions:
objects and people are arranged in actual space, which has depth as well
as height and width. This space is also a continuation of the same space
that the audience occupies, no matter how much a theatre director tries
to suggest a separate "world" on his stage.

In the cinema, mise-en-scène is somewhat more complicated, and represents a peculiar blending of the visual conventions of the theatre and the plastic arts. Like the stage director, the filmmaker also arranges objects and people within a given three-dimensional space, but once this arrangement is photographed, it's converted into a two-dimensional *image* of the real thing. The space in the "world" of the movie is not the same as that occupied by the audience, only the image exists in the same physical area, like a picture in an art gallery. Mise-en-scène in the movies resembles the art of painting in that an image of formal patterns and shapes is presented on a flat surface and enclosed within a **frame.** But because of its theatrical heritage, cinematic mise-en-scène is also an expression of a dramatic idea, which is determined by a context in time. In general, **realist** films tend to veer towards the theatrical in terms of visuals: that is, story, character, and dramatic continuity take precedence over purely formal beauty. **Expressionist** movies tend towards painting, and these films often contain visuals of striking pictorial richness and formal complexity—images which aren't necessarily dictated by the narrative context.

THE FRAME

Each movie image is enclosed by the frame of the screen, which defines the world of the film. Unlike the painter or still photographer, the film director doesn't conceive of his framed compositions as self-sufficient. Like drama, film is a temporal as well as spatial art, and consequently, the visuals are constantly in flux: the compositions are broken down, redefined, and reassembled before our eyes. A single-frame image from a movie, then, is necessarily an artificially frozen moment which was never intended to be wrenched from its context in time and motion. For critical purposes, it's sometimes necessary to analyze a still frame in isolation, but the viewer ought to make due allowances for the dramatic and temporal contexts of the image.

The frame functions as the basis of composition in a movie image. Unlike the painter or still photographer, however, the film director doesn't fit the frame to the composition, but the compositions to a single-sized frame, whose horizontal and vertical ratios usually remain constant throughout the movie. Screens come in a variety of ratios, especially since the introduction of **widescreen** in the early fifties, but prior to this time, most conventionally shaped frames were approximately 4 by 3. Widescreens are roughly 5 by 3, though they can be as extreme as 2.5 by 1—as in the movies of the Hungarian film director, Miklós Jancsó, for example. In such instances, the screen shape can be likened more to a long narrow mural than to a conventional painting (2-1).

Some films originally photographed in widescreen are cropped down to a conventional **aspect ratio** after their initial commercial release. This appalling practice is commonplace in movies which are reduced from 35 mm to 16 mm, the standard gauge used in most noncommercial exhibitions like those at colleges and museums. Needless to say, the more brilliantly the widescreen is used, the more a movie is likely to suffer when its aspect ratio is diddled with in this manner. Generally, at least a third of the

(a)

2-1a, b, c. *2001: A Space Odyssey.*
Directed by Stanley Kubrick.
The widescreen is particularly suited
to capturing the vastness of a locale.
If this image were cropped to a
conventional aspect ratio (b), much
of the feel of the infinity of space
would be sacrificed. We tend to
scan an image from left to right and
hence, in Kubrick's composition (a)
the astronaut seems to be in danger
of slipping off into the endlessness
of space. If the composition is turned
upside down, however, (c) the astronaut seems to be coming home into
the safety of the spacecraft.

(b)

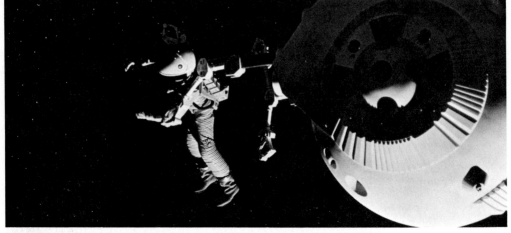

(c)

image is hacked away by lopping off the sides of the frame. This kind of cropping can result in many visual absurdities: a speaker at the edge of the frame might be totally absent in the "revised" composition, or an actor might react in horror at something that never even comes into view. When shown on television—which has a 4 by 3 aspect ratio—some of the greatest widescreen films can actually seem clumsy and poorly composed. A few movies—like Stanley Kubrick's *2001: A Space Odyssey*—probably wouldn't even make sense on TV, so subtly is the subject matter distributed over the entire surface of the widescreen.

In the plastic arts, frame dimensions are governed by the nature of the subject matter. Thus, a painting of a skyscraper is likely to be vertical in shape, and would be framed accordingly. Similarly, a vast panoramic scene would probably be more horizontal in its dimensions. But in the movies, the frame ratio is imposed from without, and isn't necessarily governed by the intrinsic nature of the materials photographed. This is not to say that all film images are therefore inorganic, however, for in this regard, the filmmaker can be likened to a sonneteer, who chooses his rigid form precisely because of the technical challenges it presents. Much of the enjoyment we derive from reading a sonnet results from the tension between the content and the form, which consists of fourteen intricately rhymed lines. When technique and subject matter are perfectly fused in

2-2. *Alphaville*.
Directed by Jean-Luc Godard.
The formal elements of this shot all conspire to suggest an upward sense of movement. The vertical lines, which slant slightly toward the center, the neutralizing masking of the shutter and window, and the triangular shape of the girl's forearms guide the viewer's eyes toward the top of the composition. The lighting from above (reflected in the window) suggests a kind of spirituality which is reinforced by the upward-directed eyes and the girl's serene and contemplative expression.

2-3. The Magnificent Ambersons.
Directed by Orson Welles.
The iris is a circular or oval mask which can close down or open out on an object or figure, thus transforming the shape of the frame. The blackness of the masking temporarily links the blocked out portions of the screen with the darkness outside the frame. In the days of the silent cinema, irises were often used merely as substitute cuts, but in many instances, iris shots can acquire symbolic significance, as in Welles's famous iris-in on an old-fashioned auto chugging comically over the crest of a hill.
(Janus Films)

this way, our aesthetic pleasure is heightened. The same principle can be applied to framing in film.

The constant size of the movie frame is especially difficult to overcome in vertical compositions: a sense of height must be conveyed in spite of the dominantly horizontal shape of the screen (2-2). One method of overcoming this problem is through **masking.** In *Intolerance,* for example, D. W. Griffith blocked out portions of some images, which in effect connected the darkened portions of the screen with the darkness of the auditorium. To emphasize the steep fall of a soldier from a wall, the sides of the image were masked out. To stress the vast horizon of a location, Griffith masked out the lower third of the image—thus creating a widescreen effect. Many kinds of masks are used in this film, including diagonal, circular, and oval shapes. Some years later, the Soviet director Eisenstein urged the adoption of a square screen, on which masked images could be projected in whatever shape was appropriate to the subject matter.

In the days of the silent film, the **iris** (a circular or oval mask which can open up or close in on a subject) was rather overused. In the hands of a master, however, the iris can be a powerful dramatic statement. In *The Magnificent Ambersons,* for instance, Orson Welles irised in on a primitive auto chugging precariously over a hill (2-3). This iris suggests a snuffing out of such nostalgic carefree scenes. It creates the effect of zeroing-in as though the charming open-air auto were being squeezed into a sinister tunnel of constricting darkness. In *The Wild Child,* François Truffaut used an iris to suggest the intense concentration of a young boy: the surrounding blackness is a metaphor for how the youngster "blocks out" his social environment while focusing on an object immediately in front of him. Iris shots of this kind can suggest psychological and symbolic ideas precisely because the odd shape of the screen violates our expectations of a stable frame ratio.

But despite occasional exceptions, masking shots fell from favor in the late twenties, perhaps because this technique tends to call attention to itself. Realist directors are especially wary of such authorial intrusions and flamboyant distortions of the frame size. Such filmmakers tend to prefer a more subtle and natural type of mask. By placing a tall object between two "framing" devices (in a doorway, for example, or between two trees), the lateral portions of the composition are in a sense neutralized, and the resultant visual effect is vertical. Low angles and a profusion of vertical lines also tend to counteract the horizontal dominance of the frame.

As an aesthetic device, the frame performs in several ways. The sensitive director is just as concerned with what's left out of the frame as with what's included. The frame selects and delimits the subject; it edits out all irrelevancies, and presents us with only a "piece" of reality. The materials included within a **shot** are unified by the frame, which in effect imposes an order on them—the order that art carves out of the chaos of reality. The frame is thus essentially an isolating device, a technique that permits the director to confer special attention on what might otherwise be overlooked in a wider context. In **close-ups** particularly the enclosing frame can pinpoint the most minute details.

The motion picture frame can function as a metaphor for other types of enclosures. Some directors use the frame voyeuristically. In many of the films of Hitchcock, for example, the frame is likened to a window through which the audience may satisfy its impulse to pry into the intimate details of the characters' lives. Indeed, *Psycho* and *Rear Window* are organized around this peeping motif. Other directors use the frame in a less voyeuristic manner. In Jean Renoir's *The Golden Coach,* for instance, the frame suggests the proscenium arch of the theatre, and appropriately so, since the controlling metaphor of the movie is the idea of life as a stage.

Most of the **metaphors** and **symbols** in cinema derive from the physical properties of the medium. Certain areas within the frame can suggest intrinsic symbolic ideas. In other words, by merely placing an object or actor within a particular section of the frame, the director can radically alter his "comment" on that object or character. Placement within the frame is another instance of how form is actually content. Each of the major portions of the frame—center, top, bottom, and edges—can be exploited for such symbolic and metaphoric purposes.

The central portions of the screen are generally reserved for the most important visual elements: this area is instinctively regarded by most people as the intrinsic "center of interest." When we take a snapshot of a friend, we generally "center" his figure within the confines of the viewfinder. Since childhood, we have been taught that a drawing must be "balanced," with the middle serving as the focal point. The center, then, is a kind of norm: we *expect* dominant visual elements to be placed there (2-4). Precisely because of this expectation, objects placed in the center tend to be visually undramatic, for this area is generally favored only when the subject matter is intrinsically compelling. Realist filmmakers, for example, prefer central dominance because formally it's the most unobtrusive kind of framing, and the viewer is allowed to concentrate on the subject matter without being distracted by visual elements that seem "off center."

The area near the top of the frame can suggest power, authority, and aspiration. A figure placed here seems to control all of the visual elements "below," and for this reason, kings and royalty are often photographed in this manner. In images suggesting spirituality, the top of the frame is often exploited to convey a God-like splendor. This grandeur can also apply to objects—a palace, for example, or the top of a mountain. If an unattrac-

(a)

(b)

(c)

2-4a, b, c, d.
Photos by Evelyn Hayes.
Various portions of the frame can be exploited for their intrinsic symbolic implications. The center (a) tends to be accepted as the norm for the placement of important figures and objects. The top of the frame (b) tends to ˙mply power, authority, triumph, and control. The edges of the frame can suggest insignificance, and in some cases a nearness to danger, oblivion, or death, since these portions of the frame are nearest to the blackness off-screen. Because the eye tends to travel from left to right across an image, a figure placed on the right edge of the frame (d) tends to be more vulnerable and in danger of "slipping off" frame than one at the extreme left edge. (c)

(d)

tive character is placed near the top of the screen, he can seem threatening and dangerous, for he's in a position of superiority over the other figures within the frame. However, these generalizations are true only when the other figures are approximately the same size or smaller than the dominating figure.

The top of the frame is not always used in this symbolic manner. In some instances, this is simply the most sensible area to place an object. In a **medium shot** of a figure, for example, the person's head is logically going to be near the top of the screen, but obviously this kind of framing isn't meant to be symbolic: it's merely reasonable, since that's where we'd *expect* the head to appear in most medium shots. Indeed, mise-en-scène is essentially an art of the **long and extreme long shot**, for when the subject matter is detailed in a close shot, the director has fewer choices open to him concerning the distribution of visual elements. In a close-up, for example, it's virtually impossible to exploit the frame for symbolic purposes, since such symbolism depends upon a certain amount of contrast with other elements within the frame.

2-5. *M.*

Directed by Fritz Lang.

Throughout this film, Lang exploits the frame with great subtlety. In this photo, for example, the psychopathic child-killer (Peter Lorre, extreme right) is trapped in the same "territory" with his threatening accusers. They tower above him, sealing off any avenue of escape, while he cowers below at the extreme edge, almost falling into the symbolic blackness outside the frame. The ***dominant contrast*** is the bright balloon, an incriminating piece of evidence.

2-6. Frenzy.
Directed by Alfred Hitchcock.
The darkness outside the frame can be exploited symbolically, to suggest ideas dealing with fear, the unknown, oblivion, and death. Out-of-frame symbolic darkness is especially common in suspense movies, horror films, and thrillers.

(Universal Pictures)

The lower part of the frame naturally suggests opposite meanings from the top: subservience, vulnerability, and powerlessness. Objects and figures placed in these "inferior" positions seem to be in danger of "slipping out" of the frame entirely, and for this reason, these areas are often exploited symbolically to suggest danger. When there are two or more figures in the frame and they are approximately the same size, the figure nearer the bottom of the screen tends to be dominated by those from above (2-5). Even when the top and middle portions of the screen are empty, figures placed near the lower part of the frame can seem particularly vulnerable, perhaps because we expect something or someone to take over or fill in the space that exists above the figures—art as well as nature abhors a vacuum.

The left and right edges of the frame tend to suggest insignificance, since these are the farthest removed areas from the center of the screen. Many mediocre films shot in widescreen can be cropped to a conventional aspect ratio precisely because their directors place only insignificant details in these portions of the screen. But when images can be cropped without significant visual damage, we can be reasonably sure that the director had only pedestrian pictorial talents to begin with, for there's not much point in using the wide screen unless one plans to exploit its artistic advantages.

Objects and figures placed near the edges of the screen are literally close to the darkness outside the frame. Many directors use this darkness to suggest those symbolic ideas traditionally associated with the lack of light—the unknown, the unseen, and the fearful (2-6). In some instances, the blackness outside the frame can symbolize oblivion or even death. In films about people who want to remain anonymous and unnoticed, the director sometimes deliberately places them off-center, near the "insignificant" edges of the screen. Suicidal characters are also occasionally placed here, for metaphorically they're attracted to the nothingness off the screen.

Finally, there are some instances when a director places the most important visual elements completely out of the frame. Particularly when a character is associated with darkness, mystery, or death, this technique can be highly effective, for the audience is most fearful of what it can't see.

(M-G-M)

2-7. Greed.
Directed by Erich von Stroheim.
Highly symmetrical designs are generally employed when a director wishes to stress stability and harmony. In this still, for example, the carefully balanced weights of the design reinforce these (temporary) qualities. The visual elements are neatly juxtaposed in units of twos, with the two beer-filled glasses forming the focal point. The main figures balance each other, as do the two converging brick walls, the two windows, the two couples in each window, the shape of the picture above the men and the shape of the resting dog below them.

In the early portions of Fritz Lang's *M*, for example, the psychotic child-killer is never seen directly. We can only "sense" his presence, for he lurks in the darkness outside the light of the frame. Occasionally, we catch a glimpse of his shadow streaking across the set, and we're aware of his presence by the eerie tune he whistles when he's excited or upset.

COMPOSITION

Although the photographable materials of movies exist in three dimensions, one of the primary problems facing the film director is much like that confronting the painter: he must arrange shapes, colors, lines, and textures on a flat rectangular surface. This arrangement is generally held in some kind of balance, or harmonious equilibrium (2-7). The desire for balance

mise-en-scène **57**

is analogous to man's balancing on his feet, and indeed, to most man-made structures which are balanced on the surface of the earth. Instinctively, we assume that balance is the norm in most human enterprises.

In movies, however, there are some important exceptions to this rule. Particularly when a visual artist wishes to stress the *lack* of balance or equilibrium, many of the standard conventions of composition are deliberately violated. In movies, the dramatic context is usually the determining factor in composition. What might be superficially regarded as a "bad composition" could actually be highly effective, depending upon its psychological context. Many films are concerned with neurotic characters, or events that are out of joint. In such cases, the director might well ignore most of the conventions of harmonious composition (2-8). **In a full shot** of a solitary character, for example, the figure is generally centered so that the image is "properly" framed. But of course not all characters in film are "well adjusted," and merely by placing the figure at the edge of the frame, the director can throw off the balance of the composition, and hence

(Columbia Pictures)

2-8. *Lightning Swords of Death.*
Directed by Kenji Misumi.
Film directors often exploit empty or "negative" space to suggest ideas dealing with loss, both physical and psychological. In this image, the decapitated victim's sudden death is viscerally reinforced by the empty space that fills his half of the screen. The symmetry and balance of the composition is destroyed with the victim's fall, releasing the tensions of the tight frame and creating a sudden sense of spatial freedom which accompanies the protagonist's victory over his adversary.

2-9. Macbeth.

Directed by Roman Polanski.

Film images are generally scanned in a structured sequence of "eye-stops." The eye is first attracted to a dominant contrast, which compels our most immediate attention by virtue of its conspicuousness, then travels to the subsidiary areas of interest within the frame. In this photo, the eye is initially attracted to the face of Lady Macbeth, which is lit in **high contrast** and is surrounded by darkness. We then scan the brightly lit "empty" space between her and her husband. The third area of interest is Macbeth's thoughtful face, which is lit in a more subdued manner. The visual interest of this photo corresponds to the dramatic context of the movie, for Lady Macbeth is slowly descending into madness and feels spiritually alienated and isolated from her husband.

present us with an image that's psychologically more appropriate to the dramatic context. (See 2-4c, d.) There are no set rules about matters of this sort. John Ford tends to use symmetrical, balanced compositions, whereas Jean-Luc Godard and Antonioni often use assymetrical compositions which exploit a kind of negative space, large areas that are left empty. In the movies, there are many techniques which can convey the same ideas and emotions. Some filmmakers favor visual techniques, others favor dialogue, still others, **editing** or acting. Ultimately, whatever *works* is right.

The human eye automatically attempts to harmonize the major formal

mise-en-scène **59**

elements of a composition into a unified whole. Apparently the eye can detect as many as seven or eight separate elements of a composition simultaneously. In most cases, however, the eye doesn't wander promiscuously over the surface of the image, but is guided to specific areas in sequence. The director accomplishes this through the use of a **dominant contrast** and several **subsidiary contrasts**. The dominant is that area to which the eye is immediately attracted because of some conspicuous and compelling contrast. It stands out in some kind of isolation from the other elements within the image (2-9). In black and white movies, the dominant contrast is generally achieved through a juxtaposition of lights and darks. For example, if the director wishes the viewer to look first at an actor's hand, rather than his face, the lighting of the hand would probably be harsher than the face, which would be lit in a more subdued manner. In color films, the dominant is often achieved by having one color stand out from the others. Virtually any formal element can be used as a dominant contrast: a shape, a line, a texture, and so on.

After the viewer takes in the dominant contrast, his eye then scans the subsidiary contrasts, which the artist has arranged to act as counterbalancing devices to the dominant. Our eyes are seldom "at rest" with visual compositions, then, even with paintings or still photographs. We look somewhere *first,* then we look at those areas of diminishing interest. None of this is accidental, for visual artists deliberately structure their images so that a specific time sequence is followed. "Movement" in film is not confined merely to objects and people that are literally in motion.

In most cases, the visual interest of the dominant contrast correlates with the dramatic interest of the image, but since films have temporal as

2-10. *The Pawnbroker.*
Directed by Sidney Lumet.
The dominant contrast of this shot would ordinarily be the police car, since it constitutes the area of greatest visual contrast. In this shot, however, the "intrinsic interest" of the wounded boy (hidden by the crowd) is the dominant.

2-11. *Alexander Nevsky*.
Directed by Sergei Eisenstein.
Particularly in scenes emphasizing confusion, a director sometimes deliberately over-
loads his compositions in order to produce a corresponding sense of visual chaos.
In this photo, for example, the diagonal lines of the swords and spears form no
discernible design, so the eye is forced to organize the subject matter into larger,
more manageable units: the sky above, the soldiers on horseback in the upper portion
of the screen, the intervening strip of white, and the masses of soldiers in the lower
portion of the screen.

well as dramatic contexts, sometimes the dominant contrast is movement
itself, and what some aestheticians call **"intrinsic interest."** Intrinsic interest simply means that the audience, through the context of a story, knows
that an object is more important dramatically than it appears to be visually.
Thus, despite the fact that a toy might occupy only a small portion of the
surface of an image, if we know that the toy is *dramatically* important, it
will assume dominance in the picture despite its lack of visual emphasis,
for in a given context, dramatic meanings tend to take precedence over
visual ones. In *The Pawnbroker,* for example, Sidney Lumet wanted to
show the relative indifference of city dwellers to a murder that has just
taken place. A young boy's body lies bleeding on the sidewalk, while people
pass by, or stare impassively. In a number of shots, the boy's body isn't
even visible to the viewer, but because of its intrinsic interest, it forms the
dominant contrast of these images (2-10).

Even a third-rate director can guide the viewer's eyes through the use
of movement, for motion is almost always an automatic dominant contrast.
For this reason, many uninspired directors simply ignore the potential
richness of their images, and rely solely on movement as a means of capturing the viewer's attention. On the other hand, a great director will vary
his dominant contrasts, sometimes emphasizing motion, other times using
movement as a subsidiary contrast only. In general, the importance of
motion varies with the kind of shot used. Movement tends to be less dis-

2-12. Psycho.
Directed by Alfred Hitchcock.
Because the eye tends to "read" a picture from left to right, film directors often compensate for the intrinsic heaviness of the right side of the composition by weighting the left side somewhat more heavily.

(*Paramount Pictures*)

tracting in the longer shots, and highly conspicuous in the closer ranges.

Unless the viewer has time to explore the surface of an image at leisure, visual confusion can result when there are more than eight or nine major compositional elements. If visual confusion is the deliberate intention of an image however—as in a battle scene, for example—the director will sometimes "overload" his composition in order to produce this effect (2-11). In general though, the eye struggles to unify various elements into an ordered pattern. For example, even in a complex design, the eye will "connect" similar shapes, colors, textures, and so forth. The very repetition of a shape, color, or line can suggest the repetition of an experience. These connections form a kind of visual "rhythm," forcing the eye to leap over the surface of the design in order to perceive the overall balance.

Visual artists often refer to compositional elements as "weights." In most cases, the artist is concerned with distributing these weights harmoniously over the surface of his visual area. In a totally symmetrical design— almost never found in movies—the visual weight is distributed evenly, with the center of the composition as the axis. (See 2-7.) Since most compositions are not so rigidly symmetrical, however, the weight of one element is often counterpoised with a different type of element. A shape, for example, counteracts the weight of a color. Psychologists and art theorists have also discovered that certain portions of most compositions are intrinsically weighted. The German art historian Wölfflin, for instance, pointed out that we tend to "read" pictures from left to right, all other compositional elements being equal. In order to be balanced, a picture must therefore be more heavily weighted on the left, to counteract the intrinsic heaviness of the right (2-12). Overweighting on the left can be conspicuous or it can be accomplished more subtly, by having a person simply look towards the left.

2-13. *Stagecoach.*

Directed by John Ford.

Because the top half of the frame tends to be intrinsically heavier than the bottom, most directors include the horizon line well above the middle of the composition. When a filmmaker wishes to emphasize the vulnerability of his characters, however, the horizon is often lowered, thus producing a sense of overwhelming vastness in the sky overhead. As in many of Ford's subsequent westerns, the director here contrasts the epic grandeur of Monument Valley, Utah with the rickety fragility of the coach as it makes its dangerous way across the enormous expanse of desert terrain.

The upper part of a composition is heavier than the lower. For this reason, skyscrapers, columns, and obelisques taper upward, or they would appear top-heavy. Images seem more balanced when the center of gravity is kept low, with most of the weights in the bottom portions of the screen. A landscape is seldom divided horizontally at the mid-point of a composition for this very reason: the sky would appear to oppress the earth. Certain directors like Eisenstein and Ford create some of their most disquieting effects with precisely this technique: they let the sky dominate through its intrinsic heaviness, and the terrain and its inhabitants seem overwhelmed (2-13).

Isolated objects and figures tend to be heavier than those in a cluster.

Sometimes one object can balance a whole group of other "equal" objects, merely by virtue of its isolation. In many films, the protagonist is shown apart from a hostile group, yet the two seem somehow equally matched despite the arithmetical differences. This effect is conveyed through the psychological weight of the hero in isolation.

Psychological experiments have revealed that certain lines suggest directional movements. Though verticals and horizontals seem to be visually "at rest," if any movement *is* perceived, horizontal lines tend to move from left to right, and vertical lines from bottom to top. Diagonal or oblique lines are naturally more dynamic, or "in transition," and also tend to sweep upward. These psychological phenomena are important to the visual artist, especially the filmmaker, for often the subject matter or dramatic context is not conducive to certain effects. For example, if a director wishes to show a character's inward agitation within a calm context, he can convey this quality through the dynamic use of line: an image composed of tense diagonal lines can suggest the character's inner turmoil, despite the apparent lack of drama in the given context. Indeed, some of the most subtle cinematic effects are achieved precisely through the contrast between the meaning of compositional elements of an image and the meaning of its dramatic context (2-14).

A design or skeletal structure underlies most visual compositions. Throughout the ages, artists have particularly favored S and X shapes, tri-

2-14. *The 400 Blows.*
Directed by François Truffaut.
Often the context of a scene does not permit a director to express emotions dramatically. Here, the boy's anxiety and tenseness are expressed in purely visual terms. His inward agitation is conveyed by the diagonal lines of the fence. His sense of entrapment is suggested by the tight framing (sides, top, and bottom), the shallow focus (rear), and the obstruction of the fence itself (foreground).

2-15. Jules and Jim.
Directed by François Truffaut.
Compositions grouped into units of 3, 5, and 7 tend to suggest dynamic, unstable relationships. The imbalance of this triangular composition is organically related to the theme of the film, which deals with the shifting love relationships between three characters (pictured). Compositions organized in units of 2, 4, or 6, on the other hand, tend to imply stable, harmonious relationships.

angular designs, and circles. These designs are often employed simply because they're thought to be inherently beautiful. The famous "S curve," for example, is regarded by many as the most graceful and feminine of all compositional structures, and is particularly favored in the Japanese cinema, most notably in the films of Kenji Mizoguchi, which usually feature female protagonists. Design is usually fused with a thematic idea, at least in the best films. In *Jules and Jim,* for example, Truffaut consistently used triangular designs, for the movie deals with a trio of characters whose relationships are constantly shifting yet always interrelated. The form of the images in this case is a symbolic representation of the romantic "eternal triangle" of the dramatic content. The tripartite structure of Truffaut's visuals makes them seem more dynamic, more "off-balance" and subject to change. Generally speaking, designs consisting of units of 3, 5, and 7 (2-15) tend to produce these effects, whereas those composed of units of 2, 4, or 6 seem more static, stable, and balanced.

In *The Seven Samurai,* Akira Kurosawa used circular and tripartite designs with great density, and these **motifs** are directly related to the theme of the film, which is a recurring preoccupation in the Japanese cinema: the need for the individual to act in harmony with the needs of his society. The movie is set in the Sengoku period of 16th century Japan —a period of class breakdowns and violent social upheavals. During this era, the traditionally revered ideals of social cooperation and civil harmony were not much in evidence in Japan. In Kurosawa's film, marauding hoards of bandits terrorize the countryside without obstruction—pillaging the villages, raping the women, and confiscating the meagre harvests. In desperation, some farmers hire seven less-than-first-rate samurai warriors to protect their village. (Traditionally, the samurai caste served as retainers to the aristocracy, and were regarded just beneath royalty in the social hierarchy of Japan. During the period of the film, however, the samurai class had fallen on hard times, and many samurai were wandering the countryside, masterless. Indeed, a good number of them turned to robbing and pillaging like common bandits.) Throughout his film, Kurosawa sharply differentiates the three groups—farmers, bandits, and samurai—and each is even characterized by its own type of music.

The circle motif is introduced at the beginning of the film, when we see the village huts constructed in a circle: only three of them lie outside this cluster (2-16a). We then see the villagers, huddled together in a circle, kneeling on the ground and lamenting their fate at the hands of the merciless bandits (16b). After seven "hungry" samurai are hired, one of

2-16a–p. The Seven Samurai.
Directed by Akira Kurosawa.

(Kurosawa Productions, Toho International Co., Ltd., and Audio-Brandon Films)

(e)

You move as a group not as individuals.

(f)

(g)

(h)

(i)

(j)

(k)

(l)

(m)

(n)

(o)

(p)

them (Toshiro Mifune) turns out to be a fake. He is actually the son of a farmer—a considerable comedown in social class. As a joke, the official flag of the village consists of six circles (one for each samurai), a written character representing the farming village, and a triangle representing the phony samurai-peasant, who doesn't seem to belong anywhere, though eventually he turns out to be one of the most flexible and intelligent of all the major characters (16c). Circles are used to symbolize both the individual and the ideal of social unity—the microcosm and the macrocosm. The villagers gather in a circle to be instructed, their individual spears arranged like spokes on a wheel, while in the center of the circle, the chief samurai (Takashi Shimura) stresses the need for the farmers to act as a unified group rather than as individuals (16d). During this scene, Kurosawa circles his circle by having the camera move around the periphery of the group, thus emphasizing its unity (16e, f). When a few farmers rebel and insist they won't sacrifice the three outlying huts, the chief samurai forces the rebels back into the circle. On the back of his robe, we can see the circular yin-yang emblem, a Buddhist symbol of mystical unity, of the reconciliation of opposites (16g). Often Kurosawa presents us with three shots of the same scene, as when the farmers are looking for impoverished but willing samurai in the city (16h, i, j). The village has a mill wheel which is attached to one of the outlying huts, and Kurosawa offers us three separate shots of this wheel—the dominant symbol of social unity in the film (16k, l, m). Later, during a bandit attack, a farmer refuses to obey orders and rushes off to his mill. This act of individualism costs him his life, and the mill and its wheel are set afire by the bandits (16n). Kurosawa uses the image of the burning wheel as a symbolic warning of what could happen to the community if individuals refuse to act in concert with each other (16o). The bandits are ultimately defeated, precisely because the strategy of the samurai leader is to isolate one or a few of the bandits from the main group. Each time one of the forty bandits is killed, the samurai chief crosses off an individual circle on his tally sheet (16p).

As we can see, some types of designs can suggest intrinsic ideas, but the dramatic context is all important in a movie (2-17). Thus, in most American westerns, the circle formed by wagon trains when attacked by Indians suggests the same symbolic ideas of unity and security as found in Kurosawa's movie. But in *Psycho,* circular designs suggest quite different ideas. Hitchcock's film deals with the guilt and corruption of virtually all the characters—even the nominally "innocent" ones. Like many of Hitch-

2-17. *Last Tango in Paris.*
Directed by Bernardo Bertolucci.
Visual motifs are not always intrinsically meaningful, but like symbols, derive their significance from the dramatic context of a film. In this movie, Bertolucci uses the circular light globes as a motif associated with sexual fantasies. The motif is found in a number of scenes, and is associated with various characters in different locations. The motif first appears in the lobby of the apartment house where the two lovers (Marlon Brando and Maria Schneider) meet for their sexual liaisons. A similar light globe is found in the lobby of the hotel of Brando's deceased wife. Her lover also has a circular globe in his room, where he and his mistress met for their sexual liaisons. The same type of light fixture is found in the apartment belonging to Schneider's mother: both of these women use the military gear which once belonged to the *pater familias* as sexual fetishes. The globe motif proliferates lyrically on the screen in the famous climactic tango sequence, shown here.

cock's works, *Psycho* also deals with the idea of voyeurism—indeed, with the idea of cinema as artistic voyeurism. In the opening sequence of the film, the "eye" of the camera enters the window of a hotel room—where we witness a scene between two semi-clad illicit lovers. Throughout the movie, Hitchcock equates images of human eyes with other circular eye-shaped objects: sinks, bathtub drains, toilets, and the empty sockets of a human skull. A profoundly pessimistic work, *Psycho* suggests that behind every human eye lies a psychological sewer, a malign repository of corruption, guilt, and violence.

TERRITORIAL SPACE AND PROXEMIC PATTERNS

Thus far, we've been concerned with the art of mise-en-scène primarily as it relates to the structuring of patterns on a two-dimensional flat surface. But since most movie images deal with the illusion of volume and depth, the film director must keep these "theatrical" considerations in mind when he composes his visuals. It's one thing to construct a pleasing arrangement of shapes, lines, colors, and textures, but movie images must also tell a story in time, a story that generally involves human beings and their problems. In a sense, striking compositions in movies are something extra, for the most basic function of these formal elements is to embody concrete objects and characters. Unlike form in music, then, form in film is seldom "pure"—film forms refer specifically to real objects.

The filmmaker who ignores or excessively minimizes this form-content balance does so at his own peril. Indeed, those movies in which human beings seem reduced to mere abstract forms often strike us as decadent, mechanical, and lacking in humanity. Even the greatest directors have

2-18a–e.
Photos by Evelyn Hayes.
The foreground information of a visual image acts as a "comment" on the subject matter found in the middle distances and the background.

(a)

(b)

(c)

(d)

(e)

fallen prey to this formalistic excess on occasion. Movies like von Sternberg's *The Devil is a Woman,* for example, strike us as mere exercises in style. Undeniably, the film is visually sumptuous, yet it's devoid of any genuine human values. Many of the scenes from the two parts of Eisenstein's *Ivan the Terrible* also seem to be composed purely for their abstract visual qualities. The human dimension is lost—though some critics argue that this is precisely Eisenstein's point, that the characters *have* no humanity to be expressed.

Directors generally emphasize volume in their images precisely because they wish to avoid an abstract, flat look in their compositions. In most cases, filmmakers compose on at least three visual planes: the midground, the foreground, and the background. Not only does this technique suggest a sense of depth, but it can also radically alter the dominant contrast of an image, serving as a kind of qualifying characteristic, either subtle or conspicuous. For example, when a figure is placed in the midground of a composition, whatever is placed in the foreground will "comment" on the figure in some way (2-18). Some foliage, for instance, is likely to suggest a certain natural blending with the environment of nature. Many of the shots of the protagonists in George Roy Hill's *Butch Cassidy and the Sundance Kid* are photographed in this manner. A gauzy curtain in the foreground can suggest mystery, eroticism, and femininity. The cross hatching of a window frame can suggest self-division, and so on. This same principle applies to backgrounds, though objects placed in these areas tend to yield in dominance to mid- and foreground ranges.

One of the most elementary yet crucial decisions the film director makes is what shot to employ for the materials photographed. That is, how much detail should be included within the frame? How "close" should the camera get to the subject—which is another way of saying how close should *we* get to the subject, since the viewer's eye tends to identify with the camera's lens. These aren't casual problems, for the amount of space included within the frame can radically affect our response to the photographed materials. With any given subject, the film director can employ a variety of shots, each of which would include or exclude a given amount of surrounding space. But how much space is "just right" in a shot? What's "too much" or "too little"?

Space is a medium of communication, and the way we respond to objects and figures within a given area is a constant source of information in life as well as art. In virtually any social situation, we receive and give off signals relating to our use of space and those people who share it. We instinctively become alerted whenever we feel that certain social conventions about space are being violated (2-19). For example, when people enter a movie theatre, they tend to seat themselves at appropriate intervals from each other. But what's "appropriate"? And who or what defines it? Why do we feel threatened when someone takes a seat next to us in a nearly empty theatre? After all, the seat isn't ours, and the other person has paid for the privilege of sitting wherever he wishes. Is it unreasonable to feel anxiety in such a situation, or is it in fact a normal instinctive response?

(R.K.O.)

2-19. *Notorious.*
Directed by Alfred Hitchcock.
Space is a symbolic medium of communication, and the nature and amount of space that a character occupies in any given area can often imply ideas dealing with power and class. In this photo, the central character (Ingrid Bergman) is dominated by the two other figures, who not only invade her personal space, but seal off the edges of the composition, and dominate her from above.

A number of psychologists and anthropologists—including Konrad Lorenz, Robert Sommers, and Edward T. Hall—have explored these and related questions. Though few film critics have concerned themselves with these anthropological findings, they can be especially revealing in terms of how space is used in the cinema. In his study *On Aggression,* for example, Lorenz discusses how most animals—including humans—are "territorial." That is, they lay claim to a given area and defend it from "outsiders." This territory is a kind of personal haven of safety, and is regarded by the organism as an extension of itself. In many cases, when this territorial imperative is violated, the intrusion can provoke aggressive and violent behavior, and sometimes a battle for dominance ensues over control of the territory.

Psychological and anthropological studies have revealed that the "friendly" organisms within a defined territory tend to take up space according to a hierarchy of power. That is, the most dominant organism of a community is literally given a wide berth, whereas the less dominant tend to be more crowded. The amount of space each organism occupies is generally in direct proportion to its importance as defined within the given territory. (See 2-12.) These spatial principles can be seen in many human communities as well. A classroom, for example, is generally divided into a teaching area and a student seating area, and the proportion of space alloted to the "authority" is considerably greater than that alloted to each of those being instructed. The spatial structure of virtually any kind of territory used by humans usually betrays a discernable concept of power and class. No matter how egalitarian we might like to think of ourselves, most of us conform to these spatial conventions. When a distinguished person enters a crowded room, for example, most people instinctively "make room" for him—though in fact they're giving him far more room than they themselves occupy.

But what has all this got to do with movies? A great deal, for space is one of the principal mediums of communication in film, and the way that people are arranged in space can tell us a good deal about their social and psychological relationships. In film, dominant characters are almost always given more space to occupy than others—unless, of course, the film directly deals with the loss of power or the social impotence of a character. The amount of space taken up by a character in a film doesn't necessarily relate to his actual social dominance, but to his dramatic importance. Authoritarian figures like kings and royalty generally occupy a larger amount of space than peasants and underlings, but if a movie is primarily about the peasant, *he* will tend to dominate spatially. In short, power, authority, and dominance are defined *contextually* in film—not necessarily the way these characteristics are defined in reality.

The movie frame is also a kind of territory, albeit a temporary one which exists only for the duration of the shot. The way space is shared within the frame is one of the major tools of the **metteur-en-scène,** for he can define, adjust, and redefine many psychological and social relationships with ease by using various spatial conventions. Furthermore, once a relationship has been established, the director can go on to other matters simply by changing his camera **set-up.** The film director, in short, is not confined to a spatial area that's permanent throughout the scene. Such masters of mise-en-scène as Welles and Antonioni can express shifting psychological and social nuances within a single shot simply by adjusting the space between characters, and by exploiting the "depths" and intrinsically weighted areas of the frame.

The amount of space permitted within the territory of the frame can be exploited for symbolic purposes (2-20). Generally speaking, the closer the shot, the more confined the photographed figures appear to be. Such shots are usually referred to as **"tightly framed."** Conversely, the longer, **"loosely framed"** shots tend to suggest freedom. Prison films often employ tightly framed close-ups and medium shots precisely because the frame functions as a kind of symbolic prison. In Robert Bresson's *A Man Escaped,* for example, the director begins his movie with a close-up of the protagonist's hands which are bound by a pair of handcuffs. Throughout the film,

2-20a-h.
Photos by Evelyn Hayes.
The frame is a given territory, and the way in which organisms and objects are placed within this territory can be even more important than the subject matter being photographed. All of these photos feature the same subject matter, yet the true content is determined by the form of each. A solitary figure photographed in the longer ranges (a, b, c) tends to seem insignificant, dominated in varying degrees by the vastness of the surrounding space. The same figure in full shot (d) suggests an equilibrium between terrain and inhabitant. In the medium range (e), the figure has major dominance, and in the closest ranges (f, g, h), the terrain becomes insignificant.

(a)

(b)

(c)

(d)

the prisoner makes elaborate preparations to escape, and Bresson preserves the tight framing to emphasize the airless sense of claustrophobia that the hero finds so unendurable. This spatial tension is not released until the end of the movie, when we see the protagonist disappear into the freedom of the darkness outside the prison walls. His triumphant escape is photographed in a loosely framed long shot—the only one in the film—which also symbolizes his psychological and spiritual sense of release. Framing and spatial metaphors of this kind are common in films dealing with confinement—either literal, as in Jean Renoir's *Grand Illusion* (2-21), or spiritual, as in Fred Zinnemann's *Member of the Wedding.*

Often a director can suggest ideas of entrapment by exploiting perfectly neutral objects and lines on the set. In such cases, the formal characteristics of these literal objects tend to close in on a figure, at least as viewed on the flat screen (2-22). In *Red Desert,* for instance, the heroine (Monica Vitti) describes a mental breakdown suffered by a friend. The audience realizes she's speaking of her own breakdown, however, for the surface of the image tends to suggest confinement. As she talks, she seems riveted to one position, her figure framed by the lines of a doorway immediately behind her, suggesting a kind of coffin or constricted enclosure. When figures are framed within a frame in this manner, a sense of enclosure is even further emphasized.

Territorial space within the frame can be exploited with considerable

(e)

(f)

(g)

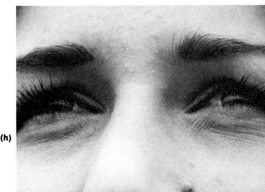

(h)

2-21. Grand Illusion.
Directed by Jean Renoir.
Tight framing allows for relatively little freedom of movement. The frame, in effect, becomes a symbolic prison, a useful technique in films dealing with entrapment, confinement, or literal imprisonment, like Renoir's World War I masterpiece.

psychological complexity. When a figure leaves the frame, for example, either the camera can adjust to this sudden vacuum in composition by panning slightly to make allowances for a new balance of weights, or it can remain stationary, thus suggesting a psychological sense of loss which is symbolized by the empty space the character has just left. The hostility and suspicion between two characters can be conveyed either by keeping them at the far edges of the composition, with a maximum of space between them (2-23), or by having the intrusive character force his physical presence into the other character's "territory," which is temporarily defined by the confines of the frame.

Spatial conventions vary from culture to culture, as anthropologist Edward T. Hall has demonstrated in such studies as *The Hidden Dimension* and *The Silent Language.* Hall discovered that **"proxemic patterns"**—the relationships of organisms within a given space—can be influenced by external considerations. Climate, noise level, and the degree of illumination all tend to alter the space between individuals. People in Anglo-Saxon and Northern European cultures tend to use more space than those in warmer climates. A great deal of noise, danger, and darkness tend to make people move closer together. Taking these cultural and external variations into account, Hall subdivides the ways people use space into

2-22a, b.
Photos by Evelyn Hayes.
Even the subtlest differences in the **(a)** form of the mise-en-scène can alter the significance of the subject matter. In these two photos, for example, the subject matter is identical: in one picture, the negative was simply printed in reverse. In (a), the distant figure seems somewhat less confined; he may not be aware that he's being observed by the figure at the left. In (b), however, his movements seem to be sealed off by the figure on the right, who appears to block off "his" space. Since our eye tends to move from left to right, we unconsciously transfer this knowledge to the distant figure, and assume he knows that he's being observed. Trivial as these differences might seem, they can be of considerable importance within a given dramatic context. Assuming we identify with the distant figure, the spatial arrangement of (b) is more menacing than (a). On the other hand, if we identify with the figure in the close range, (a) seems rather more threatening, for the distant figure seems to have **(b)** her trapped.

four major proxemic patterns: the intimate, personal, social, and public distances.

Hall defines as "intimate" those distances that range from actual skin contact to about eighteen inches away. This is the distance of physical involvement—of love, comfort, and tenderness between individuals. With strangers, such distances would be regarded as intrusive—most people would react with suspicion and hostility if "their" space were invaded by someone they didn't know very well. In many cultures, an intimate distance is considered inappropriate and in bad taste in public places.

2-23. Zabriskie Point.
Directed by Michelangelo Antonioni.
The horizontal dominance of movie screens was intensified by the introduction of scope. Some directors timidly ignored the edges of their compositions, while the more gifted exploited the new screen size by making their mise-en-scène more complex. Here, Antonioni stresses the difference in lifestyles between the two characters by placing them at the extreme edges of the composition. Psychologically, the distance between them also suggests the restraint and suspicion that each character feels for the other.

The personal distance ranges roughly from a foot and a half away to about four feet away. Individuals can touch if necessary, since they are an "arm's length" apart. These distances tend to be reserved for friends and acquaintances rather than lovers or members of a family. Personal distances preserve the privacy between individuals, yet these ranges don't necessarily suggest exclusion, as intimate distances almost always do.

Social distances range from four feet to about twelve feet. These are the distances reserved usually for impersonal business and casual social gatherings. It's a friendly range in most cases, yet somewhat more formal than the personal distance. Ordinarily, social distances are necessary when there are more than three members of a group. In some cases, it would be considered rude for two individuals to preserve an intimate or personal distance within a social situation. Such behavior might be interpreted as stand-offish and exclusive.

Hall defines as "public" those distances that extend from twelve feet to twenty-five feet and more. These ranges tend to be formal and rather detached. Displays of emotion are generally considered in bad taste at these ranges. Important public figures are often seen in the public distances, and because a considerable amount of space is involved at these ranges, people generally must exaggerate their gestures and raise their voices in order to be understood clearly.

All of these proxemic patterns are approximate, and Hall stresses their variability from culture to culture. What may be regarded as a personal distance in Egypt or Algeria would probably be regarded as intimate in Sweden or England. Furthermore, most people adjust to proxemic patterns instinctively: we don't usually say to ourselves "This guy is invading my intimate space" when a stranger happens to stand eighteen inches away from us. However, unless we're in a combative mood, we automatically tend to step away in such circumstances. Obviously, social context is also a determining factor in proxemic patterns. In a crowded subway car, for example, virtually everyone is in an intimate range, yet we generally preserve a "public" attitude by not speaking to the person whose body is literally pressed against our own.

Proxemic patterns are obvious to anyone who has bothered to observe the way people obey certain spatial conventions in actual life. But in the cinema, these patterns can be applied to the shots and their "distance" ranges. Though shots aren't necessarily defined by the literal space between the camera and the object photographed, in terms of psychological effect, shots tend to suggest physical distances. (Politicians who appear on television are often their own worst enemies because of their inability to adjust to different proxemic patterns. Old-time politicians sometimes appear pompous on TV because they're used to speaking to vast audiences which are usually in the public proxemic ranges. When the TV camera moves in to the personal range, however, the florid gestures and loud speaking voices of such politicians can seem insincere and rhetorical, even to their sympathizers. Most younger politicians, on the other hand, tend to be more conscious of the psychological effect of various proxemic ranges. Their political appearances on TV consequently tend to seem more smooth, polished, and sincere—even to their detractors.)

Usually a film director has a number of choices open to him concerning what kind of shot to use in order to convey the dramatic action of a scene. What determines his choice—though usually instinctively rather than consciously—is the emotional or intellectual impact of the different proxemic ranges. Each proxemic pattern has an approximate shot equivalent. The intimate distance, for example, can be likened to the close and **extreme close shot** ranges; the personal distance is approximately a medium-close range; the social distances correspond to the medium and full shot ranges; and the public distances are roughly within the long and extreme long shot ranges. Since our eyes identify with the camera's **lens,** in effect *we* are placed within these various ranges vis-à-vis the subject matter. When we are offered a close-up of a character, for example, in a sense we feel that we're in an intimate relationship with that character. In some instances, this technique can bind us to him, forcing us to care about him, and to identify with his problems. If the character is a villain, the close-up tends to produce an emotional revulsion in us, for in effect, he's invading our space. Sergio Leone uses this technique effectively in many of the close-ups of his various villains in *Once Upon a Time in the West.*

In general, the greater the distance between the camera and the subject, the more emotionally neutral we remain, for this is a "public" proxemic range, and tends to encourage a certain intellectual detachment. Conversely, the "closer" we are to a character, the more we feel that we're in proximity with him, and hence, the greater our emotional involvement (2-24). When we're "too close" to an action—a person slipping on a banana peel, for example—it's seldom funny, and we are concerned for the person's safety. If we see the same event from a greater distance, however, it often strikes us as comical. Chaplin used close-ups sparingly for this very reason: so long as Charlie remains in long shots, we tend to be amused by his antics and absurd predicaments. In scenes of greater emotional impact, however, Chaplin inserted a close-up, and the effect of these close shots is often devastating on the audience, for we suddenly realize that the situation we've been laughing at is no longer funny. We feel "closer" to Charlie, and identify with his feelings.

(a)

(Museum of Modern Art)

(b)

2-24a, b. Gold Rush and The Bank. *Both directed by Charles Chaplin.* "Long shot for comedy, close-up for tragedy," was one of Chaplin's most famous pronouncements. Though Chaplin probably never heard of proxemic patterns, his instincts were shrewd, for when the camera is relatively distant from an action, we tend to be more objective and detached, and are more likely to laugh at a situation (a). When the camera moves in closer, however (b), in effect *we* get close to the situation, and to the character involved. The proxemic distance between the camera and the subject forces us to identify more with his feelings, which we can no longer forget or ignore. A scene that might seem hilarious in long shot can often strike us as emotionally touching when it's photographed in close-up.

The choice of a shot is usually determined by certain practical considerations. Usually the director selects that shot which best conveys the dramatic action of a scene. If there's a conflict between the emotional effect of certain proxemic ranges and the clarity needed to convey what's going on, most directors will opt for the latter, and gain their emotional impact through some other means. In a scene from *Weekend,* however, Jean-Luc Godard sacrificed function to form, and the result is almost invariably confusion on the part of the audience. Throughout much of the movie, Godard keeps his two vicious protagonists in long shot, to prevent the audience from identifying with them in any way. Even scenes of violence are conveyed at these ranges, and consequently the brutal episodes often strike us as absurdly comical—which is Godard's deliberate intention. In one scene, however, there is an exchange of prisoners in a country farmyard. The action is conveyed in a very long shot, and without cuts, so we're unable to identify who the prisoners are because of the distance between the camera and the characters. Unwilling to offer a closer shot to clarify the situation, Godard preserves a certain sense of intellectual detachment, but unfortunately he also violates common sense and a fundamental principle of lucidity. As a result, most of the scene looses its impact.

But there are a great many situations in which the choice of shot is not necessarily determined by such functional considerations. For example, if a scene called for a shot of a man reading alone at a table, the director would have a number of options open to him, and his choice of shot would probably be determined at least in part by proxemic considerations (2-25). A functional stylist like Howard Hawks would probably photograph the scene in a medium shot, showing the upper part of the man's body and the table top. A comic realist like Chaplin would probably use a full or long shot, to prevent the audience from identifying too much with the character, and to permit us to see his social context. A predominantly expressionistic director like Hitchcock usually wants the audience to identify with his protagonists, and he would probably offer us a number of closeups of the man's face and the objects on the table to emphasize a certain emotional sequence of ideas. A director like Antonioni might portray the scene in an extreme long shot, to suggest the man's loneliness and alienation. As with virtually every other cinematic technique, then, the dramatic context determines the choice of shot and its attendant proxemic effects.

OPEN AND CLOSED FORMS

The concepts of **open** and **closed form** are generally employed by art critics and historians; these terms can also be useful in film analysis. Like most theoretical constructs, these are best employed in a relative rather than absolute sense. There are no movies that are completely open or closed in form, only works that *tend* towards these polarities. Like other critical terms, "open" and "closed form" should be applied only when such concepts are relevant and helpful in understanding what actually exists in a movie. If the concepts don't seem to be relevant, they ought to be discarded and replaced with something that *is* helpful. Criticism should always be the handmaiden of art, not vice-versa.

(a)

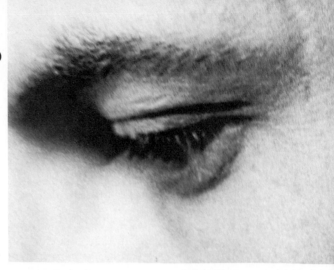
(b)

2-25a–e.

Photos by Evelyn Hayes.

The director usually has a number of different options open to him in the selection of his shots. His placement of the camera in relationship to the subject matter is often a matter of instinct, of what "feels" right. These instincts are determined in part by the emotional effects of the different proxemic ranges. The more distant the camera is from the subject, the more objective and detached our response is likely to be, for these are the public and social ranges. When the camera moves closer to the same subject matter, our emotional involvement tends to increase, for these are the personal and intimate proxemic ranges. In each of these photos, the true content is determined in large part by the proxemic implications of the shot, not merely by the subject matter alone.

(c)

(d)

(e)

Open and closed forms are not only opposing stylistic polarities, each with its own technical emphases, but also two distinct attitudes towards reality. Ultimately, open and closed forms are what can determine a film director's artistic "vision," his philosophical "universe." The two terms are also loosely related to the concepts of realism and expressionism as they've been defined in these chapters. In general, realist filmmakers tend to employ open forms, while most expressionists veer towards closed forms. Open forms tend to be stylistically subtle and recessive, whereas closed forms are generally self-conscious and conspicuous.

In terms of visual design, open form emphasizes informal, unobtrusive compositions. Often such images seem to have *no* discernible structure, and suggest an almost random form of organization. Objects and figures seem

2-26. *The Garden of the Finzi-Continis.*
Directed by Vittorio De Sica.
Realist directors are more likely to prefer open forms, which tend to suggest fragments of a larger external reality. Design and composition are generally casual and informal. Influenced by the aesthetic of the documentary, open form images seem to have been discovered rather than arranged. Excessive balance and calculated symmetry are avoided in favor of an intimate and spontaneous effect. Still photos in open form are seldom picturesque or obviously artful. Instead, they suggest a frozen instant of truth —a snapshot wrested from the fluctuations of time.

to have been found or discovered rather than deliberately arranged (2-26). Closed form emphasizes more formal designs. Though such images might suggest a certain modified realism, seldom do they have that "accidental" casualness that characterizes open forms. Objects and figures are more precisely placed within the frame, and the balance of visual weights is usually elaborately worked out (2-27).

Open forms stress apparently simple techniques because with these unself-conscious methods, the filmmaker is able to emphasize the immediate, the familiar, and the intimate aspects of reality. Sometimes such images are photographed in only partially controlled situations, and these **aleatory** conditions can produce a sense of spontaneity and directness that would be difficult to capture in a rigidly controlled context. Closed forms are more likely to emphasize the unfamiliar. The images are rich in textural contrasts and compelling visual effects. Because the mise-en-scène is more precisely controlled and stylized, there is often a deliberate artificiality in these images—a sense of visual improbability, of our being at least one remove from reality. Closed forms also tend to be more densely saturated with visual information, since economy of means usually takes precedence over considerations of superficial realism. If a conflict should arise, formal beauty is often sacrificed for truth in open forms; in closed forms, literal truth is sometimes sacrificed for beauty.

Compositions in open and closed forms exploit the frame differently. In open form images, the frame tends to be de-emphasized. It suggests a temporary masking and implies that more important information lies outside the edges of the composition. Space is continuous in these shots, and to emphasize its continuity outside the frame, directors often favor **panning** across the locale. In open form, the shot seems inadequate, too narrow in its confines to contain the copiousness of the subject matter. Like many of the paintings of Edgar Degas (who usually favored open forms), objects and even figures are arbitrarily cut off by the frame to reinforce the continuity of the subject matter beyond the formal edges of the composition

2-27. Frankenstein.
Directed by James Whale.
Expressionist directors are more likely to prefer closed forms, which tend to suggest a self-enclosed universe. Often stressing the remote or the unusual, images in closed form generally seem more self-consciously "artistic" in their effects. The beauties of line, shape, volume, and design are skillfully and sometimes flamboyantly manipulated to produce a heightened visual beauty which is seldom found in everyday reality.

(Columbia Pictures)

2-28. Black Gun.
Directed by Robert Hartford-Davis.
Movies in open form tend to exploit the frame as a temporary masking that's too narrow in its scope to include all of the relevant information. Often the frame seems to cut figures off in an arbitrary manner, suggesting that the action is continued off screen. In action films, open forms can suggest newsreel footage that was fortuitously photographed by a cameraman who was unable to superimpose an artistic form over his runaway materials.

(2-28). In closed form, the shot represents a kind of mini-universe, with all the necessary information carefully structured within the confines of the frame. Space seems enclosed and self-contained rather than continuous. Elements outside the frame are irrelevant, at least in terms of the formal properties of the individual shot, which in a sense is isolated from its spatial context (2-29).

Still photographs taken from movies that are predominantly open in form often seem artistically unimpressive, for they're seldom intrinsically striking or eye-catching. Most film books favor photographs taken from movies that are in closed form, for even these isolated fragments seem more obviously "artistic" in effect. The beauty of an open form image, on the other hand, is generally more elusive, and can be likened to a snapshot which miraculously preserves some candid expression, a kind of haphazard instant of truth. Open form also tends to value a certain visual ambiguity. Often the charm of such images lies precisely in their impenetrability—a mysterious half smile on the face of a character, for example, or an evocative shadow which casts a strange pattern across the set.

In open form movies, the dramatic action generally leads the camera. In such films as *Faces* and *Husbands,* for example, John Cassavetes emphasizes the fluidity of the camera: it dutifully follows the actors wherever they wish to lead; it seems to be placed at their disposal. Such films suggest that chance elements play an important role in determining the visual effects. (Needless to say, however, it's not what actually happens on a set that's important, but what *seems* to be happening on the screen, for many of the most "simple" effects in an open form movie are achieved only after much painstaking labor and manipulation.)

In closed form films, on the other hand, the camera tends to anticipate the dramatic action. Objects and actors are visually choreographed within the confines of a predetermined camera set-up. **Anticipatory set-ups** tend to imply fatality or determinism, for in effect, the camera seems to "know" what will happen even before it occurs. In many of the films of Fritz Lang, for example, the camera is "waiting" in a room: the door opens, the characters enter, and the action then begins. In some of Hitchcock's films, a character is seen at the edge of the composition, and the camera seems to be placed in a disadvantageous position, too far removed from where the action is apparently going to occur. But then the character "decides"

(Audio-Brandon Films)

2-29. The General.
Directed by Buster Keaton and Clyde Bruckman.
In closed form, the frame is a self-sufficient miniature universe, with all the formal elements held in careful balance. Though there may be more information outside the frame, for the duration of any given shot this information is visually irrelevant. Keaton was one of the supreme masters of framing: his comedy is essentially spatial, and derives its humor from the way in which Buster masters—or is mastered—by objects in a unified space.

mise-en-scène   **87**

2-30. *House of Wax.*
Directed by André de Toth.
The kinds of camera set-ups employed in open and closed forms can suggest certain metaphysical ideas. In open form, the camera tends to be led by the action: it generally follows the performers and seems to be at their disposal. In closed form, as in this illustration, the camera anticipates the action. Even before the characters move toward a certain space within the frame, the camera seems to know in advance where they'll go—it seems to be waiting for them: art as well as nature abhors a vacuum. In a sense, anticipatory set-ups predetermine the action, and hence tend to suggest entrapment, fate, or destiny. In open form, the minimal use of anticipatory set-ups tends to imply freedom, spontaneity, unpredictibility. The early films of Roberto Rossellini strongly emphasize these qualities. Closed forms and anticipatory set-ups, on the other hand, are common in the works of Lang and Hitchcock.

to return to that area where the camera has been waiting. When such set-ups are used in a movie, *we* also tend to anticipate actions, for instinctively we expect something to fill in the visual vacuum in the shot (2-30). Philosophically, open forms tend to suggest freedom of choice and the multiplicity of opportunities open to the characters. Closed forms, on the other hand, tend to imply destiny and the futility of will, for the characters don't seem to make the important choices, the camera does.

Open and closed forms are most effective in those movies in which these techniques are appropriate to the subject matter. A prison film employing mostly open forms is not likely to be emotionally convincing—unless of course the director is dealing with a spiritual kind of freedom within a context of physical encarceration. Most films employ both open and closed forms, depending upon the nature of the specific dramatic context. Renoir's *Grand Illusion,* for example, uses mostly closed forms for the prison camp scenes, and open forms after two of the prisoners escape. Nor do directors necessarily use the same forms for every film. The earlier works of Bergman—movies like *Wild Strawberries* and *The Seventh Seal*—tend to be predominantly closed in form. Bergman's later works, like *Shame* and *The Passion of Anna,* are mostly open in form.

Like most cinematic techniques, open and closed forms have certain limitations as well as advantages. When used badly, open forms can seem sloppy and naive, like an artless home movie. Too often open forms seem uncontrolled and even ugly. Occasionally, these techniques are so low-keyed and "unobtrusive" that the visuals can be blandly undramatic and boring. At their worst, closed forms can seem rigid and arty. The images are so overcontrolled and unspontaneous that their visual elements seem to be programmed by computer. Many viewers are turned off by the stagey, operatic flamboyance of some closed form films. Often these movies seem overwrought and decadent—all icing and no cake.

In these first two chapters, we've been concerned with the most important source of meaning in the cinema—the visual image. But of course movies exist in time, and have many other ways of communicating information. For this reason, a film image must sometimes be restrained, less saturated with meaning than a painting or still photograph, in which all the necessary information is contained within a single frame. The principles of variation and restraint exist in all temporal arts. In movies, these principles can be seen in those images which seem rather uninteresting, usually because the dominant contrast is found elsewhere. Such deliberate pictorial anticlimaxes are necessary in the cinema because of its temporal nature and its enormous technical range of expression: in a sense, then, these anticlimaxes are visual "rest areas."

A film director has literally hundreds of different ways to convey meanings. Like the painter or still photographer, he can emphasize visual dominant contrasts. In a scene portraying violence for example, he can use diagonal and zig-zag lines, aggressive colors, close-ups, extreme **low angles,** harsh lighting contrasts, unbalanced compositions, large shapes, and so on. Unlike most other visual artists, the movie director can also suggest violence through movement, either of the subject itself or of the camera. The film artist can suggest violence through his editing. Furthermore, through the use of the soundtrack, violence can be conveyed by loud or rapid dialogue, harsh sound effects, and strident music. Precisely because he does have so many ways to convey a given effect, the film director will vary his emphases, sometimes stressing image, sometimes movement, other times sound. Occasionally, especially in climactic scenes, he will employ all three.

Even the greatest films, then, have some images of only routine interest, for there are times when the dramatic context calls for a nonvisual dominant contrast, and the image thus serves as a temporary subsidiary contrast.

FURTHER READING

ARNHEIM, RUDOLF. *Art and Visual Perception: A Psychology of the Creative Eye*. Berkeley: University of California Press, 1954. (Paper) An introduction to the manner in which the human eye organizes and interprets visual information. Primarily concerned with paintings and drawings.

———. *Towards a Psychology of Art*. Berkeley: University of California Press, 1966. (Paper) A theoretical discussion of the psychology of art, utilizing a gestalt approach.

———. *Visual Thinking*. Berkeley: University of California Press, 1969. (Paper) A psychological exploration of how we apprehend visual information.

BACHELARD, GASTON. *The Poetics of Space*. New York: The Orion Press, 1964. A philosophical discussion of the medium of space in literature and the visual arts.

FREEBURG, VICTOR O. *Pictorial Beauty on the Screen*. New York: The Macmillan Co., 1923. An exploration of the conventions of composition in the cinema. Presently out of print.

HALL, EDWARD T. *The Hidden Dimension*. Garden City: Doubleday & Company, Inc., 1969. (Paper) An anthropological exploration of how animals and humans use space.

———. *The Silent Language*. Greenwich, Conn.: A Fawcett Premier Book, 1959. (Paper) An anthropological study of how people communicate with each other without the use of words.

LORENZ, KONRAD. *On Aggression*. New York: Harcourt, Brace, Jovanovich, 1966. (Paper) An anthropological study of the ways in which animals and humans respond when space is redefined for them.

NILSON, VLADIMIR. *The Cinema as a Graphic Art*. New York: Hill and Wang, 1959. (Paper) An exploration of the ways in which reality is shaped and redefined by the formal properties of the cinematic shot, with major emphasis on composition.

SOMMER, ROBERT. *Personal Space*. Englewood Cliffs: Prentice-Hall, Inc., 1969. (Paper) An anthropological study exploring how individuals use and abuse space.

3 movement

"Movies," "motion pictures," "moving pictures"—all of these phrases suggest the central importance of motion in the art of the film. "Cinema" derives from the Greek word for "movement," as do the words **"kinetic"** and "kinesthesia," terms usually associated with the art of the dance. Yet oddly enough, filmgoers and critics give surprisingly little consideration to movement per se as a medium of communication. Like the image itself, motion is usually thought of in terms of gross subject matter: we tend to remember "what happens" only in the most general sense. If we were to describe a dance sequence from *Swan Lake* in such vague terms, our discussion would certainly strike the sophisticated dance enthusiast as naive,

(a)

(b)

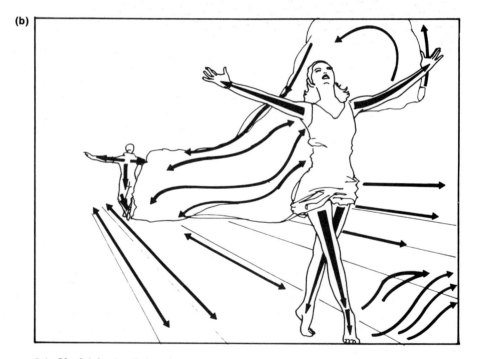

3-1. *Singin' in the Rain*.
Directed by Stanley Donen and Gene Kelly.
Dance sequences often exploit the kinetic symbolism of objects—such as the billowing veil—as well as dancers' movements to express these ideas. In effect, the fabric becomes an extension of the body. In this sequence the movements of the dancers (Cyd Charisse and Gene Kelly) suggest isolated lyrical "explosions," symbolizing the essentially private nature of the ecstasy of love, yet the two lovers are tenuously connected by the swirling veil which binds them together.

yet cinematic sequences—which can be "choreographed" with just as much or even greater complexity—are seldom appreciated for their kinetic richness and beauty.

KINESTHESIA

Like images, film movement can be literal and concrete, or highly stylized and abstract. In the kinetic arts—pantomime, mime, ballet, modern dance—we find a wide variety of movements, ranging from the **realistic** to the **expressionistic.** This stylistic spectrum can also be seen in film. For example, a highly naturalistic actor like Spencer Tracy employed only realistic movements, the same sort that could be observed in actual life. Pantomimists use more stylized movements. Chaplin, for example, tended to employ motion more **symbolically:** a swaggering gait and a twirling cane symbolized Charlie's (usually fleeting) arrogance and conceit.

Even more stylized are the movements of the performers in a musical. In this **genre,** characters express their most intense emotions through song and dance (3-1). A dance number is seldom meant to be interpreted literally: it's a stylized **convention** which we accept as a symbolic expression of certain feelings and ideas. In *Singin' in the Rain,* for example, Gene Kelly does an elaborate dance routine in a downpour. He twirls around street lamps, splashes through puddles like a happy idiot, and leaps ecstatically through the pelting rain—literally nothing can dampen the exhilaration of his love (see front cover). A wide gamut of emotions is expressed in this sequence, with each kinetic variation symbolizing the character's feelings for his girl: she can make him feel dreamy, childlike and helpless, erotically stimulated, brave and forthright, dopey and moonstruck, and finally wild with joy. In some kinds of action genres, physical contests are stylized in a similar manner. Samurai and Kung Fu films, for example, often feature elaborately choreographed sequences (3-2).

Ballet and mime are even more abstract and stylized. A great mime like Marcel Marceau is not so much concerned with expressing literal ideas (which is more properly the province of pantomime) as the *essence* of an idea, stripped of all superfluities. A twisted torso can suggest an ancient tree, bent elbows its crooked branches, fluttering fingers the rippling of its leaves. In the ballet, movements can be so stylized that we can't always assign a discernible "content" to them, though the narrative context generally provides us with at least a vague sense of what the movements represent. On this level of abstraction, however, movements begin to acquire certain self-justifying characteristics. That is, we respond to them more for their own beauty than for their function as symbolic expressions of literary or narrative ideas.

This concern with kinetic beauty for its own sake can be seen in certain schools of modern dance. Much of the choreography of Merce Cunningham and Erick Hawkins, for example, is not meant to communicate anything of a narrative nature. Abstract motion is presented for its own sake, somewhat in the same manner that pure colors, shapes, and lines are offered for their own sakes in non-representational paintings. Isadora Duncan was one of the pioneers of this school of dance, and several of the dance sequences in Karel Reisz's *Isadora* "represent" only the general feelings that the music inspires in the main character—a kind of kinetic abstract expressionism (3-3). In the movies, pure or non-representational movements are generally found in avant-garde films, in which literal representation and narrative ideas are deliberately suppressed.

In dance, movements are defined by the space that encloses the choreography, a three-dimensional stage. In film, the **frame** performs a similar function, though with each **set-up** of course, the cinematic "stage" is redefined. The intrinsic meanings associated with various portions of the frame are closely related to the significance of certain kinds of movements (3-4). For example, with vertical movements, the upward motion seems soaring and free precisely because it conforms to the eye's natural tendency to move upward over a composition. Movements in this direction often suggest aspiration, spirituality, power, and authority—precisely those ideas that are associated with the superior portions of the frame.

3-2a, b, c, d. *Enter the Dragon*.
Directed by Robert Clouse.
Physical contests such as brawls, sword fights, and oriental self-defense methods are often "choreographed" with considerable kinetic grace and elegance. The Kung-fu sequences staged by Bruce Lee are particularly stylized, almost like the dance.

(a)

(b)

(c)

(d)

3-3. *Isadora.*

Directed by Karel Reisz.

Certain schools of modern dance can be likened to abstract expressionism in the plastic arts. That is, the movements are pure and non-representational, suggesting only the private emotions and ideas that the music inspires in the dancer.

3-4.

The audience implicitly trusts that the camera will be aimed at the area of greatest interest—that the most important element of an image will appear near the center of the composition. By introducing movement from out of frame into the edge of the composition, a director can take his audience by surprise—a useful shock effect.

3-5. On the Waterfront.
Directed by Elia Kazan.
Downward motions can suggest danger, vulnerability, and insignificance, for the characters are sent into those "inferior" portions of the frame which tend to symbolize these ideas. When characters are made to move in a downward direction, a sense of tension and opposition is often suggested, for the eye's natural tendency is to move upward over a composition. In this shot, the sense of resistance and entrapment is reinforced by the enclosing walls on both sides.

Downward movements tend to suggest opposite ideas: grief, death, insignificance, depression, weakness, and so on (3-5). In some instances, movement from the top to the bottom of the frame can result in the sensation of being cramped or squeezed. Joseph Mankiewicz's *Suddenly Last Summer* exploits this psychological sensation effectively. Early in the film, several people are waiting for the mistress of the house (Katharine Hepburn) to descend in an elevator. Suddenly, she begins to address the visitors even as the elevator descends. Because the shot is from a **low angle,** the elevator seems to be slowly crushing the visitors. During the course of the film, we discover that our first impression of the lady was correct, for she ruthlessly attempts to destroy the lives of several of the characters who were in this earlier scene.

Since the eye tends to read a picture from left to right, physical movement in this direction seems psychologically natural, whereas movement from the right to left often seems inexplicably tense and uncomfortable. The sensitive filmmaker will exploit these psychological phenomena to reinforce his dramatic and thematic ideas. Frequently, for example, the

3-6. *The Red Badge of Courage.*
Directed by John Huston.
Like Griffith's *Birth of a Nation,* Huston's film exploits the two sides of the screen to keep the **continuity** of actions clear. Movements of the Union soldiers (the protagonists) are from left to right when they are attacking, from right to left when they retreat. The Confederate troops attack from the right to the left. Without these continuity aids, we would not always be able to understand the hero's physical relationship to the battles.

protagonists of a movie travel toward the right of the screen, while the antagonists move toward the left. In John Huston's *Red Badge of Courage,* the hero moves from right to left when he runs away from a battle in fear. Later, when he courageously joins an infantry charge, his movement is from left to right (3-6).

Movement can be directed toward or away from the camera. Since we identify with the camera's **lens,** the effect of such movements is somewhat like a character moving towards or away from us. If the character is a villain, walking towards the camera can seem aggressive, hostile, and threatening, for in effect, he's invading "our" space. If the character is attractive, the movement towards the camera seems friendly, inviting, sometimes even seductive. In either case, movement towards the audience is generally strong and assertive, it suggests confidence on the part of the moving character (3-7).

Movement away from the camera tends to suggest opposite meanings. Intensity is decreased and the character seems to grow remote, for in effect he's withdrawing from us. Audiences feel "safer" when a villain moves away in this manner, for he thereby increases the protective distance between him and ourselves. In some contexts, such movements can seem weak, fearful, and suspicious. Most movies end with a withdrawal of some sort, either of the camera from the locale, or of the characters from the camera. The final shot of Vittorio De Sica's *Bicycle Thief* shows the two defeated and humiliated protagonists walking away from the camera into a moving crowd: the effect is one of great delicacy and restraint, as though to pursue these characters further would be an invasion of their privacy.

There are considerable psychological differences between lateral movements on the screen and movements toward or away from the camera. A script might simply call for a character to move from one place to another, but *how* the director chooses to photograph this movement will determine

3-7. *The Garden of the Finzi-Continis.*
Directed by Vittorio De Sica.
Movements toward the camera are usually aggressive, while movements directed away from the camera tend to suggest diminution—a lessening of danger, courage, significance. When unattractive characters move toward the camera, as in this **shot** portraying a Fascist street rally, the movement is perceived as threatening and hostile, for the Fascists seem to invade our personal space, violating our sense of security and privacy.

(Cinema 5)

(a)

(Columbia Pictures)

(b)

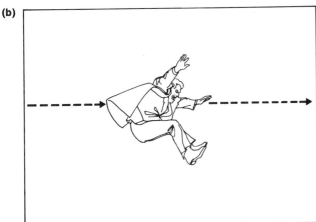

3-8. Shamus.
Directed by Buzz Kulik.
Action genres generally avoid movements into the depth of the image
in favor of lateral movements, which
emphasize speed, decisiveness, and
excitement. Such shots are usually
brief, for the amount of time required
to move from one side of the frame
to the other is minimal. Shots such
as these are generally employed in
chase sequences, and are edited
together at a rapid-fire rate.

most of its psychological implications. Generally speaking, if he moves from
right to left (or vice-versa), the character will seem determined and efficient,
a man of action (3-8). Unless the camera is at **extreme long shot** range,
these kinds of movements are necessarily photographed in brief **takes,** shots
lasting only a few seconds. Since lateral movements tend to emphasize
speed and efficiency, they're often used in action films: a staccato sequence
of quick shots **edited** together suggests a certain virile assertiveness.

On the other hand, when a character moves in or out of the "depth"
of a scene, the effect is often one of slowness and tedium. Unless the camera

(a)

(b)

3-9. *L'Avventura.*
Directed by Michelangelo Antonioni.
Psychological films often employ movements in and out of the depth of an image, especially to create a sense of tediousness and futility. Shots of this sort require anticipatory set-ups, which reinforce these qualities, for we see the destination of a character's movement long before it is completed. Here, the heroine's search for her lover in the corridors of a hotel suggests the futility of her love affair. The endless succession of doors, fixtures, and hallways implies, among other things, the repetition of the frustration she is now experiencing. Much of the meaning of shots such as these lies in their duration: space is used to suggest time.

is at close range or an extreme **wide angle lens** is used, movements towards or away from the camera take longer to photograph than lateral movements. With a **telephoto lens,** such movements can seem hopelessly dragged out. Furthermore, when a movement in depth is photographed in an uninterrupted lengthy take, the audience tends to **anticipate** the conclusion of the movement, thus intensifying the sense of tedium and frustration while we "wait" for the character to arrive at his destination. Especially when a character's goal is apparent—the end of a long corridor, for example—audiences generally grow restless if they are forced to view the entire action. Most directors would photograph the action in several different set-ups, thus compressing the time and space from the inception of the movement to its conclusion. Michelangelo Antonioni often photographs such actions in uninterrupted takes for symbolic purposes. His characters are usually engaged in a frustrating spiritual quest of some kind, a quest often symbolized by a physical journey or search. By deliberately wearing down his audiences with lengthy takes of characters moving in and out of the "depth" of his scenes, Antonioni forces us to experience some of the same fatigue that his characters are forced to endure. Needless to say, Antonioni's films "move" notoriously slowly (3-9).

The distance and angle from which movement is photographed determines much of its meaning. Distance and angle particularly influence the speed and intensity of motion. In general, the longer the shot and the higher the angle, the slower movement tends to appear. If movement is recorded from close ranges and low angles, it seems intensified and often speeded up. A film director can photograph the same subject matter—a running man, for example—in two different set-ups and produce opposite meanings. If the man is photographed in an extreme long shot from a **high angle,** he will seem hopelessly ineffectual and impotent. If he's photographed from a low angle in a **medium shot,** he will seem to be a dynamo of energy and determination. Despite the fact that the subjects of both set-ups are absolutely identical, the different forms radically alter their meaning.

Many viewers, oblivious to these perceptual relationships, tend to think of movement only in terms of gross physical action. The result has been a good deal of naive theorizing on what is "intrinsically cinematic." Such viewers tend to think that the more extravagant the movement would be perceived in real life, the more filmic it becomes. Subject matter that emphasizes **epic** events and exterior locations are presumed to be fundamentally more suited to the medium than intimate, restricted, or interior subjects. On the other hand, self-consciously highbrow viewers sometimes claim that such films are vulgar and shallow, that they're "mere action movies." Such viewers prefer "art" films, preferably European, with their de-emphasis of action in favor of "quiet" and "subtle" subjects.

Both types of viewers tend to misunderstand the nature of movement in film, though to be sure, one can use the terms "epic" and **"psychological"** in describing the general emphasis of a movie. But even on this general level, arguments about what is "intrinsically cinematic" are usually spurious. Few would claim that Tolstoy's *War and Peace* is intrinsically more novelistic than Dostoyevsky's *Crime and Punishment,* though we may refer to one as an epic and the other as a psychological novel. In a similar vein, only a naive observer would claim that Michelangelo's Sistine Ceiling is intrinsically more visual than a Vermeer domestic scene. They're different, yes. But one is not necessarily better than the other. In short, there are some good and bad epic works of art, and some good and bad psychological works. It's the treatment that counts, not the material per se.

But movement in film is more subtle than this, for it's necessarily de-

3-10a.
By Eric Zeehandelaar.
3-10b. Eclipse.
Directed by Michelangelo Antonioni.
Movement in film is always scaled to the amount of space within the frame, not necessarily to how motion might be perceived in actual life. In these photos, for example, there would be more movement involved in the extreme close-up of a man blinking his eye than there would be in the extreme long shot of the sun sinking beneath the horizon.

(a)

(b)

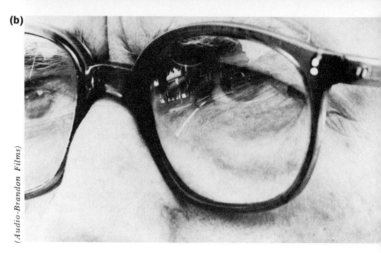

(Audio-Brandon Films)

pendent upon the kind of shot employed. The cinematic close-up can convey just as much or more movement than the most sweeping vistas in extreme long shot. Indeed, in terms of absolute movement on the screen, there's actually more action in a *close-up* showing tears running down a person's face than there is in an *extreme long shot* of a car traveling fifty feet. In the dance, movement is always scaled to the proportions of the human body, but cinematic movement is always relative to the shot. An epic film like Kurosawa's *Seven Samurai* might appear to have more movement than a claustrophobic psychological film like Carl Dreyer's *The Passion of Joan of Arc,* but in fact, Dreyer's film is photographed mostly in close-up: the movement of a feature might literally cover yards of space on the screen's surface. Yet many critics repeatedly commit the "intrinsically cinematic" fallacy, when, for example, they dismiss excellent films like William Wyler's *The Heiress* and Fred Zinnemann's *Member of the Wedding,* on the grounds that they're "too restricted in scope" for filmic treatment.

What is usually the case is that epic and psychological films employ movement in different ways, with emphasis on different shots. In general, epic movies depend on the longer shots for their effects, whereas psychological films tend to employ the closer shots. Epics are concerned with a sense of sweep and breadth, psychological movies with depth and detail. Epics often emphasize events while psychological films focus on the significance and implications of events. In good movies, as in good plays, these characteristics are matters of emphasis, not exclusion. Shakespeare's *Henry V*—which is conceived in "long shot"—is not devoid of psychological detail; nor is Chekhov's *The Cherry Orchard*—conceived in "close-up"—lacking in action (3-10).

There have been cases in which two directors have approached the same material and produced totally opposing results. *Hamlet* is a good case in point. Laurence Olivier's film version of this play is essentially an epic, with emphasis on the longer shots; Tony Richardson's version is primarily a psychological study, dominated by close and medium shots. Olivier's movie emphasizes costume and setting. There are many **long shots**, especially of the brooding castle of Elsinore. Much is made of Hamlet's interaction with this moody locale. We are informed at the beginning of the film that the movie is about "a man who could not make up his mind." The long shots are used throughout to emphasize this interpretation visually. Most of the shots are **loosely framed**, suggesting that Hamlet (played by Olivier himself) has considerable freedom of movement, freedom to act. But he refuses to use this freedom, preferring instead to sulk in dark corners, paralyzed with indecision. When he does move, the motion is generally recorded from long distances, thus reinforcing the impotence of the protagonist in relationship to his environment.

Richardson's *Hamlet* is relatively unconcerned with costumes and décor. The protagonist (Nicol Williamson) is almost always seen in **tightly framed close-ups**. Unlike Olivier's indecisive and contemplative Hamlet, Williamson's is impulsive and rash, a man who often acts before he thinks. Imprisoned by the confining close-ups, the tortured hero virtually spills off the edges of the frame into "oblivion." The unstable hand-held camera can barely keep up with him as he lunges hyperkinetically from place to place. If the very same movements were photographed from a long shot range, of course, the character would seem to move more normally. In the legitimate theatre, these two interpretations would have to be achieved through other means, for though drama is in part a visual medium, the "frame" size (the confines of the set, or the proscenium arch) remains the same for the duration of the play. The theatre, in short, is restricted to "long shots," where such distortions of movement are virtually impossible.

If there is a great deal of movement in the closer shots, its effect on the screen will be exaggerated, perhaps even disorienting (3-11). For this reason, directors tend to employ these ranges for relatively static scenes. The animation of two people talking and gesturing, for example, is more than enough movement to prevent most medium shots from appearing lifeless. A memorable **two-shot** sequence from Elia Kazan's *On the Waterfront* takes place in the cramped back seat of a taxicab. Two brothers (Marlon Brando and Rod Steiger) engage in some masculine small talk. Before long, Brando painfully reminds the older brother that he (Brando) might have been a big-time prize fighter, had the older brother not inter-

(a)

(b)

(Warner Brothers)

fered by fixing the match. The facial expressions and gestures of the two
men represent the only significant movement in the scene. Yet it seems
almost electric with energy, mostly because of the brilliance of the two
actors. Brando's pained resentment, restrained by love, is perfectly conveyed
by the subtle modulations of his face. His clumsy embarrassment is reflected in his tentative hand gestures. Steiger's uptight fury gradually di-
minishes into remembrance and shame: wild-eyed and trembling, he avoids

3-12. The Wild Child.
Directed by François Truffaut.
Unlike the dance or the legitimate theatre, cinematic movement is always relative: even gross movements are not likely to be perceived in extreme long shot, whereas the path of the tear in this photo covers over half the height of the screen.

Brando's face. Finally, recognizing his guilt, Steiger seems almost to collapse, yet the actual movement is minimal: a sigh, and a slight lowering of the head and shoulders.

Close-ups are even more subtle in their recording of movement (3-12). The so-called "chamber films" of Bergman—*The Silence* and *Persona* for example—are heavily dependent on close shots, for these films are restricted by cramped interiors, small casts, and static situations. Robert Bresson and Carl Dreyer can extract both broad and subtle movements by photographing an expressive face in close-up. Indeed, these two directors have referred to the human face as a spiritual and psychological "landscape." In Dreyer's *Passion of Joan of Arc,* for instance, one of the most powerful scenes is a close-up of Joan (Falconetti) as a tear slowly trickles down her face. Expanded thousands of times by the close-up, the path of the tear represents a cataclysmic movement on the screen, far more powerful than the inane cavalry charges and clashing armies of most conventional epic films.

Clichéd techniques are almost invariably the sign of a second-rate director. Certain emotions and ideas—like joy, love, or hatred—are so prevalent in the cinema that the serious film artist must be searching constantly for new methods of presentation, methods which can confer uniqueness to the commonplace, transform the familiar into something fresh and un-

(a)

(Janus Films)

(b)

3-13. Yojimbo.
Directed by Akira Kurosawa.
Kurosawa's movies are rich in symbolic kinetic techniques. He often creates dramatic tensions by juxtaposing static visual elements with a small but dynamic whirlpool of motion. In this scene, for example, the greatly out-numbered protagonist (Toshiro Mifune) prepares to do battle with a group of vicious hoodlums. In static visual terms, the samurai hero seems trapped by the enclosing walls and the human wall of thugs who seem to block off his space. But surrounding the protagonist is a furious whipping wind (the **dominant contrast** of the shot), which symbolizes his fury and physical power.

expected. For example, grief for the death of a loved one is a common theme in the movies; because of its popularity, it has degenerated into a cliché. Yet the theme remains universal, one that can still move audiences if handled with any degree of originality and imagination.

One method of avoiding triteness is to convey emotions through kinetic symbolism. Like the choreographer, the film director can exploit the intrinsic meanings inherent in certain types of movements. Even so-called abstract motions tend to suggest ideas and feelings (3-13). Some movements strike us as soft and yielding, for example, while others seem harsh and aggressive. Curved and swaying motions are generally graceful and feminine (3-14). Those that are straight and direct strike us as intense, stimulating, and powerful. Movements can seem whispy, jerky, exploding, withering, and so on. Furthermore, unlike the choreographer, the filmmaker can exploit these symbolic movements without even having to use people to perform them.

If a dancer were to convey a sense of grief at the loss of a loved one, his movements would probably be implosive, withdrawn, with an emphasis on slow, solemn, downward movements. A film director might exploit this same kinetic principle, but in a totally different physical context. For instance, at the beginning of *Citizen Kane,* we realize that Kane has died when we see a fragile glass globe crash to pieces on the floor. This downward motion is followed by a shot of a window shade in Kane's sickroom slowly being lowered, an act which snuffs out the only source of light. In Walter Lang's *The King and I,* we realize that the seriously ailing King (Yul Brynner) has died when we see a close-up of his hand slowly slipping towards the bottom of the frame, disappearing finally off the lower edge into the darkness. In Eisenstein's *Old and New* (also known as *The General Line*), a valuable stud bull dies, and its death has serious consequences for the agricultural commune which has purchased the animal. These consequences are expressed through two parallel shots emphasizing the same kind of kinetic symbolism. First Eisenstein shows us an extreme close-up of the dying bull's eye as it slowly closes: the mournful lowering of the eyelid is magnified many times by the closeness of the shot. Eisenstein then cuts to a shot of the sun lowering on the horizon, its streaming shafts of light slowly retracting as the sun sinks below the earth's rim. Trivial as a bull's death might seem, for the hardworking members of the commune, it has an almost cosmic significance, for their hopes and dreams for a better future die with the animal.

Of course context is all in the movies. The kind of symbolism employed in *Old and New* would probably seem pretentious and arty in a more realistic film. However, the same kinetic *principle* can be used effectively in almost any kind of context. In Norman Jewison's *In the Heat*

(Paramount Pictures)

3-14. *Blonde Venus.*
Directed by Josef von Sternberg.
Some types of movements are intrinsically symbolic, while others derive their symbolic value from the dramatic context. Here, von Sternberg exploits both types of symbolism. The sinuous undulations of the fan (a traditional symbol of feminine coquetry) suggests the insolent eroticism of the heroine, played by the director's favorite actress, Marlene Dietrich.

of the Night, for example, a police officer (Sidney Poitier) must inform a woman (Lee Grant) that her husband has been brutally murdered. When she hears the news, the woman shields her body with her arms in a kind of shrivelling, implosive gesture. In effect, she withdraws into herself, her body slowly withering as the news sinks in. She will not permit even the sympathetic officer to touch or comfort her in any way.

In Charles Vidor's *Ladies in Retirement,* these same kinetic principles are employed with superb effect. An impoverished housekeeper (Ida Lupino) has asked her aging employer for financial assistance, to prevent the housekeeper's two retarded sisters from being put away in an asylum. The employer, a vain selfish woman who acquired her wealth as the mistress of a rich man, refuses to help her distraught employee. As a last resort, the desperate housekeeper decides to kill the old woman and use her isolated cottage as a refuge for the two good-naturedly dotty sisters. The murder scene itself is conveyed through kinetic symbolism. We see the overdressed dowager playing an absurd ditty at her piano. The housekeeper, who plans to strangle the woman from behind, slowly creeps up while she plays. But instead of showing us the actual strangulation, Vidor cuts to a medium close shot of the floor, where, one by one, the dowager's pearls drop to the floor. Suddenly a whole clump of pearls splatter near the old lady's now motionless feet. The symbolism of the dropping pearls is perfectly appropriate to the context, for they embody not only the woman's superfluous wealth, but her vanity and selfishness as well. Each falling pearl suggests an elegantly encrusted drop of blood. Drop by drop, her life ebbs away, until the remaining strands of pearls crash to the floor, and the wretched creature is dead. By conveying the murder through this kinetic symbolism Vidor prevents us from witnessing the actual event, which probably would have destroyed the audience's sympathy for the housekeeper. Indeed, Vidor's presentation of the scene actually encourages the audience to identify with her, since her motives are totally selfless.

In each of these instances, the directors—Welles, Lang, Eisenstein, Jewison, and Vidor—were faced with a similar problem: how to present a death scene with freshness and originality. Each director solved the problem by exploiting similar kinetic movements: a slow, contracting, downward motion.

Kinetic symbolism can be used to suggest many other ideas and emotions as well. For example, ecstasy and joy are frequently expressed by extravagantly expansive outward motions (3-15), fear by a variety of tentative or trembling movements. Eroticism is often conveyed through the use of undulating motions. In Kurosawa's *Rashomon,* for example, the provocative sexuality of a woman is suggested by the sinuous motions of her silk veil—a movement so graceful and tantalizing that the protagonist (Toshiro Mifune) is unable to resist her erotic allure. Since most Japanese viewers would regard overt sexuality in the cinema as tasteless—even kissing is rare in their movies—sexual ideas are often expressed through these symbolic methods.

Every art form has its rebels, and cinema is no exception. Because movement is almost universally regarded as a basic component of film art, a number of directors have experimented with the idea of stasis in film. In effect, these artists are deliberately working against the nature of their

(a)

(b)

3-15. *The French Connection.*
Directed by William Friedkin.
Expansive outward movements and sunburst effects are generally associated with explosive emotions, often of joy and ecstasy. In this shot, however, the symbolism is more complex. The scene occurs at the climax of a furious chase sequence, in which the much-despised protagonist (Gene Hackman, with gun) finally triumphs over a vicious killer by shooting him just as he seems on the verge of eluding the dogged police officer once again. This kinetic outburst on the screen symbolizes not only the bullet exploding in the victim's body, but a kind of expansive release for the protagonist after his humiliating and dangerous pursuit. The kinetic "ecstasy of death" also releases much of the dramatic tension that has been built up in the audience during the chase sequence: in effect, we're seduced into sharing the protagonist's joy in the kill.

medium—stripping it of all but the most essential motions. Such film-makers as Bresson, Ozu, and Dreyer have been described as **"minimalists"** because their kinetic techniques are so austere and restrained. When virtually nothing seems to be moving in an image, even the slightest motion can take on enormous significance. In many cases, this stasis is exploited

3-16. The Last Picture Show.
Directed by Peter Bogdanovich.
Film directors will occasionally use stasis or lack of movement to suggest ideas such as exhaustion, enervation, spiritual paralysis, and even death. In such instances, even the slightest movement—such as the motion of the woman's comforting arm—tends to acquire magnified and symbolic significance.

for symbolic purposes: lack of motion can suggest spiritual or psychological paralysis (3-16). This is often the case in the films of Antonioni, for example. In Eric Rohmer's *Claire's Knee,* the director satirizes his protagonist's hyperintellectuality by showing him constantly *talking* about sex. For most of the film, talk seems to be a substitute for action. Late in the movie, he places his hand on a girl's knee and the movement seems almost cosmic— at least for the rather pathetic protagonist, whose erotic desires seem to be totally satisfied by this harmless gesture. A few directors employ these minimal techniques so rigorously that their movies seem almost anticinematic. Jean-Marie Straub's *The Chronicle of Anna Magdalena Bach,* for example, consists of less than a hundred shots (most movies average around a thousand), in which the movements are so minimal that the slightest flicker of a finger, a hand, or a page of music can rivet our attention. Andy Warhol has reduced this principle of minimalism to an absurdity. With impish perversity, Warhol made an eight hour movie, *Empire,* which consists of a single stationary shot of the Empire State Building.

THE MOVING CAMERA

Before the 1920s, directors tended to confine movement to the subject photographed. There were relatively few who moved their cameras during a shot. Expressionist directors emphasized movement through editing. When the German directors of the 1920s created something of a sensation by employing moving cameras, the Russian expressionist directors were among the most hostile in their reactions. Moving the camera within the shot was too distracting, they felt, too "unnatural." Most importantly, the moving camera would destroy the primacy of editing, which they felt was the cornerstone of film art. To this day, many directors believe that camera movements ought to be kept to a minimum, that they are permissible only in obviously necessary instances—to keep a moving subject in frame, for instance.

Such German directors as F. W. Murnau and E. A. Dupont moved the camera within the shot not only for physical reasons, but for psychological and thematic reasons as well. Certainly some of these early directors probably got carried away. In general, however, the German experiments of the 1920s permitted subsequent directors to use the mobile camera to communicate subtleties previously considered impossible. Though editing might be faster, cheaper, and less distracting, the straight cut (that is, moving the camera *between* shots) does not always suit the purpose.

One major problem of the moving camera involves time. Films that employ this technique extensively tend to seem slow moving, since moving in or out of a scene is considerably more time-consuming than a straight cut. A director must decide whether moving the camera is worth the film time involved, and whether the movement warrants the additional technical and budgetary complications. If he decides to move his camera, he must then decide how. Does he mount it on a vehicle, or simply **pan** or **tilt?** Each major type of movement implies different meanings, some obvious, some subtle. Directors can choose from four basic kinds of camera movements: **pans, tilts, crane shots,** and **dolly shots.** Several relatively recent innovations—the **zoom lens,** the hand-held camera, and **aerial shots**—are variations of these basic four.

Pan and tilt shots—those movements of the camera that scan a scene either horizontally or vertically—are taken from a stationary axis, with the camera mounted on a tripod. Such shots are time-consuming, since the camera's movement must ordinarily be smooth and slow to permit the images to be recorded clearly. Pans are also unnatural in a sense, for when the human eye moves in a similar manner, it jumps from one point to another, and tends to skip over the intervals between points.

The most common use of a pan is to keep the subject within frame (3-17, 18). If a man moves from one position to another, the camera moves horizontally to keep him in the center of the composition. Pans in extreme long shot are especially effective in epic films, where an audience can experience a sense of the sweep and vastness of the locale. John Ford, for example, often pans over vast stretches of desert before finally settling on some travelers as they slowly make their way across the enormous expanse of terrain (3-19). But pans can be just as effective at medium and close ranges. The so-called **reaction pan,** for instance, is a movement of the camera away from the central attraction—usually a speaker—in order to capture the reaction of an onlooker or listener. In such cases, the pan is an effective way of preserving the cause-effect relationship between the two subjects, for a straight cut from one shot to another would tend to emphasize their separateness.

Pans can also be used to emphasize solidarity and the psychological interrelationships between people. In François Truffaut's *Jules and Jim,*

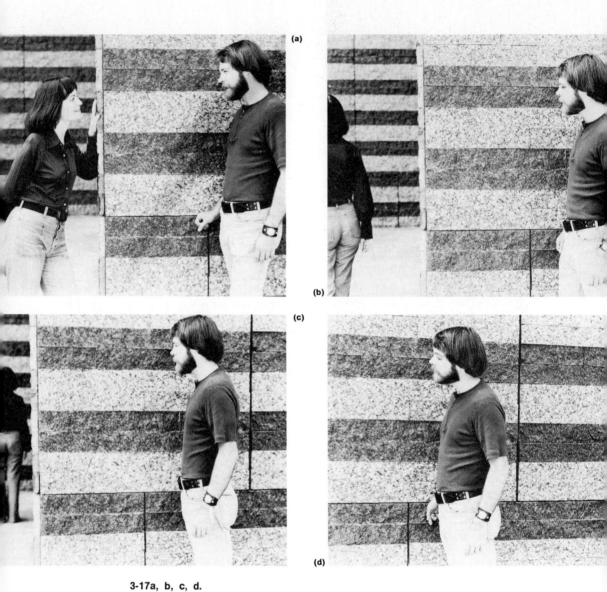

3-17a, b, c, d.
Photos by Evelyn Hayes.
If a character leaves the frame and the director simultaneously pans to correct the balance of the composition, the implication is not necessarily of loss but of adjustment and well-being, since no vacuum is created by the departure of the character.

for example, the camera pans rather than cuts between three characters in a scene. A woman is loved by two men, one her husband, the other his best friend. She stands in the middle of the frame, while the men sit at either side of her. There is a genuine sense of love that binds the three together, despite their legal and moral entanglements. To emphasize this, the director first pans to one character, then to another, and then to a third, and back and forth again, for the duration of the shot. The characters are engaged in a rather strained conversation all the while. Since the scene is photographed from a medium long range, the pan is too conspicuous to pass unnoticed—Truffaut's way of emphasizing the awareness of the characters of this awkward *ménage à trois*.

The **swish pan** (also known as a **flash pan** and a **zip pan**) is a variation of this technique and is often used for transitions between shots—as a substitute cut. What the swish pan involves is a movement of the camera so rapid that only blurred images are recorded. Despite the fact that it actually takes more time than a cut, swish pans connect one scene with another with a greater sense of simultaneity than a cut can suggest. For this reason, flash

3-18a, b, c, d.
Photos by Barry Perlus.
Significant movements in and out of the frame either create vacuums or fill them, thus suggesting important psychological ideas. Here, the movement of the young woman throws off the balance of the picture, since the original framing is preserved. A sense of loss is suggested by the spatial vacuum. If the woman had moved into the frame, a sense of completion and fulfillment would be implied, for her presence would correct the balance of the composition by filling in the void.

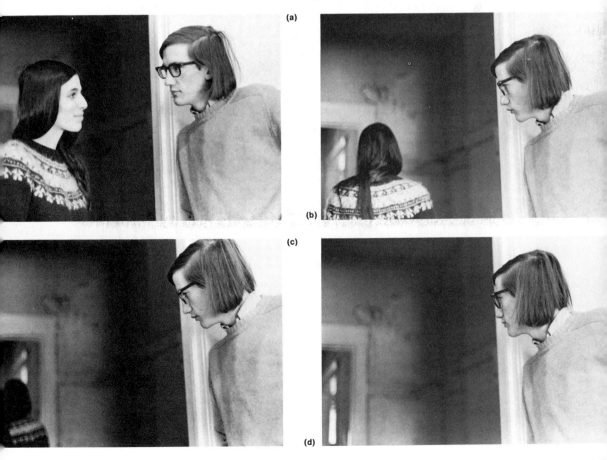

(a)

(b)

(c)

(d)

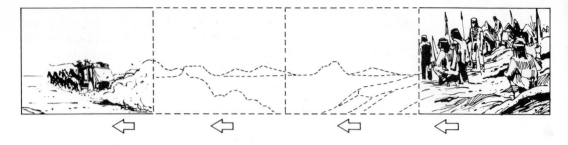

3-19.
In extreme long-shot range, the pan can suggest the vastness of a location by scanning it at length. Here, the shot opens with the Indians looking off from the edge of a bluff, pans leftward to give the viewer a sense of the desert terrain, and stops with the stagecoach making its way across the prairie. The panning shot connects the three elements in one continuous sweep.

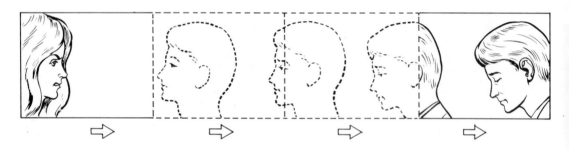

3-20.
At close-up range, the pan can suggest cause-effect relationships and the solidarity of groups. Individual shots edited together, on the other hand, would tend to suggest separateness and the individuality of the people in a group.

pans are often used to connect various events at different locales which might otherwise appear remote from each other. In *The Wild Bunch,* Sam Peckinpah used zip pans for reaction shots within the same scene. The effect is one of violence, rapidity, and simultaneity.

Because a pan shot tends to emphasize connectedness, some directors have used such shots to suggest symbolic rather than literal connections (3-20). In *The Manchurian Candidate,* for example, John Frankenheimer used a 360° pan with great daring and wit during several dream sequences. Some American prisoners of the Korean War have been brainwashed, and are being exhibited to a group of Communist observers in a laboratory amphitheatre. During the sequences, we also see what the brainwashed soldiers *think* is going on: that they're temporarily detained in a New Jersey hotel, listening half-heartedly to a lecture on horticulture which is being presented to a group of genteel dowagers. Several times Frankenheimer circles the entire assembly by beginning with the speaker's platform, scanning the audience, then circling back to the other end of the platform. But Frankenheimer interrupts these circular pans **by inter-cutting** the two "realities": genteel ladies are incongruously linked with Communist observers. The dreamers (who are still partially brainwashed many months later) are unable to make sense out of these weird mixtures of settings, characters, and events. Frankenheimer uses the circular **motif** as a metaphor of psychological determinism, a programmed pattern that begins to "short circuit" after the prisoners are released and sent back to America.

These same general principles apply to most tilt shots. A tilt involves the vertical movement of the camera around a horizontal axis. Tilts can be used to keep subjects within frame, to emphasize spatial and psychological interrelationships, to suggest simultaneity, and to emphasize cause-effect relationships. Tilts, like pans, can also be used subjectively, in **point-of-view shots:** the camera can simulate a character's looking up or down a scene, for example. Since a tilt is a change in angle, it is often used to suggest a psychological shift within a character: when an eye-level camera tilts down-

3-21. On the set of *Medium Cool*.
Directed by Haskell Wexler.
The so-called "crab dolly" does not require tracks, and can move on the ground in any direction. Note the technician's hands which pull the dolly in this traveling shot. Even on location, most directors prefer to record the sound. The overhead *boom*, of course, would not appear in the frame of the finished shot.

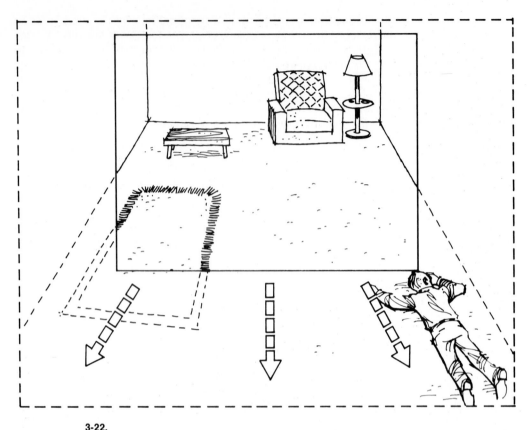

3-22.
The pull-back dolly begins by showing a restricted area. Then by withdrawing from that area the camera reveals some important detail which acts as a sudden revelation to the viewer. This technique is especially useful in suspenseful scenes.

ward, for instance, the person photographed suddenly seems more vulnerable.

Dolly shots, sometimes called **trucking** or **tracking shots,** are taken from a moving vehicle ("dolly") of some kind (3-21). Tracks are sometimes laid on the set to permit the vehicle to move smoothly—hence, the term "tracking shot." If these shots involve long distances, the tracks occasionally have to be laid or withdrawn while the camera moves in or out. Today, any vehicular movement of the camera can be referred to as a dolly shot. The camera can be mounted on a car, a train, even a horse. One of the most effective dolly shots in *Jules and Jim* was taken from a moving bicycle: the scene itself is a bicycle outing in the country, and to capture the lyrical, graceful movements of the characters on their bikes, Truffaut mounted the camera on a bicycle. A dolly need not be elaborate. To save money and to permit himself greater freedom of movement, Jean-Luc Godard has strapped his cameraman in a wheelchair, and pushed this improvised dolly himself. Such was the case in the long tracking shot at the conclusion of *Breathless,* where the camera follows the fleeing protagonist up a city street.

Tracking is a useful technique for point-of-view shots—to recreate a sense of movement in or out of a scene. If a director wants to emphasize the character's destination, he's more likely to use a straight cut between the initiation of the movement and its conclusion. If the experience of the movement itself is important, the director is more likely to track. Thus, if a character is searching for something, the time-consuming point-of-view dolly helps to elongate the suspense of the search. Similarly, the **pull-back dolly** is an effective technique for surprising the character (and audience) with a sudden revelation: by moving back, the camera reveals something startling —a corpse, for example (3-22).

A common function of tracking shots is to provide an ironic contrast with dialogue. In Jack Clayton's *The Pumpkin Eater*, a distraught wife (Anne Bancroft) returns to her ex-husband's house where she has an adulterous liaison with him. As the two lie in bed, she asks him if he had been upset over their divorce, and whether or not he missed her. He assures her that he wasn't in the least upset, but while their voices continue on the

(a)

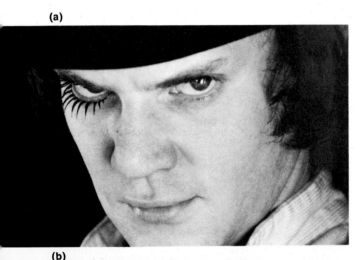

(b)

3-23a, b. *A Clockwork Orange.*

The pull-back dolly is often used to establish important psychological as well as physical information. Kubrick's movie opens with a close-up of the protagonist (Malcolm McDowell) staring brazenly at the camera. On the soundtrack, we hear his confidential commentary, which establishes an intimate if uneasy rapport between him and us: we become his confidents. Once this intimacy is established, Kubrick pulls back, and offers us a wider and longer view of the protagonist's physical surroundings, a weird "milk bar" where he and his "droogs" sit in a drug-induced stupor.

soundtrack, the camera belies his words by slowly traveling through his living room, revealing pictures, memorabilia, and mementos of the ex-wife. The shot is a kind of direct communication between the director and the audience. In a sense, shots of this sort can be compared with the **omniscient narrator** of a novel since they provide the reader with information which the characters lack. These techniques are deliberate authorial intrusions, and are particularly favored by filmmakers who view their characters with skepticism or irony—Godard and Hitchcock, for example.

Tracking shots are also used for psychological revelations. By slowly tracking in on a character, the director is getting close to something crucial. The movement itself acts as a signal to the audience, suggesting that we are about to witness something important. A cut to a close-up would emphasize the rapidity of the discovery, but a slow dolly shot suggests a more gradual and elusive revelation (3-23). For example, in Clive Donner's *The Caretaker* (also known as *The Guest*), this technique is used several times. Based on Harold Pinter's play, the film concerns two brothers and an old tramp who tries to set one brother against the other. The dialogue, as is often the case in a Pinter script, doesn't seem particularly helpful in understanding the characters: speeches seem to be wasted on totally irrelevant subjects. The brothers are dissimilar in most respects: Mick (Alan Bates) is materialistic and aggressive; Aston (Robert Shaw) is gentle and withdrawn. Each brother has a crucial scene in the film; in both the camera slowly tracks from a long range to a close-up. During these two shots, the camera gradually probes the psychological essence of the characters: with Mick, his obsessive preoccupation with "decorating" his various grubby properties; with Aston, his horrifying experience in a mental hospital where he received shock treatments which were meant to make him "like other people." Neither of the speeches is really very informative, at least not on a literal level. It is in the juxtaposition of the dialogue with the implications of the tracking shot that the audience feels it has finally "arrived" at an understanding of each character.

A stationary camera tends to convey a sense of stability and order, unless there's a great deal of movement within the frame. The moving camera—by its very instability—can create ideas of vitality, flux, and disorder. Orson Welles is fond of exploiting the mobile camera to suggest a character's dynamic energy. In his *Othello,* for example, the dolly shot becomes a thematic motif. The confident moor is often photographed in traveling shots, especially at the beginning of the film. In the ramparts scene, he and Iago walk with military briskness, as the camera moves with them at an equally energetic pace. When Iago tells him of his suspicions, the camera slows down, then comes to a halt. Once Othello's mind has been poisoned, he's photographed mostly from stationary set-ups: not only has his confident energy drained away, but a spiritual paralysis invades his soul. In the final shots of the film, he barely moves, even within the still frame. This paralysis motif is completed when Othello kills himself.

A number of film theorists have discussed the unique capacity of the cinema to convert space into time, and time into space. The simple duration of a shot—particularly a traveling shot—can sometimes be its main purpose. In other words, some directors exploit the dolly shot as a *consumer* of time. This is particularly true in some of the films of Alain Resnais and Bernardo Bertolucci, whose movies often have the theme of time (3-24). The acknowl-

3-24. The Conformist.
Directed by Bernardo Bertolucci.
A great admirer of Max Ophüls, Bertolucci has established as his trademark not only his fluid lyrical camera movements but also gracefully choreographed movements within stationary shots.

edged master of this type of dolly shot is Max Ophüls. In both *Letter From an Unknown Woman* and *The Earrings of Mme. de* . . . , the heroine throws herself into an imprudent but glorious love affair. The camera tracks relentlessly, as the women become more irrevocably involved with their lovers. As Andrew Sarris has pointed out, Ophüls uses his dolly shots as metaphors of time's cruel prodigality. His world is one of tragic flux and instability, in which love is destined to run its eventually bitter course. These lengthy tracking shots preserve the continuity of time by preserving the continuity of space: there is no time for pause and reflection "between shots" in these films. Ophüls' conversion of space into time can be overlooked by the casual viewer, for the dolly shots are at least to some degree functional: they follow characters in their daily rounds of activities. But a stationary camera could be just as functional (not to mention less expensive), for the characters could move toward or away from a fixed set-up.

In the 1950s, the introduction of a new lightweight hand-held camera permitted directors to move in or out of scenes with greater flexibility. Originally used by documentarists to permit them to shoot in nearly every kind of location, these cameras were quickly adopted by many fiction film directors as well. Hand-held shots are often jumpy and ragged. The camera's rocking

3-25. Shame.
Directed by Ingmar Bergman.
Particularly at close ranges, the hand-held camera tends to be unsteady. Here, the rocking suggests the motion of the boat. Shots like these almost always symbolize instability, impermanence, and transition.

is hard to ignore, for the screen exaggerates these movements, especially if the shots are taken from close ranges (3-25). For this reason, directors often use the hand-held camera for point-of-view shots. In Mike Nichols' *The Graduate,* a hand-held shot is used to simulate the hero's attempts to maneuver through a crowded room of people. In *Faces,* John Cassavetes used many hand-held shots to suggest an on-the-spot documentary flavor.

Crane shots are essentially airborne dolly shots. A crane is a huge mechanical arm, often more than twenty feet in length, which can lift a cameraman and camera in or out of a scene. Indeed, the crane can move in virtually any direction: up, down, diagonally, in, or out. The crane rather resembles those used by the telephone company to repair lines (3-26). Because of this flexibility, a crane shot can suggest a number of complex ideas. It can move from high long distances to low close ones, for instance, as it does

3-26. On the set of *Road to Utopia*.
Directed by Hal Walker.
When **synchronized sound** is required for a crane shot, the microphone is placed on a **boom** (pictured), a long telescoping pole which can follow the actors as they move on the set. Crane shots were especially popular during the golden years of the American studio system. Since the perfection of the zoom lens, the crane has been used with less frequency. In exterior locations, a helicopter is often used instead of a crane, for aerial shots permit a director to move his camera more extravagantly and lyrically.

in Hitchcock's *Notorious,* where the camera moves from an extreme high-angle long shot of a huge ballroom to an extreme close-up of the hand of the heroine (Ingrid Bergman), which is clasping a small key.

Because the camera can move in space, a number of filmmakers have used crane shots as metaphors of penetration. In the first Susan Alexander sequence of *Citizen Kane,* Welles used a spectacular crane shot that's been criticized for its flashiness by some critics. Through a downpouring rain, the camera cranes up to the roof of a seedy nightclub where the wretched Susan is performing, plunges through a neon sign advertising her engagement, then sinks down through the skylight of the nightclub, where Susan has collapsed in a drunken stupor. The camera's penetrating movement parallels the reporter's probe into Kane's "real" personality. Both the camera and the reporter encounter numerous obstacles—the rain, the sign, the very walls of the building must be penetrated before we can even see Susan, much less hear her speak. The shot also implies a brutal invasion of privacy, a disregard for the protective barriers that Susan has placed around her in her grief.

Like dolly shots, crane shots can be used to convert space into time. In the final sequence of Lumet's *Long Day's Journey Into Night,* the camera begins with a close-up and ends in an extreme long shot. The setting is the family living room, late at night. The mother, who is hopelessly addicted to morphine, is oblivious to her despairing family. She is vaguely reminiscing about her childhood experiences in a convent school, speaking more to herself than to the others. As she takes her journey into the past, the camera slowly moves back and up, from a close shot of the mother's face to a high extreme long shot of the entire living room. At the end of the crane's movement, the room is a dimly lighted white area, taking up less than a tenth of the screen, and surrounded by total darkness. The shot carries a multitude of symbolic meanings, all implied by the title. The "journey" is into the past, not only the mother's but the rest of the family's as well. The mother's journey into "night" is her increasing sense of isolation and oblivion, brought on by the drugs. The journey is also taken by the other members of the family, for the mother's night plunges the rest of the family into the same black despair.

The use of a zoom lens doesn't usually involve the actual movement of the camera, but its effect on the screen can be very much like a tracking or crane shot. The zoom is a combination of lenses, which are continuously variable, permitting a shift from wide-angle focal lengths to telephoto focal lengths almost instantaneously. The effect of the zoom is a breathtaking sense of being plunged into a scene, or an equally jolting sense of being plucked out of it. Zoom shots are used instead of dolly or crane shots for a number of reasons. They can zip in or out of a scene much faster than any vehicle. From the point of view of economy, they're cheaper than dolly and crane shots, for no vehicle is necessary. When filming in crowded locations, zoom lenses can be useful for photographing from long distances, away from the curious eyes of passers-by. With a single set-up of the camera, the zoom can switch from close to long ranges (and vice versa) with rapid ease. Much of the location shooting in *The Pawnbroker* required the presence of actual city crowds. Lumet shot these scenes from long unobtrusive distances, but with the help of the zoom lens, he was able to photograph close shots as well as long.

There are certain psychological differences between zoom shots and those that involve an actual moving camera. Dolly and crane shots tend to give a viewer a sense of entering into or withdrawing from a set: furniture and people stream by the edges of the screen, as the camera penetrates a three-dimensional space. Zoom lenses tend to foreshorten people and flatten space. The edges of the image simply disappear at all sides: the effect is one of sudden magnification. Instead of feeling as though we are entering a scene, we feel as though a small portion of a scene has been thrust *toward* us when we view a zoom. In shots of brief duration, these differences tend to be overlooked, but in lengthier shots, the psychological differences can be pronounced.

Since the early sixties, the zoom has been subject to overuse. Hack directors often use zoom shots to "zap up" their materials—to lend dull scenes a sense of crisis and urgency. A number of television adventure series wouldn't be possible without the indispensible zoom, for these programs seem to consist mostly of repetitive banal events which are made to seem cataclysmically significant by the rapid zooming in and out on essentially static scenes. Indeed, one of the surest signs of a desperate director is the arbitrary and frequent use of zoom shots.

In the hands of a master, however, zooms can be richly expressive and even subtle. In *The Wild Bunch,* for example, Peckinpah used a slight zooming in and out as metaphors of psychological tension and release. The wild bunch are bringing in a wagonload of weapons and munitions when they're ambushed by Mexican soldiers. Rather than give up the load to the soldiers, the bunch threaten to blow it up—and themselves with it. The decision rests with the Mexican officer in charge of the ambush. As the officer quickly sizes up the situation, Peckinpah zooms in slightly, framing the character in a tighter composition. Realizing that he's been outwitted, he smiles ironically, and agrees to let the bunch pass with their wagon. As he does so, the camera zooms back to its former position, thus releasing the tension of the tight frame. The shot functions almost like a screw, which turns in on the officer while he's under pressure to make a quick decision, then loosens up after he decides.

Aerial shots, usually taken from a helicopter, are really variations of the crane shot, for like the crane, the helicopter can move in virtually any direction. When a crane is impractical—usually on exterior locations—an aerial shot can duplicate the effect. The helicopter shot can be much more extravagant, of course, and for this reason, is occasionally used to suggest a sense of lyricism, a sweeping sense of freedom, as in the famous shot of the Beatles romping on a field in Richard Lester's *A Hard Day's Night.* In *Jules and Jim,* an aerial shot conveys Jim's transcendent sense of exhilaration when, after many years, he plans to visit his friend Jules and his wife in Germany.

MECHANICAL DISTORTIONS OF MOVEMENT

Movement in film is an optical illusion. Present-day cameras record movement at twenty-four frames per second. That is, in each second, twenty-four separate still pictures are photographed. When the film is shown in a

3-27. Snow White and the Seven Dwarfs.
By Walt Disney.
Beginning with the "Silly Symphonies" of the early thirties, the field of animation was dominated for many years by Walt Disney whose movies were ostensibly aimed at children. Disney's great feature length films—*Snow White, Bambi, Pinocchio,* and *Dumbo*—are classics of the cinema, and appeal to many adults as well.

projector at the same speed, these still photographs are "mixed" instantaneously by the human eye, giving the illusion of movement, a phenomenon called "the persistence of vision." By simply manipulating the timing mechanism of the camera and/or projector, a filmmaker can distort "natural" movement on the screen. Even at the turn of the century, Méliès was experimenting with various kinds of trick photography, and though most of these experiments were gags and clever stunts, subsequent directors have used these discoveries with great artistic results. There are five basic distortions of this kind: **animation, fast motion, slow motion, reverse motion,** and **freeze frames.**

There are two fundamental differences between animation film techniques and live-action movie methods. In animation sequences, each frame is photographed separately rather than "continuously" at the rate of twenty-four frames per second. Another difference is that animation, as the word implies, doesn't ordinarily involve the photographing of subjects that move by themselves. The subjects photographed are generally drawings, or static objects. Thus, in an animated movie, thousands of frames are separately photographed: each frame differs from its neighbor only to an infinitesimal degree. When a sequence of these frames is projected at twenty-four frames per second, the illusion is that the drawings or objects are moving, and hence, are "animated."

The common denominator of both animated and live-action film procedures is the use of the camera, the photographic process. In a sense, animation has greater affinities with the graphic arts, whereas ordinary films have closer affinities with the legitimate theatre. But in both cases, the recording camera acts as an intermediary between the subject itself and the audience. Even animated films, however, have different emphases. Many of the features of Walt Disney, for instance, are as dramatic as ordinary fiction films (3-27). Indeed, a number of parents have considered Disney's *Bambi* too frightening and violent for children. On the other hand, some of the brilliant animated films of the Canadian Norman McLaren and the Yugoslavian Zagreb School are virtually abstract expressionist paintings on celluloid.

(American International Pictures)

3-28. *Heavy Traffic.*
By Ralph Bakshi.
Many animated films are too mature or sophisticated, either in subject matter or technique, to be appreciated by young children. Bakshi's witty social satire is deliberately gross and raunchy, and was accordingly awarded an X rating.

(Apple Films)

3-29. The Yellow Submarine.
By George Dunning and Heinz Edelmann.
Feature length animated films require hundreds of thousands of separate drawings.

A popular misconception about animated films is that they're intended primarily for the entertainment of children—perhaps because the field was dominated for so many years by Walt Disney. Television has also popularized crude animation films designed almost exclusively for children. In actuality, however, the gamut of sophistication in this genre is as broad as in live-action films. The works of Disney and the puppet films of the Czech Jiri Trnka appeal to both children and adults. Some of the great Yugoslavian animated films are likely to appeal primarily to adults. There are even some X-rated animated films, most notably Ralph Bakshi's *Fritz the Cat* (based on the cartoon character by Robert Crumb) and *Heavy Traffic* (3-28). The computer-animated abstract films of John and James Whitney are dazzlingly sophisticated, and are not likely to appeal to children, nor are the mystical semi-abstract films of Jordan Belson.

Another popular misconception about animated movies is that they're more "simple" than live-action films. The contrary is usually the case. For every second of screen time, as many as twenty-four separate drawings can be photographed, though most animators use one drawing for every two frames. Thus, in an average ninety minute feature, over 648,000 drawings are usually necessary. Furthermore, some animators use transparent plastic sheets (called **"cels"**) which they layer over each other in order to give the illusion of depth to their drawings. Some single frames consist of as many as three or four layers of cels. Needless to say, most animated films are short precisely because of the overwhelming difficulty of producing all the necessary drawings for a longer movie. Most feature length animated movies are produced assembly-line fashion, with dozens of different draftsmen drawing thousands of separate frames. The animated Beatles film *The Yellow Submarine* was drawn by many different artists, though the guiding sensibilities were those of the Canadian director, George Dunning, and the designer, Heinz Edelmann (3-29).

Technically, animated films can be as complex as live-action movies. The same techniques can be used in both forms of filmmaking: traveling shots, zooms, angles, various "lenses," editing, **dissolves,** and so forth. The only difference is that animators most often *draw* these elements into their images, even though camera movements are also possible in animation. Furthermore, animators also can use most of the techniques of the painter: different kinds of paints, pens, pencils, pastels, washes, acrylics, and so on.

Some filmmakers have even combined the techniques of live-action with animation. In *Neighbours,* for example, McLaren used a technique called **"pixillation,"** which involves photographing live actors frame by frame (sometimes called "stop-motion photography"). When the sequence is projected on the screen, the actors move in abrupt, jerky motions, suggesting primitive cartoon figures. Other filmmakers have combined animation and theatrical film techniques within the same frame. This mixture is accomplished with the aid of the **optical printer.** Two film strips are superimposed, one consisting of animated frames, the other of photographs of actual people and things. **Mattes** are used to block out certain areas of the real scene where the animated drawings will appear in the finished print. Disney used this technique in many of the sequences of *Song of the South* and *Mary Poppins.* The technique is not always successful, for the reality of one style tends to contradict the plausibility of the other. The animated world has a kind of "reality" that often doesn't mesh with photographs of actual people and things.

Fast motion is accomplished by photographing events at a slower rate than twenty-four frames per second. Ordinarily, the subject photographed moves at a normal pace. When the sequence is projected at twenty-four frames per second the effect is acceleration, usually comic. Early silent comedies were photographed before the standardization of cameras and projectors to 24 fps, and so the speed of their action is exaggerated at present-day projector speeds. Even at eighteen or twenty-two fps, however, many of these early directors employed fast motion for comic effect. Without the use of acceleration, the great comedies of Mack Sennett would lose most of their vitality, and the exquisite timing of Keaton and Chaplin would be destroyed.

According to the French aesthetician, Henri Bergson, when men act mechanically, rather than flexibly, comedy is often the result. Man, unlike a machine, can think, feel, and act reasonably and appropriately. Man's intelligence is measured by his ability to be flexible. When his behavior becomes machine-like and inflexible, we laugh at him. One aspect of machine-like behavior is speed: when a man's movements are speeded up on film, he seems inhuman, ridiculous. Dignity is impossible in fast motion,

(a)

3-30a, b, c. *The Seven Samurai.*
Directed by Akira Kurosawa.
Kurosawa is a master of movements at all distance ranges,
whether he is portraying an elegantly choreographed samurai
sword fight in a very long shot
(a), a grisley slow-motion death
scene in a full shot (b), or a
medium close-up of a frightened
young man, whose fear is symbolized by the "trembling" flowers
in which he is hiding (c).

(b)

(Audio-Brandon Films)

(c)

for acceleration robs man of his humanity and reduces him to an automatic mechanism that seems wild and out of control. Even when it's used only for its own sake, fast motion tends to be funny. In Lester's *A Hard Day's Night,* acceleration is merely one of the dozens of visual gags in the film. Other directors use the technique more organically, for thematic purposes, or as an aspect of characterization. The hilarious Upton Inn mixup in Richardson's *Tom Jones* is funny precisely because the fast motion captures the machine-like predictability of all the characters: Tom flies from Mrs. Waters' bed, Mr. Fitzpatrick flies off the handle, Squire Weston screams for his daughter, and the servants scream for their lives. Fast motion is sometimes used to intensify the natural speed of a scene—one showing galloping horses, for example, or cars speeding past the camera.

Slow motion sequences are achieved by photographing events at a faster rate than twenty-four fps, and projecting the film at the standard speed. Slow motion tends to dignify and solemnize movement. Even the most commonplace action takes on a choreographic gracefulness in slow motion. Where speed tends to be the natural rhythm of comedy, slow and deliberate movements tend to be associated with tragedy. When violent scenes are photographed in slow motion, the effect is paradoxically beautiful (3-30). In *The Wild Bunch,* Peckinpah used slow-motion techniques to photograph the grisliest scenes of horror—flesh tearing, blood splattering, horses toppling: an almost endless variety. The "beauty" of these scenes of ugliness suggests why the men are so addicted to a life of violence when it seems so profitless: violence becomes almost an aesthetic credo, somewhat in the way that it is portrayed in the fiction of Hemingway. Slow-motion violence has become virtually a trademark in the works of Peckinpah, but after the mid-sixties, many other directors began imitating this technique, and it soon degenerated into a cinematic cliché.

Reverse motion simply involves photographing an action with the film running backwards. When projected forwards, the sequence of events is reversed. Since Méliès' time, reverse motion has not progressed much beyond the gag stage. Lester is fond of using this technique for absurd effects. In *A Hard Day's Night* he uses reverse motion as a comic choreographic "retake," and in *The Knack* it's used for a quick shock laugh, when an egg "returns" to its shell. One of the most expressive uses of reverse motion —combined with slow motion—is found in Jean Cocteau's *Orpheus.* The protagonist has taken a journey into Hell, to regain his lost wife. He makes a serious blunder while there and expresses a wish to return to his original point of decision to correct his mistake. Magically, he's whisked into the past before our eyes, as the previous sequence unrolls "backwards" in slow motion. The reverse motion in this sequence is a good instance of how space can be converted into time and time into space.

A freeze frame suspends all movement on the screen. A single image is selected and reprinted for as many frames as is necessary to suggest the "freezing" of motion. By interrupting a sequence with a freeze shot, the director calls attention to an image, offering it, as it were, for the audience's delectation. Sometimes the image is a fleeting, poignant moment, which is over in a fraction of a second, as in the final shot of Truffaut's *The 400*

Blows. Directors also use freeze frames for comic purposes. In *Tom Jones,* Richardson freezes the shot of Tom dangling on a rope's end, while the narrator urbanely explains to the audience why Tom should not hang.

In other instances, the freeze frame can be used for thematic purposes. The final image of Richardson's *The Loneliness of the Long Distance Runner* is frozen to emphasize the permanence of the protagonist's status at the end of the picture. Freeze frames are ideal metaphors for dealing with time, for in effect, the frozen image permits no change. At the end of *True Grit,* for example, Henry Hathaway froze a shot of the protagonist (John Wayne) and his horse leaping over a fence. By halting the shot at the crest of the leap, Hathaway creates a metaphor of timeless grandeur: the shot suggests a heroic equestrian statue, immune from the decay of time. Of course, the total absence of movement is often associated with death, and Hathaway's freeze frame also suggests this idea. Perhaps a more explicit metaphor of death can be seen in the conclusion of George Roy Hill's *Butch Cassidy and the Sundance Kid,* where the two protagonists (Paul Newman and Robert Redford) are "frozen" just before they are shot to death. Like Hathaway's freeze frame, Hill's suggests a kind of ultimate triumph over death.

Most of the mechanical distortions mentioned above were discovered by Méliès, though the zoom lens was invented much later. For many years after, these techniques were largely ignored by the majority of commercial filmmakers, until the late 1950s, when the New Wave directors in France reintroduced them. Since the early sixties, many of these techniques have been used indiscriminately. Zooms, freeze frames, and slow motion sequences have become almost *de rigueur* since that time. In many cases, the techniques degenerated into clichés, modish flourishes which were tacked onto the materials, regardless of whether or not the techniques were organic to the spirit of the subject.

Movement in film is not simply a matter of "what happens," then. The director has dozens of ways to convey motion, and what differentiates a great director from one who is merely competent is not so much a matter of what happens, but *how* things happen—how suggestive and resonant are the movements in a given dramatic context? Or, how effectively does the form of movement embody its content?

FURTHER READING

DEREN, MAYA. "Cinematography: The Creative Use of Reality," in *The Visual Arts Today,* ed. Gyorgy Kepes. Middletown, Conn.: Wesleyan University Press, 1960. An avant-garde filmmaker discusses the fusion of dance and documentary in the cinema.

FELDMAN, JOSEPH and HARRY FELDMAN. *Dynamics of Film.* New York: Hermitage House, 1952. Primarily on editing, though with many comments throughout dealing with various aspects of movement.

GIANNETTI, LOUIS D. "The Aesthetic of the Mobile Camera," in *Godard and Others: Essays in Film Form.* Cranbury, N.J.: Fairleigh Dickinson University Press, 1975. A discussion of the way in which the moving camera has been used to convey symbolic and metaphorical ideas.

JACOBS, LEWIS, *et al*. "Movement," in *The Movies as Medium,* ed. Lewis Jacobs. New York: Farrar, Straus, & Giroux, 1970. (Paper) A collection of essays on the nature of movement in film, written by Jacobs and others.

KNIGHT, ARTHUR. "The Street Films: Murnau and the Moving Camera," in *The Liveliest Art*. New York: A Mentor Book, 1957. (Paper) A succinct discussion of the contributions of the German cinema of the twenties in the art of the mobile camera.

MONTAGU, IVOR. "Film as Science," in *Film World*. Baltimore: Penguin Books, 1964. (Paper) A discussion of some of the technical aspects of movies, dealing especially with the differences between reality and the illusion of reality in film.

SARRIS, ANDREW. "Max Ophüls," in *Interviews with Film Directors,* ed. Andrew Sarris. New York: Avon Books, 1969. (Paper) A discussion of the symbolic implications of the mobile camera within the *oeuvre* of Ophüls.

STEPHENSON, RALPH. *The Animated Film*. New York: A.S. Barnes, 1973. (Paper) The most comprehensive study for laymen of the techniques and aesthetic of cinematic animation.

——, and JEAN R. DEBRIX. "Space in the Cinema: Cutting, Camera Movement, Framing," in *The Cinema as Art*. Baltimore: Penguin Books, 1965. (Paper) A discussion of some of the basic differences between the mobile camera, editing, and the art of mise-en-scène.

"The foundation of film art is editing."
—V. I. PUDOVKIN

4 editing

Thus far, we have been concerned with cinematic communication as it relates to the single **shot,** the basic unit of construction in movies. Except for traveling shots and lengthy **takes,** however, shots in film tend to acquire meaning when they are seen in juxtaposition with other shots, when they are structured into a coherent **edited** sequence. Physically, editing is simply joining one strip of film (one shot) with another. Shots are joined into **scenes,** and scenes into **sequences.** On the most mechanical level, editing eliminates unnecessary time and space. Through the association of ideas, editing connects one shot with another, one scene with another, and so on. Simple as this may now seem, the convention of editing represents one of the major cornerstones of film art. Indeed, Terry Ramsaye, an early film critic, referred to editing as the "syntax" of cinema, its grammatical language. Like linguistic grammar, the syntax of editing must be learned—we don't possess it innately.

Since 1900, editing has evolved into an art of remarkable complexity, nearly every decade providing new variations and possibilities. Before the turn of the century, most movies consisted of short anecdotes, photographed in **long shot** in one take. When the film **stock** was nearly exhausted, the vignette would be quickly concluded. The duration of the shot and the scene were equal. Essentially, these early movies were little more than stage playlets recorded on celluloid: the camera was stationary; the actors remained in long shot; the scene ran continuously, with screen time and real time roughly the same. For example, the central idea of one early film involves a man throwing a party for several girls. The man and the girls display a number of comic "bits"—flirtations, drinks being spilled, etc. Then the vignette ends with the entire cast boisterously leaving the set.

After 1900, filmmakers grew more ambitious. In France, England, and America, crude narratives made their first appearance. No longer merely vignettes, but "stories," these movies required more than a single set, and more than one continuous shot. The problem was **continuity.** Odd as it may now seem to us, the filmmakers of this period were worried that audiences would not see the relationship between one segment (shot) of a story and another. To solve their problem, they may have turned to the legitimate theatre for help. Here, the curtain was an accepted **convention,** implying a transition in time and/or place. The curtain, in effect, connected the various scenes and acts into a coherent whole. The **fade** was to film what the curtain was to drama. Quite simply, what a fade out involved was the diminishing of light at the conclusion of a scene until the screen went black; the next scene would then fade in, often revealing a different location at a different time. Usually the two scenes were unified by the presence of the same actor. As early as 1899, the Frenchman George Méliès made a short movie, *Cinderella,* in twenty "arranged scenes."

Before long, directors began cutting within scenes as well as between them. Edwin S. Porter, an American, is usually credited with this innovation, though in fact as early as 1900 the Englishman G. A. Smith inserted a **close-up** within a scene, and his countryman, James Williamson, featured an **intercut** chase sequence within one of his movies. These innovations were largely ignored, however, until Porter arrived at them independently somewhat later. Porter's *The Life of an American Fireman* (1902–3) pushed the concept of editing a step further. A simple story of a fireman's heroic rescue of a woman and her child, Porter's film contained seven scenes, the last of which featured three different shots: the firetruck arriving at the burning building; an interior shot of a woman and her child trapped in the burning building; and an exterior shot of the fireman carrying the woman down the ladder. (This last action was repeated in the rescue of the child.)

Traditionally, this scene would have been filmed in long shot, showing the entire action in one continuous take. By breaking up the scene into three different shots, Porter established the shot, and not the scene, as the basic unit of film construction. This new editing concept also introduced to film the idea of shifting points of view. Until that time, most movies were filmed in stationary long shot—roughly the same position that an actual observer would take. The duration of a scene would approximately correspond to that of the actual event. But with the breakup of shots into both exterior and interior positions, the "observer" is, in effect, at both places at once. Furthermore, since the time that elapses is not dependent upon the duration of the scene, a new subjective time is introduced, one dependent upon the duration of the various shots, not the actual event.

THE FOUNDATIONS: D. W. GRIFFITH

The American, D. W. Griffith, has been called the father of film, not only because he consolidated and expanded earlier cinematic techniques (in addition to devising many new ones), but because he was the first to go beyond gimmickry into the realm of art. One of cinema's greatest innovative geniuses, Griffith established, more than any other filmmaker in history, the basic language of film art (4-1). Within a very brief period, he explored

(Museum of Modern Art)

4-1. *Judith of Bethulia.*
Directed by D. W. Griffith.
Griffith began his experiments in editing almost as soon as he entered the film business in 1908. "The moving picture, although a growth of only a few years, is boundless in its scope and endless in its possibilities," he proclaimed. This film, made in 1913, features an elaborately intercut four-part structure, a device he was to perfect later in his 1916 masterpiece, *Intolerance.*

the three basic types of editing styles: **cutting to continuity, classical cutting** (sometimes called *découpage classique,* from the French *"découper,"* to cut up), and **thematic montage.** In his earliest movies, Griffith perfected the technique of cutting to continuity—the most basic and literal kind of editing. Classical cutting—a technique favored by most American fiction film directors until the early sixties—was refined in Griffith's masterpiece, *Birth of a Nation* (1915). A year later, in *Intolerance,* he was to explore the technique of thematic montage, though this style of editing wasn't perfected until the twenties, by the filmmakers of the Soviet Union.

Griffith recognized the principle of the association of ideas in the concept of editing and expanded this principle in a variety of ways. Cutting to continuity is a technique used in most fiction films, if only for exposition sequences. Essentially, this style of editing is a kind of shorthand, consisting of certain time-honored conventions. In general, cutting to continuity tries to preserve the fluidity of an action without literally showing all of it. For example, a scene of a man leaving work and going home might be condensed into five or six brief shots, each of which leads by association to the next: 1) the man enters a corridor as he closes the door to his office, 2) he leaves the office building, 3) he enters and starts his car, 4) he drives his car along a highway, 5) his car turns into his driveway at home. In order to keep the action logical and continuous, there must be no confusing breaks in an edited sequence of this sort. Often all the movement is carried in the same "direction" on the screen, for if the man should move from right to left in one shot and the movements are from left to right in the other shots, the viewer might think that the man is returning to his office. Cause-effect relationships must be clearly set forth: if the man slams on his brakes, for example, the director is generally obliged to offer us a shot of what prompted the driver to stop so suddenly.

The continuity of actual space and time is fragmented as unobtrusively as possible in this type of editing. Unless the audience has a clear sense of a continuous action, an edited sequence can be disorienting. (The term **"jump-cut"** means an editing transition that's abrupt or confusing in terms of space and time. Sometimes such abrupt transitions are deliberate.) In order to make his transitions smooth and continuous, Griffith carefully **established** his scenes in long shot at the beginning of a sequence. Gradually he cut to **medium shots,** then to close-ups. During the scene, he would often cut to **"re-establishing" shots** (a return to the initial long shot) in order to remind the audience of the context of the closer shots. "Between" these various shots, time and space could be expanded or contracted with considerable subtlety.

In exploring the technique of classical cutting, Griffith took the principles of cutting to continuity several steps further. Classical cutting involves editing for dramatic intensity and emotional emphasis rather than simply for reasons of continuity. Through the use of the close-up within the scene, Griffith managed to achieve a dramatic impact that was unprecedented in its time. Though close-ups had been used prior to this time, Griffith was the first to use close shots for *psychological* rather than purely physical reasons. Audiences were now permitted to see the subtlest nuances of an actor's face: no longer were the performers required to flail their arms and tear their hair. The slightest arch of an eyebrow could convey a

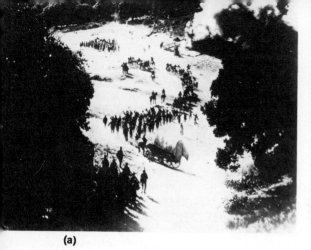

(a)

(b)

4-2a, b, c. *Birth of a Nation.*
Directed by D. W. Griffith.
Although this movie was made with rather primitive equipment, the battle scenes are still regarded as among the greatest ever photographed.
Griffith's editing in this film is masterly: despite
his enormous canvas, the continuity is always
clear. Whether he used **extreme long,** long, or
medium shots, the Confederates entered from the
left and the Union forces from the right.

(c)

(Museum of Modern Art)

multitude of emotions. By splitting the action into a series of fragmentary
shots, Griffith achieved not only a greater sense of detail, but a far greater
degree of control over his audience's reactions. In carefully selecting and
juxtaposing long, medium, and close shots, he constantly shifted the audience's point of view within the scene, excluding here, emphasizing there,
consolidating, connecting, contrasting, paralleling, and so on (4-2). The
possibilities were enormous. The spatial and temporal continuum of the
real scene was radically altered, and replaced by a substitute continuity—
the association of ideas implicit in the connected shots.

In its subtlest form, classical cutting presents a series of psychologically
connected shots—shots which aren't necessarily separated by real time and
space. For example, if four characters are seated in a room, a director
might cut from one speaker to a second with a dialogue exchange, then
cut to a reaction shot of one of the listeners, then to a **two-shot** of the
original speakers, and finally to a close-up of the fourth person. The sequence of shots in this series represents a kind of psychological cause-effect

4-3a–p. *Fat City.*

Directed by John Huston.

Classical cutting involves editing for dramatic emphasis rather than just to eliminate unnecessary time and space (b–p). Indeed, particularly during climactic scenes, this style of editing is more likely to expand time and space. The logic employed in the continuity of shots is mental and emotional rather than literal. In Huston's fight scene, for example, the entire boxing match could have been presented in a single set-up (a) though such a presentation would probably strike us as unexciting. Instead, Huston breaks up his shots according to the psychological "action" within the protagonist (Stacy Keach) and his manager and two friends in the auditorium.

(Columbia Pictures)

(a)

(b)

(c)

(d)

(e)

(f)

(g)

(h)

(i)

(j)

(k)

(l)

(m)

(n)

(o)

(p)

pattern. In other words, the breakup of shots is justified on the basis of dramatic rather than literal necessity, for the scene could be photographed just as functionally in a single **set-up,** in long shot. On this level of sophistication, classical cutting is essentially a series of shifting focuses of attention: the "action" is mental and emotional rather than physical (4-3).

During the golden years of the American studio system—roughly from 1930 to 1950—directors were often urged (or forced) to adopt the **"master shot"** technique of shooting. What this method involved was shooting an entire scene without cuts in long shot. This take contained all the dramatic variables, and hence served as the basic or "master" shot for the scene. The action was then repeated a number of times with the camera photographing medium shots and close-ups of the various principals in the scene (4-4). When all this footage was gathered together, the editor had a number of choices open to him in constructing a psychological continuity. Often disagreements arose over the proper sequence of shots. Some prestigious performers actually had clauses in their contracts stipulating a minimum number of close-ups per film, regardless of subject matter. Often the director was permitted to control the **"first cut"** (4-5). For the most part, however, the studios controlled the **"final cut"** under this system, and many directors disliked master shot techniques precisely because with so much footage available a willful producer could construct a totally different continuity. To protect himself against such interference, Hitchcock avoided master shots. To this day, his shooting techniques are so economical, virtually no changes can be made in his continuity without destroying the sense of a scene. Indeed, Hitchcock's scripts are so precise and detailed that a producer would have little to work with should he decide to re-edit a sequence. *Rear Window,* for example, yielded only a hundred feet or so of extra **footage** after the final cut!

Needless to say, Hitchcock's degree of precision is rare—indeed virtually unique—in the cinema. Master shots are still used by many directors, especially inexperienced ones, for without a master, editors often complain of inadequate footage—that the available shots "won't cut" smoothly. Even an experienced director like Arthur Penn apparently undershot in *Little Big Man.* Edited by Dede Allen (who was also responsible for the brilliant cutting of *Bonnie and Clyde*), the final military sequence of Penn's western—the Battle of the Little Big Horn—was muddled and confused, probably because of inadequate footage. The viewer is unable to tell where

(a)

4-4a, b, c, d. *Twelve Angry Men.*
Directed by Sidney Lumet.
Even with a single cramped set, the film director is able to open up limited space through the art of editing. A close shot containing a single figure (d) seems relatively spacious, even though the external dramatic context (a) is confining.

(b)

(c)

(d)

General Custer and his men are positioned, or where the Indians are coming from or going to. Particularly in complex battle scenes like this, most directors are likely to shoot many **"cover shots"**—that is, general shots which can be used as transitions to re-establish a sequence if the other shots won't cut. In *Birth of a Nation,* Griffith used multiple cameras to photograph many of the battle scenes, a technique used also by Kurosawa in some of the sequences of *The Seven Samurai*. Frank Capra used multiple cameras even in relatively simple scenes, to guarantee a sense of uniformity and spontaneity in the performances of the actors (4-6).

Griffith became particularly famous for his chase and rescue sequences which often ended his films. Most of these sequences feature **parallel editing**—or the alternation of shots of one scene with another, at a different location. By **cross cutting** back and forth between the two (or three or four) scenes, Griffith conveyed the idea of simultaneity. For example, near the end of *Birth of a Nation,* Griffith cross cuts between four groups: a besieged group of white people trapped in a cabin, a group of white vigilantes racing to their rescue, rioting Negroes on the rampage, and the heroine being forced into an undesired marriage. Despite its blatant racism, the sequence is still powerfully moving. In juxtaposing shots from these four scenes, Griffith managed to intensify the suspense by reducing the duration of the shots as the sequence peaked (4-7).

Generally speaking, the greater the number of cuts within a scene, the greater the sense of speed it conveys. To avoid the risk of monotony during this sequence, Griffith changed his set-ups many times: there are extreme long, long, medium, and close shots, varied **angles,** light contrasts, even camera movement.

If the continuity of a sequence is reasonably logical, the fragmentation of space presents no great difficulties. The problem of time, however, is more difficult to solve, since its treatment in film is more subjective than the treatment of space. Movies can compress years into two hours of film; conversely, films can also extend a few split seconds of time into many minutes. There are only a handful of films that attempt to make screen time conform to real time: Agnès Varda's *Cleo from Five to Seven* and

(a)

(Columbia Pictures)

4-5a–g. *The Last Picture Show*.
Directed by Peter Bogdanovich.
In its subtlest form, ***classical cutting*** can break up even a small area of action into smaller units of meaning. The French director-critic François Truffaut once observed that movies in which people tell lies require more shots than those in which they tell the truth. For example, if a young girl tells her mother that she thinks she is in love with a boy, and the mother responds by warning the girl of some of the emotional dangers involved, there's no reason why the scene shouldn't be done in a single set-up, with both females in the picture. Essentially, this is the way that Bogdanovich presents a similar scene (a). However, if the mother were a lying hypocrite, and the daughter suspected that the older woman might be in love with the boy herself, a director would be forced to break the scene down into five or six different shots (b, c, d, e, f, g) in order to give the viewer emotional information he would not receive from the characters themselves.

Fred Zinnemann's *High Noon* are perhaps the best known examples (4-8). Even these films "cheat" by compressing time in the expository opening sequences and by expanding time in the tense climactic scenes. In actual practice, time exists in a kind of limbo: so long as the audience is absorbed by the screen action, time is what the film says it is. The problem, then, is to hold the viewer.

On the most mechanical level, screen time is determined by the physical length of the filmstrip that contains the shot. This length is governed generally by the complexity of the image subject matter. For the most part, longer shots are more densely saturated with visual information than close-ups, and hence need to be held longer on the screen. Raymond Spot-

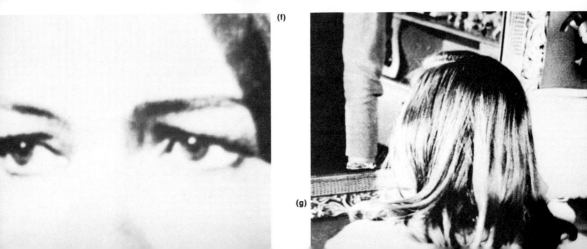

4-6. Preparing to shoot a parade sequence for *Mr. Smith Goes to Washington*.
Directed by Frank Capra (speaking at microphone).
Like many directors, Capra used multiple cameras (note the three mounted on the camera car) for crowd scenes. Unlike most filmmakers, he often used several cameras even within highly controlled studio interiors to avoid even subtle disjunctions of speech and reactions when the various shots were edited together.

tiswoode, an early film theorist, claimed that a cut must be made at the peak of the **"content curve"**: that is, that point in the shot at which the audience has been able to assimilate most of its information. Cutting after the peak of the content curve produces boredom and a sense of dragging time; cutting before the peak frustrates the audience's assimilation of information. An image with a complex **mise-en-scène** requires more time to be assimilated than a simple one, but once any image has been established, a return to it during the sequence can be considerably shorter.

But the sensitive treatment of time in editing is largely an instinctive matter, one that defies mechanical rules. Indeed, most of the great directors have edited their own films, or at least have worked in close collaboration with their editors, so crucial is this art to the success of a film. Like most great directors, Griffith had an almost unfailing sense of rhythm, and rhythm, or "pace" is what makes time in film convincing. The best edited sequences are determined by mood as well as by subject matter. Griffith, for example, generally edited love scenes in long lyrical takes, with relatively few set-ups. His chase sequences and scenes of confusion, on the other hand, were composed of many rapid shots, jammed together. Paradoxically, the love scenes actually compressed real time, whereas the rapidly cut sequences were elongations.

There are no fixed rules concerning rhythm in films. Some directors cut according to musical rhythms—the march of soldiers, for example, could be edited to the beat of a military tune. In some instances, a director will cut before the peak of the content curve. Particularly in highly suspenseful sequences, a director like Hitchcock will tease the audience by not providing enough time to assimilate all the meanings of a shot. On the other hand, Antonioni, in many of his films, cuts long after the content curve has peaked (4-9). Violent scenes are usually cut in a highly fragmented manner, but in *Bonnie and Clyde,* the exciting shoot-em-up se-

4-7. *Birth of a Nation.*
Directed by D. W. Griffith.
Famous for his last-minute rescue finales, Griffith cross cut between four different groups in the climactic sequence of this film. Despite the sense of speed suggested by the brevity of the shots, the sequence actually expands time. Griffith used 255 separate shots for about twenty minutes of screen action.

(Museum of Modern Art)

4-8. High Noon.
Directed by Fred Zinnemann.
Most movies condense time by eliminating all the undramatic stretches between the action highlights. Those few films tnat attempt to preserve real time—like *High Noon*—actually cheat somewhat by condensing in the undramatic expository sequences, and stretching time in the suspenseful climactic scenes. Most of the dramatic tension in this film was achieved through the art of editing. Throughout the movie, Zinnemann cross cut between various clocks and the worried face of the sheriff (Gary Cooper). The hero has approximately 75 minutes (the duration of the film) to try to round up some help to confront several killers who are waiting for their leader to arrive on the noonday train. Cooper was required to do little in the film other than look tense. These shots were juxtaposed with various shots of ticking clocks. The actor won an Academy Award as Best Actor of 1952, though in fact the real performance took place on the editor's bench.

quence of the motel escape is photographed in long shot, with only a few cuts. This combination is what produces the scene's bizarre blend of comedy and audacity.

Tact is another editing principle that's difficult to generalize about, since it too is dependent upon context. None of us likes to have the obvious pointed out to us, whether in real life or while watching a movie. Like personal tact, directorial tact is a matter of restraint, good taste, and respect for the intelligence and sensitivity of others. Too often directors present us with emotionally gratuitous shots, to make sure we haven't missed the point. Every emotion is milked dry by piling close-up upon close-up.

In *Intolerance,* Griffith pushed his techniques of editing to their most radical extreme: what we call thematic editing. This most sophisticated style of cutting stresses the associations of certain intellectual concepts irrespective of the continuity of real time and space. *Intolerance,* for example, is unified by the theme of man's inhumanity to man. Rather than tell just one story, Griffith presents four different examples of intolerance: one takes place in ancient Babylon; the second deals with the crucifixion of Jesus; the third with the massacre of the Huguenots in sixteenth century France; and the last takes place in America in 1916, the year the film was released. The stories are not developed separately, but in parallel fashion—with scenes of one time period intercut with scenes of another. At the conclusion of the movie, Griffith features hair-breadth chase sequences in the first and last stories, a suspenseful and brutal scene of slaughter in the third, and a slow moving tragic climax in the story of Jesus. The last sequence of the film contains literally hundreds of shots, juxtaposing images which

(Janus Films)

4-9. *L'Avventura.*
Directed by Michelangelo Antonioni.
The movies of Antonioni are among the slowest paced of the contemporary cinema. Long after the viewer has had time to absorb the visual information of a shot, it continues on the screen. Indeed, when this film was shown at the Cannes Film Festival, an audience of hostile critics kept shouting "Cut! Cut!" at the screen. The shots were so lengthy and the pace so slow that viewers assumed the director was inept at editing. But like many of Antonioni's works, this film is about enervation, exhaustion, and futility, and the rhythm of the editing is organically related to the subject matter.

4-10. The Pawnbroker.
Directed by Sidney Lumet.
The elaborate **flashback** structure and subliminal cutting in this movie represent Lumet's attempt to suggest the subjective nature of time. In this shot, the protagonist (Rod Steiger) examines some mounted butterflies in a display case which a customer wishes to pawn. The butterflies trigger the protagonist's memory, and eventually a sequence from his repressed past—also involving butterflies—displaces the present-tense scene.

are historically separated by thousands of years, and geographically by as many miles. All these different time periods and locations are unified by the central theme of intolerance. The continuity is no longer merely physical, or even primarily psychological, but rather thematic. Although *Intolerance* was not a commercial success, its influence was enormous. The filmmakers in the Soviet Union were particularly dazzled by **Griffith's** movie, and they based their own theories of *montage* on his practices in this film.

In several films, Griffith inserted "memory" shots that temporarily suspend the present. He thus established the concept of tense in the cinema—permitting future directors to interrupt the present by inserts not only of the past, but of the future as well (4-10). In Dennis Hopper's *Easy Rider,* for example, the protagonist (Peter Fonda) has a kind of prophetic vision of his own death. In Sydney Pollack's *They Shoot Horses, Don't They?,* short **flash-forwards** of a courtroom scene are interspersed throughout the present-tense story. The flash-forwards suggest a kind of hostile determinism: like the dance contest of the story proper, the future is rigged, and personal effort is equated with self-deception.

One of the most technically complicated uses of the **flashback** is found in Stanley Donen's *Two for the Road.* The story of the development and gradual disintegration of a love relationship, the narrative unfolds in a series of mixed flashbacks. That is, the flashbacks are not in chronological sequence, nor are they completed in any one scene. Rather, the flashbacks are jumbled and fragmented, somewhat in the manner of a Faulkner novel. To complicate matters, most of the flashbacks take place on the road, during various trips the couple has taken in the past. If the time periods of the film were to be designated with the letters A, B, C, D, and E, its temporal structure might be charted as follows: E (present), A (most distant past), B, C, D, B, A, C, D, B . . . ending with E. The audience gradually learns to identify each time period through various continuity clues: the women's hair styles, the modes of transportation, the particular crisis during each trip, and so on. In short, like Faulkner and other novelists, filmmakers have attempted to crack the tyranny of mechanically measured time through the manipulation of the flashback (4-11). This technique permits an artist to develop ideas thematically rather than chronologically, and allows him to stress the subjective nature of time.

From its crude beginnings, Griffith expanded the art of editing to perform a wide variety of functions: locale changes, time lapses, shot variety, emphasis of psychological and physical details, overviews, **symbolic** inserts, parallels and contrasts, associations, **point-of-view** shifts, simultaneity, and repetition of **motifs.** Furthermore, Griffith's method of editing was more economical, since related shots could be bunched together in the shooting schedule, regardless of their positions (or "time" and "place") in the finished film. Especially later, in the days of high-salaried **stars,** film budgets benefited, since directors could shoot all of the star sequences in a brief period and out of cinematic continuity, leaving details (extreme long shots, close-ups of objects, other actors) to be shot at a more convenient time. Later, all the shots would be arranged in their proper sequence on the editor's cutting bench. All film directors owe Griffith a debt of gratitude for establishing the basic conventions of cutting to continuity, and the more complex psychological techniques of classical cutting. In *Intolerance,* Griffith was years ahead of his time, for without its complex thematic cutting which virtually destroyed the literal approach to film time and space, the great experiments of the Soviet directors of the next decade would probably not have developed as they did.

SOVIET MONTAGE: V. I. PUDOVKIN AND S. M. EISENSTEIN

Griffith was a practical artist, concerned with communicating ideas and emotions in the most effective manner possible. During the years following his epic masterpieces, the Russian filmmakers expanded Griffith's associational principles and established the theoretical premises for thematic editing, or **montage,** as they called it (from the French, *"monter,"* to assemble). V. I. Pudovkin wrote the first important theoretical treatises on what he called "constructive editing." Most of his statements are explanations of Griffith's practices, but he differed with the American (whom he praises lavishly) on several important points. Griffith's use of the close-up, Pudovkin claimed, was too limited: it was used simply as a clarification of the long shot, which carried most of the meaning. The close-up, in effect, was merely an interruption, offering no meanings of its own. Pudovkin insisted that each new shot must make a new point. By the juxtaposition of a series of shots, new meanings emerge. The meanings, then, are in the juxtapositions, not in the shots alone (4-12).

To illustrate his point, Pudovkin quotes from the experiments of his colleague, Lev Kuleshov, who was also one of the first filmmakers in the Soviet Union. Kuleshov's experiments are now considered classics. The most impressive, and the most widely known, consists of a series of juxtapositions. First, he shot a close-up of an actor with a neutral expression.

4-11a–e. *Blume in Love.*
Directed by Paul Mazursky.
The dislocated flashback structure of this film permits us to contrast the present regret of the protagonist (George Segal) with the emotional stages he and his ex-wife (Susan Anspach) have gone through: a glamorous courtship (a), a romantic honeymoon in Venice (b), the first stages of marital boredom, restlessness, and guilt (c), a stormy divorce and the introduction of her new lover (played by Kris Kristofferson) (d), and finally—in the present—a solicitous reconciliation in Venice (e).

(a)

(b)

(c)

(d)

(e)

4-12a–n. An "edited sequence" from *The Golden Voyage of Sinbad*.
Directed by Gordon Hessler.

According to Pudovkin, the emotional effect of any given scene is not communicated by a single image, as in the legitimate theatre, but by the forced juxtaposition of two or more images. The continuity of an actual event has nothing to do with the continuity of shots, which can be created from completely unrelated materials. This "edited sequence," for example, was constructed from totally random publicity photographs and does not appear in the film. When shots of faces are juxtaposed with shots of the monster, the viewer assumes that the two are connected, that there is a cause-effect relationship between the shots. Pudovkin would claim that by editing together strips of movie film, a cinematic continuity could be similarly constructed, one which is not necessarily found in reality.

(Columbia Pictur

(a)

(b)

(c)

(d)

(e)

(f)

(g)

(h)

(i)

(j)

(k)

(l)

(m)

(n)

He juxtaposed this with a close-up of a bowl of soup. Then he repeated the close-up of the actor, and joined it with a shot of a coffin containing a woman's corpse. Finally, he used the same actor's neutral expression and linked it with a shot of a little girl playing. When these combinations were shown to audiences, they exclaimed at the actor's extraordinary expressiveness in portraying hunger, deep sorrow, and happiness respectively. Pudovkin's point carried. In each of the three cases, the meaning was expressed by the juxtaposition of two shots, not by one shot alone. Kuleshov's experiments also help to explain why film actors need not necessarily be skillful performers: in large part, they can be used as objects, juxtaposed with other objects. The dramatic emotion is in the juxtaposition, not in the actor's performance. In a sense, the viewer *creates* the emotional meanings, once the appropriate objects have been juxtaposed for him by the director and editor.

For Pudovkin, a sequence was not merely filmed, it was meticulously *constructed*. Using far more close-ups than Griffith, Pudovkin built a scene from many separate shots, all juxtaposed for one unified effect. The environment of the scene was the major source of the images, though long shots are relatively rare. Instead, a steady series of close-ups (often of objects) provides the audience with the necessary associations to link together the overall meaning. These juxtapositions can suggest emotional and psychological states, and even abstract ideas. The effectiveness of Pudovkin's films, especially his masterpiece, *Mother,* seems to justify his theory as a major approach to film art, though perhaps none of the great Russian films of the 1920s can justify Pudovkin's rather dogmatic assertion quoted at the beginning of this chapter.

Pudovkin, and the Soviet theorists in general, have been attacked on several counts. Some critics feel that the extensive use of close-ups not only slows the pace of a film (Pudovkin's films move notoriously slowly, despite the many cuts), but also detracts from a scene's sense of realism, for the continuity of actual time and space is almost totally restructured. But Pudovkin would claim that realism which is captured in long shot is *too* near reality. Indeed, his main criticism of Griffith was directed at his "slavish" adherence to real time and space. According to Pudovkin, the film artist must capture the essence, not merely the surface of reality, and he can do so only by conveying *expressively*—through juxtaposed close-ups of objects, textures, symbols, etc.—what is an undifferentiated jumble in real life.

Some critics feel that Pudovkin and his colleagues guide the spectator too much—that they make too many of the spectator's choices. The audience can only sit back passively, and accept the inevitable linking of associations presented to them on the screen. Political considerations are involved here, for the Soviets tended to link film with propaganda, and propaganda, no matter how artistic, usually doesn't involve free and balanced evaluations. Anti-montage film theorists, on the other hand, feel that an audience should not be passive, but should actively select and evaluate many of the relevant details on its own.

Sergei Eisenstein is almost universally regarded as one of the towering intellects of the world of cinema. A great film theorist as well as a director, for many years he was also a professor at the Higher Institute of Cinema in Moscow. Eisenstein was a man of encyclopedic erudition, and his stated aim in life was not merely to make movies, but to explore the nature of all kinds of artistic creation. In his teaching and theoretical writings on film, he constantly alluded to the other arts (especially painting, literature, and drama), to science, history, and philosophy. His contributions to the art of film editing—for which he is best known—can be fully understood only within this cultural and philosophical context.

Like many theorists, Eisenstein was interested in exploring certain general principles which could be applied to a variety of apparently different forms of creative activity. He believed that these artistic principles were organically related to the basic nature of all human activity, and ultimately to the nature of the universe itself. Needless to say, only the barest outline of his complex theories can be offered here. Like the ancient Greek philosopher Heraclites, Eisenstein believed that the essential nature of existence is based on constant change and flux. He believed that nature's eternal fluctuation was dialectical—that is, was the result of the conflict of opposites. What appears to be stationary or unified in nature is only temporary, for all phenomena are in various states of becoming (4-13). Only energy is permanent, and energy is constantly in a state of transition to other forms. Every opposite contains the seed of its own destruction in time, Eisenstein believed, and this conflict of opposites is the mother of motion and change.

The function of all artists is to capture this dynamic collision of opposites, to incorporate the concept of conflict not only in the subject matter of art, but in its techniques and forms as well. For Eisenstein, art was an organic extension of nature itself: art was a kind of mini-universe. The function of the artist is to sensitize the spectator to the eternal fluctuations of the macrocosm, to arouse in him the same conflict that can be observed everywhere in life. Conflict is universal in all the arts, according to Eisenstein, and hence, all art aspires to motion. Potentially at least, the cinema is the most comprehensive of all the arts because it can incorporate the purely visual conflicts of painting, the kinetic conflicts of dance, the tonal conflicts of music, the verbal conflicts of language, and the character and action conflicts of fiction and drama.

Eisenstein believed that the filmmaker should incorporate all of these dialectical conflicts in his techniques, but he placed particular emphasis on the art of editing. Like Pudovkin, he believed that montage was the foundation of film art. He also agreed with Pudovkin that each shot of a sequence ought to be incomplete, or "contributory," not self-contained. However, he criticized Pudovkin's concept of "linked" shots for being too mechanical and inorganic. Eisenstein thought that editing ought to be dialectical: the conflict of two shots (thesis and antithesis) produced a wholly new idea (synthesis). Thus, in film terms, the result of a conflict between shot A and shot B is not AB (Pudovkin), but a *qualitatively* new factor, C (Eisenstein). Transitions between shots should not be flowing, as Pudovkin suggested, but sharp, jolting, even violent. For Eisenstein, editing produces harsh "collisions," not smooth linkages. A smooth transition, he claimed, was an opportunity lost.

Editing, for Eisenstein, was an almost mystical process. He likened

(a)

(b)

4-13. Stagecoach.

Directed by John Ford.

According to Eisenstein, all art aspires to motion. Even a painting or still photograph is not static, but is carefully structured in a series of "eye-stops" over the surface of an image. In his classes, Eisenstein often assigned his students an exercise in the *découpage* of a still photo or painting. Their "shooting scripts" had to contain a shot-by-shot breakdown, complete with a rationale for the *sequence* of shots, which had to be inferred from the way that details were originally structured in a unified space. This photo, for example, could be broken down into at least six separate shots. Depending upon their sequence and visual emphasis, the shots could be exploited to create totally different cause-effect relationships.

it to the growth of organic cells. If each shot represents a developing cell, the cut is that "explosion" which occurs when the cell splits into two. Editing is that stage when a shot "bursts"—that is, when the tensions of the shot have reached their maximum expansion. The rhythm of editing in a movie should be like the explosions of an internal combustion engine, Eisenstein claimed. A great master of rhythm, his films are almost mesmerizing in this respect: shots of contrasting volumes, durations, shapes, designs, and lighting intensities do, indeed, collide against each other. But like objects in a torrential river, the jolting images plunge toward an inevitable destination (4-14).

The differences between Pudovkin and Eisenstein may seem to be merely theoretical. In actual practice, however, the two approaches produced sharply contrasting results. In Pudovkin's movies, the shots tend to be additive, and they are directed toward an overall emotional effect. In Eisenstein's films, the contrasting shots represent a series of essentially intellectual thrusts and parries, directed toward a predominantly abstract argument. The directors' choice of narrative structures also differed. Though both artists were didactic **Marxist** propagandists, Pudovkin's stories didn't differ radically from the kind that Griffith used: the shots are determined by the context of the narrative. On the other hand, Eisenstein's stories were much more loosely structured, usually a series of semi-connected documentary episodes, which he exploited as convenient vehicles for exploring ideas irrespective of literal time and place.

When Pudovkin wanted to express an emotion, he conveyed it in terms of physical images—objective correlatives—that were present in the actual locale. Thus, a sense of anguished drudgery is conveyed through a series of shots showing details of a cart mired in the mud: close-ups of the wheel, the mud, hands coaxing the wheel, straining faces, the muscles of an arm pulling the wheel, and so on. Eisenstein, on the other hand, wanted film to be totally free of traditional continuity. Pudovkin's correlatives, he felt, were too restricted by literal reality. Eisenstein wanted film to be as flexible as literature, particularly in its freedom to draw **metaphors** without respect to time and place. Movies should include images that are *thematically* relevant, Eisenstein felt, regardless of whether they can be found in the locale or not. Thus, in Eisenstein's earlier films, the space-time continuum is totally destroyed, and replaced by a continuity completely dependent upon the intellectual arguments of the director.

Like the dialectic in nature, the collision of two opposing elements (shots) should produce a qualitative leap, just as in literature, the yoking together of two conflicting quantitative elements can produce a metaphor which exists on a different qualitative level. Eisenstein's favorite examples were from Chinese hieroglyphs, in which two concrete characters are fused to produce an abstract idea:

the character for "door" plus "ear" means "to eavesdrop,"
the character for "mouth" plus "birds" means "to sing,"
the character for "knife" plus "heart" means "sorrow."

Even in his first feature, *Strike* (1925), Eisenstein intercut shots of workmen being machine-gunned with images of oxen being slaughtered. The oxen are not literally on location, but are intercut purely for metaphorical purposes. A famous sequence from *Potemkin* shows three shots of stone lions, one asleep, a second aroused and on the verge of rising, and a third on its feet and ready to spring. Eisenstein considered the sequence an embodiment of a metaphor: "The very stones roar." His most radical experi-

4-14a–hhh. A portion of the Odessa Steps sequence from *Potemkin*.
Directed by Sergei Eisenstein.
Perhaps the most famous instance of editing virtuosity in the history of the silent cinema, the celebrated Odessa Steps sequence is a brilliant illustration of Eisenstein's theory of collision montage in practice. The director contrasted lights with darks, vertical lines with horizontals, lengthy shots with brief ones, close-ups with long shots, static set-ups with traveling shots, and so on.

(Audio-Brandon Films)

(a)

(b)

(c)

(d)

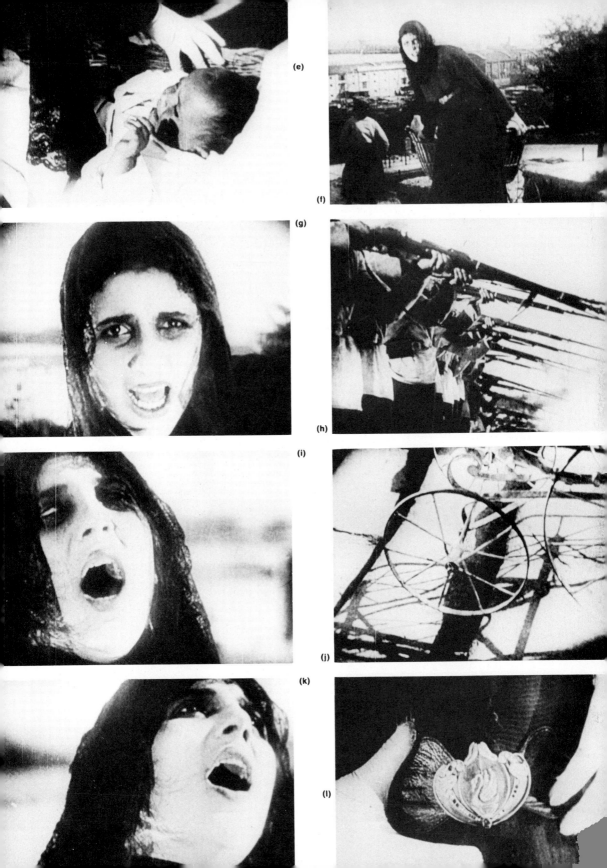

(e)

(f)

(g)

(h)

(i)

(j)

(k)

(l)

(m)

(n)

(o)

(p)

(q)

(r)

(s)

(t)

(u)

(v)

(w)

(x)

(y)

(z)

(aa)

(bb)

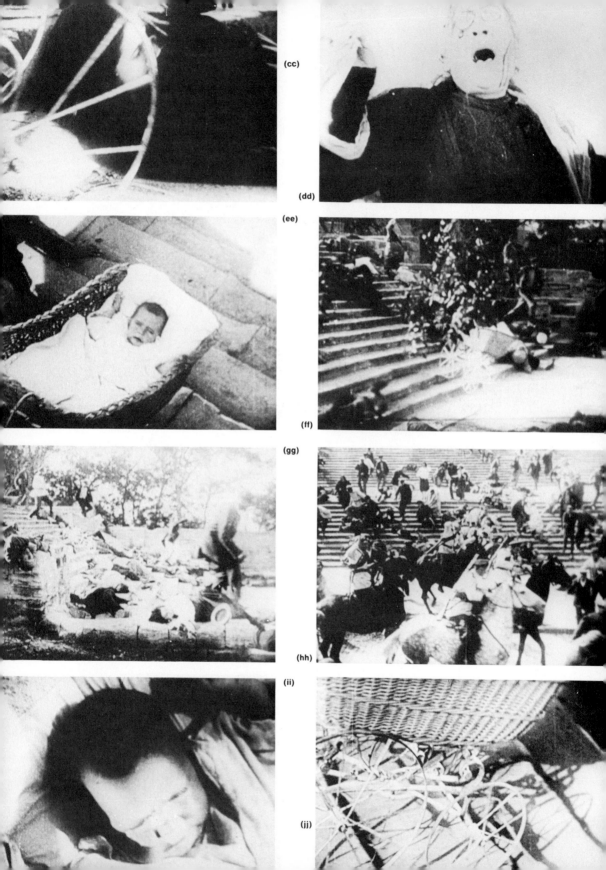

(cc)

(dd)

(ee)

(ff)

(gg)

(hh)

(ii)

(jj)

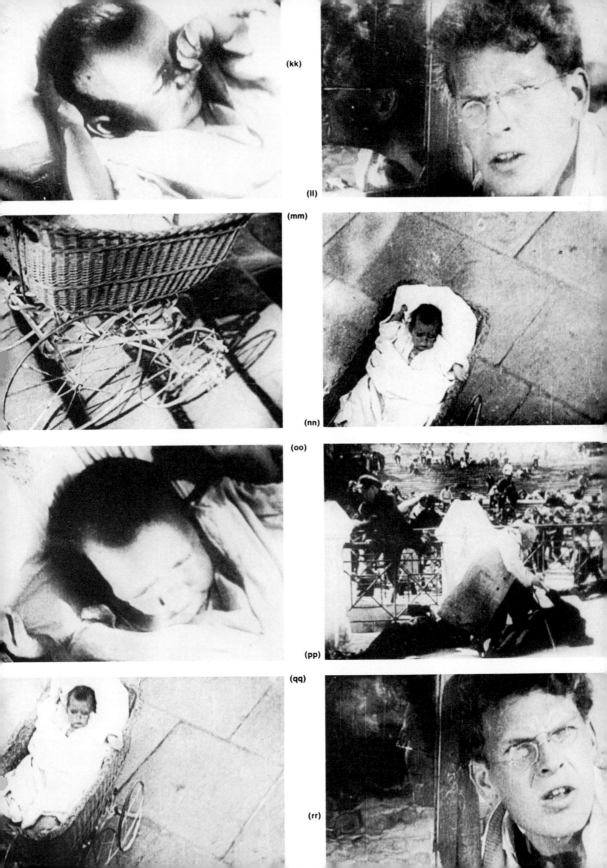

(kk)

(ll)

(mm)

(nn)

(oo)

(pp)

(qq)

(rr)

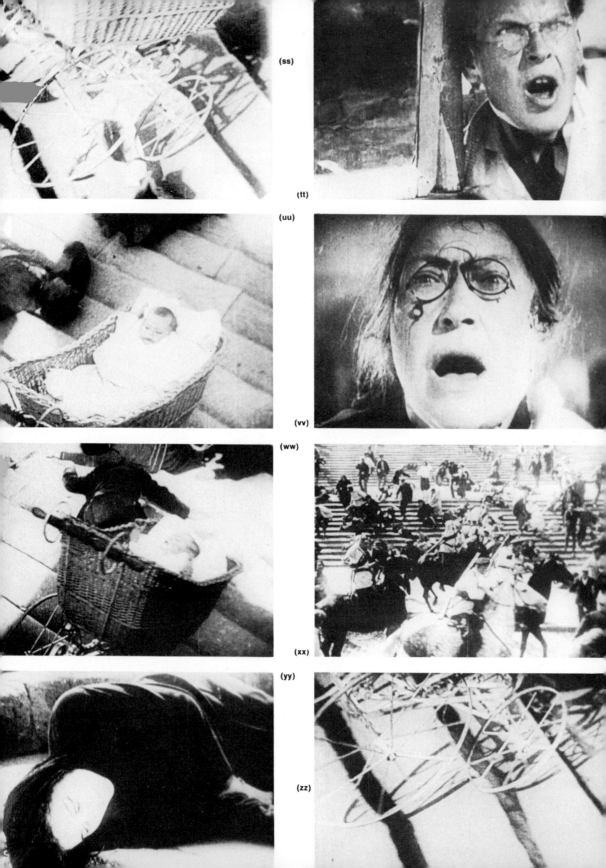

(ss)

(tt)

(uu)

(vv)

(ww)

(xx)

(yy)

(zz)

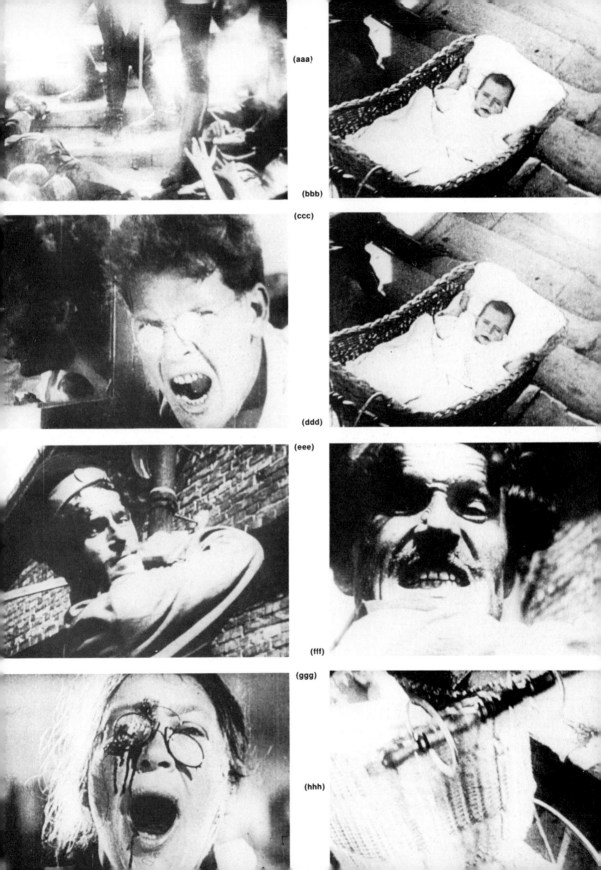

(aaa)

(bbb)

(ccc)

(ddd)

(eee)

(fff)

(ggg)

(hhh)

ments are found in *October* (also known as *Ten Days That Shook the World*). A loose documentary dealing with the earliest phases of the 1917 Revolution, the film is a good illustration of Eisenstein's theories in practice. An early sequence shows a statue of the czar being destroyed. Later, when the obsequious provisional leader Kerensky takes control, Eisenstein metaphorically describes this setback by running the statue sequence in **reverse motion.** The statue is reconstructed before our very eyes, and we thus "see" the temporary return of czarism. Many shots of Kerensky in the Winter Palace are similarly satiric: shots of Kerensky are juxtaposed with bejeweled toy peacocks, with statues of Napoleon, and so on.

Brilliant as many of these scenes are, the major problem with this kind of metaphoric editing is its tendency to be obscure. Eisenstein saw no real difficulty in overcoming the spatial and temporal differences between film and literature. But the two mediums employ metaphors and similes in different ways. We have no difficulty in understanding what is meant by the simile, "he's timid as a sheep." Or even the more abstract metaphor, "whorish time undoes us all." Both statements exist outside of time and place. The simile isn't set in a pasture, nor is the metaphor set in a brothel. Such comparisons, of course, aren't intended to be understood literally. In film, figurative devices of this kind are more difficult. Chaplin was able to express the sheep simile in the opening of *Modern Times,* but the metaphor of "whorish time" would probably be impossible to capture in film, for the materials of the cinema are concrete objects. A **multiple exposure** sequence of trees in different seasons juxtaposed with images of prostitutes might be a cinematic equivalent of this metaphor, but it's doubtful whether an audience would be able to decipher the comparison. In actual practice, editing can produce a number of figurative comparisons, but they don't work in quite the same way that they do in literature.

Eisenstein's editing theories and practices represent the most radical extreme in terms of distorting real time and space. Indeed, some of his techniques weren't revived until decades later. For the most part, however, film theorists tended to accept the Soviet line that editing was the cornerstone of all film art, despite the fact that in the United States, Germany, and elsewhere, filmmakers like Chaplin, Robert Flaherty, Erich von Stroheim, and F. W. Murnau were making movies that owed relatively little to the art of montage. These and other great realist directors found their champion eventually in the Frenchman, André Bazin, who established an aesthetic counter-tradition based on the *preservation* of real time and space.

ANDRÉ BAZIN AND
THE REALIST ALTERNATIVES

Unlike Griffith, Pudovkin, and Eisenstein, Bazin was not a film director, but solely a critic and theorist. For a number of years, he was the editor of the highly influential journal *Cahiers du Cinéma,* in which he set forth an aesthetic of film that was in direct opposition to many of the assumptions and practices of such **expressionists** as Pudovkin and Eisenstein. Furthermore, unlike the Soviet theorists, Bazin was untainted by dogmatism. Though he emphasized the **realistic** nature of the cinema, he was always generous in his praise of movies that exploited the art of editing effectively, particularly the works of Griffith, Hitchcock, and Bresson. Throughout his writings, however, Bazin maintained that montage was merely one of many techniques a director could employ in making movies. Furthermore, he believed that in many instances, editing could actually destroy the effectiveness of a scene (4-15).

Bazin's realist aesthetic is based on his belief that photography and cinema, unlike the other arts, produce images of reality automatically, with a minimum of human interference. This technological objectivity makes the cinema more immediate and credible, linking it directly with the observable physical world. A novelist or a painter must represent reality by *re*-presenting it in another medium—in this case, through language or color pigments. The filmmaker's image, on the other hand, is essentially an objective recording of what actually exists. No other art, Bazin felt, can be as literal and comprehensive in the presentation of the physical world as the cinema. No other art can be as realistic, in the most elementary sense of that word.

But Bazin's aesthetic has a moral as well as technological bias. He was strongly influenced by the philosophical movement called Personalism, which emphasized the individualistic and pluralistic nature of truth. Just as most Personalists agreed that there are many truths, not just The Truth, Bazin felt that in the cinema there are thousands of ways of portraying the real. The essence of reality, Bazin believed, lies in its ambiguity, for it can be interpreted in many different (and equally valid) ways, depending on the sensitivities and limitations of the perceiver. To capture the richness of this ambiguity, the filmmaker must be modest and self-effacing, a patient observer willing to follow where reality leads. The film artists that Bazin admired most—Robert Flaherty, Jean Renoir, and Roberto Rossellini, for example—are precisely those whose movies reflect a sense of awe and wonder before the ambiguous mysteries of reality.

Though Bazin expressed admiration for some expressionist movies, he believed that the distortions involved in using expressionistic techniques—and especially montage—often violated the complexities of reality. Such distortions superimposed a neat simplistic scheme over the infinite variability of the real world. Expressionists tend to be too egocentric and manipulative, Bazin felt, they are more concerned with imposing their willful and narrow view of reality than with allowing it to exist in all its awesome complexity (4-16). A great film historian, Bazin was among the first to point out that such directors as Chaplin, von Stroheim, and Murnau "respected" the ambiguities of reality by minimizing editing.

Unlike some of his followers, Bazin did not advocate a naive theory of film realism. He was perfectly aware, for example, that the cinema—like all art—involves a certain amount of selectivity, organization, and interpretation of reality: in short, a certain amount of distortion. He also recognized that the values of the filmmaker will inevitably influence the manner in which he perceives reality. These distortions are not only inevitable, but in most cases desirable, for Bazin believed that the best films are those in which the artist's personal "vision" is held in a delicate balance with the objective nature of the medium and its materials. Certain aspects of reality must be sacrificed for the sake of artistic coherence, then, but Bazin felt that abstraction and artifice ought to be kept to a minimum in order to allow the

(a)

(b)

4-15a, b, c. *Summer Wishes, Winter Dreams.*
Directed by Gilbert Cates.
Bazin was among the first theorists to point out that montage, with its aesthetic of fragmentation, was best suited to dealing with themes of division, separation, and estrangement (a and b). If the essence of a scene deals with ideas of reconciliation and proximity, however, (c) editing should be avoided.

(c)

materials to speak for themselves. Bazinian realism is not mere newsreel
objectivity—even if there were such a thing. He believed that reality must
be heightened somewhat in the cinema, that the director must reveal the
poetic implications of ordinary people, events, and places. Since it poeticizes
the commonplace, the cinema is neither a totally objective recording of the
physical world nor an abstracted symbolic recreation of it. In short, the
cinema occupies a unique *middle* position between the chaotic sprawl of
reality in the raw, and the necessarily artificial *imagined* worlds of the
traditional arts.

    Bazin wrote many articles which overtly or implicitly criticized the art
of editing, or at least pointed out its limitations. Montage is based on an
aesthetic of fragmentation he pointed out: actual time and space are "chopped
up" and manipulated into a new continuity which has no basis in reality. If
the dramatic essence of a scene is founded on the idea of division, separation,
or isolation, montage can be an effective technique in conveying any of these
ideas. But if the essence of a scene demands the simultaneous presence of
two or more related elements, the filmmaker ought to preserve the continuity

4-16. Gold Rush.
Directed by Charles Chaplin.
When asked why he avoided editing, the Italian neorealist director Roberto Rossellini replied, "Things are there: why manipulate them?" This statement might well serve as Bazin's theoretical motto. The essence of reality is its ambiguity, and as the most realistic of all artistic mediums, the cinema should preserve this ambiguity as much as possible. The viewer ought to decide for himself what the significance of a scene is. The director who overmanipulates his materials through excessive editing is super-imposing a simplistic interpretation on the ambiguous richness of the real world. Bazin particularly admired the restraint and tact of Chaplin's long shots and lengthy takes. Chaplin's mise-en-scène emphasizes layers and depths of meaning, Bazin pointed out, whereas editing tends to thrust visual information beneath our noses through the use of close-ups; mise-en-scène is more objective, whereas editing tends to be subjective and interpretive; mise-en-scène encourages audience participation, whereas editing preselects all the materials from reality beforehand. Philosophically, mise-en-scène emphasizes freedom and the multiplicity of choices, whereas editing tends to suggest coercion and inevitability.

of real time and space (4-17). He can do this by including all the dramatic variables within the same frame: that is, by exploiting the resources of the long shot, the **long take, deep focus,** and **widescreen.** The filmmaker can also preserve actual time and space by **panning, craning, tilting,** or **tracking** rather than cutting between individual shots.

John Huston's *The African Queen* contains a shot which illustrates Bazin's principle. In attempting to take their boat down river to a large lake, the two protagonists (Humphrey Bogart and Katharine Hepburn) get sidetracked on a tributary of the main river. The tributary dwindles into a stream, and finally trickles into a tangle of reeds and mud, where the dilapidated boat gets hopelessly mired. The exhausted travelers resign themselves to a slow death in the suffocating reeds, and eventually fall asleep on the floor of the boat. The camera then moves upward, over the reeds, and there—just a few hundred yards away—is the lake. The bitter

(Museum of Modern Art)   **(a)**   **(c)**   *(Cinema 5)*

(M-G-M)   **(b)**   **(d)**   *(Columbia Pictures)*

4-17a. *King Kong.*
Directed by Merian C. Cooper and Ernest Schoedsack.
4-17b. *A Night at the Opera.*
Directed by Sam Wood.
4-17c. *Z.*
Directed by Costa-Gavras.
4-17d. *Lightning Swords of Death.*
Directed by Kenji Misumi.
In direct opposition to Pudovkin, Bazin believed that when the essence of a scene lies in the simultaneous presence of two or more elements, editing is ruled out. Such scenes gain their emotional effect through the unity of space, not through the juxtaposition of separate shots. Particularly in films dealing with the fantastic, we are more likely to respond if the scene is presented "realistically"—with the ordinary and the extraordinary occupying the same spatial existence (a). The comic films of the Marx Brothers often derived their humor from the unity of objects and people in a single space (b). Chase sequences can seem more urgent when the pursuer and the pursued are included in the same frame (c). The desperation of a protagonist who must fight for his life can be more forcefully communicated if his enemies are shown invading his personal space (d).

irony of the scene is conveyed by the continuous movement of the camera, which preserves the physical proximity of the boat, the intervening reeds, and the lake. If Huston had cut to three separate shots, we would not understand these spatial interrelationships, and hence, the irony would be sacrificed (4-18).

Bazin pointed out that in the technological evolution of the cinema, virtually every innovation pushed the medium closer to a realistic ideal. The invention of panchromatic film stock in the mid-twenties allowed film-makers a much richer variety of grays in their images. Popularized by Flaherty's *Moana,* this stock permitted directors to eliminate the harshly contrasting blacks and whites which the orthochromatic stocks of the pre-1925 era almost inevitably produced. In the late 1920s, the invention of sound forced the cinema to become more realistic. Color and deep-focus photography in the thirties and forties pushed cinema yet closer to this realistic ideal. In the fifties, the popularization of widescreen further reduced the need to edit, as we shall see. Though Bazin wrote very little about the introduction of 3-D in the fifties, he certainly didn't dismiss it—as virtually every other critic and theorist did at the time—for like all the previous technological innovations, 3-D represented another step towards bridging the gap between reality and the "artificiality" of the screen image.

Indeed, Bazin pointed out that expressionistic techniques of editing were altered by technology, not by the critics and theorists of film. In 1927, when

(*United Artists*)

4-18. The African Queen.
Directed by John Huston.
Unified space is often necessary for purely literal reasons. In this scene, the frame excludes some crucial visual information which will be revealed later through the use of a traveling shot. If the contents outside and inside the frame were linked with a cut, the audience would be confused about the physical distance "between" the two shots, but through the aid of a mobile camera, the two areas are connected through a continuous movement which preserves the distance between them.

4-19. _All Quiet on the Western Front._
Directed by Lewis Milestone.
Even after most of the technical problems of sound had been ironed out, Bazin pointed out, movies continued to pursue a more realistic course. The highly fragmented editing styles of the twenties had become a thing of the past, for the continuity of sound anchored the shots to a more literal visual continuity, in which fewer shots were necessary. During the early sound period, dialogue sequences were generally photographed in _full shots,_ so that the source of the sound would be _visually_ apparent. Though many expressionists of this period were appalled by the more literal continuity required by **synchronous sound,** later theorists like Bazin believed that sound represented a giant leap in the evolution towards a totally realistic medium.

(Museum of Modern Art)

The Jazz Singer was released, sound eclipsed virtually all the advances made in the art of editing since Porter's day. With the coming of sound, films _had_ to be more realistic, whether their directors wished them so or not, for the microphones were placed on the set itself (4-19). Sound had to be recorded while the scene was being photographed. Usually the microphones were hidden—in a vase of flowers, a wall sconce, etc. Thus, in the earliest sound movies, not only was the camera restricted, but the actors as well, for if they strayed too far from the microphone, the dialogue couldn't be recorded properly.

The effects of these early sound films on editing were disastrous: synchronized sound anchored the images, so whole scenes were played with no cuts. Virtually all of the dramatic values were aural. The most commonplace sequences held a fascination for audiences: thus, if someone entered a room, the camera recorded the fact, whether it was dramatically important or not, and millions of viewers thrilled to the sound of the door opening and slamming shut. Critics and directors despaired: the days of the recorded stage play had apparently returned. (Later these problems were solved by the invention of the **"blimp,"** a portable soundproof camera housing which permits the camera to move with relative ease, and by the practice of **dubbing** sound after the shooting is completed.)

But sound also presented some distinct advantages. In realistic movies especially, spoken dialogue and sound effects heightened the sense of realism considerably. Acting styles had to be more sophisticated: no longer did performers have to exaggerate visually to compensate for the absence of sound. Talkies also permitted directors to tell their stories more economically, without the titles that interfered with the visuals in the silent days.

editing   **173**

4-20. *The Heiress*.

Directed by William Wyler.

Bazin was Wyler's most tireless champion. He particularly admired the American director's preference for deep-focus photography over montage. With all the visual information presented more objectively in this manner, the viewer is allowed to choose for himself what is significant or irrelevant in a shot. In this scene, for example, an edited sequence would probably focus on the faces of the two characters at the exclusion of the rather undramatic physical context. But Wyler deliberately included the empty tables and chairs as well as the waiting carriage in his shot, thus encouraging us to conclude that there is a subtle interrelationship between them and the heroine's arrogant but lonely father (Ralph Richardson, seated).

The tedious exposition scenes that began most movies could also be dispensed with, for a few lines of dialogue easily conveyed any necessary information an audience would need to understand the narrative relationships.

The use of **deep-focus** photography, re-introduced by Renoir in the thirties, also exerted a modifying influence on editing practices. Prior to this time, most lenses photographed only one focal plane clearly. These lenses could capture a sharp image of an object from virtually any distance, but unless an enormous number of extra lights were set up, other elements of the picture that weren't at the same distance from the camera remained blurred, out of **focus.** One justification for editing was purely technical then: clarity of image. If all shots—long, medium, and close—were to be equally clear, different lens adjustments were required for each.

Deep-focus photography became particularly popular after it was used in 1941 in *Citizen Kane*. Orson Welles and William Wyler are especially associated with this technique, and it's not coincidental perhaps that both these American directors had connections with the legitimate theatre. Deep focus permits composition in depth: whole scenes could be shot in one set-up, with no sacrifice of detail, for every distance appeared with equal clarity on the screen. Deep-focus tended to be most effective when it adhered to the continuity of unified space, and for this reason, the technique was thought to be more "theatrical" than cinematic: the dramatic effects are achieved primarily through the mise-en-scène rather than through the fragmented juxtaposition of shots. Bazin was particularly lavish in his praise of Wyler's "invisible" or "styleless" style, in which editing was kept to a minimum and characters maneuvered in a unified space (4-20). Some of the most effective movies to use deep focus were Wyler's adaptations of plays—especially *The Little Foxes*, *The Heiress*, and *The Children's Hour*. Similarly, Welles, who was actually trained in the theatre, has spent much of his film career adapting plays, including two exceptional adaptations of Shakespeare: *Othello* and *Falstaff*.

Bazin's admiration for *Citizen Kane* was unbounded, particularly for its brilliant exploitation of deep-focus photography, for he recognized that this technique inevitably reduced the importance of editing. In-depth photog-

(a)

(c)

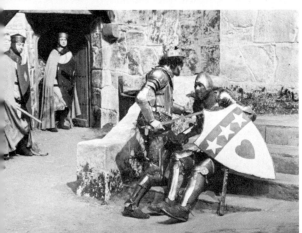

4-21a, b, c. Three frames from a lengthy take in *Macbeth*.
Directed by Roman Polanski.
Most fight sequences and scenes of violence are highly fragmented. When lengthy takes are used to preserve the temporal and spatial continuity of such sequences, a director can heighten the scene's realism by showing that the fight is not being faked through editing. Needless to say, these sequences must be painstakingly rehearsed, and the actors must be skillful swordsmen in order to avoid actually hurting each other.

(b)

4-22. The Wild Bunch.
Directed by Sam Peckinpah.
Although most filmmakers bemoaned the advent of widescreen in the fifties almost as much as they did sound in the late twenties, Bazin and other realists embraced the innovation as yet another step away from the distorting effects of montage. Widescreen tends to de-emphasize depth in favor of breadth, but Bazin believed that a horizontal presentation of visual materials could be more "democratic," and less distorting even than deep focus, which tends to emphasize visual importance in terms of an object's closeness to the camera's lens.

raphy preserved the unity of real time and space, since whole scenes could be photographed in a "mixed" shot—incorporating long, medium, and close distances simultaneously within one frame. Two, three, even four or five different spatial planes could be captured in one take, thus preserving the important psychological as well as physical relationships between people and their environments.

Bazin also liked the objectivity and tact of deep focus. Disregarding for the moment the emphatic elements of composition and movement, details within a shot could be presented more "democratically," as it were, without the special attention that a close-up inevitably confers. Thus, realist critics like Bazin felt that audiences would be forced to be more creative—less passive—in understanding the relationships between people and things. Unified space also preserved the ambiguity of life: audiences aren't led by the nose to an inevitable conclusion—à la Eisenstein—but are forced to evaluate, sort out, and eliminate "irrelevances" on their own. In short, deep-focus permits the viewer to exercise his creative powers of selectivity with the same freedom that he employs in real life.

Immediately following World War II, an informal movement called **neorealism** sprang up in Italy, and gradually influenced directors all over the world. Spearheaded by Rossellini and De Sica, two of Bazin's favorite directors, neorealism tended to reduce editing to a minimum. These film-makers favored deep focus photography, long shots, lengthy takes (4-21), and an austere restraint in the use of close-ups. Rossellini's *Paisàn* features a single-take scene which has been much admired by realist critics. An American G. I. talks to a shy Sicilian girl about his family, his life, and his dreams. Unfortunately, neither character understands the other's language, but they try to communicate in spite of this considerable obstacle. By refusing to condense time through the use of separate shots, Rossellini emphasizes the awkward pauses, hesitations and frustrations between the two characters. Through its preservation of real time, the long take forces us to experience with the characters the same tensions as they first increase, then relax. Single-take scenes like these tend to produce—often unconsciously —a sense of mounting anxiety in the viewer. We *expect* set-ups to change during a scene, and when they don't, we often get restless, hardly conscious of what's producing our uneasiness.

Like many technological innovations in film, widescreen provoked a wail of protest from most critics and directors. The new screen shape would destroy the close-up, many feared, especially of the human face. There simply was too much space to fill, even in long shots, others complained. Audiences would never be able to comprehend all the action, for they wouldn't know where to look. It was suitable only for horizontal compositions, some argued, useful for epic films, but incongruous for interior shots and "small" subjects (4-22). Fritz Lang claimed it was useful only for photographing funeral processions and snakes. Editing would be further minimized, the expression-ists complained, for there would be no necessity to cut to something if everything was already there, arranged in a long horizontal series.

At first, the most effective wide-screen films were, in fact, westerns and historical extravaganzas. But before long, a few directors began to use the new screen more subtly. Like deep-focus photography, scope meant that direc-tors had to be more careful about their mise-en-scène. More relevant details had to be included within the frame, even at the extreme edges. But this necessity also meant that films could be more densely saturated, and— potentially at least—more artistically effective. Furthermore, directors dis-covered that the most expressive parts of a person's face were his eyes and mouth, and consequently, close-ups that chopped off the tops and bottoms of actors' faces weren't as disastrous as had been previously predicted.

Not surprisingly, the realist critics were the first to reconsider the ad-vantages of widescreen. Bazin liked its "authenticity" and objectivity. Here was yet another step away from the distorting effects of editing he pointed out. As with deep focus, widescreen helped to preserve spatial and temporal continuity. Close-up images containing two or more people could now be photographed in one set-up, without suggesting inequality, as deep focus often did in its variety of depth planes. Nor were the relations between people and things fragmented as they often were with edited sequences. Scope was also more realistic because the expanse of the screen immersed the viewer in a *sense* of an experience, suggesting a kind of cinematic counterpart to the eye's peripheral vision. All of the same advantages that had been applied to sound and deep focus were now applied to widescreen: its greater fidelity to real time and space; its detail, complexity, and density;

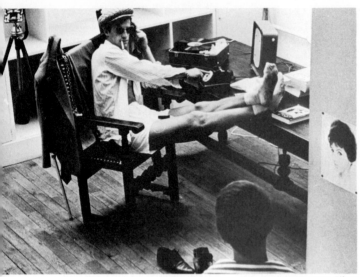

4-23. Breathless.
Directed by Jean-Luc Godard.
Perhaps more than any other single work of the New Wave, *Breathless* revolutionized film editing and set the pace for the cinema of the sixties. Godard claimed that his nervous cutting style and deliberate jump-cuts were in fact inspired by the practice of certain American **genre** directors like Samuel Fuller and Howard Hawks.

(Contemporary Films)

its more objective presentation; its more coherent continuity; its greater ambiguity; and its encouragement of creative audience "participation."

THE NEW WAVE AND AFTER

Interestingly, several of Bazin's disciples were directly responsible for a return to more expressionistic editing techniques in the late 1950s and early 1960s. Throughout the fifties, Godard and Truffaut both wrote criticism for *Cahiers du Cinéma* before turning to filmmaking in the later years of that decade. Indeed, there was an astonishing outburst of cinematic activity in France during this period, and many of these new directors had begun their careers as film critics—a pattern later to be repeated in England and the United States. The *nouvelle vague,* as this movement was called, was extraordinarily eclectic both in terms of theory and practice. The members of this group (which was never very tightly-knit) were unified by an almost obsessional enthusiasm for film culture, and the range of their enthusiasms was unusually broad: stretching from Hitchcock to Renoir, from Eisenstein to Flaherty, from Ford to Dreyer. Though these critic-directors were rather dogmatic in their personal tastes, they tended to avoid *theoretical* dogmatism. They could admire a long take from a Rossellini film as well as a highly fragmented sequence from an Eisenstein movie. For most of them, technique was meaningful only in terms of subject matter: discussions of form were usually placed within the context of content and vice versa. Indeed, it was the **New Wave** that popularized the notion that *what* a film says is inextricably bound up with *how* it's said.

The New Wave favored no "official" editing style. The movies of Agnès Varda, for example, tend to follow the Bazinian ideal of long shots and relatively lengthy takes. Her *Le Bonheur,* for instance, seems to be strongly indebted to the lyrical masterpieces of Renoir. The films of Resnais, on the other hand, tend to emphasize fragmentation. The theme of subjective time is explored primarily through *montage* in such works as *Hiroshima, Mon Amour* and *La Guerre Est Finie.* Claude Chabrol combined the influence of Hitchcock—particularly in his exploitation of the psychological thriller **genre**—and the more objective techniques of presentation advocated by Bazin.

Truffaut and Godard, the most prominent filmmakers of the New Wave, had the most encyclopedic techniques. Truffaut's first feature, *The 400 Blows,* tends to use realistic practices, with an emphasis on long shots, mise-en-scène, the moving camera, and lengthy takes. *Shoot the Piano Player,* on the other hand, is more expressionistically edited. Truffaut's first movie is strongly indebted to the films of Renoir and the theories of Bazin. His second film is more indebted to American genre films, with their stress on action, suspense, and a quick clean style of editing. Throughout his career, Truffaut has alternated styles: films like *Bed and Board* and *Stolen Kisses* reflect his profound love for the works of Renoir, whereas in *The Bride Wore Black* and *Mississippi Mermaid,* the prime influence is that of his other idol, Hitchcock. But these are generalizations only. The works of many of these artists combine styles within the same movie. Truffaut's *Jules and Jim,* for example, contains scenes of tender lyricism and liquid seductiveness that only a handful of directors would be able to equal. Yet the same film has scenes of quick sophisticated wit, in which montage plays a prominent role.

Jean-Luc Godard is the boldest innovator of the New Wave—perhaps of the entire contemporary cinema. He has turned out nearly two features a year since beginning his directing career in the late fifties. His first feature, *Breathless,* was meant to be a homage to *Scarface,* a classic gangster film by Howard Hawks, one of Godard's idols at the time. *Breathless* popularized the deliberate jump-cuts that were to become so fashionable in the sixties and seventies (4-23). Indeed, the title seemed to refer as much to the jumpy editing as to the story itself. The disorienting leaps in time and space, the disconnected sequences, the overall plotlessness—all these reflect the sense of disorder, lack of direction, and spontaneity of the central character (Jean-Paul Belmondo), a rather charming but inept gangster who self-consciously models himself on Humphrey Bogart. Godard's nervous editing style in this film is particularly suited to capturing the sense of restless and rebellious youth, though it also reflects a rather complex philosophical attitude, one emphasizing the fragmentation and dislocation of contemporary life. He was to use this style of editing often, particularly in those films dealing with youthful protagonists.

But Godard experimented with realistic alternatives to editing as well (4-24). *Les Carabiniers,* for instance, was shot mostly in long shots and lengthy takes to achieve a documentary-like objectivity, like the movies of Rossellini, another culture hero of the New Wave. *Masculine-Feminine,* one of Godard's greatest works, is a typical hybrid of styles and influences. There is one scene in this movie consisting of a single take with a stationary camera, and lasting seven minutes—an incredibly lengthy shot. Like a similar scene from *The 400 Blows,* the shot in Godard's film is an interview scene with a character, a technique borrowed from **cinéma vérité,** a docu-

4-24. La Chinoise.
Directed by Jean-Luc Godard.
Ever the compulsive experimenter, the restless Godard began exploring the artistic possibilities of lengthy takes and the art of mise-en-scène just as most other film-makers seemed to be taking up the expressionistic editing styles popularized by the early New Wave films. Here, for example, Godard uses the dividing wall rather than montage to foreshadow a split which will soon develop among the young people in a Maoist cell.

mentary movement which stressed the use of the hand-held camera and direct interview techniques. *Masculine-Feminine* also features many shots which last for only a fraction of a second.

In short, what makes so many of the New Wave films attractive is this very stylistic eclecticism: realistic *and* expressionistic techniques are exploited according to the psychological and dramatic needs of the scene. Within a few years, directors from other nations absorbed the lessons of the New Wave—usually indiscriminately. Throughout the following decade, even the trashiest hack films employed the editing techniques originally popularized by Godard and his associates. The movies of the manic, youth-obsessed sixties zoomed in and out, cross cut, **flash cut,** and jump cut—even if there was nothing in particular to cut *to*. A well written and superbly acted film like *Midnight Cowboy* was seriously flawed by John Schlesinger's zonked-out editing style—so much at odds with the intimacy and delicacy of the subject matter. Even into the seventies, some movies failed with the public in part because the editing style seemed "old fashioned" in comparison to the predominantly expressionistic modes of the day. John Huston's excellent *Fat City* was edited according to the conventions of classical cutting (a style he helped to perfect in such films as *The Maltese Falcon* and *The Treasure of Sierra Madre*), but those who saw *Fat City* tended to think that it moved too slowly and didn't have enough energy. Few people bothered

(a)

(b)

4-25a, b. Sisters.
Directed by Brian De Palma.
Although multiple images had been used as early as 1925 by Abel Gance in *Napoleon,* it was not until the late sixties that the technique was revived in such movies as *The Boston Strangler, The Ballad of Cable Hogue,* and *The Thomas Crown Affair.* Multiple images employ the aesthetic of fragmentation even more radically than Eisensteinian montage, for individual images from the past, future, or the imagination can be combined within the same frame. This technique can show two or more points of view simultaneously. De Palma's double image presents us with both a shot and a **reverse angle shot** (a), a shot and a **reaction shot** (b) at the same time. The artistic potential of multiple image movie-making is enormous, though few fiction filmmakers seem to be attracted to the technique, perhaps because of its very complexity. A new set of conventions would probably have to be established in order to permit an audience to distinguish between the different time and space contexts of each image within the frame. The number, design, and duration of the individual images could be variable, depending upon the specific needs of a dramatic scene. Editing such films would be infinitely more complex than editing single image movies, for each picture within the frame would have to be cut in coordination with the others, each with its own rhythm, **dominant contrast,** and content curve.

to note that passivity and exhaustion were the main characteristics of the people of the film, and hence, that Huston's subtle editing was organically related to these ideas.

The legacy of the New Wave is a valuable one, for it popularized the view that editing styles ought to be determined not by mere fashion, by the limitations of technology, or by dogmatic pronouncements, but by the nature of the subject matter itself (4-25).

FURTHER READING

BARR, CHARLES. "CinemaScope: Before and After," in *Film Theory and Criticism,* ed. Gerald Mast and Marshall Cohen. New York: Oxford University Press, 1974. (Paper) An attack on Eisenstein's editing theories in favor of Bazin, with particular emphasis on mise-en-scène and the widescreen.

BAZIN, ANDRÉ. *What is Cinema?* 2 vols. Edited and translated by Hugh Gray. Berkeley: University of California Press, vol. I, 1967, vol. II, 1971. (Paper) A collection of essays emphasizing the realistic nature of the film medium, with emphasis on the art of mise-en-scène over montage.

BURCH, NOËL. *Theory of Film Practice.* New York: Praeger Publishers, 1973. (Paper) An exploration of the nature of film art, strongly influenced by Bazin's theories and the actual practices of various filmmakers.

EISENSTEIN, SERGEI. *Film Form.* New York: Harcourt, Brace and Co., 1949. (Paper) One of the classic studies of montage in the cinema, written in Eisenstein's typically elliptical, difficult style.

―――. *Film Sense.* New York: Harcourt, Brace and Co., 1942. (Paper) Theoretical essays on sound, color, and editing in film.

GRAHAM, PETER, ed. *The New Wave.* London: Secker & Warburg, 1968. (Paper) A collection of essays by and about Bazin, Truffaut, Godard, and others.

JACOBS, LEWIS. "Art: Edwin S. Porter and the Editing Principle," "D. W. Griffith: *The Birth of a Nation* and *Intolerance,*" in *The Rise of the American Film.* New York: Teachers College Press, 1968. (Paper) An historical account of the evolutionary developments in editing up to the early sound period.

NIZHNY, VLADIMIR. *Lessons with Eisenstein.* Translated and edited by Ivor Montagu and Jay Leyda. New York: Hill and Wang, 1962. (Paper) An account of Eisenstein's teaching methods, with particular emphasis on montage and mise-en-scène.

PUDOVKIN, V. I. *Film Technique and Film Acting.* Translated and edited by Ivor Montagu. London: Vision, 1954. (Paper) Two of the earliest theoretical documents on editing in film, stressing the vast differences between cinema and legitimate theatre.

REISZ, KAREL. *The Technique of Film Editing.* New York: Hastings House, 1968. (Paper) The standard text on the history, practice, and theory of editing.

5 sound

There are three types of sound in film: sound effects, music, and language. These can be employed independently or in any combination. They can be used **realistically** or **expressionistically.** Realistic sounds tend to be **synchronous:** that is, they derive their source from the images, and are often recorded simultaneously with them. Many exposition sequences, for example, use synchronized dialogue with corresponding images **(two-shots).** Even **long** and **extreme long shots** are sometimes shot synchronously: to capture the actual noise of traffic in an urban location, for example. Expressionistic sounds tend to be **non-synchronous:** that is, they are detached from their sources, often acting in contrast with the image, or existing as totally separate sources of meaning.

HISTORICAL BACKGROUND

In 1927, when *The Jazz Singer* ushered in the "talkie" era, many critics felt that sound would deal a death blow to the art of the film, which would content itself merely with photographing stage plays. But in fact, the setbacks were temporary, and today sound is one of the richest sources of meaning in film art (5-1). Actually, there never really was a "silent" film, for virtually all movies prior to 1927 were accompanied by some kind of music. In the large city theatres, full orchestras provided atmospheric background to the visuals. In the small towns, a piano was often used for the same purpose. In many theatres, the "Mighty Wurlitzer" organ, with its bellowing pipes, was the standard musical accompaniment. Music was played for practical as well as artistic purposes, for these sounds muffled the noises of the patrons, who were occasionally rowdy, particularly when entering the theatre. Once the audience was settled, musical accompaniment filled the vacuum of silence in the hushed theatre.

Most of the early "100% talkies" were visually dull, since the equipment of the time required the simultaneous recording of sound and image. The camera was restricted to one position, the actors couldn't move far from the microphone, and editing was restricted to its most minimal function—primarily for scene changes. The major source of meaning was in the sound, especially the dialogue. The images tended merely to illustrate the sound track. Before long, adventurous directors began experimenting. The camera was housed in a soundproof **"blimp,"** thus permitting the camera to move in and out of a scene silently (5-2). Soon, several microphones, all on separate channels, were placed on the set (5-3). Overhead sound **booms** were constructed to follow an actor on a set, so that his voice was always within range, even when he moved about.

Despite these technical advances, the Soviet expressionistic directors remained hostile to the use of realistic (synchronous) sound recording. Eisenstein was especially wary of dialogue, and he predicted an onslaught of "highly cultured dramas," which would force the cinema back to its primitive stagey beginnings. Synchronous sound, he believed, would destroy the flexibility of **editing**, and thus kill the very soul of film art. Synchronous sound did, in fact, require a more literal **continuity**, especially in dialogue sequences. Eisenstein's metaphoric cutting, with its leaps in time and space, wouldn't make much sense if realistic sound had to be provided with each image. Indeed, to this day, Hitchcock claims that the most cinematic scenes are essentially silent—chase sequences, for example, require only some general sound effects to preserve their continuity.

Most of the talented directors of the time favored expressionistic sound. Eisenstein and Pudovkin issued a manifesto, reasserting their faith in the primacy of editing, but they saw great possibilities in the use of sound if it weren't used synchronously. They advocated the alternating use of sound and image, with each conveying different—not duplicate—meanings. Sound —especially music—should be used as an aural counterpoint to the images, they thought. The proper use of language in film, Eisenstein claimed, was in the narrated monologue, not dramatic dialogue. The monologue would

5-1. *The Jazz Singer*.
Directed by Alan Crosland.
Although there had been a number of early experiments in synchronized sound, it was not until 1927 that Warner Brothers managed to break the sound barrier with this famous talkie. Actually, Crosland's movie was mostly silent: only Al Jolson's musical numbers and a few snatches of dialogue were in synch sound.

replace the expository titles of the silent film, giving the images an uninterrupted dominance. This preference for the monologue reflected the Soviet bias toward documentary film.

Even directors of more theatrical biases, however, were opposed to strictly realistic uses of sound. The French director, René Clair, came to the same conclusions as the Soviets. Sound should be used selectively, not indiscriminately. The ear, he believed, is just as selective as the eye, and sound could be edited just as the images could. As early as 1929, he praised a Hollywood musical, *Broadway Melody,* for its imaginative experiments in sound. He observed that the film let us *hear* a door slam, so the director wisely chose not to show us the action as well. In this, and in other instances, sound could be used to replace the **shot**. Even dialogue **sequences**

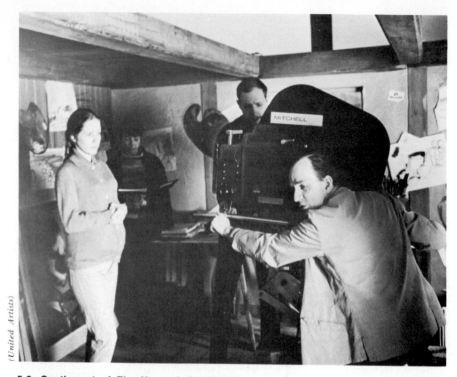

5-2. On the set of *The Hour of the Wolf*.
Directed by Ingmar Bergman (at the camera).
When shooting live sound, a large soundproof camera housing called a "blimp" is used to silence the whirr of the camera's motor.

needn't be totally synchronous, he claimed, for sound can act as a continuity device, once the relationship between image and sound has been made clear. During a sequence, there would be no need to cut back to **re-establishing shots,** since the continuity of the soundtrack would provide a perpetual continuity for all the visuals.

Clair made several musicals illustrating his theories. In his *Le Million* (1931), for example, music and song often replace dialogue. Language is juxtaposed ironically with non-synchronous images. Many of the scenes were photographed without sound, and later **dubbed** after the sequences had been edited. These charming films had virtually all of the visual freedom of the pre-sound era, and none of the stolid literalness that ruined most early talkies. Indeed, the pattern established by Clair, though ahead of its time, eventually became a major approach in sound film production.

Several American directors also experimented with sound in its first years of use. Lewis Milestone added sound effects of bombs bursting and guns firing without corresponding visuals in *All Quiet on the Western Front*. Like Clair, Ernst Lubitsch used sound and image non-synchronously to produce a number of witty and often cynical juxtapositions. In his musical *Monte Carlo*, for example, the heroine is in her bedroom, having her back rubbed by her amorous hairdresser. While she oohs and aahs in pleasurable relief, Lubitsch cuts to a shot of her maid listening outside the bedroom door, her face reflecting a mixture of lascivious awe and amazement at the sounds which continue on the sound track. In short, by the early 1930s, the practice of dubbing sound after the images had been photographed liberated the camera from the tyranny of strict synchronization.

But sound also cut off the careers of many film artists, especially actors. Most historians believe that such great silent comedians as Buster Keaton, Harold Lloyd, and Harry Langdon were put out of business by the advent of sound. Of the great American silent comics, only Chaplin managed to

(Columbia Pictures)

5-3. On the set of *From Here to Eternity.*
Directed by Fred Zinnemann (leaning over couch).
Even in relatively static, **tightly framed** scenes, sound technicians will often use more than one microphone to assure an even, crisp soundtrack.

5-4a. Monsieur Verdoux.
5-4b. Limelight.
Both directed by Charles Chaplin.
The arrival of sound wiped out the careers of many great silent film artists. Chaplin was one of the last to capitulate to the talkies, and his sound films are generally regarded as inferior to his silent masterpieces. *Monsieur Verdoux* is perhaps Chaplin's only first-rate sound movie, while the most impressive sequence in *Limelight* is the brilliant but essentially non-talking sequence between the two old music-hall performers, played by Buster Keaton and Chaplin.

(a)

(b)

(rbc films)

survive the shift (5-4). In *Modern Times* (made in 1936), Chaplin fought a gallant but ultimately futile battle against language, and this was the last film in which his tramp character was to appear. Although *Modern Times* contains sound effects and a musical score (composed by Chaplin himself), the only spoken dialogue in this movie is recited by a weird Big Brother figure on a TV monitor. Like many silent film artists, Chaplin believed that pantomime was the essence of cinema, and in this film he satirizes the superfluity of spoken language with sublime arrogance. Charlie is supposed to sing a risqué song in a rundown nightclub, but he's unable to remember the lyrics. In desperation, he improvises some gibberish "foreign" words while he suggestively pantomimes the significance of the song with his face and body. The meaning of the tune is conveyed—triumphantly—by what we see, not what we hear.

But by 1936, Chaplin's avoidance of spoken dialogue was almost universally regarded as a quixotic battle in an already lost war: the advantages of sound had long been recognized by all except the most die-hard reactionaries. The increased realism brought on by sound inevitably forced acting styles to become more natural, for performers no longer needed to compensate visually for the lack of dialogue. Like stage actors, film stars realized that the subtlest nuances of meaning could be conveyed by voice.

In the silent days, directors had to use titles to communicate nonvisual information such as dialogue and commentary. In some films, these interruptions nearly ruined the delicate rhythm of the visuals. Dreyer's *Passion of Joan of Arc,* for example, is clogged by an irritating series of explanatory titles which convey the dialogue. Other directors avoided titles by dramatizing visually as much as possible. This practice led to many visual clichés. Early in a film, for example, the villain might be established by showing him kicking a dog. A heroine could be recognized by the "spiritual" lighting that formed a halo around her head. And so on.

Even in non-dialogue sequences, sound eliminates the need for what Clair called "inflated visuals." Without sound, virtually all the necessary meanings have to be included in the images. Indeed, this problem is the basis of one expressionistic theory of art: that art forms thrive on their limitations in recording literal reality. Rudolf Arnheim, for example, claimed that the art of the film is possible precisely because it's not like reality. With no sound, the film artist must convey all his meaning with images, just as literary men must communicate their sense of reality with words, composers with sounds, and so on. But by mixing sounds and images, film is not necessarily more "like reality," as subsequent directors were to demonstrate. Sound allowed directors to expand their range of possibilities, and permitted them to convey meanings with a whole new set of juxtapositions, not all of them by any means the same as those found in reality.

In some respects, 1941 was a watershed in the history of the sound film, for this was the release year of Orson Welles' *Citizen Kane* (5-5). Here was the *Birth of a Nation* of its era. Bursting with visual brilliance in nearly every shot, the movie featured a sound track so complex that the film world seemed to gasp in astonishment. Like Griffith, Welles is often credited with "inventing" many effects when in fact he was primarily a consolidator; but also like Griffith, Welles' genius consisted of his extraordinary ability to combine and expand the piecemeal accomplishments of his predecessors. Despite his youth—he was only twenty-five years old when he made *Citizen Kane*—Welles had spent a number of years acting, writing, producing, and directing radio plays. The lessons he learned in this aural medium were to serve him well in the cinema.

In radio, sounds must evoke images: an actor speaking through an echo chamber suggests a visual context—a huge auditorium, for example; a "distant" train whistle suggests a vast landscape; and so on. Welles simply applied this aural principle to his cinematic sound track, and the results were—and still are—dazzling. With the help of his sound technician, James G. Stewart, Welles discovered that almost every visual technique has its

5-5a, b, c. *Citizen Kane.* **(a)**
Directed by Orson Welles.
Coming from the world of radio, Welles was particularly skillful in using sounds evocatively. He demonstrated that virtually every kind of visual had its aural counterpart. Even within the same frame, the qualitative moral differences between two characters could be reinforced by quantitative "distances" in the sound recording (a). With only a handful of extras and some clever ***optical printing,*** a vast auditorium filled with cheering partisans could be suggested by a reverberating public-address echo on the soundtrack (b). A visual ***montage*** sequence (c) was reinforced by an aural montage of Susan Alexander's shrieking arias, orchestral music, popping flashbulbs, and the sounds of newspaper presses rolling.

(b)

(RKO)

(c)

sound equivalent. Each of the shots, for example, has an appropriate sound quality, involving volume, degree of definition, and texture. Long and extreme long shot sounds are remote and often "distant," close-up sounds are crisp, clear, and generally loud. Two-shots are enhanced when there are two sound tracks accompanying them: if a conflict were being shown, for example, two conflicting melodic lines of music could intensify the visual and dramatic clash. **High angle shots** often feature accompanying high pitched music and sound effects; **low angles,** brooding and low pitched sounds. Abrupt cuts can be punctuated by equally abrupt sound transitions. In *Kane,* Welles cuts from a quiet low-keyed scene to a violent **flashback,** which opens with the piercing shriek of a cockatoo in close-up. Sounds can **fade** in and out, like images. Sounds can be **dissolved** and overlapped like images in a **montage** sequence. Sounds can also suggest a graceful **crane** movement with a glissando passage of music; the bobbing of a hand-held shot can be enhanced by a staccato musical phrase. The possibilities are almost limitless.

Kane is a monumental work in all areas of sound: language (the script was co-written by Welles and Herman J. Mankiewicz), music (composed by Bernard Herrmann), and sound effects. The dialogue is literate, subtle, and yet flamboyantly theatrical. While the camera leaps over time periods and different locales, the sound track forms the continuity for whole scenes. One famous scene, for example, shows Kane listening to a song sung by Susan Alexander, a girl he has just met, who will eventually become his mistress, and later his second wife. The scene is set in her dingy apartment. While the song continues on the sound track, the image dissolves to a parallel shot, revealing Kane in an opulent apartment, where an elaborately bedecked Susan finishes her song at a grand piano. In a matter of seconds, Welles establishes the relationship between Kane and his mistress, using only the song to bridge the enormous time-space gap. In another episode, Welles employs a montage sequence of Susan on her disastrous operatic tour. On the sound track, her aria can be heard, distorted into a screeching dismal wail.

In an opening sequence of the film, dialogue is spoken through an echo chamber, to suggest the pompous hollowness of Kane's onetime guardian, whose papers are stored in a tomblike archive. To demonstrate Kane's gradual estrangement from his first wife, Welles features a series of breakfast scenes, while on the sound track, Kane and his wife engage in a series of exchanges, beginning with some honeymoon sweet talk, and ending with a furious quarrel. The entire sequence contains only some thirty or so lines of dialogue. The film's very structure is based on a series of visual flashbacks during which five informants speak of their present-day opinions of Kane's paradoxical personality. Throughout the movie, Welles juxtaposes words, sound effects, and music with images of such complexity that many meanings are conveyed simultaneously.

In his next film, *The Magnificent Ambersons,* Welles refined his technique of "sound montage," in which dialogue between several groups of characters is overlapped (5-6). The language is not so important for what it expresses intellectually, but—rather like a musical composition—for the emotional effect it evokes as pure sound. One of the most brilliant episodes employing this technique is the leavetaking scene at the final Amberson ball.

5-6. The Magnificent Ambersons.
Directed by Orson Welles.
In this film, Welles perfected his technique of "sound montage," in which the dialogue of one character overlaps with that of another, or several others. The effect is almost musical, for the language is exploited not necessarily for the literal information it may convey but as "pure" sound which is orchestrated in terms of emotional tonalities.

(*Janus Films*)

Beautifully photographed by Stanley Cortez, the scene is shot in **deep focus,** with expressionistic lighting contrasts which throw most of the characters into silhouette. The dialogue of one group of characters gently overlaps with that of another, which in turn overlaps with a third group. The effect is hauntingly poetic, despite the relative simplicity of the words themselves. Each group is characterized by a particular sound texture: the young people speak rapidly in a normal to loud volume, the middle-aged couple whisper intimately and slowly. The shouts of various other family members punctuate these dialogue sequences in sudden outbursts. The entire scene seems choreographed, both visually and aurally: silhouetted figures stream in and out of the frame like graceful phantoms, their dialogue likewise floating and undulating in the shadows. The quarrels among the Amberson family are often recorded in a similar manner. Welles' actors don't wait patiently for cues: accusations and recriminations are hurled simultaneously, as they are in real life. The violent words, often irrational and disconnected, spew out in spontaneous eruptions of anger and frustration. As in many family quarrels, everyone shouts, but people only half listen.

Robert Altman used similar sound montage techniques in *M*A*S*H,* *McCabe and Mrs. Miller* and *Nashville.* Indeed, Altman's films have been harshly criticized for their "unintelligible" sound tracks. But like Welles, Altman often uses language as pure sound, particularly in some of the scenes from *McCabe and Mrs. Miller,* in which as many as twenty different sound tracks were mixed. In such scenes, many lines are deliberately "thrown away": we're able to catch only a fleeting phrase here and there, but these phrases are sufficient to give us a sense of what's really going on in a scene. More importantly, they give us a sense of how language and sounds are actually heard in reality: ambiguous, elliptical, and filled with funny incongruities.

After Welles left the United States for Europe, the quality of his sound deteriorated badly. Visually, his European movies are as dazzling as ever, but most of these films suffer from poor sound recording, apparently because of budgetary limitations (5-7). In *Falstaff* (also known as *Chimes at Midnight*), he often uses extreme long and long shots, while the dialogue seems at close-up range. Part of his problem was simply not enough time (and money) to shoot all the necessary **footage.** Because many of his actors are high-salaried **stars** who can afford to work with him only for a few weeks at a time, Welles is often forced to use stand-in actors. Because they are stand-ins, he must photograph them from long distances, so that audiences won't recognize the ruse. When the dialogue—recorded prior to shooting by the original actor—is combined with these long-distance images, many viewers find the discrepancy disorienting.

(Peppercorn-Wormser, Inc. Enterprises)

5-7. *Falstaff.*
Directed by Orson Welles.
After Welles left the United States to work in Europe and elsewhere, the quality of his sound deteriorated. In his Shakespearean adaptations, the problem of faulty sound is particularly acute, though the (essentially silent) action sequences of these films are as brilliant as ever.

But Welles is also able to create some poetic effects with this technique, paradoxically suggesting distance and intimacy at the same time, and sometimes a kind of psychological disjunction between language and action. Since the late 1950s, such image-sound discrepancies have become more common, even when there are no particular budgetary problems. John Schlesinger, for example, used long shots and close-up sound in *Midnight Cowboy*, to emphasize the insectlike insignificance of his two protagonists in New York City. The sound, in such instances, serves as a continuity device, while the audience is forced to scan the image in order to locate the source of the dialogue.

SOUND EFFECTS

Although the primary function of sound effects is generally believed to be atmospheric, they can also be surprisingly precise sources of meaning in film. Directors like Michelangelo Antonioni will spend nearly as much time with their sound effects as they do with their music and dialogue. In *L'Avventura*, Antonioni went to great lengths to recreate the desolate whine of the wind as it swept over an extinct volcano (5-8). In this same film, the insistent monotonous pounding of the ocean's waves suggested the gradual spiritual erosion of the heroine.

The pitch, volume, and tempo of sound effects can strongly affect our responses to any given noise. High pitched sounds are generally strident, and produce a sense of tension in the listener. Particularly if these types of noises are prolonged, the harsh shrillness can be totally unnerving. For this reason, high pitched sounds (including music) are often employed in suspense sequences, especially just before and during the climax. Low frequency sounds are usually heavy, full, and less tense than high pitched noises. Often low frequency sounds are used to emphasize the dignity or solemnity of a scene, like the male humming chorus in *The Seven Samurai*, for example. Low pitched sounds can also suggest anxiety and mystery: frequently a suspense sequence begins with such sounds which gradually increase in frequency as the scene peaks.

(Janus Films)

5-8. L'Avventura.
Directed by Michelangelo Antonioni. Though many film directors will settle only for general background noises in their sound effects, the most fastidious filmmakers—like Antonioni, Bergman, and Altman—will spend nearly as much time with their sound recording as with their visuals.

5-9. *A Clockwork Orange.*
Directed by Stanley Kubrick.
Sound volume—independent of its subject matter—can strongly affect our reaction to any given scene. Loud sounds tend to be aggressive, violent, and unnerving, especially over lengthy periods. In this movie, Kubrick deliberately recorded most of his sound at high volume, thus intensifying the atmosphere of violence and brutality in the world of the film. The same sounds recorded at a softened volume would have a much less abrasive effect.

Sound volume works in much the same way. Loud sounds tend to be forceful, intense, and dynamic, whereas quiet sounds strike us as delicate and hesitant. The sound track of Kubrick's *A Clockwork Orange* is almost consistently loud: noises are magnified and reverberating, dialogue is shouted rather than delivered at a normal volume (5-9). Our ears are assaulted by a barrage of relentless noises. Kubrick uses this technique to "attack" the audience aurally. In effect, the volume never permits us to relax: the noise is as violent in its intensity as the dramatic events of the film.

These same principles apply to the tempo of sound. The faster the tempo, the greater the tension produced in the listener. In the chase sequence of William Friedkin's *The French Connection,* all these sound principles are employed brilliantly. As the chase reaches its climax, the screeching wheels of the auto and the crashing sound of the runaway subway train grow louder, faster, and higher pitched. Indeed, much of the success of this sequence is due to its sound effects, which are edited as masterfully as the images.

Off-screen sounds usually bring off-screen space into play: the sound tends to expand the image beyond the confines of the **frame.** In Kubrick's *Paths of Glory,* for instance, the sounds of guns and cannons are constant reminders to the soldiers in the trenches of the dangers they must face when they enter the battlefield. Far away sounds can suggest a sense of distance between locations, both literal and **symbolic.** In *Long Day's Journey into Night,* the remote foghorn reminds the characters of the psychological journey each will take before the evening is out. Though they all desire the oblivion of forgetfulness, the foghorn brings them back to the reality of the present, which has been shaped by the past.

Sound effects can evoke terror in suspense films and thrillers. Since we tend to fear what we can't see, directors like Hitchcock and Fritz Lang will sometimes use non-synchronous sound effects to strike a note of anxiety. The sound of a creaking door in a darkened room can be more fearful than an image of someone stealing through the door. In Lang's *M,* the child murderer is identified by a tune he whistles off-screen. During the early portions of the movie, we never see him, but we recognize him by his sinister tune.

In Hitchcock's *Psycho,* the sound effects of shrill bird noises are used in a variety of ways. A shy and appealing young man (Anthony Perkins) is associated with birds early in the film. He stuffs various birds as a hobby, and his own features are intense and rather hawk-like. Later in the movie, when a brutal murder is committed, the soundtrack gives us shrill music mixed with bird screeches. The audience assumes the murderer is the boy's mother, but birds have been associated with the boy. One of Hitchcock's recurrent themes is the transference of guilt. In this film, the transfer is rather complex. The boy has dug up his long-dead mother's body and stuffed it. Often he dresses himself up in her clothing. While the audience

5-10. The Exorcist.
Directed by William Friedkin.
Sound in film is generally geared to space. When a severe discrepancy exists, the effect can be disorienting and even frightening. In this film, the devil has possessed the body of a young girl. The sounds emanating from the child's small body echo loudly, thus reinforcing a cavernous effect, as though the girl's slight figure had been spiritually expanded thousands of times in order to accommodate the many demons that inhabit it.

(Warner Brothers)

5-11. Masculine-Feminine.
Directed by Jean-Luc Godard.
Influenced by the authentic sounds of the documentary school of *cinéma vérité,* a number of fiction filmmakers refuse to "clean-up" their sound-tracks—that is, get rid of extraneous noises. Godard generally shoots synch sound even in noisy public locations. Important dialogue is sometimes drowned out by these noisy intrusions, but the director incorporates them as part of his presentation, as an aspect of his vision of contemporary urban life.

(Columbia Pictures)

thinks it sees the mother killing two victims, it has in fact seen the schizophrenic boy as his other self—his mother. The sound effects of the bird noises offer an early clue to this psychological transference.

Indeed, because images tend to dominate sounds while we're actually experiencing a movie, many sound effects work on a subconscious level. In *Psycho,* the heroine (Janet Leigh) drives her car through a severe rainstorm. On the sound track, we hear her windshield wiper blades slashing furiously against the torrential downpour. Later, when she is taking a shower in a motel, these same sounds are repeated. The source of the water noise is apparent, but the slashing sounds seem to come from nowhere—until the demented murderer breaks into the bathroom with a knife poised to strike. Similarly, throughout Sam Peckinpah's *Straw Dogs* the sound of shattering glass has an unnerving effect on the audience. Not until late in the movie, when the protagonist's eyeglasses are shattered in a vicious attack do these sound effects become more overtly relevant.

Sound effects can also serve explicit symbolic functions (5-10). Symbolic noises can be determined by the dramatic context, as they are in Luis Buñuel's *Belle de Jour,* where the sounds of jingling bells are associated with the heroine's sexual fantasies. Other symbolic sound effects are more immediately clear. In Bergman's *Wild Strawberries,* the protagonist, an elderly professor, has a nightmare. The **surrealistic** sequence is virtually silent, except for the insistent sound of a heart beat—a *momento mori* for the professor, a reminder that his life will soon end.

In reality, there's a considerable difference between hearing and listening. Our minds automatically filter out irrelevant sounds: while talking in a noisy city location, for example, we listen to the speaker, but we barely hear the sounds of traffic. The microphone is not so selective, however, and most film soundtracks are "cleaned up" of all such extraneous noises. A movie sequence might include selected city noises to suggest the urban locale, but once this context is established, these outside sounds are diminished and sometimes even eliminated in order to permit us to hear the conversation clearly.

Since the late fifties, however, a number of directors have retained these noisy soundtracks in the name of greater realism (5-11). Influenced by the documentary school of **cinéma vérité**—which avoids all simulated or recreated sounds—directors like Jean-Luc Godard have even allowed important dialogue scenes to be partly washed out by background sounds. In *Masculine-Feminine*, Godard's use of sound is especially bold. Indeed, his insistence upon natural noises—all of them, as they were recorded on the set—dismays many critics, who complain of the "cacophonous din." But the noisy soundtrack is not due to artistic sloppiness, as many of his detractors claim. The movie deals with violence, the lack of privacy, and the lack of peace and quiet. Because of the quality of his soundtrack, Godard has no need to comment overtly on these themes: they're naggingly persistent in virtually every scene. One of the most effective sound techniques in this film is the use of gun shots for transitions. Often the abruptness of the editing is punctuated by the shattering blast of these shots, which have no visual source. Other scenes are accompanied by the cracking of billiard and bowling balls, the clattering of pinball machines, and the nervous stamping of a typewriter—all of them suggesting muffled gun shots. Important dialogue is sometimes drowned out by the noise of street traffic, an adjoining conversation, or the clatter of dishes in a cafe. Because we're accustomed to a clean soundtrack, we are at first distracted by these "extraneous" noises. But this is precisely Godard's point: he wishes to remind us that serenity is almost totally absent in contemporary urban life, that even the most elementary kind of concentration of attention is difficult.

Like absolute stasis in a movie, absolute silence in a sound film tends to call attention to itself. Any significant stretch of silence creates an eerie vacuum—a sense of something impending, about to burst. Arthur Penn exploited this phenomenon in the conclusion of *Bonnie and Clyde*. The lovers stop on a country road to help a friend (actually an informer) with his car, which has presumably broken down. Clumsily, the "friend" scrambles under the car. There is a long moment of silence. The lovers exchange puzzled, then anxious glances. Suddenly, the soundtrack roars with the noise of machine guns, as the lovers are brutally cut down by policemen hiding in the bushes. In some films—Bergman's *The Silence* is a good example—the empty pauses between lines of dialogue are far more significant than the dialogue itself. These pauses suggest anxiety, fear, suspicion, and in other contexts, rage, evasion, or total exhaustion.

A world without sound is an unreal world in many ways, and some directors have exploited silence as a surrealistic device to suggest the strangeness of dreamlike states. For some reason, traveling shots are especially eerie when they are silent. F. W. Murnau's *The Last Laugh* often seems nightmarish because of this combination. Indeed, many German movies of the twenties strike us as paranoid and surrealistic because of the silent stalking camera, which almost seems to be seeking its prey.

Like the **freeze frame,** silence in a sound film is occasionally used to symbolize death, since we tend to associate sound with the presence of on-going life. Kurosawa uses this technique effectively in *Ikiru* (also known as *To Live*) after the elderly protagonist has been informed by a doctor that he will die of cancer. Totally absorbed by the reality of death, the old man exits from the medical building to an absolutely silent soundtrack. When he almost gets run over by a passing car in the street, the soundtrack suddenly roars with the noises of city traffic: the protagonist is yanked back

5-12. *Fantasia.*
By Walt Disney.
Music is perhaps the most abstract art. When fused with images, however, music automatically acquires more anecdotal significance—a fact which dismays many musicians. When Disney used Ponchielli's elegant "Dance of the Hours" to accompany a deliciously ludicrous dance between "Hyacinth Hippo" and "Ben Ali Gator" in this film, many music lovers were appalled by the "vulgarization." Similar complaints were made when Stanley Kubrick used the same witty contrasting techniques in *2001* and *A Clockwork Orange.*

(Walt Disney Productions)

into the world of the living. In Penn's *Little Big Man,* the soundtrack is similarly "dead" after the protagonist's Indian wife and child are brutally murdered by some cavalry soldiers.

MUSIC

Music is a highly abstract medium, tending towards pure form. It's very difficult, for example, to speak of the "content" of a musical phrase. When merged with lyrics, music acquires more concrete meaning, for words, of course, have more specific referents than musical sounds alone. Both words and musical notes convey meanings, but each in a different manner. With or without lyrics, music can be more specific when juxtaposed with film images. Indeed, many musicians have complained that images tend to rob music of its beauty and ambiguity precisely because visuals have a way of anchoring musical tones to specific ideas and emotions. For example, few people can listen to Richard Strauss's *Thus Spake Zarathustra* without being reminded of Kubrick's *2001: A Space Odyssey.* Many music lovers have lamented that Ponchielli's *Dance of the Hours* is utterly ruined for them because it conjures images of ridiculous dancing hippos, one of Disney's most brilliant sequences in *Fantasia* (5-12).

Most film music has not progressed much beyond the silent movie days: it's used for atmospheric effects, or merely as background filler. However, Pudovkin and Eisenstein insisted that music in film must never serve merely as accompaniment: they felt that music ought to retain its own line, its own integrity. The film critic Paul Rotha claimed that music must even be allowed to dominate the image on occasion. The use of music in film is surprisingly varied. Many directors still use it as an intensifier of the image. Some filmmakers insist on purely descriptive music—a practice referred to as **"mickeymousing."** Descriptive scores employ music as a kind of literal equivalent to the image: if a character stealthily tiptoes from a room, for example, each step has a musical note to emphasize the suspense. Other directors would hold that film music shouldn't be "too good" lest it detract from the images. Most of the great directors, however, disagree

5-13. *Music recording session at Columbia Pictures.*
In general, the musical accompaniment for a film is created after the composer has seen the **rough cut.** Once the movie is in its **final cut,** minor adjustments are made in the score to match up with the visuals. The timing of the music must be synchronized precisely with the images. In order to do so, the composer usually has a movie screen in front of him as well as the musical score. Dimitri Tiomkin (standing on platform, both hands in pockets) composed the scores of several of the films of Frank Capra (standing under microphone). Note the five overhead microphones to assure an even balance of sound.

with these views. For them, the music of even the greatest composers can be used in movies. Furthermore, music can be used for contrast as well as emphasis. Indeed, some filmmakers employ it as a totally separate source of information.

In the best films, music—whether borrowed or original—is never a careless matter. Nor is film composing a job for hacks, for the list of composers who have worked directly in film is a long and impressive one, including Darius Milhaud, Arthur Honegger, Paul Hindemith, Dimitri Shostakovitch, Arnold Schoenberg, Sergei Prokofiev, William Walton, Benjamin Britten, Aaron Copland, Quincy Jones, The Modern Jazz Quartet, Virgil Thompson, Kurt Weill, Bob Dylan, Vaughan Williams, Richard

Rogers, Cole Porter, Leonard Bernstein, and The Beatles, to mention only some of the better known.

A director doesn't need to have any technical expertise to use music effectively (5-13). As Aaron Copland has pointed out, a director must know what he wants from music *dramatically:* it's the composer's business to translate these dramatic needs into musical terms. Directors and composers work in a variety of ways. Most composers begin after they have seen the rough cut of a film—that is, the completed footage of a movie before the editor has tightened up the slackness between shots. Some composers don't begin until the film has been totally completed, except for the music. Hitchcock, on the other hand, usually works with his composers before the shooting begins, as do most directors of musicals.

In *Alexander Nevsky,* Eisenstein and Prokofiev worked out a kind of audio-visual score, in which the line of the music corresponds to the movement of the images set in a row (5-14). Eisenstein's essay, "Form and Content: Practice," relates how Prokofiev avoided purely "representational elements" in the music (mickeymousing). Instead, the two artists worked together closely, concentrating sometimes on the images first, other times on the music. The result was what Eisenstein called "vertical montage," where the line of notes on the staff, moving from left to right, parallels the movements or major lines of the images, which, set side by side, also "move" from left to right. Thus, if the lines in a series of images move from lower left to upper right, the notes of music would move in a similar direction on the musical staff. If the lines of a composition were jagged and uneven, the notes of music would also zig-zag in a corresponding manner. It's difficult to know how influential this kind of audio-visual composition has been, for there are few discussions of music in film that have gone into such visual detail. William Walton's music for Laurence Olivier's *Henry V* seems indebted to this technique, and probably most film composers have used it at least occasionally.

Music functions in a variety of ways in movies. Beginning with the opening credits, it can serve as a kind of overture, to suggest the general mood or spirit of the film as a whole. John Addison's opening music in *Tom Jones* is a witty, rapidly executed harpsichord piece. The harpsichord itself, of course, is especially associated with the eighteenth century, the period of the film. The occasionally jazzy phrases in the tune suggest a kind of sly twentieth-century overview—a musical equivalent of the peculiar blending of centuries found in the movie itself.

Certain kinds of music can suggest locales, classes, or ethnic groups. The rock songs of Dennis Hopper's *Easy Rider* aren't merely modish flourishes, as they tend to be in many American movies of the late sixties. These songs reflect the drug culture of the two protagonists, a culture that's viewed with suspicion and hostility by most of the conventional characters in the film. John Ford's westerns almost always feature simple, sentimental folk tunes, like "Red River Valley" or religious hymns like "Shall We Gather By the River" which are associated with the American frontier of the late nineteenth century. Richly nostalgic, these songs are often played on frontier instruments—a plaintive harmonica, or a concertina. Similarly, many of the Italian **neorealist** films feature sentimental and highly emotional melodies which reflect the urban culture of the working-class protagonists. The

5-14. "Audio-visual score" from
Alexander Nevsky.
Directed by Sergei Eisenstein,
music by Sergei Prokofiev.
The composer need not always subordinate his talents to those of the
film director. Here, two great Soviet
artists coordinate their contributions
into a totally fused production.

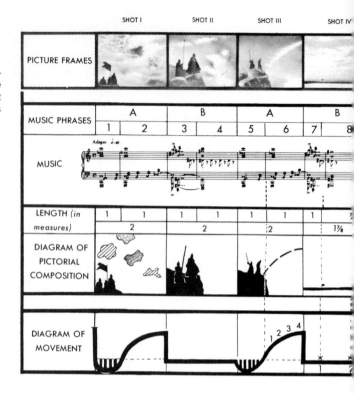

greatest composers of this kind of score are Nino Rota and Renzo Rossellini.

Music can also be used for foreshadowing, particularly when the dramatic context doesn't permit a director to prepare an audience for an
event. Hitchcock, for example, will often accompany an apparently casual
sequence with "anxious" music—a warning to the audience to be prepared.
Sometimes these musical warnings are false alarms; other times they explode
into frightening crescendos. Similarly, when actors are required to assume
restrained or neutral expressions, music can suggest their internal—hidden
—emotions. Bernard Herrmann's music functions in both ways in Hitchcock's *Psycho* and Welles's *Citizen Kane*.

Modern atonal and dissonant music generally evokes anxiety in most
listeners. Often such music seems to have no melodic line, and can even
resemble a series of strident random noises. Giovanni Fusco's music for
several of Antonioni's movies (*L'Avventura, Red Desert, Eclipse,* and others)
functions precisely to produce this sense of neurosis, lack of direction, and
paranoia. Fusco's music provides a similar function in the films of Alain
Resnais: *Hiroshima, Mon Amour* and *La Guerre Est Finie.*

Music can convey sudden emotional shifts within a continuous scene.
In John Huston's *Red Badge of Courage,* for example, the protagonist
(Audie Murphy), in an irrational outburst of daring, snatches the flag from
a dying comrade, and dashes forward onto a raging battlefield. To empha-

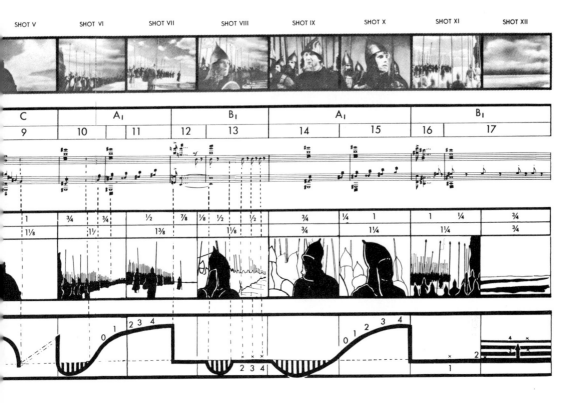

size the boy's sudden surge of patriotism, the scene is accompanied by a spirited—if not slightly satiric—rendering of Yankee fighting songs. Suddenly, the charging young man stumbles next to a wounded Confederate standard bearer, writhing in pain on the ground, his flag in tatters. With this image, the music abruptly shifts to an agonizing dirge, and gradually transforms into a grotesque distortion of "Dixie." The "heroic" excitement of the protagonist's charge might easily have overshadowed the poignance of the wounded Confederate soldier, but with the aid of the music, the audience as well as the protagonist is suddenly brought to a grim halt.

Music can also function as an ironic contrast to a sequence. Indeed, in many cases, the predominant mood of a scene can be neutralized or even reversed with contrasting music. In *Bonnie and Clyde,* the robbery scenes are often accompanied by spirited banjo music, giving these sequences a jolly sense of fun. More satirically, a scene from Kenneth Anger's *Scorpio Rising* shows a Hell's Angel motorcyclist putting on his elaborate riding gear. The scene is almost solemnly ritualistic, but the feminine fastidiousness of the young man is satirized by the banal tune, "Blue Velvet," which plays on the sound track. The homosexual undertones of his lifestyle are emphasized by the line "she wore blooo velll-vet. . . ." Contrasting music needn't always be satiric, however. In Penn's *Alice's Restaurant,* the cheerful lyrics of the title song ("You can get anything you want at Alice's Restau-

5-15. *The Last Picture Show.*
Directed by Peter Bogdanovich.
Throughout this film the director used the lyrics of pop tunes of the fifties to suggest thematic ideas and elements of characterization. A pretty, calculating opportunist (Cybill Shepherd, pictured), for example, is associated with the song, "Cold, Cold Heart."

rant") are ironically juxtaposed with a long slow **tracking shot** of Alice staring desolately past the camera.

Characterization can be suggested through musical **motifs.** In Fellini's *La Strada,* the pure sad simplicity of the heroine (Giulietta Masina) is captured by a melancholy tune she plays on a trumpet. This theme is varied and elaborated upon in Nino Rota's delicate score, suggesting that even long after her death, her spiritual influence is still pervasive. Herrmann's score for *Citizen Kane* employs motifs flamboyantly and in a more complex manner. Specific musical phrases are used to identify the major characters. These motifs are dropped, picked up again, and woven into elaborate combinations. The "Rosebud" motif, for example, is introduced early in the film, with Kane's death. The motif is repeated each time the reporter questions several of Kane's former associates about the significance of the word "Rosebud." In the final scene, the musical phrase swells grandly into dominance, as the audience (but not the characters) finally discovers the mystery of "Rosebud."

Characterization can be even more precise when lyrics are added to music. In Peter Bogdanovich's *The Last Picture Show,* for instance, pop tunes of the 1950s are used in association with specific characters (5-15).

George Lucas's *American Graffiti* uses pop tunes in a similar manner (5-16). Two young lovers who have just quarreled are shown dancing at a sock hop to the tune of "Smoke Gets in Your Eyes," and the line, "yet today my love has flown away" acquires particular poignance for the girl because the boy has just told her that he intends to date others when he goes off to college. The lovers are reconciled at the end of the film, when he decides not to leave after all. On the soundtrack, "Only You" is appropriately in-tuned, its syrupy lyrics emphasizing the "destiny of love."

Stanley Kubrick is one of the boldest—and most controversial—innovators in the use of film music. In *Dr. Strangelove,* he sardonically juxtaposed images of a twenty-first-century rocket ship gliding through the immense blueness of space with the sounds of Johann Strauss's nineteenth-century "Blue Danube Waltz"—an aural foreshadowing of man's obsolete technology in the infinitely superior technological universe beyond Jupiter. In *A Clockwork Orange,* Kubrick used music as an example of how everything—including art—is perverted in the terrifying world of the movie. The protagonist (Malcolm McDowell) is inspired with visions of sadism and violence by Beethoven's *Ninth Symphony*—especially the "Ode to Joy"

(*Universal Pictures*)

5-16. American Graffiti.
Directed by George Lucas.
Lucas's film is a bittersweet exploration of the theme of time and the ironies of history: the movie appropriately opens to the unsophisticated, insistent beat of "Rock Around the Clock." Other pop tunes of the late fifties and early sixties are used throughout the film to suggest the naïveté of this period.

5-17. *O Lucky Man!*.
Directed by Lindsay Anderson.
Music is often used as an ironic contrast to the visuals of a film. In this movie, Alan Price (pictured) and his rock group are actually shown performing their music before and after various dramatic episodes. These musical interludes function as a kind of ironic commentary on the action proper, thus distancing the spectator from too great an emotional involvement with the protagonist of the story.

(Warner Brothers)

movement, which is set to the lyrics of a poem by Schiller celebrating the triumphant transcendence of the spirit of man! Kubrick also uses music as a kind of distancing device, particularly in the violent scenes, in which the musical incongruity is exploited to undercut the realism of the sequences. An otherwise vicious gang fight takes place to the accompaniment of Rossini's elegant and witty overture to *The Thieving Magpie.* A brutal attack and rape scene is accompanied by a ludicrous song-and-dance routine set to the tune of "Singin' in the Rain." These distancing devices are also employed extensively in Lindsay Anderson's *O Lucky Man!* in which Alan Price's rock tunes are used to comment overtly on the action (5-17).

Almost since the advent of sound, filmmakers have interrupted their narratives with brief musical interludes. The protagonists might enter a nightclub, for example, and the action would come to a halt while they listened to a performer sing a song. In George Roy Hill's *Butch Cassidy and the Sundance Kid,* the leading player (Paul Newman) is photographed riding a bicycle while on the soundtrack "Raindrops Keep Fallin' on my Head" is offered for its own sake. The tune has nothing to do with the character or the action. Indeed, so pervasive were these extraneous musical sequences for a time, that one critic wittily referred to them as "S.O.L.I."— Semi-Obligatory Lyrical Interludes.

There are some musical interludes that are more organically justified, however. Michael Curtiz's *Casablanca,* for example, uses "As Time Goes By" as an important thematic motif. In Hitchcock's *The Man Who Knew Too Much,* Doris Day sings *"Che Sarà Sarà"* ("What Will Be Will Be") in a suspenseful sequence in which she is trying to hold the attention of a group at an Embassy party while her husband (James Stewart) frantically searches for their kidnapped son in the upstairs rooms. The song, with its emphasis on a child's curiosity about his future, stresses the role of fate— one of the film's major themes.

5-18. *Easy Rider.*
Directed by Dennis Hopper.
Music is used in this film to comment on various aspects of the drug and rock culture of the two protagonists. At the time of its release, several commentators interpreted the movie as a pro-drug film, though in fact the lyrics of some of the songs subtly expose the naive hypocrisy and expedient morality of the two protagonists.

Music can even be used to communicate the major theme of a film. Hopper's *Easy Rider* begins with the two likeable protagonists selling some white powder—apparently heroin—in order to stake themselves to a journey they plan to take to New Orleans (5-18). The visuals during this sequence aren't particularly condemnatory, but on the sound track, Steppenwolf's sinister rock tune "The Pusher" makes it clear what we are to think of the transaction. ("But the pusher don't care if you live or die—goddamn the pusher.") The lyrics also refer to hard drug pushers as having "tombstones in their eyes." This motif is also developed visually, for several times during the course of the film the two protagonists find themselves in cemeteries or among tombstones. The final song of the film, Roger Mc-Guinn's "Ballad of Easy Rider," explicitly develops this motif of death, with its emphasis on cleansing water, rivers, and freedom. The heroes can be free only in death, for the river flows inevitably to the repository of the sea. The death of the protagonists, in effect, is the indirect result of their selling heroin—which might possibly bring death to its users. When Wyatt (Peter Fonda) bitterly recognizes that he and his buddy "blew" their chance for real freedom, he seems to be alluding to the corrupt transaction—paradoxically, the economic basis of their idealistic search.

A frequent function of film music is to underline dialogue. A common assumption about this kind of music is that it acts merely to prop up bad dialogue or poor acting. The hundreds of mediocre love scenes performed to quivering violins have perhaps prejudiced many viewers against this kind of musical accompaniment, but in fact, some of the most gifted actors have benefited from it. In Olivier's *Hamlet,* the composer William Walton worked out his score with painstaking precision. In the "To be

(a)

5-19a, b. Cabaret.
Directed by Bob Fosse.
Realistic musicals often revolve around show business stories. A straight dramatic presentation is punctuated with musical numbers which are plausibly introduced by the action. Often these musical interludes are only peripheral to the dramatic action, but in the best works an organic relationship exists between the narrative events and the musical sequences. In Fosse's film, for example, art (a) is often used as an ironic commentary on life (b).

(b)

or not to be" soliloquy, the musical notes act in delicate counterpoint with Olivier's brilliantly modulated delivery, adding yet another dimension to this complex speech. Similarly, Franco Zeffirelli wanted two very young actors to perform in his *Romeo and Juliet*. Zeffirelli's emphasis in the film is on believability and naturalness, which at times forced him to minimize the highly stylized language. Indeed, the young principals recited their dialogue almost as though it were prose in some scenes, but Nino Rota's excellent score helps to restore the artifice to the speeches, emphasizing certain rhythms, underlining key phrases, and unifying the halts and pauses with the words. In short, the movie exploits the naturalness of prose phrasing in the dialogue delivery, while the rhythm of the poetic language is preserved by the musical accompaniment.

One of the most enduring and popular film genres is the musical—whose principal *raison d'être* is song and dance. As with opera and ballet, the narrative and dramatic elements of a musical are usually mere pretexts for the production numbers, though a great many musicals are also exceptionally sophisticated dramatically. Even musicals can be divided into the two basic types: realistic and expressionistic. The production numbers in realistic musicals are generally presented as dramatically probable. Often revolving around show business stories, such musicals justify a song or dance with a brief bit of dialogue—"Hey kids, let's rehearse the barn number"—and the barn number is then duly presented to the audience. A few realistic musicals are virtually dramas with music. In George Cukor's *A Star is Born,* for example, the narrative events would hold up perfectly well without the many musical numbers, though audiences would thereby be deprived of some of Judy Garland's most brilliant scenes. Bob Fosse's *Cabaret* is also a good example of the realistic musical (5-19). The story proper is a straight drama, but these dramatic scenes are often intercut with musical sequences (which comment obliquely on the narrative action) that take place on the stage of the shabby nightclub where the heroine (Liza Minnelli) is employed.

Expressionistic musicals make no such pretence at verisimilitude (5-20). Characters burst out in song and dance in the middle of a scene, without "easing into" the number with a realistic, plausible pretext. This **convention** must be accepted as a basic premise of such musicals, otherwise the entire film will strike the viewer as absurd. Everything is heightened and stylized in such works—sets, costumes, acting, and so on. Most of Vincente Minnelli's great musicals of the 1940s and 1950s are expressionistic: *Meet Me in St. Louis, The Pirate, The Band Wagon, An American in Paris,* and *Gigi* (5-21).

Though musicals have been produced in many countries, the genre is dominated by Americans, perhaps because it's so intimately related to the American studio system. In the 1930s, several major studios specialized in a particular type of musical. At RKO, director Mark Sandrich created the charming Fred Astaire-Ginger Rogers vehicles like *Top Hat, Shall We Dance?* and *Carefree.* Choreographer Hermes Pan was also contracted to RKO. Paramount specialized in sophisticated, intimate "Continental" musicals, like Lubitsch's *One Hour With You* and *Monte Carlo.* At Warner Brothers, director-choreographer Busby Berkeley delighted audiences with his proletarian wise-cracking show-biz stories, in which highly abstract geo-

5-20a. West Side Story.
Directed by Robert Wise.
5-20b. Godspell.
Directed by David Greene.
Musical décor and settings are often problematical. In expressionistic musicals, stylized studio sets are generally used, for when songs and dances are performed in gritty "documentary" locations, as in these two films, the effect is often jarring and incongruous: one "reality" tends to cancel out the integrity of the other.

(a)

(United Artists)

(b)

(Columbia Pictures)

metrical patterns were formed by photographing ensembles of dancers from unconventional angles (5-22).

In the forties and fifties, the genre was dominated by M-G-M, which had the two greatest musical directors under contract: Minnelli, and Stanley Donen. Indeed, this prosperous studio boasted the most talented musical personalities of the day, including Judy Garland, Gene Kelly, Frank Sinatra, Mickey Rooney, Ann Miller, Vera-Ellen, Leslie Caron, Donald O'Connor, Cyd Charisse, Howard Keel, and Kathryn Grayson. M-G-M also lured away Fred Astaire, Hermes Pan, and Busby Berkeley, who along with Michael Kidd, Bob Fosse, Gower Champion, and Gene Kelly, provided most of the

(a)

5-21a, b, c. *On The Town, An American in Paris, Gigi.*

All directed by Vincente Minnelli.

The tongue-in-cheek wit and visual elegance in the works of Minnelli were often inspired by painters and writers. *On the Town* features an amusing spoof of the "hard-boiled" fiction of such novelists as Dashiell Hammett, Raymond Chandler, and Mickey Spillane (a). *An American in Paris* features Gene Kelly as a struggling painter, and reflected Minnelli's great love for French culture (b). *Gigi* used many authentic Parisian locales, and was based on a story by Colette (c). As in the opera and ballet, the most intense emotions and significant ideas of a musical are expressed in song and dance, not through conventional dramatic means.

(M-G-M)

(b)

(c)

(a)

5-22a, b, c. *Gold Diggers of 1933*, *Gold Diggers of 1935*, *Dames*.
All directed by Busby Berkeley.
At Warner Brothers, choreographer-director Berkeley revolutionized the musical in the thirties by liberating the **genre** from the proscenium arch. Musical sequences were photographed from unpredictable angles which could not be duplicated in the theatre. Berkeley was especially fond of the **bird's-eye shot** (c), which reduced the contents of a scene to an abstract geometrical visual pattern.

(b)

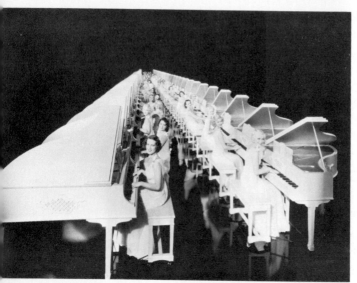

(c)

5-23a, b. Singin' in the Rain.
Directed by Stanley Donen and Gene Kelly.
Regarded by many as the greatest of all American musicals, *Singin' in the Rain* is a satiric spoof on the inanities of the Jazz Age (a) and the amusing complications which accompanied the coming of sound to the cinema (b). Gene Kelly choreographed, co-directed, and starred in this milestone work, which like many of the great M-G-M musicals, was produced by Arthur Freed.

(a)

(b)

(M-G-M)

choreography for the studio. Producer Arthur Freed was responsible for virtually all the great musicals produced there, including most of Minnelli's films, and the superb works of Donen: *On the Town, Singin' in the Rain* (both co-directed by Gene Kelly), *Seven Brides for Seven Brothers,* and the exquisite *Funny Face* (5-23).

LANGUAGE

A common misconception, held even by otherwise sophisticated moviegoers, is that language in film can't be as subtle or complex as it is in literature. The fact that Shakespeare has been successfully brought to the

(Universal Pictures)

5-24. Fahrenheit 451.
Directed by François Truffaut.
Based on a story by Ray Bradbury, this movie deals with a society that has banned all forms of written language. Appropriately, even the titles are spoken rather than printed. Though Truffaut began his career with certain reservations concerning the role of the writer in the cinema, several of his best films are based on distinguished literary sources.

screen—with no significant diminishment in either the language or the visuals—should stand as an obvious contradiction to this notion. In fact, a good number of great films aren't particularly literary, but this is not to say that movies are incapable of literary distinction, only that some film directors wish to emphasize other aspects of their art. Those who dismiss literary movies as "uncinematic" find themselves in the questionable position of condemning Welles, Bergman, Bresson, Richardson, Olivier, Godard, Truffaut, and Kurosawa—to mention only the most prominent film directors with literary sympathies.

In some respects, language in film can be more complex than in literature (5-24). In the first place, the words of a film, like those in the legitimate theatre, are spoken, not written, and the human voice is capable of far more flexibility than the cold printed page. The written word can only crudely approximate the nuances and connotations of spoken language. Thus, to take a crude example of no literary merit, the meanings of the words "I will see him tomorrow" seem obvious enough in written form. But an actor can emphasize one word over the others, and change the meaning of the sentence completely. Here are only a few possibilities:

I will *see* him tomorrow. (Implying, "but I doubt if I'll agree with him.")

I will see him *tomorrow*. (Implying, "not today, or next week either.")

I will see him tomorrow. (Implying, "not you or anyone else.")

I *will* see him tomorrow. (Implying, "and I don't care if you approve.")

I will see *him* tomorrow. (Implying, "but not his mother-in-law.")

Of course a novelist or poet could emphasize a few words by italicizing them, but unlike actors, literary people don't generally emphasize words in every sentence. On the other hand, an actor routinely goes through his speeches to see which words to stress and how, and which to "throw away" and how—in each and every sentence. With a gifted actor, the written speech is a mere blueprint, an outline, compared to the complexities of the spoken speech. A performer with an excellent voice—an Alec Guinness, for example—could wrench ten or twelve meanings from this simple sentence, let alone a Shakespearean soliloquy.

Written punctuation is likewise a crude approximation of speech rhythms. The pauses, hesitancies, and rapid slurs of speech can only be partially suggested by punctuation:

I will . . . see him—tomorrow.

I will see him: tomorrow!

I . . . will . . . see him—tomorow?

And so on. But how is one to capture all the meanings that have no punctuation equivalents? Even professional linguists, who have a vast array of diacritical marks to record speech, recognize that these symbols are primitive devices at best, capable of capturing only a fraction of the subtleties of the human voice. An actor like Laurence Olivier, for instance, has built much of his reputation on his genius for capturing the little quirks of speech—an irrepressible giggle between words, for example, or a sudden vocal upsurge on one word. Or a gulp, or an hysterical break in pitch. Indeed, the gamut of sounds and rhythms in Olivier's delivery suggests the virtuosity and richness of a musical instrument.

Because language is spoken in movies and plays, these two mediums enjoy an advantage over printed language in that the words of a text can be juxtaposed with ideas and emotions of a **sub-text** (5-25). Briefly, a sub-text refers to those meanings implicit *behind* the language of a film or play script. For example, the following lines of dialogue might be contained in a script:

Woman: May I have a cigarette, please?

Man: Yes, of course. (Lights her cigarette.)

Woman: Thank you. You're very kind.

Man: Don't mention it.

As written, these four not very exciting lines seem simple enough, and rather neutral emotionally. But, depending upon the dramatic context,

5-25. *Thieves Like Us.*
Directed by Robert Altman.
"What I am after is essentially the subtext," Altman has declared, "I want to get the quality of what's happening between people, not just the words. The words often don't matter, it's what they're really saying to each other without the words." Many commentators consider Altman the boldest innovator in sound since Orson Welles.

they can be exploited to suggest other ideas, totally independent of the apparent meaning of the words. If the woman were flirting with the man, for example, she would deliver the lines very differently from an efficient female executive. If the man and woman detested one another, the lines would take on another significance. If the man were flirting with a disinterested woman, the lines would be delivered in yet another way, suggesting other meanings. In other words, the meaning of the passage is provided by the actors, not by the language, which is merely a pretext.

The concept of a sub-text can be applied to any script meant to be spoken, even one of great literary value. A good example from a traditional text can be seen in Zeffirelli's *Romeo and Juliet,* in which Mercutio (John McEnery) is played not as the witty bon vivant who's in love with his own talk, but as a profoundly neurotic young man whose grip on reality is tenuous and fragile. This interpretation upset many traditionalists, but in the context of the film, it reinforces the loving protective bond between Romeo and his best friend, and helps to justify Romeo's impulsive (and self-destructive) act of revenge later in the movie, when Mercutio is killed by Tybalt.

Some contemporary writers and directors deliberately neutralize their language, claiming that the sub-text is what they're really after. Antonioni and Altman use their scripts merely as crude starting points. Harold Pinter, the dramatist and screenwriter, is perhaps the most famous contemporary writer who stresses the significance of the sub-text (5-26). In his play, *The Homecoming,* a scene of extraordinary eroticism is conveyed through dialogue involving the request for a glass of water! Pinter claims that language is often a kind of "cross-talk," a way of concealing certain fears and anxieties. In some respects, this technique can be even more effective in film, where close-ups can convey the real meanings behind words more subtly than can an actor on stage. Certainly Pinter's film scripts have some of the most subtle sub-texts of the contemporary cinema: *The Pumpkin Eater, The Servant, Accident, The Go-Between,* and the two adaptations of his plays, *The Caretaker* and *The Homecoming.*

But these are merely some of the advantages of language that film enjoys over literature—advantages shared, in large part, by the legitimate theatre. As an art of juxtapositions, movies can also extend the meaning of language by contrasting spoken words with images. The sentence "I will see him tomorrow" acquires still other meanings when the image shows the speaker smiling, for example, or frowning, or looking determined. All sorts of juxtapositions are possible: the sentence could be delivered with a determined emphasis, but an image of a frightened face (or eye, or a twitching mouth) can modify the verbal determination, or even cancel it out. The juxtaposed image could be a **reaction shot**—thus emphasizing the effect of the statement on the listener. Or the camera could photograph an important object, implying a connection between the speaker, the words, and the object. If the speaker is photographed in long shot, his juxtaposition with his environment could also change the meanings of the words. The same line spoken in close-up would have still another emphasis.

The advantages of simultaneity also extend to other sounds. Music and sound effects can modify the meanings of words considerably. This same sentence spoken in an echo chamber will have different connotations from

(American Film Theatre)

5-26. The Homecoming.
Directed by Peter Hall,
written by Harold Pinter.
Playwright Harold Pinter has written some of the most ambiguous scripts of the contemporary cinema. Language that seems perfectly neutral on the printed page can be charged with emotional tension when spoken by sensitive actors. The real meaning of a given scene is not in the words themselves, then, but in the dramatic tension between the words and the delivery of the performers.

5-27. Blume in Love.
Directed by Paul Mazursky.
Voice-over narratives are particularly effective in presenting us with a contrast between what is said socially and what is being thought privately. In this film, for example, Blume (George Segal) narrates what he was really feeling when he attempted to ingratiate himself with his ex-wife (Susan Anspach) and her lover (Kris Kristofferson).

(Warner Brothers)

the sentence whispered intimately. If a clap of thunder coincided with the utterance of the sentence, the effect would be different from the chirping of birds, or the moaning of the wind. Since film is also a technical medium, the sound of the sentence could be modified electronically. In short, depending upon the vocal emphasis, the visual emphasis, and the accompanying soundtrack, this simple sentence can have dozens of different meanings in film, some of them impossible to capture in written form.

There are two basic types of spoken language in movies—the monologue and dialogue. Monologues are often associated with documentaries, in which an off-screen narrator provides the audience with factual information accompanying the visuals. Most documentary theorists are agreed that the one cardinal rule in the use of this technique is to avoid duplicating the information in the image. The commentary should provide only what's not apparent on the screen. The audience, in short, is provided with two separate kinds of information, one concrete (visuals), the other more abstract (narration). The cinéma vérité documentarists have extended this technique to include interviews. Thus, instead of an anonymous narrator, the sound track conveys the actual words of the subjects of the documentary—slum dwellers, perhaps, or students. The camera can focus on the speaker, or can roam elsewhere, with the soundtrack providing the continuity.

Monologues have also been employed in fiction films. This technique is especially useful in condensing events and time. Early in *Citizen Kane* a simulated *News on the March* sequence is presented, recounting the highlights of Kane's public life. The mock "Voice of God" narrator sets up most of the major characters and events that are developed later in the movie. Narrative monologues can also be used **omnisciently,** to provide an ironic contrast with the visuals. In Richardson's *Tom Jones,* John Osborne's script features an off-screen narrator who's nearly as witty and urbane as Fielding's in the original novel, though necessarily less chatty. This nar-

(Paramount Pictures)

5-28. *Sunset Boulevard.*
Directed by Billy Wilder.
Voice-over monologues are often used to produce ironic contrasts between the past and the present. Almost inevitably, such contrasts suggest a sense of destiny and fate. Wilder, a director noted for his cynicism and audacious black humor, features a narration which is spoken by the opportunistic but decidedly dead protagonist (played by William Holden).

rator sets up the story, provides us with ironic thumbnail sketches of the characters, connects many of the episodes with necessary transitions, and comments "philosophically" on the escapades of the imprudent hero.

Off-screen narration tends to give a movie a sense of objectivity, and provides us with greater insights into the significance of the visuals. In Paul Mazursky's *Blume in Love,* this technique is used with flashbacks to produce a sense of irony between the past (visuals) and the present (sound track) (5-27). Billy Wilder's *Sunset Boulevard* is narrated by a dead man (!) while the flashback images show us how he managed to get himself killed. Narrative monologues are particularly useful in films emphasizing fatality, in which the main interest is not *what* happened, but how and why (5-28).

The interior monologue is one of the most valuable tools of the director, for with it, he can convey what a character is thinking. Originally a dramatic and novelistic device, the interior monologue is in fact frequently used in cinematic adaptations of plays and novels. Before Olivier entered the film world, most soliloquies were delivered as they are on stage: that is, the microphone "overhears" a character literally talking to himself, while the camera records the scene. Olivier's *Hamlet* introduced a more cinematic soliloquy. In the "To be or not to be" speech, several of the lines are "thought," not spoken. Suddenly, at a crucial line, Olivier spews out the words in exasperation. Using the soundtrack, both thoughts and speech can be joined in interesting combinations, with new, and often

5-29. *Richard III*.
Directed by Laurence Olivier.
In Olivier's Shakespearean film adaptations, the actor-director attempted to find cinematic equivalents to many of the stage conventions which are necessary in mounting a play. In this movie, for example, he modified Richard's soliloquies by having the villainous protagonist confide his intimate schemes directly to us—forcing us in a sense to become his accomplices.

more subtle emphases. In *Richard III*, the villain Richard (Olivier) brazenly directs his soliloquies to the camera—forcing us to be his confidants, and thereby suggesting that we are, in a sense, his accomplices (5-29).

One of the major differences between stage dialogue and screen dialogue is the degree of density. One of the necessary conventions of the theatre is articulation: if someone or something is bothering a character, we can usually assume that he will *talk* about the problem. The theatre is a visual as well as aural medium, but in general the spoken word is dominant: we tend to hear before we see. If information is conveyed visually in the theatre, it must be larger than life, for most of the audience is too far from the stage to perceive visual nuances. The convention of articulation is necessary, therefore, to compensate for this visual loss. Like most artistic conventions, stage dialogue is not usually realistic or natural, even in so-called "realistic" plays, for in real life people don't articulate their emotions and ideas with such precision. In movies, the convention of articulation can be relaxed. Since the close-up can show the most minute detail, verbal comment is often superfluous. This greater spatial flexibility means that language doesn't have to carry the heavy burden that stage dialogue does. Indeed, since the image conveys most of the dominant meaning, dialogue in film can be as realistic as it is in everyday life.

But movie dialogue doesn't have to conform to natural speech patterns. If the words are stylized, the director has several options to make the language believable. Like Olivier, he can emphasize an intimate style of delivery—sometimes even whispering the lines. Welles's Shakespearean films are characterized by a booming theatricality: the expressionistic stylization of the images in *Othello* conforms with the artificiality of the language. Generally speaking, if dialogue is nonrealistic, the images must

5-30. *Day for Night*.
Directed by François Truffaut (in leather jacket).
Foreign language films are shown in this country either in a dubbed version, or in the original language, with subtitles. Truffaut's movie was released in both forms, with the dubbed version shown primarily to popular audiences, and the subtitled version shown to smaller, more sophisticated audiences. Both methods of translation have obvious limitations. Dubbed movies often have a hollow, tinny sound, for only the crudely translated dialogue, music, and gross sound effects are recorded. Furthermore, in most cases, the dubbing is performed by actors of abilities inferior to the originals. Sound and image are difficult to match in dubbed films, especially in the closer ranges, where the movements of the actors' lips aren't synchronized with the sounds. Dubbed films also tend to lack sound "texture"—the subtleties of the sound effects are usually only approximated, thus robbing the sound of its suggestiveness and complexity. On the other hand, dubbed films permit the audience to concentrate on the visuals, rather than the subtitles, which are distracting and can absorb much of a viewer's energy. Most experienced filmgoers still prefer titles, however, despite their disadvantages. Particularly when sound is a major source of meaning, titles permit the viewer to hear what the *director* wished us to hear, not what some remote technician—however clever—decided we would settle for.

(*Warner Brothers*)

be stylistically consistent—sharp contrasts of style between language and visuals can produce jarring and often comic incongruities.

The advantages of language, then, make it indispensable to the film artist, and not merely for the director of literary tastes. As Clair foresaw many years ago, language permits a director more visual freedom, not less. Because speech can reveal a person's class, occupation, prejudices, and style the director doesn't need to waste time establishing these characteristics visually (5-30). A few lines of dialogue can convey all that is necessary, thus freeing the camera to go on to other matters, for there are many instances where language is the most economical and precise way of conveying meaning in film.

FURTHER READING

CLAIR, RENÉ. "The Art of Sound," in *Film: A Montage of Theories,* ed. Richard Dyer MacCann. New York: E. P. Dutton, 1966. (Paper) An appeal made in the early talkie era on the artistic advantages of non-synchronous sound in film.

EISENSTEIN, SERGEI. "Form and Content: Practice," in *Film Sense.* New York: Harcourt, Brace and Co., 1942. (Paper) Eisenstein modifies some of his earlier views on montage, but argues that synchronous sound would destroy many of the achievements in editing of the silent cinema.

———, V. I. PUDOVKIN, and G. V. ALEXANDROV. "A Statement on the Sound Film," in *Film Form.* New York: Harcourt, Brace and Co., 1949. (Paper) A group manifesto rejecting the use of synchronous sound in film.

EISLER, HANNS. *Composing for the Films.* New York: Oxford University Press, 1947. A standard work on the use of music in film.

Focus on Shakespearean Films, ed. Charles W. Eckert. Englewood Cliffs, N. J.: Prentice-Hall, Inc., 1972. (Paper) A collection of essays dealing with Shakespearean adaptations in film.

KNIGHT, ARTHUR. "The Movies Learn to Talk," in *The Liveliest Art.* New York: A Mentor Book, 1957. (Paper) An historical account of the early sound period.

KRACAUER, SIEGFRIED. "Dialogue and Sound," and "Music" in *Theory of Film.* New York: Oxford University Press, 1960. (Paper) A theoretical analysis of the types and functions of cinematic sound.

MANVELL, ROGER, and JOHN HUNTLEY. *The Technique of Film Music.* New York: Focal Press, 1957. A brief account of how music is employed in film.

McVAY, DOUGLAS. *The Musical Film.* New York: A. S. Barnes, & Co., 1967. (Paper) A brief history of the musical, with particular emphasis on American movies.

SPRINGER, JOHN. *All Talking, All Singing, All Dancing!* New York: Citadel, 1966. (Paper) An historical account of the musicals of the early sound period.

*"Documentary and newsreel are the noblest of
genres. They do not seek the instantaneous for its own
sake, but for what it secretes of eternity."*
—JEAN-LUC GODARD

6 documentary

Documentarists—both practitioners and theorists—are by no means agreed
on the definition of documentary film. The very term "documentary" has
been disputed: some commentators prefer the more general "nonfiction
film," while others argue for "the factual film." According to some of these
critics, "documentary" should be used to describe only those movies in
which a creative *interpretation* of factual materials is involved. A mere
presentation of information (such as industrial films, travelogues, training
films) ought to be designated by some less prestigious term. To some, then,
the term "documentary" is qualitative, suggesting at least a degree of
artistic excellence. But these distinctions are more trouble than they're

(New Yorker Films)

(a)

worth. Most fiction films (or for that matter, plays, novels, and paintings) are artistically negligible, but no one would think of differentiating them by assigning another term. As in the other arts, there are good and bad examples of documentaries, and in the following pages, the term will be used in the generic rather than qualitative sense.

THEORETICAL BACKGROUND

The distinction between fiction films and documentaries is also difficult to make in some instances. For example, critics have argued over the classification of such movies as Eisenstein's *Ten Days That Shook the World,* Pontecorvo's *The Battle of Algiers,* Rossellini's *The Rise of Louis XIV,* and *Fellini's Roma,* to mention only a few (6-1). No sooner does one begin to describe the main features of the documentary than a number of prominent exceptions come to mind. Despite individual exceptions, however, there are certain general characteristics that most examples of this genre share.

The most obvious of these, of course, is that documentaries deal with fact rather than fiction, with real people, places, and events rather than imagined ones (6-2). This authenticity is at once the greatest glory and the greatest potential source of controversy in the nonfiction film. In fiction movies, "authenticity" is generally defined internally, in terms of the "world" of the film. But no matter how convincing the "reality" of a fiction film might be, in the back of our minds, we're always aware that "it's only a movie," that the events are simulated. Hence, we are able to watch scenes of the most gruesome violence—as in Sam Peckinpah's *Straw Dogs,* for example—without losing our sense of the world outside the film. We willingly suspend our disbelief in order to respond fully to a fiction movie, but at the same time, we have enough **aesthetic distance** to realize that the screen events have been staged for us. Fiction films are faked—at least on this

(Rizzoli Films)

(b)

(Paramount Pictures)

(c)

6-1a. Paisàn.
Directed by Roberto Rossellini.
6-1b. The Battle of Algiers.
Directed by Gillo Pontecorvo.
6-1c. Medium Cool.
Directed by Haskell Wexler.
As an eclectic art which defies neat categories, the cinema abounds in hybrid **genres.** The distinctions between fiction and documentary are especially difficult to make among **realist** filmmakers. Rossellini began his career as a documentarist, and in such films as *Paisàn* (a), he used nonprofessional actors to recreate scenes that were based on actual events which took place in Italy during World War II. Because most of these events were dramatically heightened and synthesized from a variety of sources, film historians tend to consider the movie essentially fictional, though with a strong documentary flavor. Pontecorvo's movie (b) was totally recreated, yet the grainy images, the shaky camera work, and the film's gripping sense of immediacy mislead viewers into believing that the **footage** was photographed while the revolutionary events were actually taking place. Wexler's film (c) incorporates some authentic documentary footage of the 1968 Chicago political demonstrations within a fictional framework dealing with the television coverage of the Democratic National Convention held in that city.

literal level. The desire of the fiction filmmaker—or any artist who creates an imaginary world—is that the audience will accept the *symbolic* truth of his situations and characters. Indeed, Aristotle valued art over history precisely because he believed in the greater universality of art. History deals with authentic events and people, and hence may be too narrowly specific and idiosyncratic to have universal significance.

The documentarist—like the historian—is likely to reject these views. We arrive at truth through authentic facts, not artistic "falsehoods," he believes. Because authenticity is his artistic trump card, the documentarist is acutely sensitive to charges of inaccuracy, distortion, or fakery. Perhaps

6-2. A Hard Day's Night.
Directed by Richard Lester.
Even **expressionist** filmmakers have incorporated documentary elements into their works. Lester's Beatles film is a whimsical and bewildering mixture of the techniques of musicals, TV commercials, and documentaries.

the ultimate condemnation of a documentary is to accuse it of being "fictional"—that is, too slick, too contrived, and emotionally hyped up in order to cater to an audience's desire for "drama" which doesn't actually exist in the material. For these reasons, many documentarists are suspicious of "the beautiful **shot**," for it tends to suggest the manipulative tampering of the fiction filmmaker. A shaky, blurry shot of an actual murder is far more emotionally moving than a glossily photographed recreation of the event, many documentarists believe, even if the filmmaker tries to reconstruct the event as authentically as possible (6-3).

To many documentarists, then, literal truth has a beauty that transcends mere formal excellence. To many fiction filmmakers, on the other hand, beauty has a symbolic truth that transcends mere factual authenticity. The argument is an old and tedious one. There are great documentaries and great fiction films, though the kind of artistry involved in each tends to be different. Perhaps Jean-Luc Godard, who has made both kinds of films, has expressed it best:

> Beauty—the splendor of truth—has two poles. There are directors who seek the truth, which, if they find it, will necessarily be beautiful; others seek beauty, which, if they find it, will also be true. One finds these two poles in documentary and fiction.

The documentarist believes that he is not creating a world so much as he is observing the one that already exists. He is no mere recorder of external reality, however, for like the fiction filmmaker, he must shape his raw materials through his selection of details. These details are organized into a coherent artistic pattern, though many documentarists deliberately keep the structure of their movies simple and unobtrusive: they want their films to suggest the copiousness and apparent randomness of life itself. Details are exploited differently in fiction films and documentaries. In most fiction movies, the director invents certain details to enhance the credibility

(Zipporah Films)

6-3. Law and Order.
Directed by Frederick Wiseman.
The documentarist is more likely to value truth above beauty. Or rather, he is more likely to find a higher beauty *in* truth, a beauty that transcends mere picturesqueness. For these reasons, documentarists are sometimes suspicious of carefully **framed** and "artistically" composed images. A grainy, haphazard shot of an actual event will be more genuinely beautiful, these filmmakers believe, than any slickly photographed recreation, which will inevitably distort the truth—and hence the beauty—of the original event.

documentary **227**

of his characters and story, which may or may not resemble people and events of the real world. The major problem of the fiction filmmaker, then, is not fidelity to external reality, but internal consistency and probability. That is, how is such-and-such a character *likely* to react in a given situation?

The documentarist tends to withhold judgment until he observes how the person reacts *in fact*. Whether or not the reaction is consistent or probable, the documentarist prefers the actual thing to the likely thing. For example, in any documentary dealing with the life of Robert Frost, one would expect at least one episode of the poet on a lonely road, perhaps meditating upon a natural scene. But in *Robert Frost: A Lover's Quarrel With the World*, Robert Hughes avoided the probable, and concentrated

(Museum of Modern Art)

6-4. Divide and Conquer.
Directed by Frank Capra and Anatole Litvak.
Because most documentaries are structured around a theme rather than a plot, the shots can be arranged with much greater freedom than in most fiction films. Indeed, many theorists believe that documentaries are created on the **editor's** bench, for the genre often gains its major effects through the juxtaposition of shots for *thematic* continuity. It was precisely the propagandistic potential of thematic montage which appealed to the great Soviet film theorists and directors of the twenties, and had such a profound influence on Capra and Litvak in works like this, one of the "Why We Fight" movies produced by the U.S. War Department during World War II. This series, consisting of seven films, was supervised by Capra, who did virtually no "directing" in the conventional sense, but re-edited existing footage, much of it taken from captured enemy newsreels and Nazi propaganda films. By restructuring the footage and accompanying this new **continuity** with an anti-Nazi commentary, Capra altered the significance of the original visuals.

on what Frost actually was: a rather snappish, not altogether pleasant man, shrewd and thoroughly contemporary. The final image of the movie is not of the "Celebrated Contemplative Poet" walking down a country road, but of a weary professional in a station wagon, driving off to yet another tiresome speaking engagement.

Most fiction films tell a story, while documentaries are primarily concerned with revealing facts, usually within non-narrative frameworks. Fiction movies deal with conflicts, often between a protagonist and an antagonist. The selection and placement of shots and scenes are determined primarily by these considerations of plot and character. A cause-effect pattern is generally quite apparent in fiction films: once the conflict is established, each subsequent scene represents a progressive intensification until the climax is reached, and the conflict is resolved. This cause-effect pattern of development in most fiction movies means that the sequence of scenes is pretty much fixed by the demands of the narrative structure. One couldn't rearrange such sequences without damaging the logic of the rising action. Of course, some fiction films are more rigorously story oriented than others: it's a matter of degree. Most of Hitchcock's films, for example, are structured almost exclusively in terms of narrative. The movies of Renoir, on the other hand, have more leisurely and casual structures.

Documentaries tend to be thematically rather than narratively structured. The filmmaker is more concerned with presenting a problem or an argument than with telling a story. Consequently, the documentarist generally has greater freedom in arranging and structuring his materials. In many cases, the sequence of shots and even entire scenes could be rearranged with relatively little loss of comprehension or logic (6-4). Frequently there is no dramatic conflict in a documentary, merely a given situation. Climaxes are usually not overt in factual films: the most effective argument or the most telling scene is generally saved till late in the movie, but there isn't the sense of inevitability that characterizes most fictional climaxes. Relatively few documentaries are concerned with the complexities of "character" in the fictional sense. Indeed, one of the most persistent criticisms leveled at the documentary is its preoccupation with social issues and abstract ideas rather than with real people. Generally speaking, it was not until the sixties that many documentaries began to explore the ambiguities of the human personality in any great depth (6-5).

Perhaps no other type of movie is as suited to the analysis of social problems as the documentary. Many factual films are concerned with exposing immediate social ills, and for this reason, documentaries tend to seem dated once the problem has been resolved. Only the greatest nonfiction movies retain their universality long after their release date, though of course there are many thematically dated documentaries that are still technically brilliant. Since documentaries tend to be socially oriented, the emphasis is often on the interrelationship between man and his environment. Particular stress is placed on political institutions and their degree of responsiveness to the needs of citizens. Not surprisingly, a great many documentaries are government sponsored, and are intended primarily for educational and propagandistic purposes. For example, in the United States during the 1930s, such documentaries as Pare Lorentz's *The River* publicized the work of the TVA and its various benefits (6-6).

(Warner Brothers)

6-5. Jimi Hendrix.
Directed by Joe Boyd, John Head, and Gary Weis.
Throughout most of its history, the documentary has concentrated primarily on social issues rather than individuals, though the works of Robert Flaherty and a handful of others constitute some important exceptions. In general, however, it was not until the sixties that the complexities of character and the ambiguities of human nature were explored by documentarists on a wide scale. The interest in rock stars particularly continued into the seventies.

Not content merely to analyze social problems, many documentarists also offer specific solutions. In the thirties, the desire to expose abuses and suggest reforms was particularly strong, especially in Great Britain, where the documentary movement was dominated by the Scotsman, John Grierson. It was Grierson who originally coined the term "documentary," and defined it as "the creative treatment of actuality." Along with his disciple Paul Rotha, Grierson insisted that the documentarist must be a political and social analyst. He or she must take a position and make a moral commitment (6-7). Grierson scoffed at the concept of "objectivity" in nonfiction films. The so-called objective documentary is mere newsreel, he insisted, for it only reports information, and doesn't suggest causes and cures of specific social problems.

This issue of objectivity versus subjectivity has plagued the documentary movement almost since its inception. Critics and theorists seem to have been more preoccupied with the problem than filmmakers, who generally view

6-6. The River.
Directed by Pare Lorentz.
Many documentaries are government sponsored. Lorentz's film, for example was commissioned by the Federal government of the United States to publicize the achievements of the Tennessee Valley Authority in curbing the disastrous soil erosion which had devastated the lives of many Americans living in the Mississippi River basin.

6-7. The Spanish Earth.
Directed by Joris Ivens.
Many documentarists disdain the notion of objectivity. Some events, they claim, are simply too morally outrageous to allow for a "balanced view." In this film, the great Dutch documentarist Ivens, in collaboration with the American novelist Ernest Hemingway, exposed the mass slaughter of civilians during the Spanish Civil War in the late thirties. With planes and bombs provided by his Fascist cronies Hitler and Mussolini, Franco wrecked devastation on thousands of innocent Spaniards, many of them women and children. Hemingway's moving commentary, spoken by the novelist himself, forcefully communicates the sense of helpless terror brought on by the bombing: "Before, death came when you were old and sick. But now it comes to all in this village. High in the sky and shining silver, it comes to all who have no place to run, no place to hide."

(a)

6-8a, b, c. *Fellini's Roma*.
Directed by Federico Fellini.
Total objectivity is an impossible goal
in any documentary enterprise, for a
director's perception of actual events
will inevitably be influenced by his
values, prejudices, and preconceptions.
The choice of subject matter and the
principles of selectivity are determined
by what the *director* thinks is important,
not necessarily what someone else
might regard as essential. Indeed, in this
work, Fellini makes no pretense whatever at objectivity: as the title suggests,
the film is an exploration of the city of
Rome as seen through *Fellini's* eyes,
which has little to do with what an
average tourist might see in the city.
To varying degrees, the same principle
could be applied to virtually any documentary. Like fiction films, then, great
documentaries are valuable not only because of the subject matter but the way
in which the subject matter is interpreted
and presented. Most critics would regard Fellini's outrageously theatrical
scenes, like the "ecclesiastical fashion
show'' (a) or the hilarious eating habits
of the Romans (b) as more aesthetically
effective than the uninteresting episode
in the subways of Rome (c), which is
rather more objective and traditional in
its presentation.

(b)

(United Artists)

(c)

the entire issue as naive. After the mid-1960s, however, the issue erupted into a national controversy in the United States, where the major television networks were widely criticized for their "slanted" coverage of the Vietnam conflict and the Protest Movement. But the problem of subjectivity is a complex one, involving epistemological dilemmas that go far beyond the relatively narrow confines of documentary filmmaking.

The naive layman tends to believe that film directors ought to capture any event as it "really happened." The truth of the matter of course is that an event must be *perceived,* and the very act of perception involves distortions. Relevant and significant facts must be sorted out from the vast multitude of irrelevant details. But what's relevant to one person might seem merely incidental to another observer. The sifting of "significant" details, then, is already a gross distortion of an actual event, rather like the digest of a novel in relationship to the unexpurgated version.

Different people react differently to the same event—just as varying eyewitness accounts of an accident often differ. Furthermore, people with different backgrounds and different sets of values will perceive an event differently (6-8). A left-wing filmmaker will interpret an event from a totally different ideological and moral perspective than a right-winger, though both may sincerely believe that they're portraying the event truthfully. Throughout the turbulent sixties, for example, the three major American TV networks presented news coverage of the same events, yet each tended to "see" the events from a slightly different ideological perspective. The selection of details, the use of certain **angles** and **lenses,** the style of editing, were different with each network, yet they all believed that they were portraying the events responsibly and fairly.

We have seen how the use of certain techniques can alter the "content" of a shot. By using certain angles and editing styles, a student protest could be made to look like a flower-child convention or a teeming mass of rampaging anarchists. Objectivity, then, is an impossible goal in documentary filmmaking. Even Frederick Wiseman, arguably the most objective of all major documentarists, would insist that his movies are a subjective *interpretation* of actual events, people, and places—though he does try to be as "fair" as possible in rendering his subjects.

Like many cinematic concepts, "objectivity" and "subjectivity" are best used as relative terms. As in fiction films, the degree of distortion in documentaries ranges over a surprisingly wide spectrum. Indeed, the concepts of Realism and Expressionism are almost equally useful in discussing documentaries as they are in discussing fiction movies, though the overwhelming majority of documentarists would insist that their principal interest is with subject matter rather than technique. Nonetheless, many of the same characteristics of fiction films can be discerned in certain types of documentaries. Realistic documentaries tend to be more content oriented, with an emphasis on **mise-en-scène** rather than editing, which is more typical of expressionistic nonfiction films. Realistic documentaries tend to de-emphasize technique, whereas expressionistic films are stylistically more flamboyant. Most viewers would accept the "objectivity" of a realistic documentary because of its emphasis on **long takes,** neutral **set-ups,** and the avoidance of "forced" juxtapositions. Expressionistic documentaries, on the other hand, tend to strike viewers as "subjective," more manipulative (for better or worse), more

6-9. *The Battle of Russia.*

Directed by Frank Capra and Anatole Litvak.

Although the techniques used in the "Why We Fight" series tend to be highly manipulative, especially in terms of editing and accompanying commentary, Capra had the wisdom to realize that certain images needed no further comment. Here, for example, some Soviet newsreel footage conveys all the remorseless arrogance of some captured Nazi officers who were responsible for reducing the city of Stalingrad to a heap of rubble, and for starving, maiming, and killing many of its inhabitants.

(Museum of Modern Art)

personal and interpretive (6-9). Realists tend to find truth on the surface of reality; expressionists believe that the truth often lies embedded beneath the surface, and needs to be heightened in order to be recognized.

Of course, most documentarists fall somewhere between these two extremes. Indeed, some filmmakers believe that the tension resulting from the conflict between subject matter (content) and treatment (form) is what gives many documentaries their vitality. Albert Maysles, for example, has remarked on this artistic tension:

> We can see two kinds of truth here. One is in the raw material, which is the footage, the kind of truth that you get in literature in the diary form—it's immediate, no one has tampered with it. Then there's the other kind of truth that comes in extracting and juxtaposing the raw material into a more meaningful and coherent storytelling form, which finally can be said to be more than just raw data. In a way, the interests of the people in shooting and the people editing (even if it's the same individual) are in conflict with one another, because the raw material doesn't want to be shaped. It wants to maintain its truthfulness. One discipline says that if you begin to put it into another form, you're going to lose some of the veracity. The other discipline says if you don't let me put this into a form, no one is going to see it and the elements of truth in the raw material will never reach the audience with any impact, with any artistry, or whatever. So there are these things which are in conflict with one another and the thing is to put it all together, deriving the best from both. It comes almost to an argument of content and form, and you can't do one without the other.

The documentarist, then, is faced with many of the same artistic problems that beset the fiction filmmaker. Needless to say, arguments over which approach or emphasis is "better" are doomed to futility.

ROBERT FLAHERTY AND THE
REALIST TRADITION

The American Robert Flaherty is generally regarded as the father of the documentary movement. Even though factual elements had been present in the cinema from its beginnings, Flaherty's first movie, *Nanook of the North* (1922) is almost universally considered the first masterpiece of the documentary movement. Actually, Flaherty began his career as an explorer and amateur ethnologist, and in some respects, his films can be considered the artifacts of his continuing explorations of remote cultures. Originally, Flaherty brought a movie camera along simply to record some scenes of Eskimo life beyond the Arctic Circle. He knew virtually nothing about filmmaking, and throughout his career, he preferred a simple direct approach.

Prior to filming *Nanook,* Flaherty had lived several years in the Arctic regions of Canada, and had developed a profound admiration for the life and culture of the Eskimo. Essentially a nineteenth-century Romantic, Flaherty was disdainful of the tepid "civilized" lifestyles of modern technological societies (6-10). His imagination was stirred by "primitive" cultures, in which people lived constantly on the edge of extinction, where self-sacrifice, fortitude, and sheer guts were the requisites of survival. These were the highest virtues for Flaherty, **epic** virtues which seemed in short supply in contemporary urban societies. The Arctic and its Eskimos provided him with a conflict on an epic scale, in which a noble, courageous protagonist fought a life-or-death battle with a harsh, unyielding environment.

Nanook is loosely structured in three parts. The first third takes place in the warm season, in which Nanook repairs his primitive equipment. The second third shows us the harsh life of the Eskimo during the long winter. The final third of the film encompasses a single episode which takes place during a fierce blizzard. The constant quest for food is the major thematic spine of the movie. Each season involves its own problems, and we see the resourceful Nanook meet these problems with incredible ingenuity. He and his family are portrayed as totally natural—they *use* their environment and blend into it with amazing skill. The blizzard sequence is thrillingly conveyed. With the wind tearing relentlessly at 100 m.p.h. and the temperature at 90° below zero, we see the family desperately sledding across the vast Arctic expanses in search of shelter. Finally, through a stroke of good luck, they find an abandoned igloo to which they scramble for protection for the night.

Even when the film was first released it was criticized for being factually distorted and irrelevant to contemporary urban audiences. But the movie was far from the sentimentalized adventure yarn that some critics claimed: two years after the film was completed, the brave and gentle Nanook died of starvation while trying to hunt deer to feed his family.

Flaherty's approach to filmmaking was almost mystical—much to the annoyance of his associates, who were often exasperated by his time- and money-consuming methods. Using no prepared script, he would shoot thousands of feet of film before deciding how he would use the material—if at

(a)

6-10a, b, c. *Nanook of the North.*
Directed by Robert Flaherty.
In many respects, Flaherty's masterpiece seems to exist in a timeless
void. Most of the scenes depict a
rugged heroic existence which had
not significantly altered in hundreds
of years. Nanook hunted seals in the
same manner as his ancient ances-
tors, and with the same primitive
weapons (a). Judging from Flaherty's
account, family life among the Eskimos had not been affected by the
technology of the twentieth century
or the white man's incursion into the
Arctic (b). When Flaherty does depict
some aspect of contemporary technology, as in the rather comic scene
showing Nanook listening to a phono-
graph (c), the scenes are very brief
and presented as essentially irrelevant to the everyday lives of the
protagonists.

(b)

(Museum of Modern Art)

(c)

6-11. *Nanook of the North.*
Directed by Robert Flaherty.
The first great realistic documentarist, Flaherty distrusted editing and attempted as much as possible to include all the relevant dramatic variables within the same frame. Spatial interrelationships are emphasized by **deep-focus** photography, and real time is preserved by the frequent use of lengthy takes.

(Museum of Modern Art)

all. His shooting ratios were very high, at least for the time. (The 7000-foot-long *Man of Aran,* for example, was edited from a total of 200,000 feet of film.) Flaherty believed that only by shooting massive amounts of footage would the theme of his film emerge. He was hostile to the idea of imposing a structure on his materials, and insisted that the rhythm of a film sequence ought to be the same as the rhythm of the event in life (6-11). The artist merely "discovers" what's already there, both in life and in the raw footage.

Paul Rotha, the English documentarist and film critic, suggested that Flaherty may have taken these ideas from Eskimo culture. Eskimo ivory carvers, for example, don't think of themselves as creators so much as discoverers of art objects. The piece of crude ivory, in their view, is a formless mass in which is hidden a given shape. The carver merely "releases" or "frees" this shape from its surroundings. The carving process is viewed as "exploratory" until the hidden subject begins to make itself apparent, at which point the artist cuts away the remaining excess materials so that the form may be viewed without obstructions. To the Eskimo, art is a process of revelation, not "creation" in the usual sense of the term.

Flaherty's theory of documentary art is very close to this view. Ironically, he was often accused of arrogance because of his uneconomical methods of filmmaking, when actually his attitude reflected a good deal of humility. To Flaherty, the integrity of the material itself was paramount, and he went to considerable lengths to avoid the arbitrary superimposition of a form which was not an organic extension of the content. Deeply suspicious of the "distortions" of editing, Flaherty tried to reveal his subject in and through the camera. Reality was best served through the mise-en-scène, he believed, not by juxtaposing shots which chopped reality into a series of separate fragments.

Throughout *Nanook,* Flaherty employs **open forms,** implying that there

(a)

6-12a, b, c. _Nanook of the North._
Directed by Robert Flaherty.
Like most realists, Flaherty preferred
open forms, and his films are filled
with **_loosely framed extreme long
shots,_** which reveal much of the
harsh terrain (a). Nanook's heroic
stature is often expressed by the
mise-en-scène, with the courageous
protagonist poised triumphantly at
the top of the frame (b). To suggest
spontaneity and freedom, Flaherty
avoids **_anticipatory set-ups:_** his camera dutifully follows the protagonist
(c).

(b)

(Museum of Modern Art)

(c)

6-13. Nanook of the North.
Directed by Robert Flaherty.
Some of the most human and moving scenes in Flaherty's work involve the protagonist's acknowledgement of the audience. Particularly after an amusing or daring incident, Nanook sometimes turns to the camera with a winning grin of triumph.

is more information outside the frame (6-12). As in his other films, the director includes a number of sweeping **pan shots** to suggest the vastness of the terrain. Nanook's heroism is visually suggested in shots which show his figure at the top of the picture, dominating the remaining elements within the frame. In scenes emphasizing vulnerability, as in the blizzard sequence, Nanook's sled races precariously near the bottom of the frame, at times almost slipping out into the dark oblivion below. Whenever possible, Flaherty tries to preserve the unity of time and space by using long takes, and including all the relevant variables within a single shot. While Nanook is hunting walrus, for example, Flaherty keeps both the hunter and the hunted within the same frame, capturing not only the specific distance between them but thereby also preserving the suspense, for with one false step, Nanook could scatter the herd away.

In a number of **sequences**, Flaherty refuses to reveal too much too soon. In one scene, for example, Nanook harpoons something through a hole in the ice. After a fierce struggle, the exhausted hunter pulls a harpooned seal through the hole. This type of elementary suspense was no mere gimmick for Flaherty, for he believed that art—like reality—doesn't yield up its secrets without a fight. In effect, Flaherty forces the audience to "work," to actively participate in interpreting the scene (6-13). Like most realists, he instinctively distrusted an artistic reality that lacked ambiguity, that was too glibly clear.

Although *Nanook* was almost universally praised, a number of commentators criticized its inaccuracies and distortions. For example, several observers noted that in the famous seal fishing episode, the limp creature that was finally pulled through the hole in the ice was obviously dead—yet moments before, it was fighting frantically. Other critics scoffed at the size of Nanook's igloo. Flaherty explained that a conventional igloo was too small and dark to permit his bulky camera to function properly. In order to show Nanook's family life from inside the igloo, a special dwelling had to be constructed, one that was twenty-five feet in diameter, with a hole in the roof to permit the light to enter. "Sometimes you have to lie," Flaherty explained, "one often has to distort a thing to catch its true spirit." In light of the extraordinary overall achievement of *Nanook,* these criticisms seem rather carping. In Flaherty's subsequent films, however, his distortions became less and less excusable.

Man of Aran is perhaps Flaherty's greatest film, yet ironically, it's also the least authentic—in the documentary sense of that term. The movie is an exploration of the harsh life on the Aran Islands, which lie off the western coast of Ireland. The only other film by Flaherty in which the "Nanook formula" was successful, *Man of Aran* is a heroic saga of a courageous people fighting an eternal battle against the sea. As in *Nanook,* Flaherty focused on a single family as the symbol of an entire people.

Like the Arctic in *Nanook,* the Aran Islands are barren: only the barest subsistence can be eked out by the rugged inhabitants. Lacking even soil, the Islanders must create a synthetic earth by mixing crushed rocks with seaweed, in which they grow potatoes, their subsistence crop. Tiger King, the husband, is shown engaged in the back-breaking task of smashing rocks, while his wife Maggie hauls seaweed up a steep cliff. Their young son Mikeleen is also a hard worker, and helps his parents with many of their arduous tasks.

The central episode of the movie deals with the harpooning of a huge basking shark, some twenty-seven feet long—"the biggest fish found in the Atlantic," as one of the titles informs us. Tiger King and some other men go off in pursuit of the shark in a curragh, a lightweight boat consisting of a ribbed frame over which is stretched a tarred canvas covering. The shark is successfully harpooned, but so great is its strength, the men are forced to remain at sea for two days, while they are hauled across the water's surface by the wounded creature.

While the men are at sea, Maggie, Mikeleen, and some other Islanders begin preparations for boiling out the oil from the shark's enormous liver. A huge black cauldron is set up at the edge of the 300 foot cliff. When the shark is finally brought in, the Islanders cut up its liver and place huge chunks in the cauldron. As Maggie stirs the greasy mixture, her handsome features are highlighted by a smile of triumph, for now there will be plenty of oil for their lamps.

Like *Nanook,* this film ends with a ferocious storm sequence. Tiger King and his friends are trapped at sea in their fragile curragh while gigantic waves toss the boat about as though it were a twig. There is an epic battle between Man and Sea. Maggie and Mikeleen wait and watch helplessly on the steep cliff, their black outlines dwarfed into insignificance by the vast sky and the sea, which sprays to a height of 450 feet at the cliff's edge.

Miraculously, the skillful oarsmen maneuver their curragh near the shore, but the boat is pulverized by the waves and jagged rocks moments after the men leap off to safety. The film ends with the family looking back in awe at the implacable fury of their ancient enemy—the Sea.

There's no question that Flaherty's movie produces an overwhelming aesthetic experience in the viewer. The film is a noble testament to man's indestructibility in the face of monumental hardships. But the movie is not quite fact and not quite fiction, and for this reason, it created a storm of controversy when it was first released in 1934. Because it was presented as a factual account of life on the Aran Islands, the film was attacked for the dishonesty of its scenes. What was left out of the movie created an even greater furor (6-14).

Virtually every sequence (except the rock and seaweed episode) is inauthentic. Even the family was Flaherty's own creation, for Maggie, Tiger

6-14. *Man of Aran.*
Directed by Robert Flaherty.
Although arguably the director's greatest film, this "documentary" account of life on the Aran Islands aroused a storm of controversy in the thirties. Flaherty concentrated on the eternal struggle of Man versus Sea, but according to many social critics of the period, the real enemies of the people were the appalling conditions of poverty on the islands, the exploitation of absentee landlords, the religious bigotry, ignorance, and superstitiousness of the people. Flaherty ignored virtually all of these social facts in favor of a more romantic fictionalized approach.

(Museum of Modern Art)

King, and Mikeleen scarcely knew each other in real life: they were selected for their handsome appearance. The entire shark episode is fanciful, to say the least. In the first place, the basking shark is not a man-killer, as Flaherty implies, but a gentle plankton-eating creature. Furthermore, the Aran Islanders had been using paraffin for their lamps for well over fifty years, and the men on the island didn't even know how to hunt basking sharks. Like the women who boiled down the shark liver in the cauldron, the "hunters" had to be taught how to perform their activities.

This is certainly not to deny the extraordinary courage of the Islanders. In some respects, their bravery was even greater than Flaherty showed. For example, odd as it may seem, almost none of the Islanders could swim. When Flaherty asked the men to go out on very rough seas so he could photograph the storm sequences, they were actually taking greater risks than is shown in the film. If their curragh had scraped against just one rock, all the men would have drowned in a matter of seconds. Against their better judgment, these sturdy boatmen ventured out time and again, mostly because they wanted to please Flaherty.

Actual life on the Aran Islands was considerably less romantic than Flaherty depicted. In fact, it was hopelessly wretched. When the movie was being made, Europe and the Americas were plunged in one of the cruelest economic depressions in modern history, yet there's no reference to this anywhere in the film. The island itself was rife with class conflicts. Impoverished families were being evicted almost daily from their homes by the police, who were following the orders of absentee landlords on the mainland or in England.

There was also an intense religious conflict on the island which went back many years. Indeed, the male lead in the film was a Protestant, and for some time, many of the Catholics on the island refused to cooperate with Flaherty for fear that Tiger King would sprinkle their youngsters with "magic water" and turn their children into Protestants. Yet there is no mention of any religious strife in *Man of Aran*.

The ignorance and superstitiousness of the Islanders were exploited at every turn. When Maggie was hired to act in the movie, for example, her children were spindly from undernourishment. Yet three months after the film unit left Aran, she was persuaded by a missionary priest from the mainland to give him all her earnings from the movie. For some time, the destitute Islanders refused to work for Flaherty (who was politically rather conservative) because they had heard that he was a "socialist"—even though no one really knew what the term meant.

Marxist critics were especially harsh in their denunciation of Flaherty's film. One hardly had to be a Marxist, however, to recognize that *Man of Aran* wasn't likely to be of much assistance in improving social conditions on the islands. Grinding poverty, ignorance, squalor, and heartless exploitation—these were the true enemies of the people of Aran. And these were the documentary facts that Flaherty ignored while he pursued his romantic chimeras and "sea monsters." In England, where the documentary movement was mildly Marxist in its ideology, Flaherty was accused of bourgeois condescension towards the Islanders by sentimentalizing their ignorance and conservatism. The Griersonians would have approached the subject in a totally different way, asking totally different questions: "Who is responsible for these conditions?" "Who benefits from them?" "Why is no one working to improve them?" To the English, Flaherty's film—which they acknowledged was visually stunning—was not only personally irresponsible, but ultimately artistically irresponsible as well, for it was based on dangerous romantic sentimentality, not facts.

Perhaps *Man of Aran* will always occupy its own special category in the history of the documentary, if for nothing else, for the extraordinary beauty of its images. Ironically, in its own time, the film seemed hopelessly anachronistic, at least in social terms. Today it outshines virtually every nonfiction film made during the same period—precisely because of its timelessness. Furthermore, since the postwar period, the range of documentary art has expanded considerably, and most documentarists would concede that there are a number of subjects that aren't particularly political or even social, yet are still worthy of treatment.

Although many subsequent documentarists paid homage to Flaherty, his influence was not strong until the late fifties and sixties, when **cinéma vérité** became the dominant school in the documentary movement. Throughout the thirties, the war years, and up to the mid-fifties, however, the most important documentaries were influenced primarily by the techniques and theories that had been developed in the Soviet Union and Great Britain during the twenties and thirties.

DZIGA VERTOV AND THE EXPRESSIONIST TRADITION

After the 1917 Revolution in Russia, many young Soviet cinéastes came forward to offer their services to the new society. Among them was the Polish-born Dziga Vertov, who was experimenting in documentary forms and theory at about the same time that Flaherty was producing *Nanook*. Like Eisenstein, Vertov was enthusiastic about the vast potential of film as an educational and propagandistic tool of the Revolution. A new society needs new forms of expression, Vertov believed, and a society composed overwhelmingly of illiterate workers and peasants needed to be instructed about the workers' historical struggle, and about the ideals of the Revolution. Vertov believed that documentary film could carry out this mission better than any other art form, and that documentaries ought to be revolutionary in technique as well as subject matter. "Art," he once wrote, "is not a *mirror* which reflects the historical struggle, but a *weapon* of that struggle."

Vertov believed that fiction films were counter-revolutionary. He considered them variations of traditional bourgeois literature and drama, only "furnished with cinematic illustrations." Fiction films were mere "aesthetic hash-hish," Vertov felt, for they provide an escape from—not a confrontation with—reality. The raw material of the cinema must be the observable material world—real people, places, and things. Recreations of reality will inevitably falsify it, will render it fictional, even if the filmmaker sincerely strives for authenticity. An actor impersonating a peasant will always strike the viewer as precisely that—not the genuine article. Condemning all acted films as opiates, Vertov criticized even Eisenstein's historical reconstructions, which he called "acted films in documentary trousers" (6-15).

6-15. Potemkin.
Directed by Sergei Eisenstein.
Vertov believed that the documentary would sensitize citizens to the poetry of everyday life, and train them to value facts and authentic details, not merely the "artistic inventions" which are inspired by these facts and details. Eisenstein's historical reconstructions, according to Vertov, are merely "acted films in documentary trousers," for the raw materials are not taken from the observable world, but from a world of the past which must be imagined rather than recorded as it now exists.

(Audio-Brandon Films)

But like most expressionists, Vertov believed that the filmmaker doesn't merely record external reality, he exploits it. He must see beneath the surface chaos of the external world in order to discover underlying truths. The revolutionary documentarist must point out ideological lessons in his films, explaining social and economic relationships which aren't always apparent, especially in capitalist societies. He must reveal who produces goods, who consumes them, and who actually profits by them. He must demystify social institutions, exposing those that don't serve the needs of the people, and praising those that do. Reality is too complex, too sprawling to be understood by those who are uninstructed in revolutionary ideology. Hence, the documentarist uses the actual world merely as a repository of unsystematized data. Vertov likened the shaping of the raw footage of this reality to bricklaying: by themselves, pieces of film are useless, but the documentarist uses these "bricks" to construct cinematic buildings. By selecting, interpreting, and manipulating the raw footage he helps workers and peasants to view reality through a new revolutionary consciousness.

Like Eisenstein and Pudovkin, Vertov believed that the foundation of cinematic art was editing. Influenced by the elaborate thematic **cross-cutting** of Griffith's *Intolerance,* Vertov believed that montage could unite elements which are apparently unrelated in life. Indeed, editing can "contrast any points in the universe," without regard to the restrictions of space and time. Going beyond even Eisenstein, Vertov felt that **continuity** in film should be *totally* thematic, that shots ought to be linked poetically, not "logically," as they are in fiction films and in conventional documentaries (6-16).

Like the poet, he felt, the film artist is essentially a fuser of images. Indeed, Vertov did very little actual shooting himself, so little did he emphasize the mise-en-scène aspect of the cinematic process. Beginning with the three-hour long *Anniversary of the October Revolution* (1918), the first Soviet feature, Vertov conducted a series of editing experiments which became progressively more audacious. In 1922, he created a series of newsreels entitled *Kino-Pravda* ("Film-Truth"), which were unabashedly subjective. The *Kino-Pravda* films not only informed the proletariat of current events, they simultaneously instructed the audience on how to view these events from a revolutionary perspective.

Nor did Vertov edit all of his movies in the same style. His concept of **montage** was generally geared to the nature of his subject matter. His so-called "cine-poems," for example, tended to be edited more lyrically, as were his "cine-symphonies." *The Man with a Movie Camera,* Vertov's best-known work, is edited in a variety of rhythms. The film tends to be relatively

6-16. *The Man With a Movie Camera.*
Directed by Dziga Vertov.
The documentary artist, according to Vertov, is a poet, a fuser of disparate images. The cine-poet can yoke together any elements in the universe to form new combinations, and without regard to considerations of literal continuity. The unique fusion of poetry with technology, of art with science, was particularly appealing to the filmmakers of the Soviet Union.

slow paced in scenes featuring Moscovites awakening in the morning. As the people accelerate their pace at work, the shots quicken to four or two seconds in length. At the height of the work day, some of the shots are less than a second long.

Even more than Eisenstein, Vertov experimented widely with a metaphoric kind of montage. In *The Man with a Movie Camera,* for example, he employed an eye **motif** throughout the film to create a startling assortment of comparisons. The human eye is likened to the camera's **lens**—what Vertov called the "cine-eye." In the opening morning sequence, we see shades lifted from windows, and doors to airplane hangars being raised like huge steel eyelids. A girl washing herself is juxtaposed with a shot of a man washing down merchandise, and with workers cleaning windows. A woman putting on a slip is compared to a photographer putting a new lens on his camera; cutting hair is likened to cutting film; sewing machines are linked analogously with editing machines. All of these comparisons are purely visual, for the film is silent and doesn't contain a single title.

Since movies can fuse images with ease, Vertov considered cinema the ultimate poetic art. But like most Soviet directors, he also enthusiastically praised the mechanical aspects of filmmaking, and considered it the ultimate technological art as well. Perhaps nothing appealed more to Soviet filmmakers than this unique fusion of art with science, of imagination with material reality, of feeling with fact. The scientific properties of the photographic process were precisely what made some of the most poetic effects possible in the cinema, Vertov believed. Unlike most documentarists, he thought that nonfiction filmmakers ought to use the full range of special effects that are available to the fiction film director. In his own movies, the technical brilliance is dazzling in its variety: Vertov uses subliminal shots which are only one or two frames long, tinted stock for emotional emphasis, virtually every kind of lens and **filter, fast motion, slow motion, reverse motion, freeze frames, multiple exposures,** split screens, even **animation!**

Furthermore, Vertov hailed the advent of sound in film, and foresaw great new possibilities for the juxtaposition of sounds with images. His *Three Songs of Lenin* (1934), for example, leaps through time and space not only in its images but in its soundtrack as well. Archive shots of Lenin are linked to old newsreels and contemporary interview scenes with breathtaking agility. The soundtrack likewise juxtaposes recordings of Lenin's speeches with Soviet songs and a wide range of **synchronous** and **non-synchronous sound** effects. As early as 1922, Vertov was eagerly awaiting the arrival of color photography, and even 3-D. Everything was possible in this extraordinary new medium, the enthusiastic Vertov proclaimed.

Indeed, so excited was he about the possibilities of cinema that some of his movies are as much a joyous celebration of the filmmaking process as they are documents of reality. In *The Man with the Movie Camera,* Vertov chronicles various events that take place in Moscow within a day's span. He also chronicles how these events are used as raw material by the filmmaker. The opening sequence features a trick shot showing a movie camera on a tripod, pointed at us. Through a double exposure technique, a "little" cameraman walks on top of the camera. We then see people filing into a theatre to see a movie, then Vertov's film proper begins. Within the work itself, Vertov shows us an event, then a cameraman photographing the

**6-17. *The Man With a Movie Camera.*
*Directed by Dziga Vertov.***
Employing a profusion of eye images
from a wide variety of sources, Vertov's best known film is a celebration
of the extraordinary resources of the
cinema. Some of his images, though
taken from everyday reality, have an
abstract, flat quality that has influenced the pop poster styles of contemporary filmmakers like Jean-Luc
Godard.

(Museum of Modern Art)

event, then an editor cutting the film strip on which the event is recorded,
then a shot of an audience looking at the image of the event! Perhaps no
director in film history—with the possible exception of Godard—took such
witty delight in reminding an audience that what they were viewing was not
reality, but an *image* of reality, one that had been manipulated by many
artists and technicians (6-17).

Vertov died in 1954, but his career was killed long before that, in the
mid-thirties. Along with Eisenstein and a number of other great Soviet
artists, Vertov was criticized and ultimately condemned for "formalism," or
a decadent preoccupation with form and technique at the expense of content.
By 1932, much of the experimentation that had previously characterized
Soviet art was brought to a halt. After 1934, **Socialist Realism** was decreed
the official style of Soviet art. Sometimes known as the "Stalin School,"
Socialist Realism was conservative technically, and rather standardized in
terms of its range of themes and subjects, at least until the death of Stalin.
Like Eisenstein, Vertov fell into semi-official disgrace with his government.
He spent most of the remainder of his life as a hack editor of government
newsreels.

Most documentarists have avoided the freewheeling extravagance of
Vertov's techniques. Because of their undisguised subjectivity, Vertov's
movies are effective only with those who are already in agreement with
the director's views, his critics have argued. To persuade a neutral observer,
a more "objective" presentation of factual materials must be practiced, a
presentation which seems to take in both sides of an argument. There have
been a few political documentarists who have taken over Vertov's methods,
however—particularly his editing techniques and his tendency to remind
audiences that what they are watching is a manipulated *image* of reality.

6-18. Point of Order!.
Directed by Emile de Antonio.
Like most of the great Soviet filmmakers, Vertov's principal emphasis was on the art of editing. Materials which might seem politically neutral can acquire enormous ideological impact when the footage is re-cut to emphasize startling juxtapositions. Many documentaries in the Vertov mold, like *Point of Order!* were photographed by relatively impartial newsreel cameramen: the political significance is conveyed by the way in which this neutral material is manipulated on the editing bench.

In his "Maoist" documentaries like *Wind from the East, See You at Mao,* and *Vladimir and Rosa,* the Frenchman, Jean-Luc Godard has consciously adopted a number of Vertov's subjective techniques, though not always with complete success.

Perhaps the most effective Vertovian documentarist is the American, Emile de Antonio, whose films—*Point of Order!, In the Year of the Pig, Rush to Judgment,* and *Millhouse*—are polemical and unashamedly one-sided (6-18). Probably the best of these is *In the Year of the Pig,* a scathing attack on the American involvement in Vietnam. Much of de Antonio's footage is taken from archives—old newsreels, TV film clips, and even still photographs. This footage is intercut—usually with maximum ironic impact —with interview scenes featuring anti-war political and military specialists. Battle footage of the civilian carnage in Vietnam is juxtaposed with inter-views of American leaders of both parties piously justifying their motives for involving the United States in "the battle for men's minds and souls." The juxtapositions in de Antonio's film are not limited only to visuals. In one sequence, for example, we see the French army ignominiously sur-rendering to General Giap at Dienbienphu. On the soundtrack, we hear a wittily orientalized rendition of "The Marseillaise," the French national anthem.

Ultimately, Vertov's influence in the cinema has probably been greatest with fiction filmmakers, especially those in the **avant-garde.** In somewhat diluted form, however, the editing theories of the great Soviet film director were to exert a profound influence on the documentary movement in the thirties and forties, particularly in western Europe and in the English-speaking countries.

JOHN GRIERSON AND THE BRITISH SCHOOL

Although he personally directed only one movie (*Drifters,* 1929), John Grierson was probably the single most influential force in the documentary movement. His importance was primarily inspirational. As a teacher, publicist, producer, distributor, and organizer, Grierson was the main guiding force of the documentary movement not only in Great Britain, but in Canada, and, to a lesser extent, in Australia, New Zealand, and the United States. Throughout his career, this crusty old warrior fought a continuing battle—wheedling, cajoling, scolding, and charming various government officials into recognizing the importance of the documentary as an instrument of public education. "I look upon the cinema as a pulpit," he once declared, "and use it as a propagandist."

For the didactic Grierson, film had to be *useful*—it fulfilled a specific and important public function. He believed that documentary film was essential if a democracy hoped to survive. Only when citizens are aware of what's going on in the public sector are they likely to select the best leaders and the most responsive social programs. The Scotsman believed that documentary was primarily an instrument of communication and persuasion, and only secondarily an art form. If nonfiction films educated citizens in an artistically pleasing manner, so much the better, but function always took precedence over form. Throughout his career, he admired good craftsmanship and innovative techniques, but he was suspicious of anything smacking of aestheticism in documentary films: "The conscious pursuit of art carries with it, in periods of public difficulty, a certain shallowness of outlook," he once remarked.

Grierson's somewhat Calvinistic philosophy is no longer very fashionable among contemporary filmmakers. But during the period of his greatest influence—throughout the Great Depression and the Second World War—his attitude certainly seemed the most responsible, humane, and relevant (6-19). Furthermore, he was never dogmatic about matters of style—so long as the technique didn't overwhelm the subject matter. For example, he was much impressed by the Continental documentaries of the twenties, particularly Alberto Cavalcanti's *Rien que les heures* and Walther Ruttmann's *Berlin: The Symphony of a Great City,* but he expressed annoyance at what he viewed as their preoccupation with form at the expense of serious social analysis.

In many respects, the British school can be viewed as a compromise between the traditions of Flaherty and the Soviet documentarists. Grierson himself often acknowledged his indebtedness to Flaherty's *Nanook* and Eisenstein's *Potemkin,* though Grierson always expressed impatience with what he viewed as their shortcomings and excesses. With Flaherty, he had a lifelong love-hate professional relationship, though personally they were great friends. What Grierson admired in the American's work was his poetic delicacy, his love of natural and intimate scenes, his sincere respect for the dignity of manual labor. Grierson also felt that Flaherty demonstrated a profound sensitivity toward individuals, a quality conspicuously lacking in the Soviet cinema, which tended to emphasize masses of people and communal units.

But Grierson was always dismayed by what he called Flaherty's "Neo-Rousseauism": his romantic exoticism, his sentimentalization of a bygone era, his avoidance of social issues, his lack of reformist zeal, and his glorification of an obsolete notion of the "Noble Savage." The problems facing the twentieth century were essentially urban and technological, Grierson insisted, and these require collective and public solutions. Beautiful as they were, Flaherty's movies were simply irrelevant in solving contemporary problems. After seeing Flaherty's *Louisiana Story*, Grierson once again complained of the American's lack of relevance: "Yet another brilliant evocation of the damn fool sense of innocence this wonderful old character pursues," he lamented.

Grierson's response to the Soviet cinema was just as ambivalent. He always acknowledged the enormous technical contributions of the Russians, particularly their editing innovations. He also admired the strong sense of social purpose of most Soviet documentarists—at any rate, in their theory, if not always their practice. Like the Russian filmmakers, Grierson insisted that the cinema is not a passive mirror of the material world, but a dynamic hammer which helps to shape reality, and gives a society a sense of purpose and direction.

But Grierson was sharply critical of what he believed to be an *idée fixe* of the Soviet documentary—the Revolution. So long as Russian filmmakers dwelt on this one obsession, their films were exciting and effective—in a flashy, rhetorical sort of way. But the real problems of any society involve peacetime activities and programs, Grierson believed, and in this realm, the Soviet cinema was dull and pedantic. Eisenstein's *Old and New* (also known as *The General Line*) was trifling and hackneyed in comparison with *October* or *Potemkin*, Grierson felt, for nowhere does the Russian show the same fervor and sincerity in dealing with an agricultural commune that he displayed in dealing with the Revolution. Even the Revolutionary films were excessively fictionalized for Grierson's taste: their structures were forced and melodramatic, filled with false climaxes and hysterical crescendos. Furthermore, their neglect of individuals in favor of mass movements and groups gave these films a cold inhumanity.

Grierson was especially critical of Dziga Vertov, who inspired the Scotsman to new heights of indignation and wit. He duly noted Vertov's technical brilliance, but condemned his "exhibitionism." *The Man with a Movie Camera* was mere virtuosity, Grierson scoffed. The shots move along so rapidly that the film seemed more like a "snapshot album" than a documentary. He dismissed Vertov's *Enthusiasm* as "all dazzle-dazzle and bits and pieces, whoopee for this, whoopee for that." Ultimately, he found Vertov's work even more irresponsible than Flaherty's and in many respects, Grierson felt that the charge of "formalism" in Vertov's case was justified.

6-19. *Prelude to War.*
Directed by Frank Capra.
More than any other single person John Grierson popularized the idea of using the documentary as an instrument of public education. By 1945, Capra's film had been seen by a total of 9,000,000 people. The purpose of the movie was to inform Allied troops of the course of events leading up to World War II, to help soldiers to understand the human and ideological background to the war.

Grierson's concept of documentary tended to be pragmatic, efficient, and rational—all the virtues he himself displayed in abundance. He emphasized pre-planning, especially in the script-writing stage. A certain amount of discovery and improvisation was allowable, but he didn't sanction the kind of random experimentation that characterized the approaches of Flaherty and Vertov, neither of whom used scripts at all. Flaherty believed that documentary was essentially a creation of the camera, whereas Vertov thought that films were created on the editor's bench. Grierson, on the other hand, tended to believe that the script was the major force behind a documentary, though of course the collaborative nature of the filmmaking process doesn't always permit such easy distinctions, and he was the first to acknowledge this fact.

In general, Grierson encouraged a problem-causes-solutions approach to the documentary. He was always suspicious of the "aestheticky" method

6-20. Night Mail.
Directed by Basil Wright and Harry Watt.
The British documentaries produced under Grierson often dealt with materials which were not intrinsically very dramatic or exciting. The success of these films was due, in large part, to their excellent craftsmanship.

(Museum of Modern Art)

that the Russians tended to favor—that is, films which "celebrated" rather than analyzed events and institutions. For the most part, British documentaries produced under Grierson's guidance tended to be brief and deliberately narrow thematically. They dealt with specific national issues and institutions of public concern: *Housing Problems, Coalface, Night Mail, Children at School, The Smoke Menace*—the very titles suggest their limited scope and analytical orientation.

This is not to suggest that British documentaries of this period are dull or ploddingly didactic. Some of them are witty, subtle, and even poetic, despite their utilitarian goals. *Night Mail*, for example, deals with the mail express train that travels from London to Glasgow and the ordinary workmen who are responsible for processing the mail along the way (6-20). On the surface, not a very exciting topic, yet the movie is rather romantic in its treatment, and especially innovative in its use of sound, featuring a musical score by Benjamin Britten and a verse narration by W. H. Auden.

Perhaps the greatest filmmaker to emerge from the British school is Humphrey Jennings, whose major work was produced during World War II. Poetic, lyrical, and inspirational in the best sense, Jennings' films are probably the least propagandistic of all the major documentaries produced during this period. His concern was always with people rather than abstract ideas—with their courage, fortitude, and determination to stand up to all the punishment the Nazi war machine could dish out. Movies like *London Can Take It, Listen to Britain*, and *Fires Were Started*—all produced during England's darkest hours—are still moving accounts of the capacity of a beleaguered nation to endure and fight on (6-21). Although the war years produced some brilliant documentaries—most notably the Nazi *Triumph of the Will*, directed by Leni Riefenstahl, and the "Why We Fight" Series, under the supervision of the American, Frank Capra—few of them surpassed Jennings' achievement in emotional richness, and perhaps none of them could match his universality and subtlety.

Grierson was one of the first to recognize that a new "film generation"

6-21. Fires Were Started.
Directed by Humphrey Jennings.
Generally regarded as the greatest of all the British documentarists, Jennings' works are impressionistic, understated, and poetic. In this film, released in 1943, he recounts the heroism of some English firemen within the course of a twenty-four hour period during the London Blitz. Unlike most wartime documentaries, Jennings' film minimizes political propaganda in favor of celebrating the grandeur of individuals.

was emerging—one that was less oriented towards print and public speaking for its sources of information. He was able to persuade a number of high ranking public officials that it was in the national interest to exploit the film medium as an essential channel of communication between government and citizenry. The overwhelming number of important British documentaries produced during the years of Grierson's influence (roughly from 1928 to the end of the war) were *publicly* funded. The concept of governmental support for the production of documentary films was also adopted in the United States during the thirties, though Congressional funding was rather sporadic and niggardly. During the war years of course, all the major powers committed themselves to large-scale documentary production to boost morale (6-22).

In 1938, Grierson helped to establish the prestigious Canadian National

Film Board, and in the following year, he became its first Film Commissioner. After the war, Grierson's interests became more international. In 1947, he served as Director of Mass Communications and Public Information for UNESCO at the United Nations. During this same period, he lamented the serious decline of the documentary movement in all countries except Canada and the Socialist nations of Eastern Europe (6-23). In the fifties, he developed a greater interest in the public possibilities of television, which was quickly displacing cinema as the major visual mass medium, and which he rightly predicted would take over the main thrust of the documentary movement. In 1972, the old warhorse of the documentary movement died.

(a)

6-22a. *Triumph of the Will.*
Directed by Leni Riefenstahl.
6-22b. *The Battle of San Pietro.*
Directed by John Huston.
Some of the greatest documentary films were produced just before and during World War II. Riefenstahl is generally regarded as the most gifted of the German documentarists. Her 1936 glorification of the Nazi mystique was a brilliantly effective piece of propaganda, so inflammatory and powerful that the Allied powers banned it from circulation for some years after the war. In contrast to Riefenstahl's grandly theatrical images and bravura style, Huston's small masterpiece is far more human and tragic in its impact. Indeed, the film was not received warmly by the Pentagon, which believed that its tone of ironic bitterness, emphasizing the futility and waste of war, was virtually a condemnation of all military activity—hardly the kind of movie to inspire soldiers and civilians with a sense of the justness of their cause.

(b)

6-23. The Quiet One.
Directed by Sidney Meyers.
Documentaries produced in the immediate post-war period tended to be less ideological
in emphasis. Meyers' film, for example, deals with the loneliness and alienation of an
emotionally disturbed youngster living in Harlem. The film's emphasis is not on the
protagonist's blackness or his social environment so much as his individual and
personal needs. Meyers stresses psychological and symbolic concepts rather than
social ideas or propaganda.

TELEVISION AND CINÉMA VÉRITÉ

A good many commentators see no significant difference between documentaries produced for TV and those made for the cinema. There are considerable
distinctions, both technological and aesthetic, though in fact these tended
to blur somewhat after the mid-sixties. Perhaps the most important difference concerns sponsorship. Prior to TV, documentaries were either independently produced, or—as in Canada and Great Britain—sponsored by
governments which exercised extraordinary restraint by allowing their film
production units to go pretty much their own way. In the Soviet Union,
film production was rigorously controlled, especially after 1934. Grierson
complained occasionally that certain important subjects were considered by
the government as too controversial for cinematic treatment, but in general,
no one interfered seriously with the activities of his film units.

6-24. The Sorrow and the Pity.
Directed by Marcel Ophüls.
The problems of censorship tend to be acute with TV documentaries, for airwaves are controlled by governments, and in most of the countries of the world, a documentary criticizing the government would not be permitted on the air. Even in less repressive societies, TV networks have been coerced into journalistic "restraint" and "balanced presentations"—polite terms for self-censorship. Ophüls' film, originally commissioned by the French television network, is a less than flattering exploration of the Resistance Movement during World War II; because of its frankness, the movie was not permitted on the air.

Television is another matter, however. In the first place, in most countries, the airwaves are controlled by the government (6-24). Even in the United States, the Federal Communications Commission is empowered to regulate all major uses of this publicly owned resource. In the majority of countries, a documentary criticizing the government simply wouldn't be permitted on the air. Consequently, most TV documentaries are either nonpolitical or pro-government. In the United States, the so-called "Fairness Doctrine" can have a similarly coercive effect, though there's considerable leeway in interpreting this regulation, which postulates that every significant position ought to be given a fair hearing in the treatment of controversial issues. The TV networks are particularly sensitive to any charges of distortion or slanted reporting, and whenever a documentary creates a controversy—like *Harvest of Shame* or *The Selling of the Pentagon* (both produced by CBS)—the repercussions can be severe. Almost invariably, the networks subsequently respond with caution and "self-restraint," which can be just a polite term for self-censorship.

There are also significant aesthetic distinctions between television and films. Though both are visual mediums, the degree of visual density differs in each. Because of its small screen, television tends to favor detailed shots, especially **close-ups** and **medium shots**. Beyond the **full shot** range, the TV screen begins to lose definition, and small details are lost. A movie like *Man of Aran*, with its **long** and extreme long shots, is likely to lose much of its effectiveness on TV. Conversely, many films made for television tend to look technically inferior in the theatre. Visual blemishes that would hardly appear on the small screen are exaggerated when they're blown up for the movies.

Because of its greater effectiveness in the closer ranges, TV tends to emphasize editing rather than mise-en-scène, for cutting between shots is more effective in pointing out a sequence of specific details than mise-en-scène which encourages the viewer to analyze the contents of a longer shot on his own. The result is that most TV documentaries are not characterized by the same visual beauty found in theatrical nonfiction films, for the aesthetic resources of the long and extreme long shots must be sacrificed. As a compensation, however, TV documentaries often seem more emotionally involving because of their concentration on the closer shots.

Sound is also used differently in each medium. Perhaps because many TV journalists received their early training in radio, they tend to be more dependent upon language than the majority of theatrical documentarists. The continuity of many TV nonfiction films is provided by the spoken narration, not the pictures. The visuals in such documentaries tend to be *illustrative* rather than definitive. That is, the major source of information is provided by the language, while the pictures serve merely to illustrate these ideas. In the best theatrical documentaries, on the other hand, narration generally serves a secondary purpose—to bridge transitions, for example, or to provide abstract (i.e., non-visual) information.

In their fondness for the direct interview, TV documentaries are especially likely to seem tedious in the theatre. On television, such interviews are generally rather brief, but even longer interviews can hold our interest so long as what is being *said* is important. In the cinema, interviews must be visually compelling as well, or we tend to lose interest. The most absorbing interview scenes in theatrical documentaries are generally those in which there is a tension or conflict of some kind between what the subject is saying and what he actually seems to be feeling. For example, in *The Sorrow and the Pity* (which was originally made for French TV), Marcel Ophüls used a great many interviews; the most successful are those in which the subject was trying to evade the question. The straightforward interviews, on the other hand, tend to be visually boring, even though what is being *said* is important.

Despite these technical and legal restrictions, television was responsible for producing most of the interesting documentaries in the United States throughout the fifties and early sixties. Edward R. Murrow's *See It Now* program for CBS was perhaps the best-known and most widely praised documentary series in America. Along with Fred W. Friendly, Murrow produced a number of programs which were surprisingly partisan, and very much in the Griersonian tradition of social exposé and humane reform. NBC's *White Paper* series, produced by Irving Gitlin, performed a similar public service.

But it was ABC's *Close-Up!* that altered most of the characteristics of TV nonfiction films. Indeed, this series, inaugurated in 1960 and produced by Robert Drew, was to exert a profound influence on the entire documentary movement. Drew Associates employed some of the most exciting American documentarists of the sixties, including Richard Leacock, Albert and David Maysles, and D. A. Pennebaker. Together, these artists launched

6-25. On the set of *Groupies*.
Directed by Peter Nevard and Ron Dorfman.
Cinéma vérité introduced a whole new technology to the documentary movement. The lightweight hand-held camera, portable synch sound equipment, and new *fast stocks* permitted filmmakers to travel virtually anywhere in their search for authenticity. Scenes which previously required careful pre-planning, elaborate equipment, and relatively large crews could now be captured on the spot with a crew of two or three people. Eventually this technology had an enormous impact on fiction filmmaking, ushering in a new era of authenticity, particularly in terms of settings.

the school of "direct cinema," or cinéma vérité (film-truth) as it's most often called. At about the same time that Drew Associates was exploring the possibilities of direct cinema, Jean Rouch, Chris Marker, and others were experimenting with some of the same techniques and theories in France. But the French branch of cinéma vérité tended to be influenced by the tradition of Dziga Vertov, whereas in America and Canada the principal influence was Robert Flaherty, at least until the mid-sixties at which time direct cinema became more eclectic technically.

The rise of cinéma vérité provides a good instance of how technology can affect aesthetics in film (6-25). Because of the need to be able to capture news stories quickly, efficiently, and with a minimal crew, television journalism was responsible for the development of a new technology, which in turn eventually led to a new philosophy of truth in documentary cinema. A lightweight 16 mm hand-held camera was perfected, allowing cameramen to move around more easily. Adjustable **zoom lenses** were devised, allowing cameramen to go from 12 mm **wide angle** positions to 120 mm **telephoto**

6-26a, b, c. Gimme Shelter.
Directed by David and Albert Maysles and Charlotte Zwerin.
Cinéma vérité virtually eliminated the need for recreations, for this school of documentary emphasized a *direct* recording of events while they are actually occurring. Due to the impossibility of planning in advance, filmmakers were often frustrated because they could never be certain where the most interesting action would occur. To cover themselves, many documentarists employed multiple cameras, particularly within sprawling uncontrollable contexts, like the notorious Altamont Rock Festival of 1969, featuring Mick Jagger and the Rolling Stones.

(a)

(b)

(Maysles Films, Inc.)

(c)

positions with a flick of the wrist. New fast film stocks were also developed, permitting scenes to be photographed without the necessity of setting up special lights. So sensitive were these stocks to **available lighting,** that even nighttime scenes could be recorded with acceptable clarity. A lightweight tape recorder was invented, allowing a technician to record sound directly, in automatic synchronization with the visuals. This equipment was so easy to use that only two individuals—the cameraman and the soundman—were now required to bring in a news story.

Their more flexible equipment permitted the filmmakers at Drew Associates to redefine the concept of documentary authenticity. In effect, this new aesthetic amounted to a rejection of the Grierson tradition, with its emphasis on pre-planning and carefully detailed scripts. A script involves preconceptions about reality, and tends to cancel out spontaneity and ambiguity. Direct cinema rejected such preconceptions as essentially fictional: in the Grierson tradition reality was not being *observed* but was being *arranged* to conform to what the script says it was. But now, recreations of *any* kind were no longer necessary, because so long as the members of the crew are present while an event is actually taking place they can capture it *directly,* in all its sprawling, ambiguous complexity (6-26).

The concept of minimal interference with reality became the dominating preoccupation of the American and Canadian schools of cinéma vérité, at least during the early sixties. Most of the traditional techniques of documentary film were discarded in favor of a totally **aleatory** approach, with a strong emphasis on open forms. Attempts to alter or comment on reality were rejected as fictional. The filmmaker must not control events in any way, he must be guided by them. Recreations—even with the people and places actually involved—were unacceptable. Editing was kept to a minimum, for otherwise it could lead to a false impression of the sequence of events. Actual time and space were preserved whenever possible by using long takes. If a close-up was required, the cameraman tended to zoom in rather than cut, so the unities of space and time were preserved. Anticipatory set-ups were likewise avoided, for to anticipate the contents of a shot was to impose a form on events before they actually occurred. If people or events moved, the cameraman was expected to pursue them, either by panning, zooming, **tilting,** or simply walking—with the camera mounted on a shoulder harness.

Needless to say, the realist aesthetic of cinéma vérité tends to place enormous burdens on the cameraman, for he must be able to make snap judgments—often in the midst of turbulent events. For this reason, many directors also serve as their own cameramen. (Leacock, Pennebaker, and Albert Maysles, for example, do most of their own shooting.) He must know *what* to shoot and how to shoot it. Vast amounts of footage are often expended, for the cameraman often has no idea when something is going to happen, and once it does, there's no going back to get the shot if he has missed it the first time. He must be patient and self-effacing, waiting and watching until he senses that an important event is about to occur.

Because much of the footage in these movies was caught on the run, as it were, a good many of the shots are necessarily shaky, blurred, and clumsily framed. Occasionally there are zoom-ins indicating that the cameraman expected a moment of revelation; but sometimes the revelation doesn't

6-27. *Law and Order.*
Directed by Frederick Wiseman.
Some of the most scrupulously rigorous direct cinema advocates, like Wiseman, refuse to use non-synch sound. The subjects are allowed to speak for themselves, and the burden of interpretation is placed on the viewer, who must analyze the significance of the materials on his own.

occur, and the sheepish cameraman is forced to zoom back to a looser shot. At times the lighting of these films is also inadequate, notwithstanding the highly sensitive stocks that were used. Sound is sometimes muffled; distracting street noises often drown out voices. But these blemishes were considered a part of the aesthetic of cinéma vérité—a testament, in a way, to its utter authenticity. Indeed, most of these filmmakers believed that picturesque visuals and crisp soundtracks are highly suspect: they suggest a manipulation of reality. By sacrificing the "craftsmanship" associated with the traditional documentary, the direct cinema filmmakers believed that they were able to capture an event with far greater immediacy and intimacy —qualities that they felt took precedence over formal beauty.

In its attempt to eliminate all barriers between the subject and the audience, direct cinema also used sound cautiously. For the most part, non-synchronous music is avoided and dismissed as a fictional technique. These artists were especially hostile to the "Voice of God" commentaries that accompanied many traditional documentaries. Narration tends to interpret images for the audience, they believed, thus relieving the viewer of the necessity of analyzing for himself. If narration *was* used, it tended to be used sparingly—offering only necessary factual data, and delivered in an emotionally neutral voice. Some filmmakers dispensed with narration entirely. In the works of Frederick Wiseman, for example, only direct sound is employed (6-27). The people in the films are allowed to speak for themselves. Perhaps more than any American filmmaker, Wiseman insists that the ambiguities and contradictions of actual life must be preserved

6-28. Warrendale.
Directed by Allan King.
Because the advocates of direct cinema must work within uncontrollable contexts, some of the technical craftsmanship of the traditional documentary must necessarily be sacrificed. But most of these filmmakers would argue that the resultant intimacy allows us to observe "privileged moments" of intense poignance and authenticity— moments which would have been impossible to capture using traditional documentary techniques.

in documentaries, that films which are too neat and clear-cut are probably false reflections of reality.

Perhaps what the practitioners of direct cinema value above all is the "privileged moment"—those brief glimpses into reality that are so intimate, so genuine, that the screen seems to disappear and we feel that we're in the presence of the event itself (6-28). A good example of this kind of intimacy can be seen in *The Chair,* which was made by Leacock, Penne-baker, and Gregory Shuker. The movie deals with a convicted murderer, Paul Crump, and his lawyer's attempts to have Crump's death sentence commuted to life imprisonment, since he is obviously rehabilitated. We follow Donald Moore, the lawyer, as he desperately tries everything in his power to postpone the impending execution. At one point, he receives a telephone call informing him that some high Church officials will issue a statement urging clemency—an important break for which Moore has been praying. Overcome with relief, Moore silently and thoughtfully puts out his cigarette, then, unable to control his emotions, he bursts into tears. It's a powerful scene, so touching in its emotional depth that it moves many of its viewers to tears as well.

Like most schools of documentary, cinéma vérité is better at some subjects than others. Certainly few traditional documentaries can offer the same degree of intimacy, emotional directness, and spontaneity (6-29). On the other hand, these techniques would be rather dull if employed on a subject like a mail train express. Indeed, even Pennebaker eventually expressed concern that direct cinema tends to depend too much on its "marvelous moments" for justification. A number of critics have complained that audiences are forced to endure a great deal of tedious footage in order to arrive at these privileged moments.

Direct cinema is also effective with materials that are intrinsically dramatic, such as crisis situations in which a conflict is about to reach its climax. But here too critics have complained of the lack of aesthetic distance in such films as Leacock's *The Children Were Watching*, which deals with a highly explosive civil rights confrontation in 1960 in the city of New Orleans. The hand-held camera captures all the fear, hatred, and tension of the situation, with angry white bigots on one side and terrified black children and their parents on the other. But critics complained that in such emotionally charged situations, what is needed is sobriety, reason,

6-29. *Monterey Pop*.
Directed by D. A. Pennebaker.
Cinéma vérité is particularly suited to capturing the spontaneity of events, especially crisis situations, and theatrical occasions. The tremendous popularity of such performers as Janis Joplin introduced a new sub-genre, the rock documentary.

(Leacock-Pennebaker Films)

(a)

(b)

(Warner Brothers)

and calm objectivity in the cinematic treatment, not a whirling camera that's plunged right in the middle of the most volatile confrontations. Such films merely encourage more hysteria, these critics argued, not rational alternatives.

In the later sixties, rock stars and music festivals were also popular subjects for direct cinema. Indeed, feature length documentaries like *Don't Look Back* and *Monterey Pop,* both by Pennebaker, were enormously successful in theatres, as was the Rolling Stones film, *Gimme Shelter,* by the Maysles brothers and Charlotte Zwerin. These films were already beginning to abandon some of the earlier techniques of direct cinema (though even in the early sixties, there was a considerable gap between the ideals and the practices of the filmmakers at Drew Associates). Editing styles became more complex, as can be seen in the elaborate flashback structure of *Gimme Shelter*. By the time Michael Wadleigh's *Woodstock* was released (1970), artful compositions, multiple images, and sound juxtapositions of all kinds had replaced the long take, direct sound recording, and blurry zoom shots. What began as a realistic movement eventually evolved into an eclectic, pragmatic attitude towards filmmaking which mixed realistic and expressionistic techniques with casual nonchalance (6-30).

FURTHER READING

BARSAM, RICHARD MERAN. *Nonfiction Film*. New York: E. P. Dutton & Co., Inc., 1973. (Paper) A critical history of the documentary, from *Nanook* to cinéma vérité.

BLUEM, A. WILLIAM. *Documentary in American Television*. New York: Hastings House, 1965. A critical history of television documentaries in the United States, with some background information on the influence of radio and print journalism.

GRIERSON, JOHN. *Grierson on Documentary,* ed. Forsyth Hardy. New York: Praeger Publishers, Rev. Ed., 1971. (Paper) A collection of critical and theoretical essays spanning most of Grierson's career.

ISSARI, M. ALI. *Cinéma Vérité*. East Lansing: Michigan State University Press, 1971. An exploration of the technical and aesthetic characteristics of cinéma vérité, with major emphasis on American and French documentarists.

JACOBS, LEWIS, ed. *The Documentary Tradition: From Nanook to Woodstock*. New York: Hopkinson and Blake, 1971. (Paper) A comprehensive collection of essays about documentary films and filmmakers from every period and most of the major film producing nations.

LEVIN, G. ROY, ed. *Documentary Explorations*. Garden City: Doubleday & Co., Inc., 1971. (Paper) A collection of fifteen interviews with such famous documentarists as Rouch, Leacock, Pennebaker, the Maysles brothers, Wiseman, and others.

LOVELL, ALAN, and JIM HILLIER. *Studies in Documentary*. New York: The Viking Press, 1972. (Paper) A critical study of the British documentary, with major emphasis on Grierson, Jennings, and the Free Cinema movement of the 1950s.

MAMBER, STEPHEN. *"Cinéma Vérité* in America," in *Screen* (Part I, Summer, 1972; Part II, Autumn, 1972). A discussion of the major films and filmmakers of the American cinéma vérité movement.

ROSENTHAL, ALAN. *The New Documentary in Action*. Berkeley: University of California Press, 1971. (Paper) A collection of interviews with famous documentarists, including Allan King, Albert Maysles, Charlotte Zwerin, Peter Watkins, and others.

ROTHA, PAUL, in collaboration with Sinclair Road and Richard Griffith. *Documentary Film*. New York: Hastings House, Rev. Ed., 1970. A critical history of the documentary film, written (primarily) by Grierson's most famous disciple, Rotha.

"The function of the cinema is to reveal, to bring to light certain details that the stage would have left untreated."
—ANDRÉ BAZIN

7 drama

Many people cling to the naive belief that theatre and film are two aspects of the same art, the only major difference being that drama is "live," while movies are "recorded." Certainly there are undeniable similarities between the two arts. Most obvious, perhaps, is that both employ action as a principal mode: what people *do* is a major source of meaning. The theatre and movies are also collaborative enterprises, involving the coordination of writers, directors, actors, and technicians. Drama and film are both social arts, performed before groups of people, and experienced publicly as well as individually.

TIME, SPACE, AND LANGUAGE

But films are not mere recordings of plays. The language and materials of the two mediums are fundamentally different, especially in their treatment of space and time. The basic unit of construction in the theatre is the **scene,** and the amount of dramatic time that elapses during a scene is roughly equal to the length of time the scene takes to perform. To be sure, some plays cover many years, but in general, these years pass "between curtains." We're informed that it is "seven years later," either by a stage direction or by the dialogue. The basic unit of construction in movies is the **shot,** which can lengthen or shorten time more subtly, since the average shot lasts only ten or fifteen seconds. Drama has to chop out huge blocks of time between the relatively few scenes and acts; films can expand or contract time between the many hundreds of shots.

Space in the theatre is also dependent upon the basic unit of the scene. Theatrical space is continuous: the action takes place in a unified area, which has specific limits, usually defined by the proscenium arch (7-1). A synthetic art, theatre confines all the relevant meanings within this given area. Drama, then, almost always deals with **closed forms:** we don't imagine that the action is being continued in the wings and dressing rooms of the theatre. The "proscenium arch" in film is the frame—a masking device that isolates objects and people only temporarily. As an analytical art, movies deal with a series of space fragments (7-2). Though shots can be either open or closed in form, a closed form image is still only a temporary piece of a larger whole. Beyond the frame of a given shot, another aspect of the action waits to be photographed. A **close-up** of an object, for example, is generally a detail of a subsequent **long shot,** which will give us the context of the close-up. In the theatre, it's much more difficult to withhold information in this manner.

The relationship between the audience and the work of art is also different in these two mediums. In the theatre, the viewer remains in a stationary position: the distance between him and the stage is constant. To be sure, an actor can move close to an audience, but compared to the fluid space in the cinema, distance variation in the legitimate theatre is negligible. The film viewer, on the other hand, identifies with the camera's **lens** which permits him to "move" in any direction, and from any distance. An **extreme close-up** allows him to count the lashes of an eye; an **extreme long shot** permits him to see miles in each direction. In short, the cinema has the advantages over the stage of **editing** and the moving camera. Most theatrical equivalents to these techniques have been crude at best.

These spatial differences don't necessarily favor one medium over the other. In the theatre, space is three-dimensional, occupied by tangible people and objects, and hence, is more **realistic,** since our perception of space and volume is essentially the same as it is in real life. The living presence of actors, with their subtle interactions—both with other actors and the audience—is impossible to duplicate in film. Movies provide us with a two-dimensional *image* of space and objects, and no interaction exists between the screen actors and the audience. For this reason, nudity

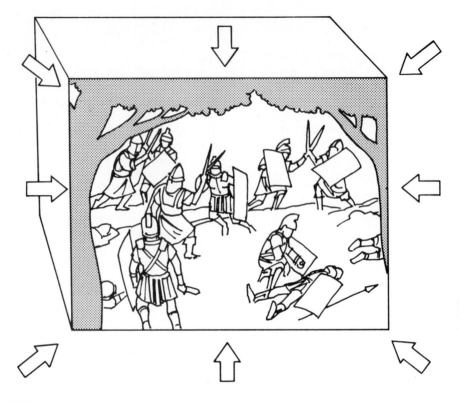

7-1.
Somewhat like painting, the legitimate theatre is a synthetic art, usually employing *closed forms.* All the relevant variables are included within the *frame*—the proscenium arch or its equivalent. We don't imagine that the action is continued in the wings or dressing rooms of the theatre. The dimensions of the playing area are permanent: when its contents no longer serve the playwright's needs, the scene is concluded and a new time and/or place is presented.

is not so controversial an issue on the screen as in the theatre, for on stage the naked people are real, whereas on film they're "only pictures." The stage performer interacts with his viewers: he must establish a delicate rapport with each different audience. The screen actor, on the other hand, is inexorably fixed on celluloid: he can't readjust to each audience, for the worlds of the screen and the viewer aren't connected and continuous. Movies often seem dated because acting styles can't be adjusted to newer audiences; stage actors, on the other hand, can make even a four-hundred year old play seem fresh and relevant, for though the words remain the same, their interpretation and delivery can always be changed to suit contemporary tastes.

Because of these spatial differences, the viewer's participation is different in each medium. In the theatre, the audience generally must be more active. Since all of the visual elements are provided within a given space, the viewer must sort out what's essential from what's incidental. Disre-

7-2.
As an analytical art, cinema tends to chop up time and space. Whether in *open* or closed form, the frame is temporary, an isolating device which presents us with only a small portion of the setting. Beyond the frame, another aspect of the action waits to be photographed. The basic unit of construction in cinema is the shot; in the theatre, the scene.

garding for the moment the importance of language in the theatre, drama is a medium of low visual saturation: that is, the audience must fill in certain meanings in the absence of visual detail. A film audience, on the other hand, is generally more passive. All the necessary details are provided by close-ups and by edited juxtapositions. Film, then, is a medium of high visual saturation: that is, the pictures are densely detailed with information, requiring little or no filling in (7-3). These generalizations are relative, of course. Realist film directors tend to be more theatrical in their handling of space, forcing their audiences to participate more than they would in viewing an **expressionist** or highly fragmented film.

Though both drama and film are eclectic arts, the theatre is a narrower medium, specializing in spoken language. That is, most of the meanings

7-3a, b. Macbeth.
Directed by Roman Polanski.
Film is a medium of high visual saturation. Certain types of information—like Macbeth's prowess as a warrior—can be presented in visual as well as verbal detail (a). Unlike the theatre, the cinema can also present intimate exchanges of dialogue more realistically by simply moving into a closer range while the wider social context is temporarily kept in abeyance (b).

(a)

(b)

(Columbia Pictures)

in the theatre are found in words, which are usually densely saturated with information. For this reason, drama is generally considered a writer's medium. The primacy of the text is what makes drama a kind of special branch of literature. In the theatre, we tend to hear before we see. The film director René Clair once observed that a blind man could still grasp the essentials of most stage plays. Movies, on the other hand, are generally regarded as a visual art, and therefore a director's medium. Clair observed that a deaf man could still grasp most of the essentials of a film. But these generalizations are also relative, for some movies—many of the works of Welles, for example—are densely saturated both visually and aurally.

Since plays stress the primacy of language, one of the major problems in adapting them for the screen is determining how much of the language is necessary in a predominantly visual art like movies. George Cukor's version of Shakespeare's *Romeo and Juliet* was a conservative film adaptation. Virtually all the dialogue was retained, even the exposition and purely functional speeches of no particular poetic merit. The result was a respectful but often tedious film, in which the visuals tended merely to illustrate the language. Often images and dialogue contained the same information, producing an overblown, static quality that actually contradicted the swift sense of action in the stage play.

Zeffirelli's film version of this play was much more successful (7-4). Verbal exposition was cut almost completely and replaced (just as effectively) by visual exposition. Single lines were pruned meticulously if the same information could be conveyed by images. Most of the great poetry was preserved, but often with **non-synchronous** visuals, to expand—not duplicate —the language. The close-ups looked like a series of exquisite Renaissance portraits. The camera recorded the most intimate details of the lives of the lovers, and the soundtrack picked up the most delicate sighs. The fight scenes were more thrilling than any stage presentation could hope to be, for the camera raced and whirled with the combatants. In short, Zeffirelli's movie, though technically less faithful to the stage script, was actually more Shakespearean in spirit than the scrupulously literal version of Cukor.

Both theatre and cinema are audio-visual mediums, then, but they differ in their stress of certain **conventions.** The two major sources of information in drama are action and dialogue. We observe what people do and what they say. The action of a play is no mere illustration of the words. Hedda Gabler's burning of Lovbörg's manuscript, for example, embodies emotional and intellectual information that can't be adequately paraphrased in language. The contrast between what people say and do is a common source of irony on the stage: Chekhov built several of his plays around this ironic contrast. Even in a talky play like Shaw's *Man and Superman,* the audience delights in watching Ann Whitefield vamping John Tanner, while he talks on and on.

Action in the theatre is restricted primarily to objective long shots, to use a cinematic metaphor. That is, only fairly large actions are effective: the duel between Hamlet and Laertes, Amanda helping Laura to dress in *The Glass Menagerie,* and so on. Extreme long shot ranges—to continue the cinematic metaphor—must be stylized in the theatre. The **epic** battles of Shakespeare's history plays, for example, would appear ridiculous if staged realistically. Likewise, close-up actions would be missed by all but those in the front rows unless the actions were exaggerated and stylized by the actors. Hamlet's distaste for Claudius must be expressed visually either by exaggerated facial expressions, or by the prince's larger-than-life gestures and movements. Except in the most intimate theatres, close-up actions in the drama have to be verbalized. That is, the subtlest actions and reactions of stage characters are usually conveyed by language rather than by visual means. We know of Hamlet's attitude toward Claudius primarily through Hamlet's soliloquies and dialogue. On the close-up level of action, then, what we see on stage is often not what people do, but what people *talk* about doing, or what's been done.

Because of these visual problems, most plays avoid actions requiring vast or minute spaces. Theatrical action is usually confined to the **full** and long shot ranges. If vast or minute spaces are required, the theatre tends to resort to unrealistic conventions: to ballets and stylized tableaux for extreme long shot actions, and to the convention of verbal articulation for close-up actions. Movies, on the other hand, can move easily among all these ranges. For this reason, the cinema often dramatizes the action that takes place on stage only "between the curtains." This is not to say that the cinema doesn't have its own set of conventions. The moveable camera, expressionistic sound, and editing are just as unrealistic as the conventions of the legitimate theatre. In both cases, the audience accepts these conventions as the rules of the game.

There's a certain obviousness in the theatre precisely because of some of these problems. Most dramatic plots, for example, involve a clear-cut, linear conflict between a protagonist and an antagonist: between Antigone and Creon, Lear and his two daughters, Stanley Kowalski and Blanche Dubois. A clear problem or conflict is presented early in the play. This conflict intensifies progressively over the course of the ensuing scenes, resulting finally in a climactic confrontation in which either protagonist or antagonist triumphs. Not all plays conform to this Aristotelian, linear structure of action, but a surprising number of them do, even a delicate "nontheatrical" play like Chekhov's *The Cherry Orchard,* where the protagonists are the members of the Ranevsky family, and the antagonists are the forces of a changing society, which ultimately deprive the family of their orchard, their estate, and a whole way of life.

In the cinema, the dramatic or Aristotelian mode is only one of several that can be employed, though it's easily the most popular, especially in the United States. Because of the greater spatial and temporal flexibility of movies, film can employ a number of other modes and structures as well: the epic (*Birth of a Nation*), the lyric (*Easy Rider*), the stream-of-consciousness (Buñuel's *An Andalusian Dog*), the documentary (Frederick Wiseman's *High School*), the essay (Godard's *Masculine-Feminine*), even the purely formal (the abstract films of the Whitney brothers). In short, movies can dispense with overt conflicts, climaxes, and even plots, for cinematic action can be theatrical or nontheatrical with equal ease.

The human being is central to the aesthetic of the theatre: words must be recited by people, conflicts must be embodied by actors. The cinema is not so dependent upon humans. The aesthetic of film is based on photography, and anything that can be photographed can be the subject matter of a film. In general, drama tends to emphasize people's relationships with each other; movies can also deal with people's relationships with things (7-5). For this reason, adapting a play to the screen, while difficult, is hardly impossible, for much of what the stage can do the screen can do also. To adapt most movies to the stage, however, would be much more difficult. Movies with exterior locations would be almost automatically ruled out, of course (7-6). How would one go about adapting John Ford's great westerns, like *Stagecoach* and *The Searchers?* But even films with interior locations are often impossible to translate into theatrical terms. True, the words would present no problem, and some actions would be transferable. But how would one deal with the time fragmentation of

Resnais' *Last Year at Marienbad?* Or the kaleidoscopic fragmentation of space in Richard Lester's *A Hard Day's Night?* Theme and characterization in Joseph Losey's *The Servant* are communicated primarily through the use of camera **angles**—impossible to duplicate in the theatre. The theme of Bergman's *The Silence* is conveyed primarily through images of empty corridors, doors, and windows. How could one transfer this technique to the stage?

Nor is the best method of adapting a play for the screen necessarily to "open it up"—to substitute exterior locations for interiors. Cinema doesn't always mean extreme long shots, sweeping **pans,** and flashy editing. Hitchcock once observed that many filmed versions of plays fail precisely because the tight, compact structure of the original is lost when the film director "loosens it up" with inappropriate cinematic techniques. Particularly when

(a)

(b)

7-4a, b. Romeo and Juliet.
Directed by Franco Zeffirelli.
The essence of Shakespeare's play is found in the impulsive haste and imprudence of its very youthful protagonists, the swift sense of catastrophe piled upon catastrophe, and the violence of much of the action. Zeffirelli's film version heightened these characteristics by avoiding visual-verbal redundancies, which would have impeded the catapulting sense of inevitability in Shakespeare's original.

7-5. *Eclipse.*
Directed by Michelangelo Antonioni.
Virtually all plays are social in emphasis. That is, they deal with the interrelationships between people. The cinema can also deal with the relationship of people with things. Antonioni is particularly interested in the way that environment—both natural and man-made—can affect humans, and vice-versa. Such themes are difficult to convey in the theatre, for the environment must be created on the artificial "world" of the stage, which usually bears only a ***symbolic*** resemblance to outside environments.

a play emphasizes a sense of confinement—and a great many of them do, either physical or psychological—the best adaptors respect the spirit of the original by finding filmic equivalents (7-7). Tony Richardson's *Hamlet* is photographed almost exclusively in **medium shots** and close-ups. The sets are constricted interiors, except one, where the camera moves back to a longer distance. The scene fails precisely because it releases all the tensions that have been built up in the earlier portions of the movie, because it violates the sense of psychological and spiritual claustrophobia that's so carefully preserved in the other scenes.

THE DIRECTOR

In the mid-1950s, the French periodical, *Cahiers du Cinéma,* popularized the **"auteur" theory,** a view which stressed the dominance of the director in film art. According to this theory, whoever controls the **mise-en-scène** is

7-6. *The Wild Bunch.*
Directed by Sam Peckinpah.
Because it is virtually limitless in its use of space, the cinema is particularly suited to dealing with man's relationship to nature—a rare theme in the drama, in which the limitations of space are much more severe. A stage western, for example, is almost unthinkable, since most of the conventions of the **genre** are associated with wide open exteriors.

the true "author" of a movie. The other collaborators (writers, **cinematographer**, actors, editor) are merely his technical assistants. No doubt the auteur critics exaggerated the primacy of the director, particularly in America, where many film directors were at the mercy of the studio system, which tended to emphasize group work rather than individual expression, **"stars"** rather than directors, and box-office success before artistic distinction. If a director could control the financing of a film—that is, act as producer as well as director—then he might be freer to control the final product. Some of the best movies of John Huston and Alfred Hitchcock were produced as well as directed by these men.

Despite the many anonymous hacks who merely seem to have directed traffic on their sound stages, the *auteur* critics are essentially correct in assigning authorship primarily to the director—at least with most of the best films. To refer to a movie as "good except for its direction" seems as contradictory as referring to a play as "good except for its script." To be sure, we can enjoy a poorly directed movie, or a badly written play, but what we enjoy are usually the secondary aspects of the art—an effective performance, or a suggestive set, or some interesting costumes. In movies especially, the cinematography and the acting can often redeem an otherwise banal film. Such enjoyable elements generally represent the individual triumph of a gifted interpretive artist (actors, set designers, costumers, cinematographers) over the mediocrity of the dominant artist—the director in film, the writer in the theatre.

On the stage, then, the director is essentially an interpretive artist. If we see a rotten production of *King Lear,* we don't dismiss Shakespeare's play, but only that specific interpretation of the play. True, the stage director creates certain patterns of movement, appropriate gestures for his actors, and spatial relationships, but all of these visual elements take second place to the language of the script, which is created by the playwright. The theatrical director's relation to the text is similar to the stage actor's relation to a role: he can add much to what's written down, but what he contributes is usually secondary to the text itself—an improvisation, as it were, which is circumscribed by the limits set down by the author.

The stage director is a kind of go-between for the author and the cast and production staff. That is, the director is responsible for the general interpretation of the script, and usually defines the limits for the other interpretive artists: actors, designers, technicians. The director must see to it that all the production elements are harmonized and subordinated to the overall interpretation. His influence tends to be stronger during rehearsals than in the actual performance. Once the curtain opens before an audience, he is powerless to control what then takes place.

On the other hand, the screen director has a good deal more control over the final product (7-8). He too dominates the pre-production activities, but unlike the stage director, he controls virtually every aspect of the finished work as well. The degree of precision a film director can achieve is impossible on the stage, for the movie director can rephotograph people and objects until he gets exactly what he wants. As we have seen, films communicate *primarily* through moving images, and it's the director who determines most of the visual elements: the choice of shots, angles, lighting effects, **filters**, optical effects, framing, composition, camera movement, and editing.

7-7. *The Member of the Wedding.*
Directed by Fred Zinnemann.
Because of its spatial limitations, the theatre is an ideal medium for dealing with the theme of confinement. One of the problems facing the film director who wishes to adapt a play is whether to "open it up"—that is, whether to dramatize off-stage actions on the screen. To do so would run the risk of releasing the spatial tensions of the original—which the dramatist exploits as part of his artistic form. Zinnemann's adaptation of Carson McCuller's play (itself based on her own novel) opened up the action only once (pictured). The theme of the novel, the play, and the film is the same: the sense of entrapment of a girl about to enter young womanhood. In the novel, her isolation and confinement are conveyed primarily by a limited **point-of-view** narration; in the play, the theme is spatially symbolized by the narrow confines of a single set; in the movie, this idea is communicated principally by the close, **tightly framed** shots which seem to imprison the young heroine (Julie Harris, pictured). Much of the language of the novel is sacrificed in the play, and even more is cut out of the movie version, which uses spatial equivalents for many of the verbal ideas.

(Columbia Pictures)

7-8. On the set of *The Last Picture Show.*
Directed by Peter Bogdanovich.
The major influence of the theatrical director is in the pre-production and rehearsal stages, when he presents his interpretation of a play to his actors and staff. Once a play is performed live in front of an audience, however, the actors are in complete control, at least until the end of the scene. The film director, on the other hand, deals with shorter units of time and space—the shot—which allows him a far greater degree of precision. He can order dozens of separate *takes* to be photographed until he gets exactly what he wants. Some filmmakers have been known to shoot over a hundred different takes of the same shot. Furthermore, the film director is generally more precise in his instructions to his actors, for if the shot is to be tightly framed, a difference of a mere few inches of space can ruin the shot. Here Bogdanovich (right) tells Jeff Bridges (left) and Timothy Bottoms where he wants them to stand for a shot.

The differences in control and precision between stage and film direction can be best illustrated perhaps by examining the handling of the mise-en-scène. The stage director is much more restricted: he must work with only one setting per scene. All the actors, objects, and patterns of movement are placed within this given area. Since this is a three-dimensional space, he has the advantage of depth as well as breadth to work with. Through the use of platforms, he can also exploit height on the stage. The theatrical director must use certain conventions to assure maximum clarity. Thus, with a proscenium stage, the audience pretends it's peeping into a room where one wall has been removed. Naturally no furniture is placed against this "wall," nor do actors turn their backs to it for very long periods, for the dialogue would not be audible. If a thrust stage is used, the audience surrounds the acting area on three sides, forcing the performers to play to three sides instead of one. Again, this convention is necessary to assure maximum clarity.

In the cinema, the director converts three-dimensional space into a two-dimensional image of space. Even with **deep-focus** photography, "depth" is not literal. But the flat image has certain advantages. Since a camera can be placed virtually anywhere, the film director is not confined to a single set with a given number of "walls." The **eye-level** long shot more-or-less corresponds to the view the theatrical proscenium arch gives. But in movies, the close-up also constitutes a given space—in effect, a cinematic "roomlet," with its own "walls" (the frame). Each shot, then, represents a new given space, with different (and temporary) dimensions (7-9). Eisenstein referred to this volume arrangement as the "mise-en-shot." Furthermore, the moveable camera permits the director to rearrange his "walls" many times for maximum expressiveness, with no sacrifice in clarity. Thus, in film, a character can enter the frame from below, from above, from either side, and from any angle. By **dollying** or **craning,** a camera can also take us "into" a set, permitting objects to pass by us.

(Janus Films)

7-9a, b. Richard III.
Directed by Laurence Olivier.
When adapting a play to the screen, the film director instinctively places his camera according to the **proxemic** implications of the dialogue. When the action deals with social and public events, the camera tends to be further away (a), but when the action is essentially private and intimate (b), the camera moves closer to exclude any visual distractions. On the stage, these ideas are generally communicated with lights and through the actors' voices.

(a)

(b)

7-10. Macbeth.
Directed by Roman Polanski.
On the stage, important dialogue is almost never delivered with the actors' backs turned to the audience, for the lines would not be completely audible. In the cinema, however, sound is independent of space. The warning of the three witches in *Macbeth* (shown here) can be staged in virtually any manner with maximum visual impact, for the recorded soundtrack guarantees audibility.

Because of the audience's identification with the camera's lens, the viewer in the cinema is, in a sense, mobile.

Since the stage director's mise-en-scène is confined to the unit of the scene, a certain amount of compromise is inevitable. He must combine a maximum of expressiveness with a maximum of clarity—not always an easy task, especially in realistic productions. The film director has to make fewer compromises of this sort, for he has a greater number of "scene-lets" (shots) at his disposal: some movies average over a thousand shots. He can give us a half dozen shots of the same object—some emphasizing clarity, others emphasizing expressiveness. Some shots can show a character with his back to the camera: the soundtrack guarantees the clarity of his speech (7-10). A character can be photographed through an obstruction of some kind—a pane of glass, or the dense foliage of a forest. Eisenstein occasionally had one actor block out another by having the first stand before the camera. Such "impediments" are usually employed for symbolic reasons, but since the cinematic shot need not be lengthy, clarity can be suspended temporarily in favor of expressiveness.

These generalizations are postulated upon the assumption that the stage is essentially realistic in its handling of time and space, whereas the cinema is basically expressionistic. But the differences are relative, of course. Indeed, a good argument could be made that Strindberg's expressionistic plays—*The Dream Play,* for example—are more fragmented and subjective than a realistic movie like Chaplin's *Gold Rush,* which emphasizes the continuity of time and space. Certainly it's true that most realistic film directors (the Italian **neorealists,** for example) treat time and space theatrically, while some expressionistic dramatists (the Absurdists, for example) handle time and space cinematically. In each case, however, we use the terms "theatrical" and "cinematic" as metaphors: when all is said, the differences in time and space remain fundamental.

THE ACTOR

Space and time also determine the differences between stage acting and screen acting. In general, the stage seems to be a more satisfactory medium for the actor, for once the curtain goes up, he tends to dominate the proceedings. In movies, this is not necessarily the case. The essential requisites for the stage performer are that he be seen and heard clearly. Thus, the ideal theatrical actor must have a flexible, trained voice. Most obviously, his voice must be powerful enough to be heard even in a theatre containing thousands of seats. Since language is the major source of meaning in the theatre, the stage actor's voice is of paramount importance. It must be capable of much variety: he or she must know which words to stress and how; how to phrase properly for different types of lines; when to pause and for how long; how fast or slow a line or speech ought to be delivered. Above all, the stage actor must be totally *believable,* even when reciting dialogue that's highly stylized and unnatural. Most of the credit for an exciting theatrical production is given to the performers, but most of the burdens are also theirs, for when we're bored by a production of a play, we tend to assign the responsibility to the actors.

Physical requirements are different in the theatre and movies (7-11). Most obviously, the stage actor must be seen—even from the back of the auditorium. Thus, it helps to be tall, for small actors tend to get lost on a large stage. It also helps to have large and regular features, though makeup can cover a multitude of deficiencies. For this reason, casting a forty-year old actress as Juliet is not necessarily a disaster in the theatre, for her age won't show beyond the first few rows of seats. Because of the distance between actors and audience in most theatres, performers can play roles ranging twenty or even thirty years beyond their actual age, providing their voices and bodies are flexible enough.

The stage actor's entire body is always in view, and for this reason, he must be able to control it with some degree of precision. Some obvious activities as sitting, walking, and standing are performed differently on the stage than they are in real life. An actor must usually learn how to dance a little, how to fence, and how to move in period costume naturally. He must know what to do with his hands—when to let them hang, and when to use them for an expressive gesture. Furthermore, an actor must know how to adjust his body to different characters: a twenty-year old youth moves differently from a man of thirty; an aristocrat moves differently from a clerk of the same age. The body must communicate a wide variety of emotions in pantomime: a happy man even stands differently from a dejected man or a fearful one. And so on.

7-11. On the set of _Magnum Force._
Directed by Ted Post.
In the legitimate theatre, actors are selected not only on the basis of their looks and talent, but also on how well they match up with the other actors on stage. A theatrical director must always conceive of his productions in terms of an ensemble effect. In the cinema, these considerations are secondary. In this film, Clint Eastwood, who stands 6' 4", is romantically paired with Adele Yoshioka, who is 5' 4". On stage, this height discrepancy would be an absurd sight gag, but on the screen (or more accurately, off-screen), the problem was easily resolved through the art of exclusion: their love scenes were photographed close in, with the actress standing on a box.

(Warner Brothers)

Theatrical acting is sustained for lengthy periods of time. The performer must build—scene by scene—toward the climactic scene near the end of the play. Usually the stage actor begins at a relatively low energy level, then increases this energy with each progressive scene, until, in the climax, the energy reaches its bursting point, then quickly tapers off in the resolution of the play. In short, the actor generates in psychic energy the play's own structure. Within this overall structure, the stage performer "builds" within each scene, though not every scene is automatically played at a greater intensity than its predecessor, for different plays build in different ways. What's essential for the stage actor is to sustain an energy level for the duration of a scene. Once the curtain rises, he's alone on the stage: mistakes aren't easily corrected, nor can a scene be replayed or cut out.

In general, the film actor can get along quite well with a minimum

7-12. It Happened One Night.
Directed by Frank Capra.
Film stars—as opposed to straight actors—play variations of the same personality in most of their roles. Often this personality is identical with or similiar to their actual personalities. Virtually every performance by Clark Gable, for example, displayed the same manly virility and rugged charm. An actor of limited technical skills, Gable was nonetheless able to exploit this roguish swagger with great popular success for nearly four decades. Similarly, Claudette Colbert was noted for playing wealthy, high-spirited women whose warmth was sometimes obscured by a certain veneer of upper-class fastidiousness.

7-13. *Midnight Cowboy.*
Directed by John Schlesinger.
Straight actors are likely to play roles that differ widely from film to film, and their actual personalities are seldom allowed to intrude on a performance unless a given trait is relevant to the role. Unlike most stars, straight actors will often play unattractive and unglamorous characters, for frequently these are the roles that offer the greatest technical challenges. Jon Voight and Dustin Hoffman are often referred to as "stars" because of their box-office popularity, but they are essentially straight actors in the sense that the term is used here.

of stage technique. The essential requisite for a performer in the movies is what Antonioni calls "expressiveness." That is, he must *look* interesting. No amount of technique will compensate for an unphotogenic face. Furthermore, some of the most famous stage actors in history—including Sarah Bernhardt—looked preposterous on film: her technique was mannered and stagey to the point of hamminess. In movies, then, too much histrionic technique can actually undercut a performance, can make it seem unnatural and unbelievable.

At about the turn of the last century, George Bernard Shaw (who was then a theatre critic) wrote a famous essay comparing the two foremost stage actresses of the day—Elenora Duse and Sarah Bernhardt. Shaw's comparison is a useful springboard for a discussion of different types of film acting. Bernhardt, Shaw wrote, was a great personality and she managed

(a)

(Warner Brothers)

(b)

(Warner Brothers)

to tailor each different role to fit this personality, which is what her fans both expected and desired. Her enormous personal charm was larger-than-life and undeniably captivating. Her performances were filled with brilliant effects that had come to be associated with her personality over the years. Duse, on the other hand, possessed a more quiet talent, less dazzling in its initial impact. She was totally different with each role and her own personality never seemed to intrude on the playwright's character. Hers was an "invisible" art, but her impersonations were so totally absorbing, believable, and moving, the viewer was likely to forget that they *were* imper-

(c)   (United Artists)

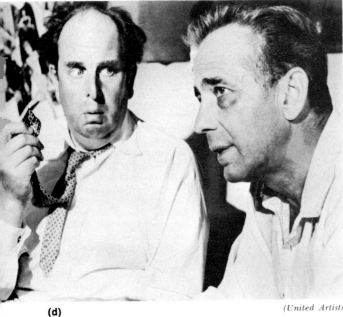

(d)   (United Artists)

7-14a. *The Maltese Falcon.*
7-14b. *The Treasure of Sierra Madre.*
7-14c. *The African Queen.*
7-14d. *Beat the Devil.*
All directed by John Huston.
Casting against type—that is, violating an established star's popular image—can have its glories as well as its dangers. For many years, Humphrey Bogart played sardonic hard-boiled types, such as the cynical detective Sam Spade in *The Maltese Falcon* (a) and the crafty prospector Fred C. Dobbs in *The Treasure of Sierra Madre* (b). In *The African Queen* (c), Bogart went against type, and played Charlie Allnut, a lovable, funny drunk whose poetic vulnerability endeared him to audiences and won Bogart an Academy Award as best actor. In *Beat the Devil* (d), the actor assayed a role beyond his powers—a sophisticated adventurer stranded with a motley assortment of rogues, fakers, and weirdos. Truman Capote's witty tongue-in-cheek dialogue fell flat in Bogart's confused and self-conscious performance. Cary Grant could have played the role with much greater believability and grace.

sonations. In effect, Shaw was pointing out some of the major distinctions between a great "star" and a great actor.

Actually, in film there are three broad categories of performers, though there can be a considerable amount of overlapping: the star (7-12), the actor (7-13), and the nonprofessional. Stars are made—and in many respects controlled—by the public. A film star can be a good technical actor or not, but the essential requisite of the star is that he or she tailors each role to fit his or her personality, which remains relatively constant from role to role. Whenever a star deviates significantly from his image, the public often reacts unfavorably. Throughout the teens and early twenties, the most popular star in the United States was Mary Pickford—"America's Sweetheart." With her coy golden curls, her "angelic" sexual innocence, and a certain waggish charm, Pickford was to remain the eternal little girl for virtually her entire career. A clever and sophisticated woman in actual life, she tried several times to change her image to something more in keeping with the jazz age—not to speak of her chronological age. She was heartily weary of playing twelve-year old Pollyannas, but her public refused to let her grow up. In desperation, she defiantly cut off her curls in 1929—at the age of thirty-seven! Her new flapper's bob was her emancipation proclamation, but she appeared in only a few more films after that,

(M-G-M)

(Paramount Pictures)

7-15a. *Romeo and Juliet.*
Directed by George Cukor.
7-15b. *Romeo and Juliet.*
Directed by Franco Zeffirelli.
The differences between the ages of an actor and a character are far more important on the screen than on the stage, for the cinematic close-up can be merciless in revealing age. Despite the intelligence of the director and many of the actors, Cukor's film abounded in visual absurdities: Norma Shearer and Leslie Howard (pictured) were a far cry from the youngsters called for in Shakespeare's script. Shearer was thirty-seven when she played the thirteen-year-old Juliet, Leslie Howard, as Romeo, was forty-four. At fifty-five, John Barrymore seemed preposterous as Mercutio, Romeo's firebrand friend. Zeffirelli's version of the play was much more successful because he cast by sight rather than sound, and awarded the principal **(a)** roles to two teenagers, Olivia Hussey and Leonard Whiting **(b)**.

(b)

and none of them was popular with the public. She retired in disgust at the age of forty—just as most actresses are at the peak of their powers.

But most stars are not so narrowly confined to a single role (7-14). Many of them—particularly gifted performers like Audrey Hepburn, James Stewart, Cary Grant, and Ingrid Bergman—have played wider variations of certain types of roles. Nonetheless, we can't imagine Miss Hepburn playing a woman of weak character, or a coarse or lower-class woman, for example, so firmly entrenched is her image as an elegant and rather aristocratic female. Similarly, most people know what's meant by an "Ingrid Bergman role," just as they understand such terms as "the Jimmy Stewart type."

The star system is not necessarily a bad thing. In the first place, there are a number of performers who are excellent at playing one type of character. And why not, since no one is likely to play John Wayne as well as John Wayne himself? So long as Marilyn Monroe played vulnerable, wide-eyed sex kittens, as in *Some Like It Hot,* she was a charming performer, but when she attempted to play *femme fatale* roles in earnest, as in *Niagara,* she was embarrassingly inept. Nor does the star system necessarily exploit a person's actual personality. For many years, Barbara Stanwyck specialized in playing intense, tough, and even cynical women-of-the-world roles, yet in real life, she's almost universally admired for the sweetness of her disposition and her helpful and encouraging attitude toward her fellow performers.

In the movies, there's usually a certain amount of casting to type whether the performers are stars, straight actors, or nonprofessionals. Though it's a much abused practice, typecasting can often produce some excellent results. Cukor's *Romeo and Juliet* is an example of the disasters that can befall a movie when a director miscasts—or casts against type (7-15). The film boasted some of M-G-M's most "distinguished" (i.e., stage-trained) performers. Leslie Howard played Romeo, Norma Shearer Juliet, John Barrymore was Mercutio. On stage, it would have been an impressive production, for Shakespeare's language was delivered with feeling. But the movie abounded in visual absurdities: Juliet had clearly not seen thirteen in many years; Romeo was middle-aged and balding; Mercutio was paunchy and fiftyish. That such mature people would behave so childishly made the whole dramatic action seem ludicrous. Thirty years later, Franco Zeffirelli filmed the same work (7-15b), using teenagers in the major roles, and the movie was totally believable, in large part because the director cast his principals according to type.

Rather than be victimized by the star system, Hitchcock—with characteristic cunning—often exploits it (7-16). His villains are usually actors of enormous personal charm—like James Mason in *North by Northwest.* Hitchcock counts on the audience's good will towards an established star, thus permitting the director to have his "heroes" behave in ways that can only be described as morally dubious. In *Rear Window,* for example, James Stewart is literally a voyeur, yet we can't bring ourselves to condemn such a wholesome type as Jimmy Stewart. Audiences also assume that a star will dominate an entire film—an assumption Hitchcock was counting on when he outrageously killed off Janet Leigh even before the mid-point of *Psycho.*

There are some great actors who are sometimes called "stars" because of their boxoffice popularity, but they are not stars in the narrower sense that we have been using the term. Bette Davis, Laurence Olivier, and Marlon Brando are all in the Duse rather than the Bernhardt mold. That is, they subordinate their own personalities in favor of exploring the various facets of the characters they are playing. For example, just as Brando was being typed as the sexy young working-class stud (*A Streetcar Named Desire, On the Waterfront*), he completely reversed his image with a Shakespearean role (*Julius Caesar*) and a stint at musical comedy (*Guys and Dolls*). In *The Teahouse of the August Moon,* he played a diminutive Japanese houseboy, and in *The Young Lions,* an effete German aristocrat. His Fletcher Christian in *Mutiny on the Bounty* was not the standard star vehicle that Clark Gable had made of the role in the earlier version of this film, but a performance which stressed the character's fastidious and rather effeminate snobbishness. In *The Godfather,* Brando astonished his public by playing an elderly Mafia don, and in his brilliant performance in *Last Tango in Paris,* he played a neurotic middle-aged romantic, totally obsessed with sexuality.

Other great actors who are not stars in the Bernhardtian sense are Liv Ullmann, Joanne Woodward, Jack Nicholson, Vanessa Redgrave, Dustin Hoffman, Anne Bancroft, Jon Voight, and Marcello Mastroianni, to name only some of the best known. A few actors have spent years performing in a variety of character roles, only to achieve star status later in their careers, after a particularly popular single performance: George C. Scott, Lee Marvin, and Rod Steiger are some prominent examples. There was a time when the phrase "a George C. Scott role" would have been meaningless, but today this is far from the case.

Some directors prefer using nonprofessional actors precisely because they haven't been seen in repetitive and familiar roles. In a sense, such performers are neutral in the eyes of the audience, and the filmmaker can exploit only those aspects of their personalities—usually their physical appearance—that are relevant to the character in the film. Generally, the more familiar an actor is to the public, the more he tends to bring with him an automatic kind of characterization—those qualities we associate with his previous roles. In *Last Tango in Paris,* Bertolucci was able to exploit these automatic associations, for the movie—on one level—is virtually an exploration of Brando's various roles, both artistic and private. But in other types of films, these associations can be disastrous.

The post-war Italian neorealists were especially fond of using nonprofessional actors (7-17). Coming from a background in documentary film, Roberto Rossellini established the viability of using nonprofessionals in fiction films with his movie, *Open City.* This was followed by *Paisàn,* which featured only nonprofessionals, though with somewhat less striking success, for the voices of some of his actors betrayed their amateur status. Vittorio De Sica's *Bicycle Thief* is an artistic triumph in large part because of the utter authenticity of the characters. When De Sica was trying to finance the film, one producer agreed to put up the money provided that the leading role—an ordinary working-class laborer—were played by Cary Grant! Needless to say, De Sica couldn't imagine an elegant and graceful actor like Grant in the role, and the director wisely went elsewhere for his financing. The role was finally given to an actual laborer, Lamberto Maggiorani. Other

(a)

(RKO)

(b)

(M-G-M)

(c)

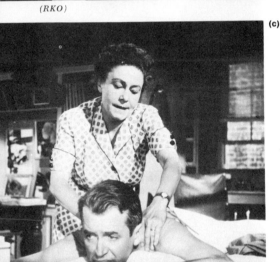

(Paramount Pictures)

(d)

(Paramount Pictures)

7-16a. *Notorious.*
7-16b. *North by Northwest.*
7-16c. *Rear Window.*
7-16d. *Psycho.*
All directed by Alfred Hitchcock.
In casting his films, Hitchcock usually exploits the star system by creating a tension between the unattractive traits of a character as written, and the attractive qualities which a star automatically brings with him or her. In *Notorious* (a) Ingrid Bergman lends a great deal of warmth and femininity to the role of a woman whose life has been dominated by excessive drinking and sexual promiscuity. Gentle, soft-spoken Claude Rains plays her Nazi husband. In *North by Northwest* (b) Cary Grant is a complacent huckster, while the elegantly suave James Mason is an enemy agent. Eva Marie Saint, delicate, ladylike, and vulnerable, plays his mistress. In *Rear Window* (c) James Stewart, the all-American boy, plays a casual voyeur who spies on his neighbors. In *Psycho* (d), Hitchcock exploited Anthony Perkins' boyish charm in the role of Norman Bates, a dangerously unstable schizophrenic. Virtually all of Hitchcock's greatest films deal with the theme of appearance versus reality, and his exploitation of the star system is an organic part of this theme.

7-17. Shoeshine.
Directed by Vittorio De Sica.
Nonprofessional actors often seem more believable in fiction films precisely because they haven't had a chance to develop slick actorish mannerisms from role to role. Such performers are usually cast because of their physical appearance rather than any histrionic skill they might possess—though the two are by no means incompatible. In the hands of a gifted and sensitive director like De Sica, nonprofessionals often turn in performances of great poignance and delicacy.

directors have used nonprofessionals for the same reason: they seem more authentic. Robert Bresson, for example, feels that a movie can be made by "bypassing the will of those who appear in them, using not what they do, but what they are." Antonioni agrees: "Film actors need not understand, but simply be." Eisenstein once asked, why use an actor to impersonate a peasant when one can go out and photograph a real peasant?

Whether a director prefers to use stars, straight actors, or nonprofessionals, acting in movies is almost totally dependent upon the filmmaker's approach to his materials. In general, the more realistic the director's techniques, the more he has to rely on the abilities of his actors. Realists tend to favor long shots, which keep the performer's entire body within the frame. This is the camera distance that corresponds to the proscenium arch of the legitimate theatre. The realist also favors **long takes**—thus permitting the actors to sustain performances for relatively lengthy periods without interruption. In short, the more realistic the directorial techniques, the more theatrical are the acting techniques. From the audience's point of view, it's easier to evaluate acting in a realist movie than in an expressionist film, for we're permitted to see sustained scenes without any apparent directorial interference. Indeed, the camera remains essentially a recording device.

The more expressionist the director, the less likely he is to value the actor's contribution. For Bresson, for example, the actor is not an interpretive artist, but merely one of the "raw materials" of the cinema. Indeed, Bresson avoids professionals precisely because they tend to want to convey emotions through acting. Like Pudovkin, Bresson feels that emotions and ideas in film shouldn't be communicated theatrically, but cinematically—by

7-18a, b. The Passion of Anna.
Directed by Ingmar Bergman.
Even with important dialogue, some directors insist that the major information a viewer receives is derived from the image, not the language. The same line of dialogue delivered straight on (a) or off-screen (b) can be altered significantly by the visuals accompanying the dialogue.

(United Artists)

(a)

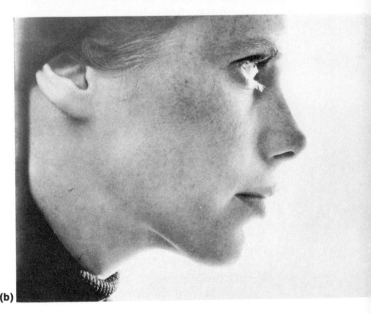

(b)

juxtaposing shots to produce linked associations. Thus, in his *Une Femme Douce,* a fierce domestic conflict is conveyed almost exclusively through the use of images of doors and windows, juxtaposed with the neutral expressions of his two leading actors, who were nonprofessionals at the time. In this same film, a suicide is portrayed through a sequence of nontheatrical images: the young wife is shown in long shot looking from a balcony; next, a medium shot of a balcony chair tipping over; next, a shot showing the empty balcony; finally, a shot showing the wife's delicate scarf floating in the air beyond the balcony's railing.

Antonioni has stated that he uses his actors only as a part of the composition—"like a tree, a wall, or a cloud." Many of the major themes of his films are conveyed through long shots in which the juxtaposition of people and their settings suggests complex psychological and spiritual states. Perhaps more than any other contemporary director, Antonioni is sensitive to how meanings change, depending upon the mise-en-scène. Thus, the significance of a line of dialogue can be totally changed if an actor delivers it standing before a brick wall rather than on a deserted street. Antonioni has also pointed out that a line spoken by an actor in profile may have a totally different meaning from one delivered facing the camera (7-18).

Though he's by no means an exclusive expressionist, some of Hitchcock's most stunning cinematic effects have been achieved by minimizing the contribution of actors. In a movie called *Sabotage,* Hitchcock was working with Sylvia Sidney, a stage actress who burst into tears on the set because she wasn't permitted to act a crucial scene. The episode involved a murder, where the sympathetic heroine kills her brutish husband in revenge for his murder of her young brother. On stage of course her feelings and thoughts would be communicated by the actress's exaggerated facial expressions. But in real life, Hitchcock has observed, people's faces don't necessarily reveal what they think or feel. For a number of reasons, Hitchcock preferred to convey these ideas and emotions through edited juxtapositions (7-19).

The setting for the scene is a dinner table. The heroine looks at her husband (a) who is eating as usual (b). Then a close-up shows a dish containing meat and vegetables, with a knife and fork lying next to it (d); the wife's hands are seen behind the dish. Hitchcock then cuts to a medium shot of the wife thoughtfully slicing some meat (f). Next, a medium shot of the brother's empty chair (g). Close-up of the wife's hands with knife and fork (i). Close-up of a bird cage with canaries—a reminder to the heroine of her dead brother (k). Close-up of wife's thoughtful face (l). Close-up of the plate and knife (m). Suddenly a close-up of the husband's suspicious face (n). He notices the connection between the knife and her thoughtful expression, for the camera pans, rather than cuts, back to the knife. He gets up next to her (p). Hitchcock quickly cuts to a close-up of her hand reaching for the knife (r). Cut to an extreme close-up of the knife entering his body (s). Cut to a **two-shot** of their faces, his convulsed with pain, hers with fear (t). Cut to a medium shot, in which his dead body drops out of the frame (u).

One of Hitchcock's recurrent themes is the idea of complicity. By forcing the audience to identify with his .protagonists, he involves us in their behavior. In effect, we share the responsibility for certain questionable acts because of this identification. In *Sabotage,* we must somehow excuse the heroine's act of murder by participating in it. He forces this identification by fragmenting the sequence at the dinner table. Like the heroine, we too connect the knife with the dead brother and the guilty husband. The knife gradually seems to acquire a will of its own, a kind of destiny. Before we (or the heroine) realize what's happening, the knife is in the husband's body—almost as though it were predestined to find its home there. The revenge is complete, yet we don't really blame the distraught wife, for in effect we have helped commit the act. When Miss Sidney saw the finished product, she was delighted with the results, and exclaimed at Hitchcock's brilliance. The entire scene, of course, required very little acting in the conventional sense.

But it's difficult to make too many generalizations about acting in film, for directors don't approach every movie with the same attitudes. In some films they'll use predominantly realistic techniques, and in others, expressionistic. In *Rope,* for example, Hitchcock includes no edited sequences, for the director was experimenting with ten-minute takes which preserved actual time. In *Psycho,* on the other hand, the most effective scenes are highly fragmented. Men like Elia Kazan and Ingmar Bergman, who are distinguished stage directors as well as filmmakers, will vary their technique considerably, depending upon the dramatic needs of the film. Nor is there any "correct" approach to filming a scene. A director like Bergman might convey a specific idea through acting, whereas Carl Dreyer might approach the very same idea through editing or composition. Each version could be effective: whatever *works* is right.

But whether a director is a realist or expressionist, the differences between film acting and stage acting remain fundamental. For example, a performer in film is not so restricted by vocal requirements, since sound volume is controlled electronically. Marilyn Monroe's small breathy voice wouldn't have projected beyond the first few rows in the theatre, but on film it was perfect for conveying that childlike vulnerability that gave her performances such poetic delicacy. Some film actors are popular precisely because of the off-beat charm of their voices: James Stewart's twangy nasality, for example, is an essential aspect of his country-boy unpretentiousness. Since acting in movies isn't so dependent upon vocal flexibility, many performers have succeeded despite their wooden, inexpressive voices: Gary Cooper, John Wayne, and Gregory Peck, for example.

Even the *quality* of a movie actor's voice can be controlled electronically. Music and sound effects can totally change the meaning of a line of dialogue. Through electronic devices, a voice can be made to sound garbled, or booming, or hollow. Indeed, Antonioni claims that language in film is primarily pure sound, and only secondarily meaningful dialogue. Since dialogue in a movie can be **dubbed,** a director can re-record a line until it's perfect (7-20). Sometimes he'll select one or two words from one recorded take, and splice them with the words of another. This kind of synthesizing can be carried even further—by combining one actor's face with another actor's voice.

Similarly, the physical requirements for a film actor are different from those for a stage performer. The movie actor doesn't have to be tall, even if he's a leading man. Alan Ladd, for example, was quite short. His directors simply avoided showing his body in full unless there was no one else

(a)

(b)

(c)

(g)

(h)

(i)

(m)

(n)

(o)

(s)

(t)

(u)

7-19. Sabotage sequence.
Directed by Alfred Hitchcock.
Through the art of editing, a director can construct a highly emotional "performance" by juxtaposing shots of his actors with shots of objects. In scenes such as these, the actor's contribution tends to be minimal: the effect is achieved through the linking of two or more shots. This associational process is the basis of Pudovkin's theory of "constructive editing."

7-20. La Dolce Vita.
Directed by Federico Fellini.
In the Italian cinema, live sound recording is rare: virtually all films are dubbed after the **footage** has been photographed, and often even after it's been edited. Because sound is not recorded on the set, some directors don't even bother with dialogue at the time of performance. Fellini, for example, has been known to instruct his actors to recite numbers rather than words while enacting a scene. Later, appropriate dialogue is written to match the visuals. Needless to say, such techniques place the actor (as well as the writer) in the director's hands even more than conventional methods of performance.

in frame to contrast with his height. He played love scenes standing on a box, the lovers' bodies cut off at the waist. **Low angle shots** also tended to make him seem taller. A film actor's features don't have to be large, only expressive—particularly the eyes and mouth. An actor who moves badly is not necessarily at a disadvantage in film. The director can work around the problem by not using many long shots and by photographing the actor *after* he has moved. Complicated movements can be faked by using stuntmen or doubles. Elaborate sword fights for example are usually performed by specially trained stuntmen, dressed like the principal actors. These shots are **intercut** with closer shots of the leading actor, and the edited juxtaposition leads the audience to assume that the main performer is involved in all the shots. Even in close-up, the film performer's physical appearance can

7-21. On the set of *The Big Heat*.
Directed by Fritz Lang.
Film actors are expected to perform under the most distracting conditions. Their concentration must be extraordinary, for even highly intense and intimate scenes are performed while the camera and dozens of technicians are just a few feet away. Lang (wearing glasses) was particularly notorious for giving his actors instructions off camera while the performers were enacting a scene. Pictured are Gloria Grahame and Glenn Ford.

be changed through the use of special lenses, filters, and lights.

Since the shot is the basic building unit in film, the movie actor doesn't have to sustain a performance for very long—even in realistic films, in which the takes can run to two or three minutes. In an expressionistic movie—in which shots can last for less than a second—one can scarcely refer to the performer's contribution as acting at all: he simply *is*. Furthermore, the shooting schedule of a film is determined by economic considerations. Thus, the shooting of various sequences isn't always artistically logical. An actor may be required to perform the climactic scene first, and low-keyed exposition shots later. The screen actor, then, doesn't "build" emotionally, as the stage actor must. The film performer must be capable of an intense degree of concentration—turning emotions on and off for very short periods of time. Most of the time he must seem totally natural, as though he weren't acting at all (7-21). Certainly he's almost always at the mercy of his director, who later constructs the various shots into a coherent performance. Some directors have tricked actors into a performance. Hitchcock and Antonioni have at times deliberately lied to their actors, asking for one quality in order to get another.

Since acting in the cinema is confined to short segments of time and space, the film performer doesn't need a long rehearsal period to establish a sense of ease with other actors, the set, or his costumes. Sometimes the film performer hasn't even seen the set when he arrives at the studio or on location, yet he's expected to pretend that he's been living there all his life. Unlike the stage actor, he doesn't have to establish an intimate rapport with other performers: sometimes he has not even met his co-stars. Many directors don't bother rehearsing some scenes, especially for shots of brief duration. Actors occasionally don't know their lines: this is remedied by having a prompter on the set, or by writing the lines on a blackboard off camera, where the actor can read them. Furthermore, a film actor is expected to play even the most intimate scenes with dozens of technicians on the set, working or observing. He must seem totally at ease, even though the lights are unbearably hot, and his running make-up must be corrected between shots. Since the camera distorts, actors are required to perform some scenes unnaturally. In an embrace, for example, the lovers can't really look at each other, or they will appear cross-eyed on the screen. In point-of-view shots, an actor must direct his lines at the camera rather than at another actor. Much of the time the movie actor has no idea what he's doing, or where a shot might appear in the finished film, if indeed it appears at all, for many an actor's performance has been left on the cutting room floor. In short, the lack of theatrical **continuity** in the cinema places the film actor almost totally in the hands of the director.

COSTUMES, MAKEUP, AND SETTINGS

In the most sensitive films and plays, costumes aren't merely frills added to enhance an illusion, but aspects of character and theme. The style of a costume can suggest certain psychological states. In Jack Clayton's *The Pumpkin Eater,* for instance, the hair styles and costumes of the heroine (Anne Bancroft) are used to convey her sense of freedom or confinement. Whenever she's happy—usually when she is pregnant or with her young children—her costumes are casual and a bit sloppy, her hair loose and wild. When she feels unhappy and useless, her costumes are neat, fashionable, yet oddly sterile. One especially effective outfit of this sort is a smart tailored suit, and a severe Garbo-type hat which conceals her hair. The effect is somewhat like a chic straitjacket.

Depending upon their cut, texture, and bulk, certain costumes can suggest agitation, fastidiousness, delicacy, dignity, and so on. A costume, then, is a medium, especially in the cinema where a close-up of a fabric can suggest information that's independent even of the wearer. One of the directors most sensitive to the meanings of costumes was Sergei Eisenstein. In his *Alexander Nevsky,* the invading German hordes are made terrifying primarily through their costumes. The soldiers' helmets, for example, don't reveal the eyes: two sinister slits are cut into the fronts of the metal helmets (7-22). In Eisenstein's *Ivan the Terrible,* the evil boyars are portrayed as

(a)

7-22a, b, c. *Alexander Nevsky.*
Directed by Sergei Eisenstein.
In both theatre and film, a costume is a medium: it conveys information by suggesting ideas and emotions. Eisenstein's costumes often violated historical accuracy in order to suggest a symbolic truth. In this movie, the ruthless mechanization of the German soldiers is conveyed by the medieval metal helmets which dehumanize the invaders by obscuring the features of their faces (a). The German officers wear truncated human hands and animal appendages as insignia on their helmets, and their horses seem mechanized with their stylized metal head plates (b). Nevsky and the Russian soldiers, on the other hand, wear helmets that suggest Russian Church spires, and their chain mail allows for more flexibility of movement (c). This netting also recalls the fishing nets used by the peasant fishermen earlier in the film.

(b)

(Audio-Brandon Films)

(c)

7-23. Juliet of the Spirits.
Directed by Federico Fellini.
After *La Dolce Vita*, Fellini's works became progressively more fantastic, more **surreal.**
In this movie, the women's costumes are grotesquely extravagant in their opulence
and gaudiness. Fellini contrasts these women with his protagonist (Giulietta Masina,
extreme right), a woman of directness and simplicity—qualities emphasized by her
more conventional mode of dress.

animal-like, especially the boyar princess, whose bulky black headdress,
cape, and dress suggest a huge, sinister vulture. Ivan, on the other hand,
is Christ-like (at least in the first half of this two-part film), with his simple
flowing hair, beard, and unpretentious white robes.

Fellini's costumes in *Juliet of the Spirits* are deliberately theatrical and
bizarre (7-23). The gaudy reds and yellows, the elaborate feather boas, and
the fantastic extravagance of the women's outfits are used especially to
convey the vulgar show-biz world of the heroine's husband—a world that
seems to combine the features of a circus with those of a brothel. Color
symbolism is used by Zeffirelli in *Romeo and Juliet*. Juliet's family, the
Capulets, are characterized as aggressive parvenues: their colors are appropriately rich reds, yellows, and oranges. Romeo's family, on the other hand,
is older and perhaps more established, but in obvious decline. They are

costumed in blues, deep greens, and purples. These two color schemes are echoed in the liveries of the servants of each house, which helps the audience identify the combatants in the brawling scenes. The color of the costumes can also be used to suggest change and transition. The first view of Juliet, for example, shows her in a vibrant red dress. After she marries Romeo, however, she wears blues. Line as well as color can be used to suggest psychological qualities. Verticals, for example, tend to emphasize stateliness and dignity (Lady Montague); horizontal lines tend to emphasize earthiness and comicality (Juliet's nurse).

Perhaps the most famous costume in film history is Chaplin's Charlie the tramp outfit. The costume was an indication of both class and character, conveying the complex mixture of vanity and clumsiness that makes Charlie so universally appealing. The moustache, derby hat, and cane all suggested the fastidious dandy. The cane particularly was used to give the impression of self-importance, as Charlie swaggered confidently before a hostile world. But the baggy trousers, several sizes too large, and belted often by a piece of rope, the oversized shoes, the too tight coat—all these suggested Charlie's social insignificance and poverty. Chaplin's view of mankind is symbolized by that costume: self-deceived, vain, absurd, and—finally—pathetically vulnerable.

Makeup in the cinema is generally more subtle than on stage. The theatrical actor tends to use makeup primarily to enlarge his features so that they'll be visible from long distances. On the screen, makeup tends to be more understated, though Chaplin used stage makeup for the tramp character, since he was generally photographed in long shot. Even the most delicate changes in makeup can be perceived in the cinema. Mia Farrow's pale green face in Roman Polanski's *Rosemary's Baby*, for example, was used to suggest the progressive corruption of her body while she was pregnant with the devil's child. Similarly, the ghoulish makeup of the actors in *Fellini Satyricon* suggests the degeneracy and death-in-life of the entire Roman population of the period. In *Tom Jones*, Richardson used elaborate, artificial makeup on the city characters like Lady Bellaston, to suggest their deceitfulness and decadence. (In the eighteenth-century comedy of manners, cosmetics are a favorite source of imagery to suggest falseness and hypocrisy.) The country characters, on the other hand, especially Sophy Weston, were more naturally made up, with no wigs, powder, and patches.

Cinematic makeup is closely associated with the type of performer wearing it. In general, stars prefer makeup that tends to glamorize them (7-24). Dietrich, Garbo, and Monroe usually had an ethereal quality in which each feature was subtly heightened to an exquisite perfection. Straight actors are less concerned with glamor, unless the characters they're playing are in fact glamorous. In an effort to submerge their own personalities, such performers often use makeup to attenuate the familiarity of their features. Brando and Olivier are particularly likely to wear false noses, wigs, and distorting cosmetics. Though Orson Welles is known primarily for playing strong domineering roles, he too has resorted to such tricks in makeup to maximize the differences between his roles. Nonprofessional

7-24. Makeup for Marlene Dietrich as she appears in *Blonde Venus.*
Directed by Josef von Sternberg.
Dietrich and von Sternberg were amused by the Trilby-Svengali publicity put out by Paramount Studios where the star and director made a number of films together in the early thirties. The publicity had some basis in fact, for von Sternberg taught Dietrich much about the technical aspects of lighting, camera filters and lenses, and about the effects of certain costumes and makeup. No matter how preposterously Dietrich was wigged and costumed, her shimmering ethereal beauty was usually preserved by the glamorous makeup she wore. The exquisite Dietrich face, with its perfect bone structure, was always heightened by von Sternberg's painstaking calculation.

actors usually wear the least amount of makeup, since they're chosen precisely because of their interesting and authentic physical appearance.

In the best movies and stage productions, the setting is not merely a backdrop for the action, but an extension of the theme and characterization. Like lights, costumes, and makeup, settings convey information. They not only tell us what the tastes and habits of the characters are, they can be used also to suggest certain symbolic ideas, especially in the cinema. Sets can be realistic or expressionistic, depending upon the nature of the work of art. In either case, however, stage sets need not be so detailed as film sets, for the audience is too distant from the stage to perceive many details. The stage director generally must work with fewer sets, usually one per act, and thus he must inevitably settle for less precision and variety than a screen director, who faces virtually no limits of this kind, especially if he's shooting on location.

Problems of space force the stage director to make constant compromises with his sets. If he uses too much of the upstage (rear) area, the audience won't be able to see or hear well. If he uses high platforms to give an actor dominance, the director then has the problem of getting his actor back on the main level quickly and plausibly. The stage director must also use a constant sized space: his settings are confined to "long shots." If he wants to suggest a vast field, for example, he must resort to certain conventions. He can stage an action in such a way as to suggest that the playing area is only a small corner of the field. Or he can stylize his set with the aid of a cyclorama, which gives the illusion of a vast sky in the background (7-25). If he wants to suggest a confined area, generally he can do so only for short periods, for an audience grows restless when actors are restricted to a small playing area for long periods. Stage directors can use vertical, horizontal and oblique lines in a set to suggest psychological states, but unlike the film director, these lines (or colors or objects) can't then be cut out in scenes in which they are inappropriate.

The film director has far more freedom in his use of settings. Most importantly, of course, the cinema permits a director to shoot out-of-doors —an enormous advantage. The major works of a number of great directors would have been impossible without this freedom: Griffith, Eisenstein, Keaton, Kurosawa, Fellini, Antonioni, De Sica, Godard, Truffaut, Renoir. Antonioni often structures his films around a location. In *Red Desert,* for example, the main "character" of the film is really the polluted industrial wastelands of Ravenna, a northern Italian city. In *Zabriskie Point,* the middle portion of the film takes place in Death Valley, which Antonioni uses as a metaphor for the sterility of contemporary America. Epic films would be virtually impossible without the extreme long shots of vast expanses of land. The poetry in the epic films of John Ford, for example, is largely found in the exquisite photography of the American plains, mountains, and deserts.

Certain film genres traditionally have been shot out-of-doors, most notably the western, samurai movies, many documentaries, and those films dealing with nature. Other genres, particularly those requiring a certain degree of stylization or deliberate unreality, have been associated with the studio: musicals, horror films, and many period films, for example (7-26). Such genres often stress a kind of magical, sealed-off universe, and images taken from real life tend to clash with these essentially claustrophobic qualities. Even a good musical like *On the Town* contains some jarring incongruities which result from the clash between studio footage and location shots of New York City, which are intercut with it.

In the golden days of the American studio system, sets were constructed within the studio whenever possible: most directors felt that such sets permitted them greater precision and control (7-27). Even the gangster films of the early thirties were largely photographed indoors, despite their urban settings. Studio sets of exterior locations usually lend films a kind of airlessness, which is often psychologically appropriate. The horror films of this same period, for example, benefit from this kind of stylized unreality.

However, these are merely generalizations. There are some westerns that have been shot mostly indoors (7-28), and some musicals which have been photographed on location: it all depends on how it's done. If a locale

7-25. A Midsummer Night's Dream.
Directed by Max Reinhardt and William Dieterle.
The magic and wonder of Shakespeare's enchanted wood is conveyed effectively in this movie thanks to the magic and wonder of Warner Brothers' special effects department. The famous German theatre director Reinhardt was brought over specifically to stage the enchanted forest scenes, and his genius is evident in all the fairy sequences. Reinhardt's cinematic treatment would have been impossible on the narrow confines of a theatrical stage. Unfortunately, the straight dramatic scenes, directed by Dieterle, are considerably less than brilliant, in part because of inappropriate actors.

is extravagantly romantic, for instance, there's no reason why a musical can't exploit such a setting. The Parisian scenes of Minnelli's *Gigi* are a good example of how locations can enhance a stylized genre. Similarly, a period film like *Tom Jones* uses a number of exterior settings in London. *Rosemary's Baby* is a realistic horror film—that is, the movie attempts to show supernatural elements in everyday life, and director Polanski wisely chose to shoot on location whenever possible.

Since the 1950s, most directors have preferred location shooting to the studio—at least for exteriors. There are some filmmakers who insist on authentic settings even for interiors; which are relatively easy to construct in a studio. Perhaps the most famous—if not infamous—example of this passion for authenticity is Erich von Stroheim, who detested the studio (7-29). In *Greed,* Stroheim insisted that his actors actually live in a seedy boarding house to get the "feel" of the film's low-life setting. He forced them to wear shabby clothes, and deprived them of all the amenities that their characters would lack in real life. Perhaps because of the severe hardships his cast and crew suffered, the film's authenticity is incontestable. Among contemporary directors, Jean-Luc Godard avoids studio sets, claiming that they can diminish a film's authenticity in a thousand small ways.

Settings can be used to suggest a sense of progression or development. In Fellini's *La Strada,* for instance, the protagonist and his simple-minded assistant are shown as reasonably happy as they travel together from town to town with their theatrical act. After he abandons her, he heads for the mountains. Gradually, the landscape changes: the trees are stripped of their foliage, snow and dirty slush cover the ground, the sky is a murky gray. The changing setting becomes a metaphor for the protagonist's spiritual condition, and nature itself seems to grieve when the helpless girl is left to die alone.

7-26. Miniature set for *Letter From an Unknown Woman.*
Directed by Max Ophüls.
Period films often benefit from the slight sense of unreality of studio sets. If a set is needed only for **establishing** purposes, miniatures are often constructed, though these scaled-down sets can be as tall as six or eight feet, depending upon the amount of detail and realism needed. Note the two studio flood lights behind the houses of this miniature, and the flat, two-dimensional apartment dwellings on the horizon in the upper right.

(Universal Studio)

In *Tom Jones,* Richardson employs a progressive drainage of color in his settings to suggest the moral qualities of the three main locations: the Allworthy estate, the road to London, and London itself. Brilliant colors are used to suggest the full-bodied richness of Tom's earlier life in the country. As he gets closer to the city, the color becomes more diffuse, more grayish and sickly. London itself is virtually colorless, save for the gaudy clothes of the rich and powerful. The cinema, then, is an ideal medium for dealing with themes of man's relationship with nature. Such themes are rare in the theatre, but in film they are commonplace: *The General, Gold Rush, The Rules of the Game, The Searchers, McCabe and Mrs. Miller,* are a few examples.

Even with interiors, the cinema can get more mileage from its settings. On the stage, a setting is generally admired with the opening of the curtain, then quickly forgotten as the actors take over as the center of interest. In the movies, a director can keep cutting back to the setting to remind the audience of its significance. Indeed, the setting in a film can have the dramatic power of a character—as does Kane's opulent palace Xanadu in *Citizen Kane.* The lavish estate is used to externalize Kane's fantastic wealth and growing dominance over others. During the course of his life, he keeps adding more and more clutter to the palace. Even his second wife is essentially an object to be stored in his vast warehouse. The castle is a bizarre

7-27a, b. Process shot from
The Sands of Iwo Jima.
Directed by Allan Dwan.
Because a studio allowed a director more control and precision than an actual location, some filmmakers used the so-called "process" shot in scenes requiring exterior locations. What this technique involved was a rear projection of a moving image on a translucent screen. Live actors and a portion of a set were placed in front of this screen, and the entire action and background were then photographed by a camera which was synchronized with the rear projector. The finished product (b) looked reasonably authentic, though backgrounds tended to look suspiciously washed out and flat in comparison to foreground elements.

7-28. "Exterior" set at Universal Studios.
The western is usually thought to be a genre requiring exterior locations. During the golden years of the studio system, however, particularly when the budget was limited and a movie had to be shot quickly and efficiently, even "exteriors" could be created indoors with reasonable success.

7-29. Greed.

Directed by Erich von Stroheim.

Notorious for his insistence on absolute authenticity, von Stroheim shot his 1925 masterpiece entirely on location in a shabby section of San Francisco and in Death Valley. During the production, his actors were required to live in a seedy boarding house (the locale for much of the action in the film) and were permitted only those amenities that the characters were likely to enjoy.

mixture of styles and periods—just as Kane's personality is an inconsistent blend of psychological contradictions. Finally, the mansion becomes a grotesque prison, for Kane discovers too late that a man can become possessed by his possessions.

A film can fragment a set into a series of shots, now emphasizing one aspect of a room, now another, depending upon the needs of the director in finding appropriate visual analogues for thematic and psychological ideas. In Losey's *The Servant,* a stairway is used as a major thematic symbol. The film deals with a servant who gradually takes control over his master. Losey uses the stairway as a kind of psychological battlefield, where the relative positions of the two men on the stairs give the audience a sense of who's winning the battle. Losey also uses the rails on the stairway to suggest prison bars: the "master" of the house is often photographed from behind these bars. In John Frankenheimer's *All Fall Down,* the separate rooms and corridors of a house are used to suggest the emotional fragmentation

7-30.
The objects of a set are often used as symbols. Eisenstein pointed out how a circular table suggests social equality, with no seat dominating. A rectangular table tends to suggest social stratification, with a "head" at one end and positions of less social importance descending from this dominant seat.

of a family. The father is usually seen in the cellar, the mother on the ground floor, the two sons in the upper bedrooms.

Even the furniture of a room can be exploited for psychological and thematic reasons. In one of his classes, Eisenstein once discussed at length the significance of a table for a set (7-30). The class exercise was centered on an adaptation of Balzac's novel, *Père Goriot.* The scene takes place at the dinner table, which Balzac describes as circular. But Eisenstein convincingly argues that a round table is wrong cinematically, for it implies equality, with each person linked in a circle. To convey the highly stratified class structure of the boarding house, Eisenstein suggests the use of a long rectangular table, with the mistress of the house at the head, the favored tenants close to her sides, and the lowly Goriot alone, near the base of the table.

Such careful attention to the details of a set often distinguishes a master of film from a mere technician, who settles for only a general effect. Indeed, some directors feel that the set is so important that they will even construct different versions for separate shots. In *The Graduate,* Nichols wanted to underline the sudden sense of loss and humiliation of Anne Bancroft when she's betrayed by Dustin Hoffman. To convey the effect more forcefully, a separate set was constructed, with an oversized doorway towering above her. With the camera at a **high angle,** a vast expanse of white wall to one side, and a huge empty doorway at the other side, Miss Bancroft appeared as physically dwarfed as she felt.

The setting of a movie—far more than the setting of a play—can even take over as the central interest of a film. In Kubrick's *2001: A Space Odyssey,* the director spends most of his time lovingly photographing the instruments of a space ship, various space stations, and the enormous expanses of space itself. Indeed, the few people in the film seem almost incidental, and certainly far less interesting than the real center of concern—the setting. It would be impossible to produce *2001* on the stage: the "language" of the film is not theatrically convertible. And though the movie is perhaps an extreme instance of how the cinema communicates, it represents nonetheless a logical extension of Bazin's observation, quoted at the head of this chapter.

FURTHER READING

BAZIN, ANDRÉ. "Theatre and Cinema," in *What is Cinema?* Edited and translated by Hugh Gray. Berkeley: University of California Press, 1967. (Paper) A classic essay dealing with the similarities as well as the differences between the two mediums.

CARRICK, EDWARD. *Designing for Moving Pictures.* London: Studio, 1947. A discussion of the problems and techniques of set designing in film.

HASKELL, MOLLY. *From Reverence to Rape.* Baltimore: Penguin Books, 1974. (Paper) A critical history of the treatment of women in film, with principal emphasis on the American cinema, written from a feminist perspective.

HURT, JAMES, ed. *Focus on Film and Theatre.* Englewood Cliffs: Prentice-Hall, 1974. (Paper) A collection of essays dealing with the similarities and differences between the two mediums.

NICOLL, ALLARDYCE. *Film and Theatre.* New York: Crowell, 1936. A standard, if somewhat outdated, exploration of the differences and similarities between the two mediums.

NIZHNY, VLADIMIR. *Lessons with Eisenstein.* Translated and edited by Ivor Montagu and Jay Leyda. New York: Hill and Wang, 1969. (Paper) An exploration of some of the practical problems facing the movie director in adapting plays and novels into film.

PUDOVKIN, V. I. *Film Technique and Film Acting.* Translated and edited by Ivor Montagu. New York: Grove Press, 1960. (Paper) An early treatise on the differences between acting in movies and on the stage, with major emphasis on the art of editing.

ROACH, MARY ELLEN, and JOANNE BUBOLZ EICHER, eds. *Dress, Adornment, and the Social Order.* New York: John Wiley and Sons, 1965. An analysis of how dress and adornment have been used symbolically through the ages.

ROSEN, MARJORIE. *Popcorn Venus.* New York: Coward, McCann & Geoghegan, 1973. A history of the treatment of women in the American cinema, written from a feminist perspective.

"The film-maker/author writes with his camera
as a writer writes with his pen."
—ALEXANDRE ASTRUC

8 literature

It's been variously estimated that from one-fourth to one-fifth of all feature films have been literary adaptations. Nor has the relationship between movies and literature been one way: many commentators have remarked upon the cinematic quality of much modern fiction and poetry, including classics such as Dos Passos's *U.S.A.,* Joyce's *Ulysses,* and Eliot's "The Love Song of J. Alfred Prufrock" (8-1). The relationship between these two mediums can be traced back almost to film's infancy. At the turn of the century, George Méliès used literary materials as a basis for several of his movies. Griffith claimed that many of his cinematic innovations were in fact taken straight from the pages of Dickens. In his essay, "Dickens, Griffith, and the

8-1. Cabaret.
Directed by Bob Fosse.
Some stories have been adapted in so many mediums that the artistic permutations seem almost incestuous. Christopher Isherwood first created the main characters and the corrupt milieu of the early Nazi period in his collection of short stories, *Goodbye to Berlin.* Some of the materials of these stories were adapted by John Van Druten in a play entitled *I Am a Camera,* which itself was adapted into a nonmusical film of the same title, with Julie Harris playing Sally Bowles. Some years later, these materials were adapted into a stage musical entitled *Cabaret.* Fosse's musical film, adapted by Jay Allen and Hugh Wheeler, used much of the stage music, but also incorporated a good deal of the original Isherwood material.

(Allied Artists)

Film Today," Eisenstein shows how Dickens's novels provided Griffith with a number of techniques, including equivalents to **fades, dissolves, frame composition,** the breakdown into **shots,** special modifying **lenses,** and—most important—the concept of **parallel editing.** Eisenstein even converts Chapter 21 of *Oliver Twist* into a shooting script to demonstrate Dickens's "cinematic" sensibility (8-2).

THE WRITER

Perhaps more than any of the director's other collaborators, the script writer has been suggested from time to time as the main "author" of a film. After all, the writer is generally responsible for the dialogue, he outlines most of the action (sometimes in great detail), and he usually sets forth the main theme of a film (8-3). Particularly after the advent of sound, when movie scripts became more elaborate, precise, and—most of all—verbal, many established literary figures were attracted to the new audio-visual medium. In the United States, some of our greatest writers—including William Faulkner, Nathanael West, John Dos Passos, and F. Scott Fitzgerald, to name only a handful of the most famous—went to Hollywood with great expectations.

Most of these writers became embittered and cynical. Notwithstanding the encouragement of such powerful producers as Irving Thalberg, Darryl F. Zanuck, and later, Stanley Kramer (who all tended to believe that cinema is essentially a writer's medium), most of these literary figures were thwarted and artistically frustrated. The majority of them produced only hack work. Indeed, one could make a convincing argument that with few exceptions, great novelists, poets, and dramatists seldom make good screenwriters, simply because they tend to misunderstand the nature of the medium. Certainly most of the best film writers have made their *major* contribution in movies, not in other forms of literary expression.

But assessing the writer's contribution in the movie-making process is a labyrinthine exercise, and perhaps one doomed to futility, since the writer's role varies immensely from film to film and from director to director. In the first place, some directors hardly bother with a script. Godard, for example, usually begins a movie with only a few ideas jotted down on a scrap of paper. Of course many of the greatest filmmakers write their own scripts: Bergman, Cocteau, Eisenstein, and Renoir, to name only a few (8-4). In the American cinema, there are also many writer-directors: Griffith, Chaplin, Keaton, von Stroheim, Huston, Welles, Joseph L. Mankiewicz, Billy Wilder, Preston Sturges, Samuel Fuller, and John Cassevetes, are among the most famous.

Most great directors take a major hand in writing their scripts, but they bring in other writers to expand on their ideas. Fellini, Truffaut, Kurosawa, and Antonioni all work in this manner. The American studio system also tended to encourage multiple authorship of scripts. Often writers had a certain specialty, such as dialogue, comedy, construction, atmosphere, and so on. Some writers were best at "doctoring" weak scripts, others were good

(Columbia Pictures)

8-2. Oliver!.
Directed by Carol Reed.
D. W. Griffith claimed that most of his "innovations" were in fact techniques suggested by Charles Dickens in such novels as *Oliver Twist*. Sergei Eisenstein converted a chapter of this novel into a shooting script. A film version of the novel was finally made by David Lean in 1948. Reed's movie was loosely based on a stage musical, also entitled *Oliver!*

8-3. Deliverance.
Directed by John Boorman, written by James Dickey.
Movies based on novels and plays are seldom written by the original novelists and dramatists—usually for good reason. Filmmakers have complained that the scripts written by such writers are frequently too "literary," too unvisual and talky. Dickey's screenplay, adapted from his own novel, was an exception to this rule. A comparison between the novel and the movie demonstrates some of the advantages and limitations of each medium. The novel tends to be superior in the reflective passages and those sections dealing with abstract ideas. The movie is superior in conveying the visceral impact of the action sequences.

"idea" people but perhaps lacked the skill to execute their ideas. In such collaborative enterprises, the screen credits are not always an accurate reflection of who contributed what to a movie. Furthermore, even though many directors—like Hitchcock—contribute a great deal to the final shape of their scripts, they often refuse to take screen credit for their work, allowing the official writer to take it all. Surprisingly few major directors depend entirely upon others for their scripts. Joseph Losey and Harold Pinter, Marcel Carné and Jacques Prévert, and Vittorio De Sica and Cesare Zavattini are perhaps the most famous director-writer teams.

On the other hand, there are some movies in which the writer seems more dominant than the director. This certainly seems to be the case in the films scripted by Paddy Chayevsky, for example, in which the dialogue tends to dominate the visuals. In general, the more literary the movie, the greater the contribution of the writer. Indeed, some directors enjoy considerable prestige at the expense of their excellent writers, who are either forgotten or relegated to dependent clauses in critical commentaries. Howard Hawks seems to be such a filmmaker, for though he has directed some of the most enjoyable works of the American cinema, most of them were scripted by the cream of Hollywood's screenwriters: William Faulkner, Jules Furthman, Ben Hecht, Leigh Brackett, and Charles Lederer (8-5). In many ways, Hawks seems to have all the virtues of a good stage director: he's gifted in directing actors, he has an energetic sense of pace, and an unpretentious, functional visual style. But all of these considerable virtues would be wasted were it not for the first-rate scripts Hawks had to work with (not to speak of his excellent actors), particularly in such charming films as *His Girl Friday, The Big Sleep* (written by Faulkner, Brackett, and Furthman, from the novel by Raymond Chandler), and *Rio Bravo* (written by Furthman and Brackett, from a story by B. H. McCampbell). On the other hand, not even Hawks's most fervent enthusiasts would praise *Red Line 7000,* which was written mainly by Hawks in collaboration with George Kirgo.

For many years American intellectuals were inclined to dismiss the virile, clean scripts of Hawks's movies in favor of those that dealt overtly with "serious" themes. To this day, many filmgoers believe that art must be solemn—if not actually dull—to be respectable. Indeed, even in the heyday of the Hollywood studio system, such "intellectual" writers as Dalton

(New World Pictures)

8-4. Cries and Whispers.
Written and directed by Ingmar Bergman.
A good number of the best film-makers write as well as direct their own films. Bergman is perhaps the most famous writer-director in the cinema. Unlike most screenplays, his are eminently readable, and a number of them have appeared in published form.

(Columbia Pictures)

8-5. His Girl Friday.
Directed by Howard Hawks, written by Charles Lederer, adapted from the play, The Front Page, *by Ben Hecht and Charles MacArthur.*
While it's not necessarily true that a movie can never be better than its script (a common canard among film commentators), a great many films seem to succeed primarily because of their excellent scripts. Hawks has enjoyed the services of some of the best screenwriters in Hollywood history, including William Faulkner, Ben Hecht, Leigh Brackett, and Charles Lederer.

literature **315**

8-6. *Chloe in the Afternoon.*
Written and directed by Eric Rohmer.
In dealing with abstract ideas, the screenwriter is at a distinct disadvantage when compared to the novelist. For the most part, the only characters who are likely to discuss ideas without self-consciousness are students, artists, and intellectuals—the kind of characters often found in the works of Rohmer. A novelist has more freedom in these matters. Even if his characters are intellectually unsophisticated and imperceptive, the novelist can communicate even the most complex ideas through the use of an all-knowing narrator who "speaks" directly to the reader.

(Columbia Pictures)

Trumbo, Dudley Nichols, and Carl Foreman enjoyed tremendous prestige because their scripts were filled with "fine speeches" dealing with Justice, Brotherhood, and Democracy. Today these purple patches of dialogue seem clumsy, self-consciously school-marmish, and ultimately dishonest, for often even rough, unlettered characters would burst forth with eloquent speeches that were totally out of character. Not that these themes aren't important, but to be effective artistically, ideas must be dramatized with tact and honesty, not simply parcelled out to the characters like high-sounding speeches on a patriotic holiday. Generally speaking, only students, artists, and intellectuals discuss ideas and abstractions without a sense of self-consciousness. Perhaps this is why the films of Eric Rohmer—like *Claire's Knee* and *My Night at Maud's*—are so convincing: the main characters are intellectuals who prefer discussing ideas to other topics (8-6). In order to be convincing, then, eloquent language must be dramatically probable: we must believe that the eloquence belongs to the *character,* and is not merely the writer's "message" dressed up as dialogue.

Even great directors like Bergman and Ford have been hoodwinked by "fine writing"—sometimes even by their own. For example, a good many of Ford's movies are pretentious and earnestly "literary" in the worst sense of that term. Many of the scripts to these films—*The Informer, Mary of Scotland, The Plough and the Stars, The Fugitive*—were adapted by that incorrigible preacher, Dudley Nichols, from well-known literary works. But Ford is at his best with laconic, even inarticulate characters. Indeed, the scripts to his greatest films—especially his westerns—are lean, spare, and genuinely poetic precisely because the writing is so understated. Frank S. Nugent wrote many of these movies: *Fort Apache, She Wore a Yellow Ribbon, Wagon Master, The Quiet Man,* and *The Searchers,* for example.

Ultimately, however, generalizations about what constitutes good screen-writing are very difficult to make. It all depends on how it's done. In Penn's *Little Big Man,* for example, the protagonist's Indian grandfather (Chief Dan George) discusses abstract ideas and moral issues with complete believ-ability. Indeed, much of the charm and humor of his speeches results from the tension between the sophistication of his ideas and the naive racism of most viewers, who expect Indians to grunt in monosyllables. Calder Willing-ham's script (based on the novel by Thomas Berger) avoids sentimental clichés. Just as the Indian chief seems to be slipping into a Noble Savage stereotype, for example, the writing subtly and humorously undercuts the potential bathos. In a scene late in the movie, the elderly chief climbs a high hill where he plans to die. He performs several solemn death rituals,

8-7. Crime and Punishment.
Directed by Josef von Sternberg, screenplay by S. K. Lauren and Joseph Anthony, after the novel by Fyodor Dostoyevsky.
Adapting a distinguished literary work is usually more difficult than adapting a second-rate book, for literary masterpieces are densely saturated with information, and the filmmaker is often hard-pressed to find cinematic equivalents without distorting the nature of the original material. Although von Sternberg's film adaptation of *Crime and Punishment* contains some excellent scenes, the work as a whole is cinematically inferior to his greatest movies, which were based on relatively undistinguished literary sources, or featured original screenplays.

then lies down on the ground, while his sorrowing grandson (Dustin Hoffman) watches helplessly. Inexplicably, the chief doesn't die. Shrugging philosophically, he rises and remarks to his grandson, "Sometimes the magic works, sometimes it doesn't." Undaunted, the chief returns with his grandson to the Indian village in the valley, to the land of the living.

Despite the enormous importance that the script can play in a sound film, some directors scoff at the notion that a writer can ever be the dominant artist in the cinema. When asked what value he placed on his scripts, for example, Josef von Sternberg replied that the narrative or story elements of his works were of "no importance whatsoever" to him (8-7). Antonioni once remarked that *Crime and Punishment* was a rather ordinary story—the genius of the novel lies in *how* it's told, not in the subject matter *per se*. Certainly the large number of excellent movies based on routine, or even mediocre scripts seems to bear out such anti-literary views.

Movie scripts seldom make for interesting reading precisely because they are mere blueprints of the finished product. Unlike a play script, which usually can be read with pleasure, too much is missing in a screenplay. Even highly detailed scripts seldom offer us a sense of a film's **mise-en-scène,** one of the principal methods of expression at the director's disposal (8-8). With characteristic wit, Andrew Sarris has pointed out how the director's choice of shot—*how* the action is photographed—is the crucial element in most films, not merely the action *as* action:

> The choice between a close-up and a long-shot, for example, may quite often transcend the plot. If the story of Little Red Riding Hood is told with the Wolf in close-up and Little Red Riding Hood in long shot, the director is concerned primarily with the emotional problems of a wolf with a compulsion to eat little girls. If Little Red Riding Hood is in close-up and the Wolf in long shot, the emphasis is shifted to the emotional problems of vestigial virginity in a wicked world. Thus, two different stories are being told with the same basic anecdotal material. What is at stake in the two versions of Little Red Riding Hood are two contrasting directorial attitudes toward life. One director identifies more with the Wolf—the male, the compulsive, the corrupted, even evil itself. The second director identifies with the little girl—the innocence, the illusion, the ideal and hope of the race. Needless to say, few critics bother to make any distinction, proving perhaps that direction as creation is still only dimly understood.

Sarris' observations reinforce the thesis of this book: that subject matter alone can never be a reliable index of quality in a film, for the artist must translate his subject into the *forms* of his medium before its true content can be fully experienced and appraised. In these terms, then, the screenwriter generally provides the subject matter of a film, but the director creates its true content.

THE SCRIPT

There are a few published screenplays which can provide the reader with a certain amount of pleasure, though seldom as much as the finished film itself. Ernest Lehman's script for Hitchcock's *North by Northwest* is such

(a)

8-8a. The Scarlet Letter.
Directed by Victor Seastrom, based on the novel by Nathaniel Hawthorne.
8-8b. Gulliver's Travels.
By Max Fleischer, based on the tale by Jonathan Swift.
8-8c. The Conformist.
Directed by Bernardo Bertolucci, based on a novel by Alberto Moravia.
Although lovers of literature are often quick to point out the shortcomings of film adaptations, seldom do these critics notice the advantages of the adapting medium. In general, novels can easily explore internal realities—that is, what a character is thinking or feeling. Movies tend to be better at presenting external realities—what a character is doing and how actions seem to affect others (a). In literature, fantastic elements have to be imagined, but because the cinema is virtually unlimited in its pictorial possibilities, fantasy materials can be presented concretely (b). Because novelists must communicate through an ordered *sequence* of individual words, simultaneity is difficult to convey in literature. In the cinema, on the other hand, we are presented with a great deal of information simultaneously: we can absorb many actions and reactions at the same time (c).

(b)

(c)

a work. Lehman has the novelist's gift for suggesting interior states by describing exterior events, and the dramatist's fluency with crisp, understated dialogue. Indeed, the script to *North by Northwest*—like most published screenplays—is essentially a blending of the techniques of the novelist and the playwright. That is, it provides us with an essentially literary experience of the subject matter. Screenplays of this sort are intended to give a reader a reasonably coherent *general* description of what the characters do and say. Seldom do they contain much technical information, such as the **découpage** of shots, their length, or the detailed contents of the mise-en-scène. Lehman's script, then, provides us with the **continuity** of *actions* rather than the continuity of shots, which is what a shooting script contains, as we shall see when we examine Hitchcock's *découpage* of Lehman's literary text.

Like many of Hitchcock's films, *North by Northwest* revolves around the idea of mistaken identity: an innocent man is accused of and persecuted for a crime he didn't commit. The protagonist, Roger Thornhill (Cary Grant) is a rather glib but charming advertising executive who's accidentally mistaken for a government agent named Kaplan. Thornhill is abducted by enemy agents, almost murdered by them, then fatefully implicated in the murder of a U. N. diplomat. Pursued by both the police and the enemy agents, Thornhill flees to Chicago in desperation, hoping to discover the real Kaplan who presumably will establish Thornhill's innocence. In Chicago he is told that Kaplan will meet him alone at a designated location. The following excerpt from Lehman's script relates what then takes place:

Helicopter Shot—Exterior, Highway 41—Afternoon

We START CLOSE on a Greyhound bus, SHOOTING DOWN on it and TRAVELING ALONG with it as it speeds in an easterly direction at seventy m.p.h. Gradually, CAMERA DRAWS AWAY from the bus, going higher but never losing sight of the vehicle, which recedes into the distance below and becomes a toylike object on an endless ribbon of deserted highway that stretches across miles of flat prairie. Now the bus is slowing down. It is nearing a junction where a small dirt road coming from nowhere crosses the highway and continues on to nowhere. The bus stops. A man gets out. It is THORNHILL. But to us he is only a tiny figure. The bus starts away, moves on out of sight. And now THORNHILL stands alone beside the road—a tiny figure in the middle of nowhere.

On the Ground—with Thornhill—(Master Scene)

He glances about, studying his surroundings. The terrain is flat and treeless, even more desolate from this vantage point than it seemed from the air. Here and there patches of low-growing farm crops add some contour to the land. A hot sun beats down. UTTER SILENCE hangs heavily in the air. THORNHILL glances at his wristwatch. It is three twenty-five.

In the distance, the FAINT HUM of a MOTOR VEHICLE is HEARD. THORNHILL looks off to the west. The HUM GROWS LOUDER as the car draws nearer. THORNHILL steps closer to the edge of the highway. A black sedan looms up, traveling at high speed. For a moment we are not sure it is not hurtling right at THORNHILL. And then it ZOOMS past him, recedes into the distance, becoming a FAINT HUM, a tiny speck, and then SILENCE again.

THORNHILL takes out a handkerchief, mops his face. He is beginning to sweat now. It could be from nervousness, as well as the heat. Another FAINT HUM, coming from the east, GROWING LOUDER as he glances off and sees another distant speck becoming a speeding car, this one a closed convertible. Again, anticipation on THORNHILL's face. Again, the vague uneasiness of indefinable danger approaching at high speed. And again, ZOOM—a cloud of dust—a car receding into the distance—a FAINT HUM—and SILENCE.

His lips tighten. He glances at his watch again. He steps out into the middle of the highway, looks first in one direction, then the other. Nothing in sight. He loosens his tie, opens his shirt collar, looks up at the sun. Behind him, in the distance, another vehicle is HEARD approaching. He turns, looks off to the west. This one is a huge transcontinental moving van, ROARING TOWARD HIM at high speed. With quick apprehension he moves off the highway to the dusty side of the road as the van thunders past and disappears. Its FADING SOUND is replaced with a NEW SOUND, the CHUGGING of an OLD FLIVVER.

THORNHILL looks off in the direction of the approaching SOUND, sees a flivver nearing the highway from the intersecting dirt road. When the car reaches the highway, it comes to a stop. A middle-aged woman is behind the wheel. Her passenger is a nondescript MAN of about fifty. He could certainly be a farmer. He gets out of the car. It makes a U-turn and drives off in the direction from which it came. THORNHILL watches the MAN and takes up a position across the highway from him. The MAN glances at THORNHILL without visible interest, then looks off up the highway toward the east as though waiting for something to come along.

THORNHILL stares at the MAN, wondering if this is George Kaplan.

The MAN looks idly across the highway at THORNHILL, his face expressionless.

THORNHILL wipes his face with his handkerchief, never taking his eyes off the MAN across the highway. The FAINT SOUND of an APPROACHING PLANE has gradually come up over the scene. As the SOUND GROWS LOUDER, THORNHILL looks up to his left and sees a low-flying biplane approach from the northwest. He watches it with mounting interest as it heads straight for the spot where he and the stranger face each other across the highway. Suddenly it is upon them, only a hundred feet above the ground, and then, like a giant bird, as THORNHILL turns with the plane's passage, it flies over them and continues on. THORNHILL stares after the plane, his back to the highway. When the plane has gone several hundred yards beyond the highway, it loses altitude, levels off only a few feet above the ground and begins to fly back and forth in straight lines parallel to the highway, letting loose a trail of powered dust from beneath its fuselage as it goes. Any farmer would recognize the operation as simple crop-dusting.

THORNHILL looks across the highway, sees that the stranger is watching the plane with idle interest. THORNHILL's lips set with determination. He crosses over and goes up to the MAN.

THORNHILL: Hot day.

MAN: Seen worse.

THORNHILL: Are you . . . uh . . . by any chance supposed to be meeting someone here?

MAN (still watching the plane): Waitin' for the bus. Due any minute.

THORNHILL: Oh . . .

MAN (idly): Some of them crop-duster pilots get rich, if they live long enough . . .

THORNHILL: Then your name isn't . . . Kaplan.

MAN (glances at him): Can't say it is, 'cause it ain't. (He looks off up the highway) Well—here she comes, right on time.

THORNHILL looks off to the east, sees a Greyhound bus approaching. The MAN peers off at the plane again, and frowns.

MAN: That's funny.

THORNHILL: What?

MAN: That plane's dustin' crops where there ain't no crops.

THORNHILL looks across at the droning plane with growing suspicion as the stranger steps out onto the highway and flags the bus to a stop. THORNHILL turns toward the stranger as though to say something to him. But it is too late. The man has boarded the bus, its doors are closing, and it is pulling away. THORNHILL is alone again.

Almost immediately, he HEARS the PLANE ENGINE BEING GUNNED TO A HIGHER SPEED. He glances off sharply, sees the plane veering off its parallel course and heading toward him. He stands there wide-eyed, rooted to the spot. The plane roars on, a few feet off the ground. There are two men in the twin cockpits, goggled, unrecognizable, menacing. He yells out to them, but his voice is lost in the NOISE of the PLANE. In a moment it will be upon him and decapitate him. Desperately he drops to the ground and presses himself flat as the plane zooms over him with a great noise, almost combing his hair with a landing wheel.

THORNHILL scrambles to his feet, sees the plane banking and turning. He looks about wildly, sees a telephone pole and dashes for it as the plane comes at him again. He ducks behind the pole. The plane heads straight for him, veers to the right at the last moment. We HEAR two sharp CRACKS of GUNFIRE mixed with the SOUND of the ENGINE, as two bullets slam into the pole just above THORNHILL's head.

THORNHILL reacts to this new peril, sees the plane banking for another run at him. A car is speeding along the highway from the west. THORNHILL dashes out onto the road, tries to flag the car down but the driver ignores him and races by, leaving him exposed and vulnerable as the plane roars in on him. He dives into a ditch and rolls away as another series of SHOTS are HEARD and bullets rake the ground that he has just occupied.

He gets to his feet, looks about, sees a cornfield about fifty yards from the highway, glances up at the plane making its turn, and decides to make a dash for the cover of the tall-growing corn.

SHOOTING DOWN FROM A HELICOPTER about one hundred feet above the ground, we SEE THORNHILL running toward the cornfield and the plane in pursuit.

SHOOTING FROM WITHIN THE CORNFIELD, WE SEE THORNHILL come crashing in, scuttling to the right and lying flat and motionless as WE HEAR THE PLANE ZOOM OVER HIM WITH A BURST OF GUNFIRE and bullets rip into the corn, but at a safe distance from THORNHILL. He raises his head cautiously, gasping for breath, as he HEARS THE PLANE MOVE OFF AND INTO ITS TURN.

SHOOTING DOWN FROM THE HELICOPTER, we SEE the plane leveling off and starting a run over the cornfield, which betrays no sign of the hidden THORNHILL. Skimming over the top of the cornstalks, the plane gives forth no burst of gunfire now. Instead, it lets loose thick clouds of poisonous dust which settle down into the corn.

WITHIN THE CORNFIELD, THORNHILL, still lying flat, begins to gasp and choke as the poisonous dust envelops him. Tears stream from his eyes but he does not dare move as he HEARS THE PLANE COMING OVER THE FIELD AGAIN. When the plane zooms by and another cloud of dust hits him, he jumps to his feet and crashes out into the open, half blinded and gasping for breath. Far off down the highway to the right, he SEES a huge Diesel gasoline-tanker approaching. He starts running toward the highway to intercept it.

SHOOTING FROM THE HELICOPTER, WE SEE THORNHILL dashing for the highway, the plane leveling off for another run at him, and the Diesel tanker speeding closer.

SHOOTING ACROSS THE HIGHWAY, WE SEE THORNHILL running and stumbling TOWARD CAMERA, the plane closing in between him, and the Diesel tanker approaching from the left. He dashes out into the middle of the highway and waves his arms wildly.

The Diesel tanker THUNDERS down the highway toward THORNHILL, KLAXON BLASTING impatiently.

The plane speeds relentlessly toward THORNHILL from the field bordering the highway.

THORNHILL stands alone and helpless in the middle of the highway, waving his arms. The plane draws closer. The tanker is almost upon him. It isn't going to stop. He can HEAR THE KLAXON BLASTING him out of the way. There is nothing he can do. The plane has caught up with him. The tanker won't stop. It's GOT to stop. He hurls himself to the pavement directly in its path. There is a SCREAM OF BRAKES and SKIDDING TIRES, THE ROAR OF THE PLANE ENGINE and then a tremendous BOOM as the Diesel truck grinds to a stop inches from Thornhill's body just as the plane, hopelessly committed and caught unprepared by the sudden stop, slams into the traveling gasoline tanker and plane and gasoline explode into a great sheet of flame.

In the next few moments, all is confusion. THORNHILL, unhurt, rolls out from under the wheels of the Diesel truck. The drivers clamber out of the front seat and drop to the highway. Black clouds of smoke billow up from the funeral pyre of the plane and its cremated occupants. We recognize the flaming body of one of the men in the plane. It is LIGHT, one of THORNHILL's original abductors. An elderly open pick-up truck with a second-hand refrigerator standing in it, which has been approaching from the east, pulls up at the side of the road. Its driver, a FARMER, jumps out and hurries toward the wreckage.

FARMER: What happened? What happened?

The Diesel truck drivers are too dazed to answer. Flames and smoke drive them all back. THORNHILL, unnoticed, heads toward the unoccupied pick-up truck. Another car comes up from the west, stops, and its driver runs toward the other men. They stare, transfixed, at the holocaust. Suddenly, from behind them, they HEAR the PICK-UP TRUCK'S MOTOR STARTING. The FARMER who owns the truck turns, and is startled to see his truck being driven away by an utter stranger.

FARMER: Hey!

He runs after the truck. But the stranger—who is THORNHILL—steps harder on the accelerator and speeds off in the direction of Chicago.

Hitchcock's working methods are legendary—and virtually unique. Unlike most directors, he has almost every detail planned in advance in his shooting script. Nothing is left to chance, and he disdains the very notion of improvising on the set. In most cases, he works closely with his writers, offering them suggestions for locations, character quirks, and thematic de-

(Universal Pictures)

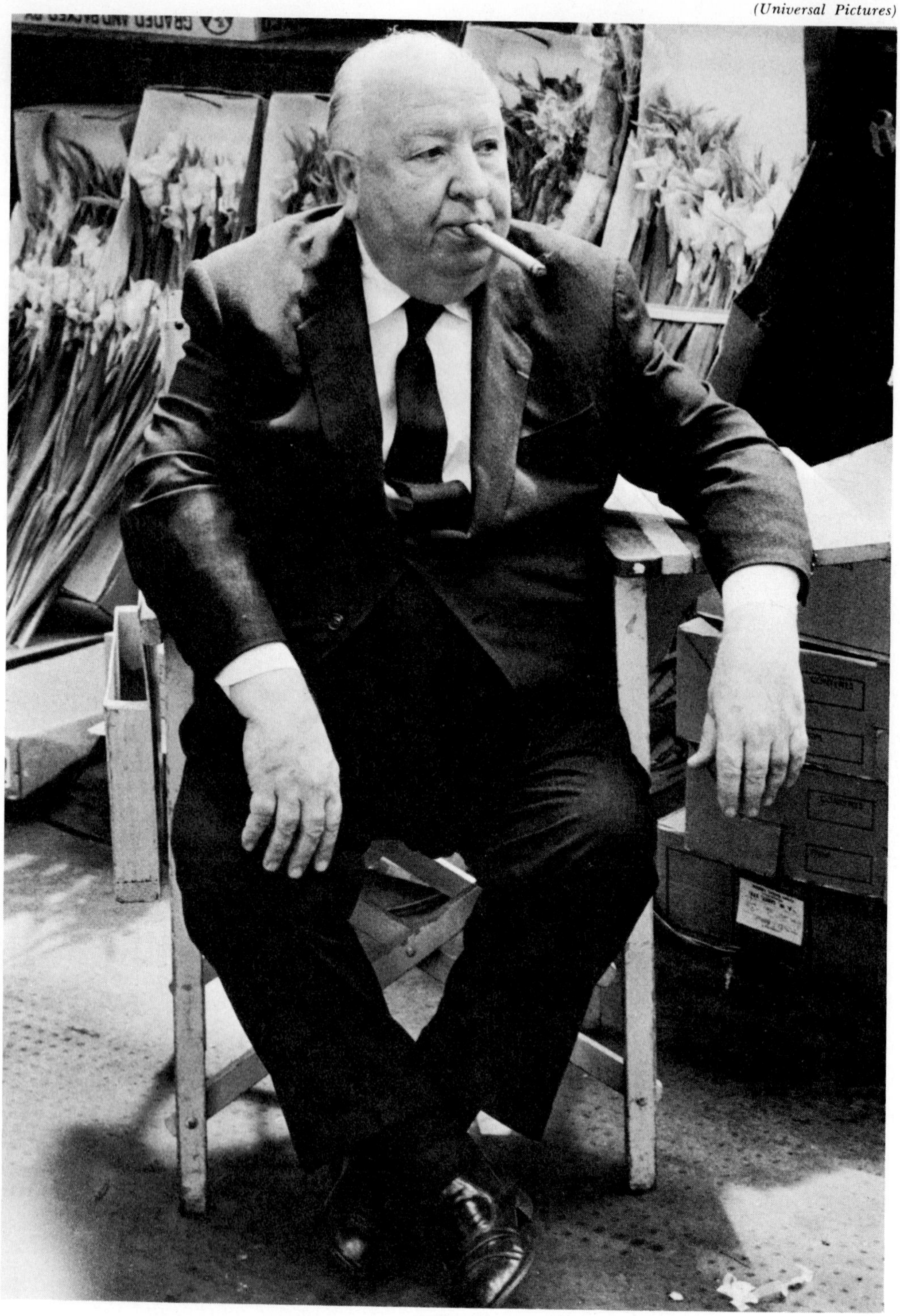

8-9. Alfred Hitchcock "directing" on the set of *Frenzy*.

According to Hitchcock, his shooting scripts are so precise and detailed, the actual filming is merely a "technicality." After observing the shooting of several scenes from a Hitchcock movie, the critic André Bazin marveled: "I had been watching for a good hour, during which time Hitchcock did not have to intervene more than twice; settled in his armchair, he gave the impression of being prodigiously bored and of musing about something completely different."

tails. With mock fiendishness, he enjoys recounting how he will suggest to his writer: "Wouldn't it be fun to kill him this way?" After they finish the script, Hitchcock then begins his shooting script, which for him is the most exciting part of making movies. Indeed, he claims that the actual shooting is a tedious process for him, since all the creative work has already been completed on paper. Included in most of his shooting scripts are the *découpage* of shots, their length, and individual sketches for each. He also includes the sound elements and any technical data such as special **lenses** or **filters** that might be required (8-9). André Bazin once noted that when he was allowed to watch a scene from *To Catch a Thief* being filmed, Hitchcock himself was seated off to the side, giving "the impression of being prodigeously bored." A far cry indeed from the semi-organized chaos that exists on most movie sets.

The following excerpt is not Hitchcock's shooting script of Lehman's text but perhaps the next best thing: a reconstruction of the sequence taken directly from the film by Albert J. LaValley, which appears in his volume, *Focus on Hitchcock*. Though certain elements (textures, rhythms, movements, acting nuances, etc.) in this reconstruction are necessarily modified, it nonetheless offers some useful insights into the difference between the film writer's function and the director's role. Each number represents a separate shot; drawings identified with a letter represent a continuation of the previous shot, though with enough new action to warrant an additional sketch. The numbers in parentheses indicate the approximate length of the shots in seconds. The following abbreviations are used: E.L.S., **extreme long shot**; L.S., **long shot**; M.S., **medium shot**; C.U., **close-up**; P.O.V., a shot taken from Thornhill's **point-of-view.**

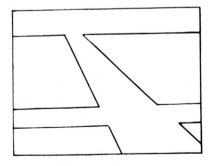

1. E.L.S., aerial. Dissolve to empty road across fields where rendezvous with KAPLAN is to take place. We see and hear bus arriving, door opening.

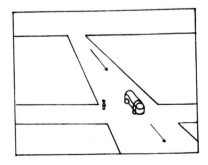

1b. THORNHILL emerges, bus leaves. He is alone. (52)

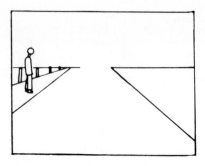

2. L.S., low angle. THORNHILL at roadside, waiting. (5)

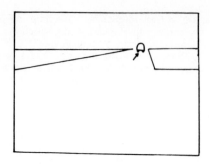

3. E.L.S., P.O.V. Looking down main road: bus going away in distance. (4)

4. M.S. THORNHILL near sign, turns left to right, looking for someone. (3 2/3)

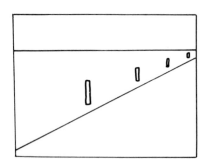

5. L.S., P.O.V. View across road, empty fields with posts. (4)

6. M.S. THORNHILL by sign, turns from right to left, looking. (3)

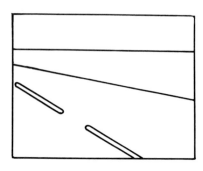

7. L.S., P.O.V. Across fields. (4)

8. M.S. THORNHILL by sign again, waiting, turns head and looks behind him. (3)

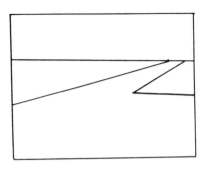

9. E.L.S., P.O.V. The field behind him, road. (4)

10. M.S. THORNHILL by sign, waiting, turning forward—long waiting feeling. (6 1/2)

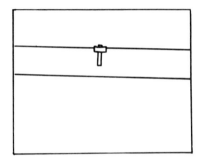

11. E.L.S. Empty landscape across road, signs, post. (3)

12. M.S. THORNHILL by sign. Turns right. (2)

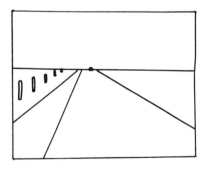

13. E.L.S. Empty main road, car coming in distance. (4)

14. M.S. THORNHILL by sign, looking at car approaching. (3/4)

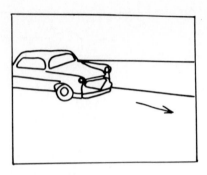

15. L.S. Car goes by fast, whizzing sound, camera pans slightly to right. (1 3/4)

16. M.S. THORNHILL by sign, moves back to left, follows car with his eyes. (2)

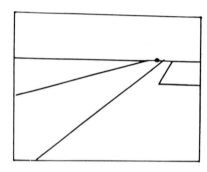

17. E.L.S., P.O.V. Road, car going, sound recedes. (4)

18. M.S. THORNHILL by sign, hands in pockets, turns from left to right. (3)

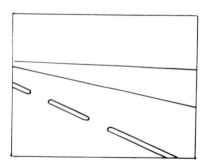

19. L.S., P.O.V. Field across road again. (3)

20. M.S. THORNHILL by sign, same pose, still looking, turns from right to left. (2 3/4)

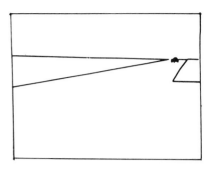

21. E.L.S. Road, car in distance, sounds begin. (3 1/2)

22. M.S. THORNHILL by sign, looking at car, no movement. (2 1/2)

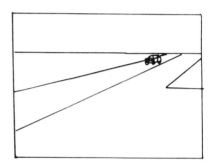

23. E.L.S. Car coming closer, sound increasing. (3 3/4)

24. M.S. THORNHILL by sign, looking at car coming. (3)

25. L.S. Car closer, rushes past, camera pans a bit to follow it. (3)

26. M.S. THORNHILL by sign, takes hands from pockets, turns left to right to follow car. (3)

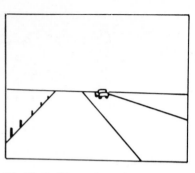

27. E.L.S. View of road, car in distance receding. (3 3/4)

28. M.S. THORNHILL by sign, waiting again. (2 1/4)

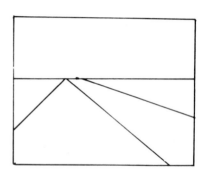

29. E.L.S. Road, truck coming; we hear its sound. (4)

30. M.S. THORNHILL by sign, sound of truck increasing. (3)

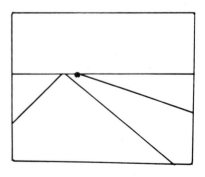

31. E.L.S. Truck coming down road, sound still increasing. (3 3/4)

32. M.S. THORNHILL by sign (2 1/4)

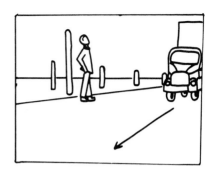

33. L.S. Truck whizzes by.

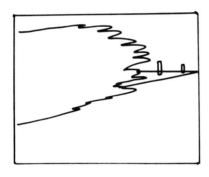

33b. Kicking up dust, obscuring THORNHILL, camera pans slightly left, and he emerges out of the dust gradually. (4)

34. M.S. THORNHILL wiping dust from his eyes, turns to right. (7)

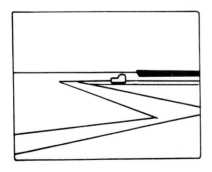

35. E.L.S. Fields across way, car coming out behind corn. (5)

36. M.S. THORNHILL by sign puzzled by car. (5)

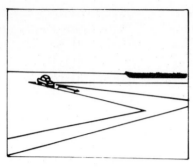

37. E.L.S. Car making turn on dirt road. (4)

38. M.S. THORNHILL awaiting car. (3 2/3)

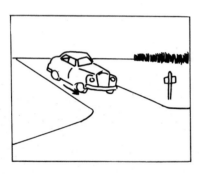

39. L.S. Car nearing main road, camera pans following it to right, a sign there. (4)

40. M.S. THORNHILL waiting to see what will happen. (3 1/3)

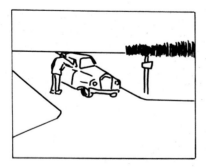

41. L.S. MAN getting out of car, talking to driver, we hear the door of the car slam. (3 1/2)

42. M.S. THORNHILL reacting, wondering, getting ready to meet this man. (2)

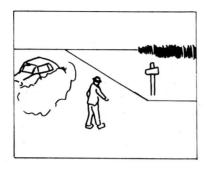

43. L.S. Sound of car turning around, dust raised, car turns around and the MAN walks towards main road opposite THORNHILL, looking back at the car leaving. (1 4/5)

44. M.S. THORNHILL, closer than previous shots, eyeing the man. (1 1/2)

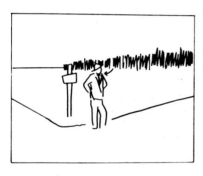

45. L.S. Camera pans right slightly; the MAN goes over by the sign and turns his head to look up the road and over at THORNHILL. (4 1/3)

46. M.S. Same as 44. THORNHILL's reaction, his head tilts and he looks across the road. (3 4/5)

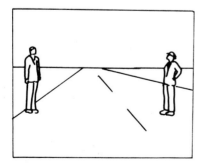

47. L.S. low angle. Road in the middle stretching to infinity, two men oddly stationed on either side of road, the other MAN looking up the road a bit. (7)

48. M.S. THORNHILL's reaction, takes hands out of pockets, opens coat, puts hands on hips, contemplates situation. (6 1/3)

49. L.S. Same as 45, only the MAN turns his head looking the other way. (3 1/2)

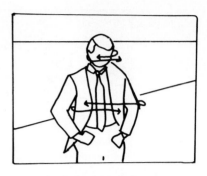

50. M.S. Same as 48, but THORN-HILL has both hands on hips now, his head looking across. His head turns up road to see if anyone is coming; he looks back, one hand on hip, other at side, at MAN across way.

50b. Starts walking across road part way. (10)

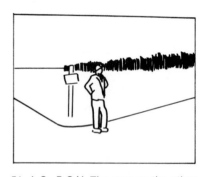

51. L.S., P.O.V. The man on the other side of road, as THORNHILL crosses, camera tracks across road part way, acting as his eyes. (2 2/3)

52. M.S. THORNHILL walks across road; synchronous tracking camera continuing movement begun in 50b.

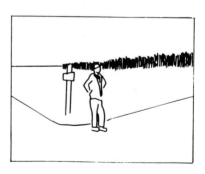

53. L.S., P.O.V. Same as 49, 51 of other MAN across road, but camera tracks in on him, acting as THORN-HILL's eyes, continues movement begun in 50b.

54. M.S. THORNHILL on other side of road, but camera tracks to continue movement of 50, 52.

54b. Camera continues tracking to other side of road until other man comes into view and THORNHILL begins to talk to him. THORNHILL's hands are a bit nervous in movement; he plays with his little finger; the other man has hands in pockets.

> THORNHILL (after a long wait): Hi! (a long pause follows) Hot day. (Another pause.)
> MAN: Seen worse.
> THORNHILL (after a long pause): Are you supposed to be meeting someone here?
> MAN: Waitin' for the bus. Due any minute.
> THORNHILL: Oh. (another pause)
> MAN: Some of them crop duster pilots get rich if they live long enough.
> THORNHILL: Yeah! (very softly) (21)

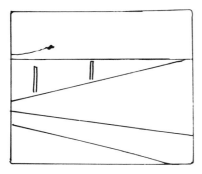

55. E.L.S. Fields with plane at great distance in far left of frame coming right. (2 2/3)

56. M.S. Reaction shot of both looking at plane.

> THORNHILL: Then . . . a . . . (pause) then your name isn't Kaplan?
> MAN: Can't say that it is 'cause it ain't. (pause) Here she comes (as he looks down the road). (11)

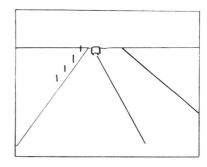

57. E.L.S. Bus coming down the road.

> MAN: (voice off) . . . right on time. (2 2/3)

58. M.S. Same as 56, two talking then looking again across road at crop duster.

    MAN: That's funny.
    THORNHILL: (very softly) What?
    MAN: That plane's dustin' crops where there ain't no crops.
    THORNHILL turns to look. (8)

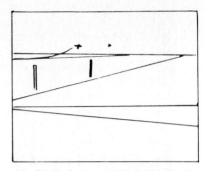

59. E.L.S. Same as 55, field with the plane over it. (4)

60. M.S. Two men off center looking at plane. THORNHILL's hands continue nervous movements; the other's are in his pockets as before. Sound of approaching bus. (3 1/3)

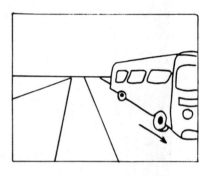

61. L.S. Bus arriving and coming quite close to camera. (1 4/5)

62. M.S. MAN gets on as door of bus opens and seems to shut THORN-HILL out. The bus leaves.

62b. THORNHILL puts hands on hips and looks across, then looks at his watch. For a second he is alone in the frame as the bus goes out of sight. (2 1/3)

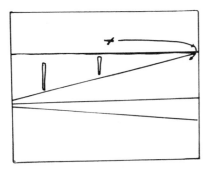

63. E.L.S., P.O.V. Same as 59, what THORNHILL sees across the road; the plane goes to end of frame and turns right, toward him. (5 1/5)

64. M.S. THORNHILL in front of road by sign, puzzled and rather innocent looking; sound of plane approaching. (2 1/3)

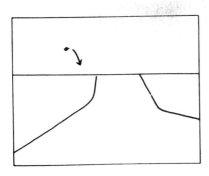

65. E.L.S. Plane coming toward camera, still far, but closer and with sound increasing. (3 4/5)

66. M.S. Same as 64. THORNHILL reacting. (2 1/4)

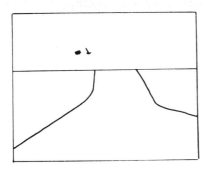

67. E.L.S. Same as 65 but plane closer and louder. (2 1/8)

68. M.S. Closer shot of THORNHILL, still puzzled and confused as plane comes at him. (4 1/2)

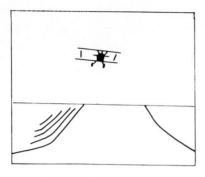

69. L.S. Plane clearly coming at him, filling mid-frame, very loud. (1 1/3)

70. M.S. THORNHILL drops, a short held shot, he falls out of frame at bottom. (2/3)

71. L.S. THORNHILL falling on ground, both arms on ground, plane behind him, he in a hole. (3 1/2)

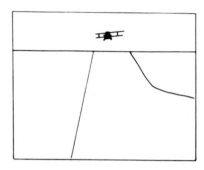

72. L.S. Plane going away from him. (3)

73. L.S. THORNHILL on ground getting up, kneeling on left knee. (3 1/2)

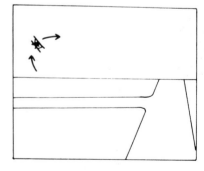

74. E.L.S. Plane going farther away and sound receding. (2 4/5)

75. L.S. THORNHILL getting up.
(2 1/5)

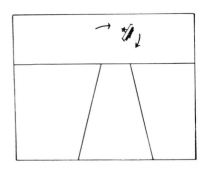

76. E.L.S. Plane in distance banking. (2 1/3)

77. M.S. THORNHILL up and about
to run. (2 1/3)

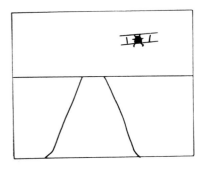

78. L.S. Plane approaching again,
sound getting louder. (2)

79. M.S. THORNHILL runs and falls
in ditch. (1 1/2)

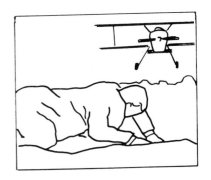

80. L.S. THORNHILL in ditch, sound
of plane and bullets sprayed on him,
smoke; he turns head to left and
faces camera to watch when plane is
gone. (5 1/3)

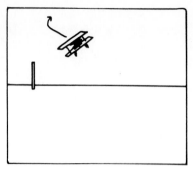

81. L.S. Plane getting ready again, banking. (5 1/5)

82. M.S. THORNHILL in ditch coming up, gets up on left arm, sound of receding plane. (2 1/2)

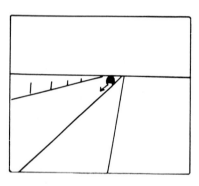

83. E.L.S., P.O.V. The road as THORNHILL sees it, car in distance. (2 1/2)

84. M.S. Same as 82, THORNHILL rising from ditch, receding plane sound. (1 1/2)

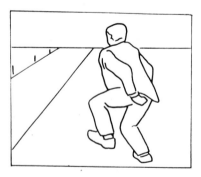

85. L.S., low angle. THORNHILL runs to road to try to stop car.

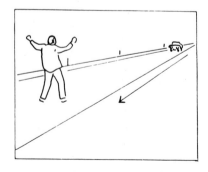

85b. He tries to flag it down. Car sounds approach and it whizzes by. (9 1/2)

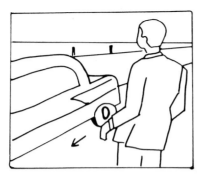

86. M.S. THORNHILL's back after turning left as the car whizzes by. (4 2/3)

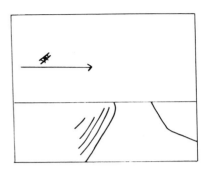

87. E.L.S. Plane in distance, sounds again. (2 1/3)

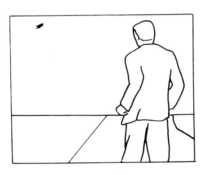

88. L.S. THORNHILL's back with plane in distance at far left coming at him.

88b. L.S. He looks at plane, turns around looking for a place to hide, looks at plane again, turns around and runs towards camera. Camera reverse tracks.

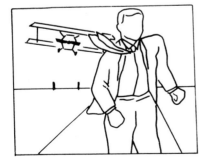

88c. THORNHILL running toward camera, camera reverse tracking. He turns around twice while running to look at plane; it goes over his head just missing him. (13 1/2)

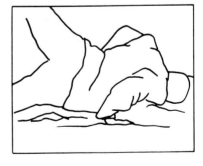

89. M.S. THORNHILL falling, side view, legs up, bullet and plane sounds. (5)

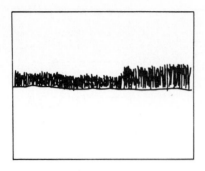

90. L.S., P.O.V. Cornfield, a place to hide. (2 1/2)

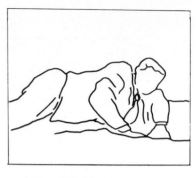

91. M.S. THORNHILL lying flat on ground, looking. (1 2/3)

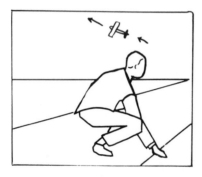

92. L.S. THORNHILL getting up, plane in distance banking again for new attack. (3)

93. M.S. THORNHILL running, turns back to look at plane, camera tracks with him as he runs to cornfield. (4 1/2)

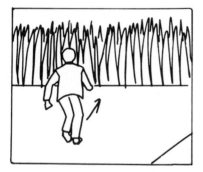

94. L.S., low angle. THORNHILL's back as he runs into cornfield; low camera angle shows lots of ground, stalks. He disappears into corn. (2 3/4)

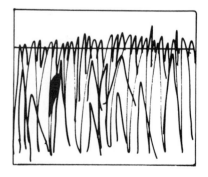

95. L.S. Picture of corn; a patch reveals where THORNHILL is hiding. The corn rustles. (2)

96. M.S. Camera follows THORNHILL down as he falls on ground inside the corn patch. He turns back to look up to see if plane is coming. A cornstalk falls; then he looks down again, up again, down again, up. (7 3/4)

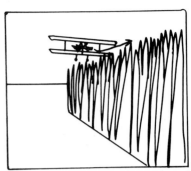

97. L.S. Plane coming along edge of cornfield and over it; it gets very loud. (4 1/2)

98. M.S. Same as 96. Corn rustles, wind from the plane blows over. THORNHILL sees he's out of danger, and smiles a bit, feeling that he's outwitted his pursuers. (15 4/5)

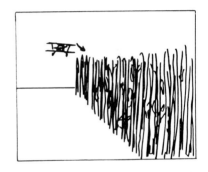

99. L.S. Plane coming in on bend, repeating pattern of 97; it gets louder. (3 1/4)

100. M.S. Same as 96, 98. THORN-HILL in corn, getting up, looking around, suddenly aware of plane in new way; he's startled that it's coming back. (4 4/5)

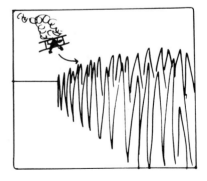

101. L.S. Plane over corn, repeating pattern of 97, only dust coming out of it; plane comes closer to camera. (7)

102. M.S. Same as 96, 98, 100; THORNHILL's reaction to dust, which fills up screen: he coughs, takes out handkerchief, camera follows him as he raises himself up and down; coughing sounds (12 1/4)

103. M.S. THORNHILL in corn, new shot; he runs towards camera trying to get out of corn; rustling corn, he looks out of field. (4 1/2)

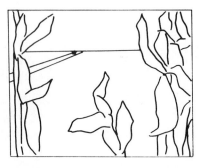

104. E.L.S., P.O.V. Out of cornfield, view of road as framed by corn; tiny speck on road in distance is truck. (2 3/4)

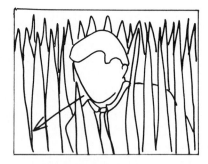

105. M.S. THORNHILL in corn, but he is standing; he moves forward, looks back up for plane, makes dash for the truck coming down road; he goes out of frame for moment at the end. (3 1/2)

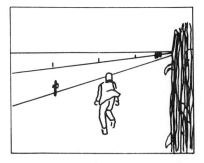

106. L.S. THORNHILL running toward truck, gets to road from corn; truck farther along the road, sounds of truck (4)

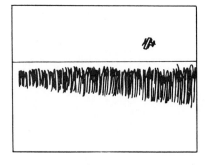

107. E.L.S. Plane banking over corn, getting ready to turn toward him; faint plane sounds; horn of truck. (2)

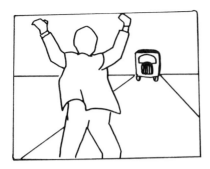

108. L.S., low angle. THORNHILL in road, truck coming, he waves at it. (1 2/3)

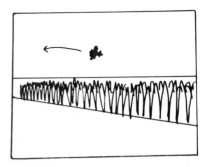

109. E.L.S. Continuation of 107, plane further left. (2)

110. M.S. THORNHILL trying to stop truck, sounds of horns, brakes. (2)

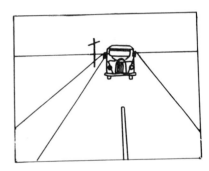

111. L.S. Truck approaching, getting bigger. (2)

112. M.S. Same as 110, but he looks at plane coming in on his left, then puts up both hands instead of one, and bites his tongue. (1 1/2)

113. L.S. Truck even closer, about fifty feet in front of camera. (1)

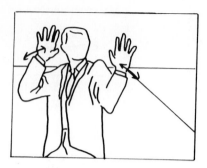

114. M.S. Same as 112, 110. THORN-HILL waving frantically now. (1)

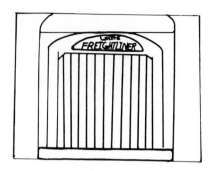

115. C.U. Grille of truck as it tries to halt; brake sounds. (1)

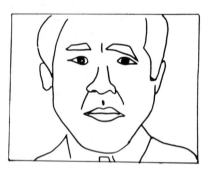

116. C.U. THORNHILL's face in anguish about to be hit.

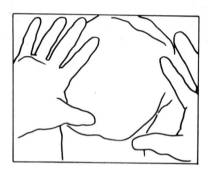

116b. His hands go up and his head goes down. (4/5)

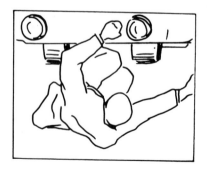

117. L.S. THORNHILL falls under the truck, front view. (1)

118. M.S. THORNHILL under the truck, side view. (2 1/2)

119. L.S., low angle. Plane comes toward truck (and camera). (1 3/4)

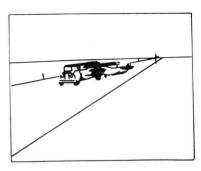

120. L.S. Plane hits truck, view from across road. (1)

121. L.S. Truck bursts into flames; another angle of truck and plane; music begins and continues to end of scene. (2 1/2)

122. L.S. Shot of truck in flames from in front, two men scramble hurriedly from cab.
DRIVER: Let's get out of here. It's going to explode. (6 1/2)

123. L.S. Backs of men running somewhat comically to cornfield. (2)

124. L.S. THORNHILL runs toward camera from explosions of oil truck behind him. Music tends to mute explosion sounds (2 3/4)

125. L.S. Reverse angle of THORN-HILL as he now backs away from explosion. A car has just pulled to side of road, followed by a pickup truck with a refrigerator, which pulls to the side in front of it. Doors open and people get out. THORNHILL goes over and talks to them. No sounds are heard (the music continues), but we see his motions of explanation. (9)

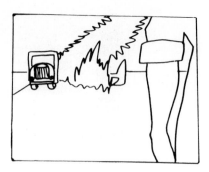

126. L.S. View of explosion in distance with close-up of farmer's arm on right. (2)

127. L.S. THORNHILL and others watch explosion. He backs away from scene to right of frame while they all move closer to the wreck as THORNHILL retreats unnoticed by them. (11)

128. L.S. Backs of others watching explosion. (6 1/3)

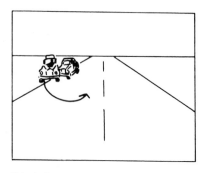

129. L.S. THORNHILL takes the pickup truck with refrigerator in back and pulls out while they are watching the explosion. (3 4/5)

130. L.S. Same as 128, but the FARMER turns, seeing his truck being taken, and shouts "Hey." (2 1/2)

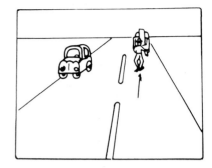

131. L.S. Chase by the FARMER, bow-legged and comic; he finally stops as the truck recedes into the distance. "Come back, come back," he is shouting. Dissolve to next sequence. (15)

Of course a shooting script is no substitute for the experience of the film itself, but this shot breakdown does help to demonstrate that even if Hitchcock had nothing to do with the subject matter (an extremely unlikely supposition, since it has all the earmarks of a classic Hitchcockian **sequence**), its effectiveness is due primarily to the director's cinematic manipulation of the materials. Hitchcock transforms Lehman's verbal description of the events into a sequence of such gripping terror that most viewers are paralyzed with fear, yet simultaneously—and paradoxically—delighted by the many unexpected touches of wit.

To encourage us to identify with Thornhill, Hitchcock often employs point-of-view shots, thus literally forcing us to see things through the protagonist's eyes. These shots are particularly effective when combined with a **tracking** camera. Hitchcock exploits the emotional effects of **proxemic** distances with great economy: there are only two close-ups in the entire sequence: the onrushing truck's grille and Thornhill's face just before he's hit by the truck. These close-ups are offered in tandem to maximize the sense of physical impact. The rhythms of the **editing** are brilliant: the earlier shots are lengthier and seem to contain "nothing"— a deliberate attempt on Hitchcock's part to induce a sense of relaxation and then boredom in the viewer. In the climax, the staccato shots machine-gun by at an explosive pace. Even with a visually uninteresting setting, Hitchcock's mise-en-scène—especially his subtle use of the frame—is exemplary. "I do not follow the geography of a set," he has explained, "I follow the geography of the screen."

MOTIFS, SYMBOLS, METAPHORS, AND ALLUSIONS

In his 1948 essay, *"La Caméra-Stylo,"* Alexandre Astruc observed that one of the traditional problems of film had been its difficulty in expressing ideas. The invention of sound, of course, was an enormous advantage to

(Paramount Pictures)

8-10. Psycho.
Directed by Alfred Hitchcock.
Motifs are generally so unobtrusive in a film that they can pass unnoticed even after repeated viewings. In *Psycho,* for example, Hitchcock employed the "doubles" motif with great density. The two pairs of leading actors (Janet Leigh/Vera Miles and Anthony Perkins/John Gavin) were cast according to physical resemblances, which suggest psychological similarities. Many of the scenes feature mirrors, which reinforce the doubles motif, as well as suggesting themes of reality versus illusion, truth versus deception, and conscious behavior versus irrational impulse.

the filmmaker, for with spoken language, he could express virtually any kind of abstract thought. But film directors also wanted to explore the possibilities of the image as a conveyor of abstract ideas. Indeed, even before the sound era, filmmakers had devised a number of nonverbal figurative techniques.

A figurative technique can be defined as an artistic device in which an object suggests abstract ideas and emotions over and beyond what the object literally means. There are a number of these techniques in both literature and cinema, but perhaps the most common are **motifs, symbols,** and **metaphors.** In actual practice, there's a considerable amount of overlapping among these terms. All of these are "symbolic" devices since they impute a significance to an object or event beyond its limited denotative meaning, but perhaps the most pragmatic method of differentiating among these techniques is to describe the degree of obtrusiveness of each of them.

A motif is the least obtrusive extreme, a metaphor is the most conspicuous, and a symbol is a more general term which falls somewhere in between—although each category overlaps somewhat with its neighbor.

Motifs are so totally integrated within the realistic texture of a film that we can almost refer to them as "submerged" or "invisible" symbols. A motif is any device that's systematically repeated in a movie yet doesn't call attention to itself. Even after repeated viewings, a motif is not always apparent, for its symbolic significance is never permitted to emerge or "detach" itself from its literalness (8-10). The circular shapes of *The Seven Samurai* are a good instance of a visual motif, but motifs can also be musical, kinetic (like the travelling shots in *8½*), verbal (like the term "Rosebud" in *Citizen Kane*) or aural (like the pounding of the waves in *L'Avventura*).

A symbol doesn't have to be repeated to suggest ideas, for its significance is usually clear from its specific dramatic context. Like motifs, symbols can be palpable objects, but there is *additional* meaning implied. Furthermore, the symbolic meanings of these objects can shift with the dramatic context. A good example of the shifting implications of a symbol can be seen in the uncut version of Kurosawa's *The Seven Samurai*. In this movie, a young samurai and a peasant girl are attracted to each other, but their class differences present insurmountable barriers. In a scene that takes place late at night, the two accidentally meet. Kurosawa emphasizes their separation by keeping them in separate frames, a raging outdoor fire acting as a kind of barrier (8-11a, b). But their attraction is too strong, and they then appear in the same shot, the fire between them now suggesting the only obstacle, yet paradoxically, also suggesting the sexual passion they both feel (8-11c). They draw towards each other, and the fire is now to one side, its sexual symbolism dominating (8-11d). They go inside a hut, and the light from the fire outside emphasizes the eroticism of the scene (8-11e). As they begin to make love in a dark corner of the hut, the shadows cast by the fire's light on the reeds of the hut seem to streak across their bodies (8-11f). Suddenly, the girl's father discovers the lovers, and now the billowing flames of the fire suggest his moral outrage (8-11g). Indeed, he is so incensed that he must be restrained by the samurai chief, their images

8-11a–j. *The Seven Samurai.*
Directed by Akira Kurosawa.

(a)

(b)

(c)

(d)

(e)

(f)

(g)

(h)

What do you mean - falling for a samurai?

(i)

(j)

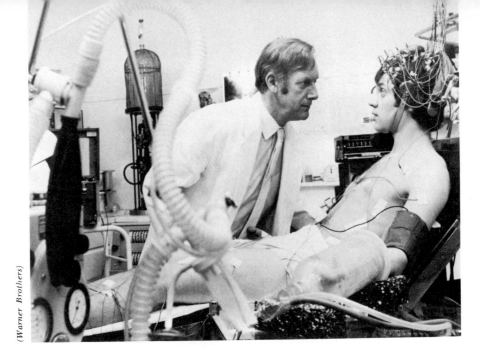

8-12. O Lucky Man!.
Directed by Lindsay Anderson. Screenplay by David Sherwin, based on an idea by Malcolm McDowell.
Like their literary counterparts, cinematic allegories usually feature an Everyman figure as the protagonist, someone who seems to typify Mankind in general. Similarly, each character and sequence in an allegory usually represents some broad aspect of contemporary society. Here, for example, the "mad scientist" figure represents the inhuman excesses of Modern Scientific Experimentation. Other scenes in the movie deal with Religion, Big Business, Politics, Art, and so on.

almost washed out by the intensity of the fire's light (8-11h). It begins to rain, and the sorrowing young samurai walks away despondently (8-11i). At the end of the sequence, Kurosawa offers a close-up of the fire, as the rain extinguishes its flames (8-11j).

A metaphor is usually defined as a comparison of some kind that could not literally be true. Two terms that aren't ordinarily associated are yoked together, producing a certain sense of literal incongruity. "Poisonous time," "torn with grief," "devoured by love" are all verbal metaphors. Editing is a frequent source of metaphor in film, for two shots can be linked together to produce a third—symbolic—idea. This is the basis of Eisenstein's theory of montage. In *October,* for example, he satirized the fears and anxieties of an anti-revolutionary politician by intercutting shots of a "heavenly choir" of female harpists with shots of the politician delivering his cowardly speech. The row of pretty harp players is brought in "from nowhere": that is, they are certainly not found in the locale (a meeting hall), but are introduced solely for metaphoric purposes. Special effects cinematography is also used to create metaphoric ideas, for through the use of the **optical printer** two or more objects can be yoked together in the same frame to create ideas that have no literal counterparts in reality. Cinematic metaphors are always somewhat obtrusive then; unlike motifs and most symbols, metaphors are less integrated contextually, less "realistic" in terms of our ordinary perceptions.

There are two other figurative techniques used in film and literature: **allegory** and **allusion**. The first is seldom employed in movies since it tends towards simplemindedness. In allegory, a one-to-one correspondence exists between a character or situation and a broad and rather apparent symbolic idea. Allegorical narratives, like Penn's *Mickey One,* usually deal with the idea of Life in general (8-12). One of the most famous examples of allegory is the character of Death in Bergman's *The Seventh Seal.* Needless to say, there's not much ambiguity involved in what the character is supposed to symbolize. Indeed, allegory is generally avoided precisely because of its

8-13. *Cries and Whispers.*
Written and directed by Ingmar Bergman.
An allusion is an indirect reference, usually to a well-known event, person, or work of art. Here, Bergman's image recalls Michelangelo's celebrated religious sculpture, the *Pietà.* The anguished comforting maternal figure also alludes to a number of Renaissance paintings which deal with the Madonna Dolorosa theme.

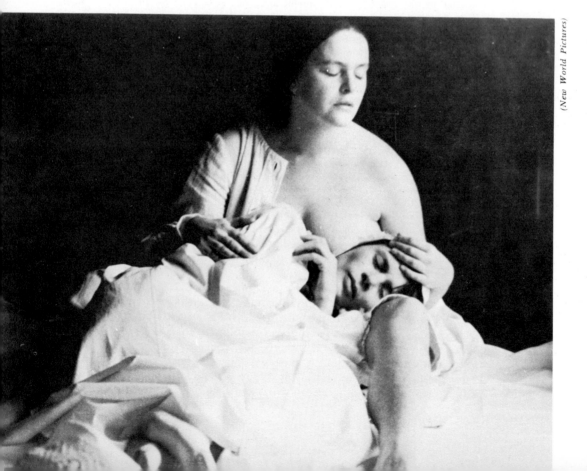

8-14. *A Woman is a Woman.*
Written and directed by Jean-Luc Godard.
The cinematic homage, or *hommage* as it's called in French, is a respectful and often playful tribute to another movie or cinéaste. Here, the characters burst out in spontaneous song and dance, while expressing their desire to appear in an M-G-M musical by Gene Kelly, choreographed by Bob Fosse.

(Contemporary Films)

lack of resonance, suggestiveness, and ambiguity, which are often what make motifs, symbols, and metaphors so intriguing.

An allusion is a common type of literary analogy. It's an implied reference, usually to a well-known event, person, or work of art (8-13). Dennis Hopper's *Easy Rider* contains several allusions to persons and events from American history. The leading character's name, Wyatt, seems to be an allusion to Wyatt Earp; his contentious side-kick, Billy, dresses in a buckskin jacket, suggesting Wild Bill Hickok. Some young people of a hippie commune dress in Indian outfits. We learn that they almost starved the previous winter, and now they are planting corn for the winter ahead. The clothing allusion suggests that like most of the American Indians of the past, the hippies will either starve or be destroyed.

In the cinema, an overt reference or allusion to another movie, director, or memorable shot is sometimes called a **homage.** The cinematic homage is not only a kind of "quote," but the director's tribute to a previous cinematic master or a contemporary colleague (8-14). In Bogdanovich's *The Last Picture Show,* for example, the young protagonists go to the movies on their last night together. The film they see is Howard Hawks' *Red River,* a classic western of the late forties. The footage from Hawks' movie is organically integrated into Bogdanovich's film, for the idealized heroic west of *Red River* is ironically juxtaposed with the decaying contemporary Texas town that is the setting of *The Last Picture Show.* Homages were popularized by Godard and Truffaut, whose films are rich in such tributes.

Perhaps the most practical method of seeing how motifs, symbols, metaphors, and allusions actually function in motion pictures is to explore in detail their use in a single movie. Bergman's *Persona* is one of the most complex films ever created, its richness and density resulting largely from Bergman's profuse employment of these techniques. The director uses virtually every kind of cinematic metaphor including editing juxtapositions as well as **kinetic,** aural, and optical metaphors. There are also many allusions and motifs in *Persona*. Two motifs in particular stand out: the "doubles" theme (implying the splitting and merging of personalities), and motifs of paralysis and immobility (suggesting catonia and perhaps even death). There are also motifs of blood, hands, and eyes.

The basic theme of the film is schizophrenia, which Bergman exploits as a symbolic basis for more philosophical and metaphysical concerns. A well-known actress, Elisabeth Vogler (Liv Ullmann) suddenly stops speaking while performing on stage in the title role of *Electra*. After many days of total silence, during which she refuses to talk even to her husband and young son, she is referred to a psychiatric hospital. Alma, an impressionable young nurse (Bibi Andersson) is asked to take charge of the actress at the summer cottage of the psychiatrist, where the doctor hopes that the young nurse might induce the actress to speak. Alone on the barren rocky island, the two women are drawn together emotionally, though Elisabeth continues to remain silent. Encouraged by Elisabeth's flattering attention, Alma painfully recounts a story of an orgy she once took part in. As a result, the nurse got pregnant and eventually decided to have an abortion. In telling the story, Alma only now begins to feel the anguish and guilt of her past acts. After this shared confidence, the nurse is drawn to Elisabeth more than ever, even to the point of imagining that the two are very much alike, both physically and temperamentally.

All the while, the mysterious Elisabeth listens attentively, sometimes with apparent compassion, at other times with a certain affectionate amusement. Alma's life seems so trivial in comparison with the horrors that Elisabeth has apparently experienced. When Alma offers to mail her patient's letter, the nurse is unable to resist the temptation to read it, for Elisabeth has neglected (deliberately?) to seal the envelope. In her letter, the actress writes with detached curiosity of Alma's sexual experiences. Elisabeth can't resist "studying" her friend. (Possibly for a future role?) This casual betrayal has a traumatic effect on Alma. From this point on in the movie, we're never sure whether we are watching real events or imagined ones. Nor are we certain whether the fantasist is Alma or Elisabeth—though most likely it is Alma. The two women quarrel violently. Their identities begin to merge, subtly at first, then dramatically, uncontrollably. Alma even makes love with Mr. Vogler, while his wife watches with detachment, sorrow, and hopelessness. Bergman includes a number of other fantasy sequences between the two women which take place in a kind of timeless void. Alma tries desperately to resist merging personalities with Elisabeth, but is unsuccessful. Suddenly, Elisabeth mysteriously disappears. Soon after, we see Alma packing her clothes, shutting up the cottage, and departing alone on an empty bus. The psychiatric story ends here—with an unresolved, ambiguous conclusion.

Despite its tremendous dramatic power, this is only the narrative scaffolding of Bergman's movie, for the film is also an elaborate philosophical exploration of the problems and responsibilities of the artist in relationship to his political and social environment. The story of the two women is enclosed by a kind of frame, which consists of a series of brief, almost subliminal shots. Many of these shots are not contextually related to the story proper, but serve as metaphors for Bergman's philosophical themes. These editing metaphors are found not only at the beginning and ending of the movie, but also at the midpoint, where they erupt violently as Alma's love for Elisabeth turns to hatred.

The elaborate pre-credit sequence functions like a musical overture, briefly introducing most of the important ideas that will be developed in the story proper. Some of the shots in this sequence defy precise analysis, and even Bergman is unsure of what a few of them mean. At this point in viewing the film, of course, we aren't expected to know the significance of most of these shots. They function mostly on a visceral level: they're intended to jolt us out of our passivity. The opening shot of the movie shows us the carbon arc lamp of a film projector lighting up (8-15a). Then, in quick succession, we see a film strip coming off the sprockets of a projector, and some movie images whirling out of control on a screen. Bergman then cuts to a shot of an upside-down cartoon figure washing her face in the water of a rocky-banked harbor (15b). The sprocket holes of this **animated** film can be seen plainly. All of these images suggest that *Persona* will deal at least in part with the problems of making movies, perhaps that the figures of Alma and Elisabeth are themselves "personas" or masks for Bergman's own artistic and psychological experiences. The mechanical breakdown of the projector certainly suggests a metaphorical foreshadowing of the breakdown of the emotional mechanisms of the two women.

8-15a–zz. *Persona*.
Written and Directed by Ingmar Bergman.

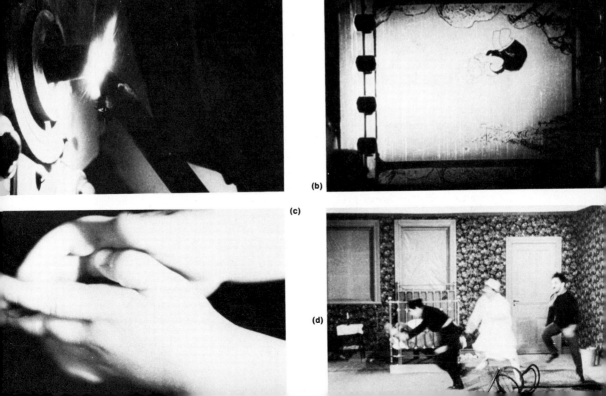

(a)

(b)

(c)

(d)

The shot of the animated woman washing is followed by a close-up of two real hands washing (15c). Perhaps this juxtaposition is a comment on the pitiful ineffectuality of art in capturing real experiences in all their complexity. That is, that art, no matter how complex, must always seem a ludicrously inadequate caricature of the real thing to the artist who is trying to externalize his feelings and ideas. The juxtaposition might also be an indication of the various levels of reality that Bergman will be using throughout the film.

The director then cuts to a **fast motion** sequence which seems to be an old silent movie farce, with a man being pursued by the devil and a skeleton (15d). Again, one is tempted to view this scene as an implied comment on the inadequacies of film art in dealing with such complex themes as evil and death. Bergman then **intercuts** three shots which suggest religious allusions. First, there's a shot of a black spider, which is apparently an allusion to Bergman's earlier *Through a Glass Darkly*. (In that movie, an artist—in this case a novelist—was fascinated by his own daughter's descent into madness, and was using her experiences as material for his art. At the end of the film, the girl imagines that she sees God—a terrifying black spider.)

The second shot is an **overexposed** image of a dead lamb being slashed open. A hand reaches into its belly and dredges out its guts. The camera **pans** slightly, and we see the lamb's glassy eye staring dumbly (15e). The third shot shows a spike being driven into a hand, an obvious crucifixion allusion (15f). It's difficult to know whether Bergman is suggesting the Christ-like agony of the artist in creating, or the agony of his "victims," his subject matter from real life. Perhaps both ideas are implied, for in the story proper, both Elisabeth (the artist figure) and Alma (the "raw material" of art) undergo terrible anguish.

Bergman then offers a shot of a blank concrete wall, the first example of the motif of immobility. This dissolves to a shot of some trees stripped of their foliage in a bleak winter setting. Next, we see an image of a spiked iron fence, with a pile of snow in front of it. This in turn leads to a series of close shots of an old woman lying silently in what seems to be a hospital, or perhaps a morgue, for one shot is a close-up of her hand dangling lifelessly off the edge of the bed (15g). On the soundtrack, we hear some eerie dripping sounds, metaphors perhaps for the passage of time, or drops of blood, life's basic substance.

Bergman then begins one of the most ambiguous series of shots in this pre-credit sequence. We see a pubescent boy lying naked under a white sheet. Unable to sleep, the boy sits up on his bed, puts on his glasses and tries to read, but he is too restless (15h). He then looks at the camera—at us—and his hand gropes slowly towards the lens (15i). The movement seems to suggest a reaching out, but also a kind of conjuring effect. Bergman then gives us a **reverse angle shot,** and we see that the boy is reaching toward an out-of-focus image of a woman's face—the face of Bibi Andersson, who plays Alma (15j). This sequence has been interpreted in various ways, but Bergman deliberately keeps its symbolism ambiguous. The boy could represent Elisabeth's son, whom she has guiltily rejected. He could also be an embodiment of Alma's aborted child: his groping for her face could

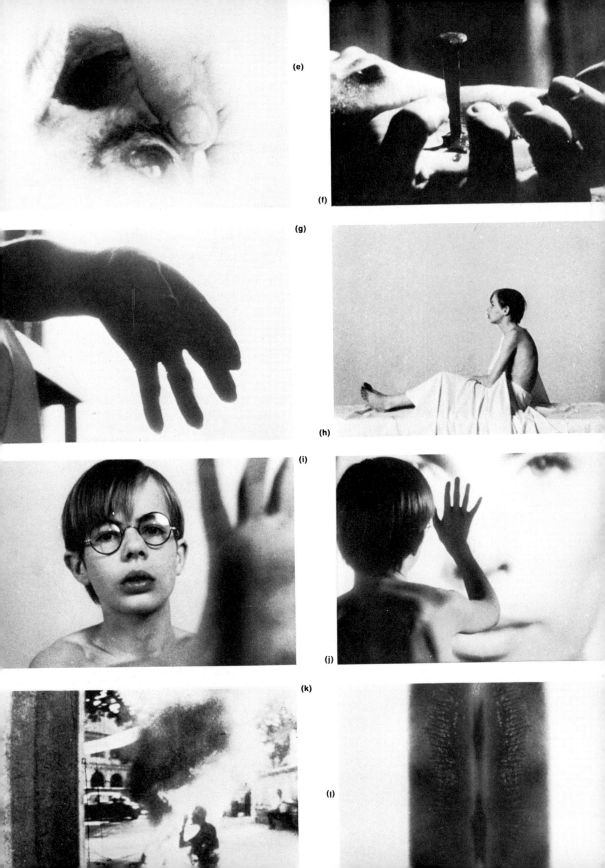

(e)

(f)

(g)

(h)

(i)

(j)

(k)

(l)

represent Alma's subjective projection of guilt. But the boy is also a kind of conjurer of images, and as such he could represent Bergman himself, child-like before his own creations, who seem to overpower him.

At this point, Bergman begins his credits, but interspersed with them are various shots that are actually a continuation of the pre-credit sequence. Included in these shots is an image of Liv Ullmann as Elisabeth playing Electra. There is also a shot of a barren, rocky seacoast, which will be the major setting of the story proper, and a television image of a Buddhist monk immolating himself (15k). There is also an **extreme close-up** of a pair of lips, only photographed vertically so that the lips seem to resemble a vagina (15l). Possibly the shot is meant to suggest the idea of giving birth: George Bernard Shaw as well as Freud believed that the artist is essentially a neurotic, who in creating a work of art is subconsciously trying to mimic a woman's giving birth "normally." The fact that this image appears at the "birth" of the film itself tends to confirm this interpretation. Bergman then intercuts three close-ups with his concluding titles. The boy's close-up is repeated a number of times. We are then offered a shot of Alma (15m) and one of Elisabeth (15n), both of them, like the boy, staring directly into the camera. The two women are photographed in such a way that their striking physical resemblance is emphasized. The fact that these shots are so conspicuously parallel seems to suggest that they all represent aspects of the same single consciousness.

All of these shots take no longer than a few minutes of screen time. The story proper begins with the psychiatrist recounting Elisabeth's breakdown to Alma. The fact that the actress began to giggle while playing

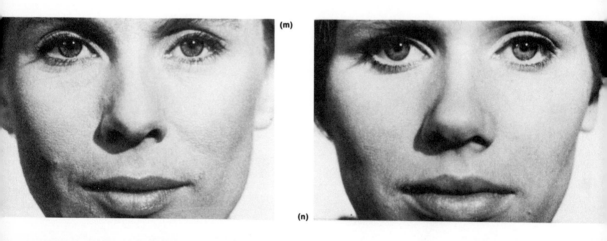

(m)

(n)

(o)

(p)

She stopped in the middle of a scene...

Electra is significant. The theme of *Electra* is of matricide: a child's revenge for a mother's betrayal (15o). We later learn that Elisabeth hated being a mother because it interfered with her artistic career. The complex pattern of guilt this hatred produced in Elisabeth is apparently what precipitated her giggles and later silent withdrawal. Art seems so *simple* in comparison with life, with all its messy ambiguities and contradictions. Later, in the hospital room, Elisabeth again begins to giggle when she hears a radio melodrama which strikes her as a ludicrous caricature of real life. Bergman never offers us an explicit explanation for Elisabeth's withdrawal, but by permitting us to watch Alma's step-by-step deterioration, we can infer the causes underlying the actress's condition, for they are virtually the same: the betrayals, compromises, deceptions, and self-deceptions of everyday life are what destroy both women.

In a powerful scene which is photographed in a very **long take,** Bergman gives us a close-up of Elisabeth lying in bed in the hospital. Slowly, very slowly, her face gradually submerges into total darkness (15p). Another hospital scene tends to confirm this interpretation of Elisabeth as a despairing artist figure. The actress is watching TV, where she sees a newsreel of the war in Vietnam (15q). Suddenly the television screen is filled with a shot of a Buddhist monk setting fire to himself in protest. Elisabeth recoils in horror, withdrawing to a corner of the room, and the very edge of Bergman's frame (15r). In a series of shots that cut closer and closer to Elisabeth's face, in which the symbolic effects of the **proxemic ranges** are brilliantly exploited, we see all the anguish and despair that has precipitated her revolt of silence (15s, t). But no matter how much

(q)

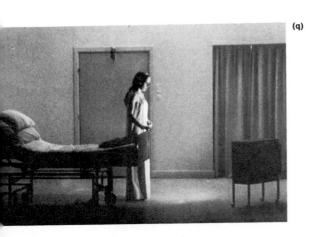

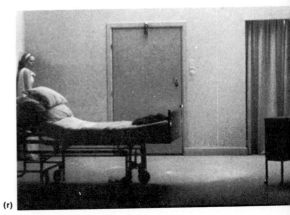

(r)

(s)

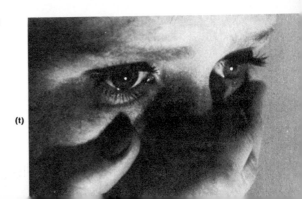

(t)

(u)

(v)

(w)

(x)

(y)

(z)

(aa)

(bb)

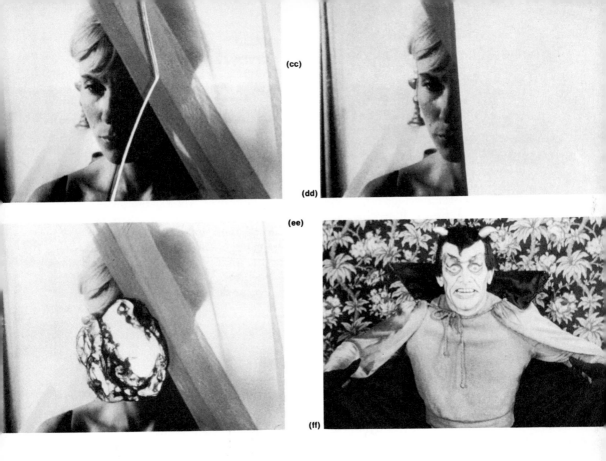

(cc)

(dd)

(ee)

(ff)

she withdraws, the horrors of reality are always there—even if at second hand on a TV screen.

Once the scene shifts to the island retreat, Elisabeth's condition seems to improve, though Bergman often cuts to shots of the barren immobile rocks, which act as constant reminders of the essential sterility of such an isolated existence (15u). As the women draw closer, Bergman photographs them in complementary costumes, uses parallel set-ups, and even blocks their movement so that their bodies seem to merge (15v). This "doubles" motif is carried over into a dream sequence (probably Alma's) in which Elisabeth enters the nurse's room through one door (15w) and leaves through another parallel to it (15x). Photographed mostly in **slow motion** through a gauzy lens, this graceful sequence is one of the first overt dramatizations of the merging of personalities. Both women stand before a dark mirror, where Elisabeth pulls back Alma's hair to reveal their extraordinary physical resemblance (15y).

Bergman even brings the reality of the audience into the film. Lest we become too complacent in viewing this "freak show," the director begins one sequence with a shot of the rocky shore. Suddenly, from beneath the frame, Elisabeth emerges into view with a still camera and clicks "our" picture (15z). *Persona* is as much a portrait of ourselves as it is a study of the "neurotic" characters of the film.

Roughly at the midpoint of the movie, Alma learns of Elisabeth's betrayal. After reading the letter, the nurse stands thoughtfully at the edge of a pool of water—a shot which emphasizes the doubles theme by including her full reflection (15aa). Seething with anger, Alma leaves a jagged piece of glass on the walkway, where she hopes Elisabeth will step on it. When she does, Bergman cuts to a shot of Alma looking at the scene from behind a window and curtain (15bb). Suddenly the soundtrack reverberates with a cracking noise, and we observe a rip in the film image (15cc). Half the image drops from sight, literally splitting Alma's face into two (15dd).

This "crack-up" of course is a metaphor of Alma's emotional collapse. A burning hole then penetrates Alma's face, and consumes the image (15ee). Through the burn hole, incongruous images of the silent movie devil (15ff) and the skeleton (15gg) emerge—Bergman's reminders of the primitiveness and inadequacies of his medium in conveying intense passions. After the two women quarrel, Alma withdraws to the rocks where she remains for hours (15hh), silently huddled in a kind of immobile trance (15ii).

In her bedroom, Elisabeth finds a photograph of a Nazi concentration camp and its victims (15jj). Again, she is struck by the horrors of the real world, particularly by a small Jewish boy who is among those being herded (15kk). The boy reminds her of her own son perhaps, whom we saw earlier in a photograph. The fact that Elisabeth is jolted back to reality by several "documentary" images possibly reflects Bergman's own despair in trying to capture honest and uncompromised emotions in a "fictional" image. After this, we're never sure whether what we are seeing are fantasies or events that actually take place. Probably mostly fantasies.

In one particularly dream-like sequence, Elisabeth's husband (who is apparently blind) visits the cottage. Mr. Vogler speaks to Alma as though she were his wife. At first Alma resists (15ll), but prodded by the mysterious Elisabeth, Alma pretends to be his wife, even going so far as to make love with him (15mm). All the while, the silent Elisabeth seems to recall her marital relationship with tender, futile sorrow, her face half in darkness, or symbolically cut off by the frame (15nn).

In another sequence, Alma sees Elisabeth guiltily covering the torn photograph of her boy, with her hands. The nurse prods the mother to speak of her son, but Elisabeth refuses (15oo). Instead, Alma tells the story, almost as though it were her own. As she recounts Elisabeth's horror at being pregnant and giving birth to an unwanted child, the camera moves from an **over-the-shoulder two-shot** to a close-up of Elisabeth listening—half her face plunged in symbolic darkness (15pp). Then Alma repeats the story of guilt and anguish, only this time the camera focuses on *her,* the opposite side of her face similarly in darkness (15qq). The repetition of the story in two opposite shots suggests the merging of personalities. Alma denies this fusion of identity (15rr) but suddenly, using special effects photography, Bergman fuses the faces of the two women into one (15ss).

Near the end of the film, we see Elisabeth packing her clothes. Later, we see Alma doing the same. She looks into a mirror, and again we see an image of fused identities, dreamily shot in **double exposure** (15tt). As Alma leaves the cottage with her suitcase, Bergman crowds her figure with the face of a wooden ship's masthead (15uu). He then cuts to a close-up of Elisabeth's frozen features as Electra, another striking motif

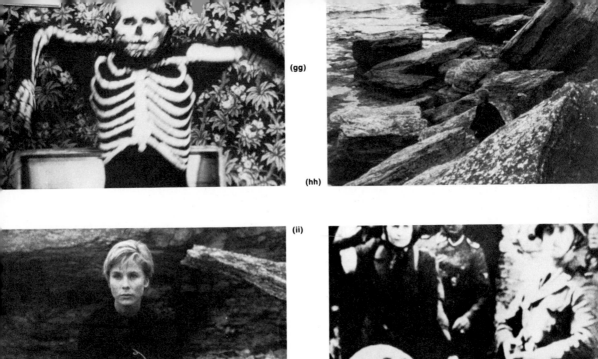

(gg)

(hh)

(ii)

(jj)

(kk)

Mr. Vogler, I am not your wife.

(ll)

(mm)

(nn)

(oo)

(pp)

(qq)

Tell me about it, Elisabeth.

Tell me about it, Elisabeth.

I am not Elisabeth Vogler.
You are Elisabeth Vogler.

(rr)

(ss)

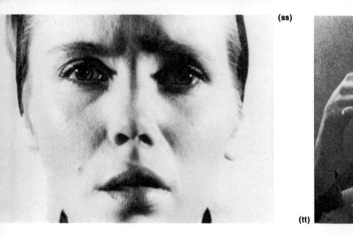

(tt)

(uu)

(vv)

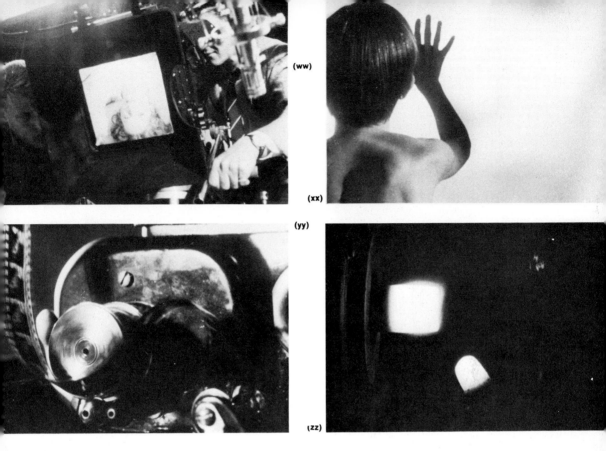

(ww)

(xx)

(yy)

(zz)

of immobility (15vv). This in turn is intercut with a shot of Bergman and his great **cinematographer** Sven Nykvist behind a camera, which is descending slowing on a **crane** (15ww). The juxtaposition of these three shots once again suggests their parallelism, implying that Alma and Elisabeth are two sides of Bergman's own personality.

The film concludes with a reversal of some of the opening shots. We see the boy reaching for a totally out-of-focus image of the fused Bibi Andersson-Liv Ullmann face (15xx). The soundtrack seems to whirl out of control as we see an image of a film strip uncoiling wildly off its sprocket (15yy). Finally, the carbon arc lamp of the projector sputters out (15zz), and there is only darkness.

POINT-OF-VIEW
AND LITERARY ADAPTATIONS

Point-of-view in fiction determines the relationship between the materials and the narrator, through whose eyes the events of a story are viewed. That is, the ideas and incidents are sifted through the consciousness and language of the story teller, who may or may not be a participant in the action, and who may or may not be a reliable guide for the reader to follow. There are four basic types of point-of-view in fiction: the **first person**, the **omnisci-**

8-16. A Clockwork Orange.
Written and directed by Stanley Kubrick, based on the novel by Anthony Burgess.
In the cinema, first person narration takes two forms. A point-of-view shot is visual, while a character's voice-over on the soundtrack is aural. Generally, when a character narrates his own story on the soundtrack, the visuals present us with another point of view. Kubrick reinforced the intimacy between the audience and the storyteller (Malcolm McDowell) by occasionally having the protagonist direct his eyes at the camera—at us.

ent, the **third person,** and the objective. In the movies, point-of-view tends to be less rigorous than in fiction, for though there are cinematic equivalents for the four basic types of narration, feature films tend to fall naturally into the omniscient form.

The first person narrator tells his *own* story (8-16). In some cases, he is an objective observer who can be relied upon to relate the events accurately. Nick Carraway in Fitzgerald's *The Great Gatsby* is a good example of this kind of narrator. Other first person narrators are subjectively involved in the main action, and can't be totally relied upon. In *Huckleberry Finn,* the immature Huck relates all the events as he experiences them. Huck obviously can't supply his readers with all the necessary information when he himself does not possess it. In employing this type of first person narrator, the novelist must somehow permit the reader to see the truth without destroying or straining the plausibility of the narrator. Generally, a novelist solves this problem by providing the reader with clues, which permit him to see more clearly than the narrator himself. For example, when Huck enthusiastically recounts the glamor of a circus and the "amazing feats" of its performers, the more sophisticated reader sees beyond Huck's words and infers that the performers are in fact a rather shabby crew, and their theatrical acts merely cheap deceptions.

8-17. Rashomon.
Directed by Akira Kurosawa, screenplay by Kurosawa and Shinobu Hashimoto, based on two stories by Ryunosuke Akutagawa.
In this movie, Kurosawa tells the "same" story four times, each from the perspective of a different (and far from disinterested) observer: a young samurai, his wife, a bandit (Toshiro Mifune, pictured) and a compassionate woodcutter. The visual presentation in each instance is slanted, representing the biases and self-interests of each narrator.

Many films make some use of first person narrative techniques, but only sporadically. The cinematic equivalent to the "voice" of the literary narrator is the "eye" of the camera, and this difference is an important one. In fiction, the distinction between the narrator and the reader is clear: it's as though the reader were listening to a friend tell a story. In film, however, the viewer identifies with the lens, and he thus tends to fuse with the narrator. To produce first person narration in film, the camera would have to record all the action through the eyes of the character, which —in effect—would also make the viewer the protagonist.

In *The Lady of the Lake,* Robert Montgomery attempted to use the first person camera throughout the film. It was a noble and interesting experiment, but a failure, for several reasons. In the first place, the director was forced into a number of absurdities. Having the characters address the camera was not too much of a problem, for point-of-view shots are common in most movies. However, there were several actions where the device simply broke down. When a girl walked up to the hero and kissed him, for example, she had to slink toward the camera and begin to embrace it, while her face came closer to the lens. Similarly, when the hero was involved in a fist fight, the antagonist literally had to attack the camera, which jarred appropriately whenever the "narrator" was dealt a blow. The problem with the exclusive use of the first person camera, then, is its literalness. Furthermore, it tends to create a sense of frustration in the viewer, who wants to *see* the hero. In fiction, we get to know the first person through his words, through his judgments and values, which are reflected in his language. But in movies, we get to know a character by seeing how he reacts to people and events. Unless the director breaks the first person camera **convention,** we can never see the hero, we can only see what he sees. Montgomery partially solved this problem by using many mirror shots, in which the hero's reflected image permitted the viewer to see what the protagonist looked like. But the real problem still remained, for these mirror shots are usually included in the least dramatic sequences, in which the need for a close-up of the hero's face is least necessary.

A useful first person technique in film is to have a narrator tell his story in words on the soundtrack, while the camera records the events, usually through a variety of narrative shots. An interesting variation of this sound technique is multiple first person narration (8-17). In *Citizen Kane,* five different people give us their own characterizations of Charles Foster Kane. Each narration is accompanied by a **flashback** sequence, though not in the first person camera. The flashbacks present Kane in somewhat contradictory terms, each reflecting the prejudices of the story teller. Where one narrator leaves off, another who knew Kane in a different period of his life picks up the narrative line and develops it further, until the final story teller concludes with a tale of Kane's last days.

The omniscient narrator is often associated with the nineteenth-century novel. Generally, such narrators are not participants in a story but all-knowing observers who supply the reader with all the facts he needs in order to appreciate the story (8-18). Such narrators can span many locations and time periods, they can enter the consciousness of a number of different characters, telling us what they think and feel. Omniscient narrators can be relatively detached from the story, as in *War and Peace,* or they can take on a distinct personality of their own, as in *Tom Jones,* where the amiable story teller amuses us with his wry observations and judgments.

Omniscient narration is almost inevitable in film. In literature, the first person and the omniscient voice are mutually exclusive, for if a first-person character tells us his own thoughts directly, he can't also tell us— with certainty—the thoughts of others. But in movies, the combination of first person and omniscient narration is common. Each time the director moves his camera—either within a shot or between shots—we are offered a new point-of-view from which to evaluate the scene. He can cut easily from a subjective point-of-view shot (first person) to a variety of objective shots. He can concentrate on a single reaction (close-up) or the simultaneous reactions of several characters (long shot). Within a matter of seconds, the film director can show us a cause and an effect, an action and a reaction. He can connect various time periods and locations almost instantaneously (parallel editing), or literally superimpose different time periods (dissolve or **multiple exposure**). The omniscient camera can be a dispassionate observer, as it is in many of Chaplin's films, or it can be a witty commentator—an evaluater of events—as it often is in Hitchcock's films or those of Lubitsch.

The third person point-of-view is essentially a variation of the omniscient. In the third person, a non-participating narrator tells a story from the consciousness of a single character. In some novels, this narrator completely penetrates the mind of the leading character; in others, there is virtually no penetration. In Jane Austen's *Pride and Prejudice,* for example, we learn what Elizabeth Bennett thinks and feels about events, but we're never permitted to enter the consciousness of the other characters.

8-18. *War and Peace.*
Directed by Sergei Bondarchuk, based on the novel by Leo Tolstoy.
Except for mysteries and suspense films, in which the audience is deliberately kept in ignorance of certain facts, the cinema tends to fall into omniscient narration automatically. As in omnisciently narrated novels like *War and Peace,* the film director provides us with all the necessary information we need to know in order to comprehend the characters and events of a story.

We can only guess what they feel through Elizabeth's interpretations—which are often inaccurate. Her interpretations are not offered directly to the reader as in the first person, but through the intermediacy of the narrator, who tells us her responses.

In movies, there is a rough equivalent to the third person, but it's not so rigorous as in literature. Usually, third person narration is found in documentaries, where an anonymous commentator tells us about the background of a central character. In Sidney Meyer's *The Quiet One,* for example, the visuals dramatize certain traumatic events in the life of an impoverished youngster, Donald. On the soundtrack, James Agee's commentary tells us some of the reasons why Donald behaves as he does, how he feels about his parents, his peers, and his teachers. The verbal third person is also used in some literary adaptations, such as John Huston's version of Crane's *The Red Badge of Courage.* Perhaps the visual equivalent of the third person is a shot of the central character. Most movies

(Warner Brothers)

8-19. Moby Dick.
Directed by John Huston, screenplay by Ray Bradbury, based on the novel by Herman Melville.
The events of **epic** novels are generally too sprawling to be transferred to the screen without some condensation. Because of its dense visual saturation, however, the cinema can add a great deal that's not found in the original—atmospheric details, reactions to speeches, and so on. Bradbury's script concentrated on Melville's characters and dramatic events. The historical and symbolic materials on whaling found in the original were eliminated as uncinematic.

8-20. *Throne of Blood.*
Directed by Akira Kurosawa, based on Shakespeare's Macbeth.
The loose film adaptation takes a few general ideas from an original source, then develops them independently. Many commentators consider Kurosawa's film the greatest of all Shakespearean adaptations precisely because the filmmaker doesn't attempt to compete with the dramatist. Kurosawa's samurai movie is a *cinematic* masterpiece, these commentators claim, owing relatively little to its language for its effects. Its similarities to Shakespeare's literary masterpiece are superficial, just as the play's similarities to Holinshed's *Chronicles of England, Scotland, and Ireland* (Shakespeare's primary source) are of no great artistic significance.

combine the first and third persons. Hitchcock, for instance, often permits us to identify with a character's experiences through a point-of-view shot (first person), then gives us a close-up of the character's face (third person).

The objective point-of-view is seldom used in novels, though writers occasionally employ it in short stories, such as Crane's "The Blue Hotel." The objective voice is also a variation of the omniscient. Objective narration is the most detached of all: it doesn't enter the consciousness of any character, but merely reports events from the outside. Indeed, this voice has been likened to a camera, which records events impartially and without bias. It presents facts, and allows the reader to interpret for himself. The objective voice is more congenial to film than to literature, for the movies literally employ a recording camera. The cinematic objective point-of-view is generally used by **realistic** directors, who keep their camera at

8-21. Greed.

Written and directed by Erich von Stroheim, based on the novel McTeague, *by Frank Norris.*

The extraordinary richness of detail that characterizes von Stroheim's faithful adaptation is a reflection of the director's profound respect for Norris' naturalistic novel. The director boasted that every word of the literary original had its cinematic counterpart. Unfortunately, the movie version was nine hours long, an impractical length which even the extravagant von Stroheim conceded was excessive. By order of Irving Thalberg, production head at M-G-M, the movie was re-edited to a running time of two hours. To the incredulous horror of later film historians, all of the discarded remaining footage was burned and lost forever. Though the finished product is still regarded as one of the greatest films of all time, von Stroheim disowned the work, referring to it as his "mutilated child."

long shot, and avoid all distortions that would "comment" such as unusual **angles**, lenses, and filters.

A great many movies are adaptations of literary sources. In some respects, adapting a novel or play requires more skill than an original screenplay. Furthermore, the better the literary work, the more difficult the adaptation. For this reason, many film adaptations are based on mediocre sources, for few people will get upset at the modifications required in film if the source itself isn't of the highest calibre. There are many adaptations that are considerably superior to their originals: *Birth of a Nation*, for instance, was based on Thomas Dixon's trashy novel, *The Klansman*. Some commentators believe that if a work of art has reached its fullest artistic expression in one form, an adaptation will inevitably be inferior (8-19). According to this argument, no film adaptation of *Pride and Prejudice* could equal the original, nor could any novel hope to capture the richness of *Gold Rush,* or even *Citizen Kane,* which is a rather literary movie. There's a good deal of sense in this view, for we've seen how literature and film tend to solve problems differently, how the true content of each medium is organically governed by its forms.

The real problem of the adapter is not how to reproduce the *content* of a literary work (an impossibility), but how close he should remain to the raw data of his *subject matter,* in the sense that these terms have been used throughout this chapter. This degree of fidelity is what determines the three general categories of adaptations: the **loose,** the **faithful,** and the **literal.** Of course these classifications are for convenience only, for in actual practice, most movies fall somewhere in between.

The loose adaptation is barely that. Generally, only an idea, a situation, or a character is taken from a literary source, then developed independently. Loose film adaptations can be likened to Shakespeare's treatment of a story from Plutarch, or to the ancient Greek dramatists who often drew upon a common mythology (8-20). A film that falls into this class is Kurosawa's *Throne of Blood,* which transforms Shakespeare's *Macbeth* into quite a different tale set in medieval Japan, though the filmmaker retains several plot elements from Shakespeare's original.

Faithful adaptations, as the phrase implies, attempt to recreate the literary source in filmic terms, keeping as close to the *spirit* of the original as possible. André Bazin likened the faithful adapter to a translator, who tries to find equivalents to the original. Of course, Bazin realized that

(American Film Theatre)

8-22. The Iceman Cometh.
Directed by John Frankenheimer, based on the play by Eugene O'Neill. Virtually all literal adaptations were originally stage plays, for the language and actions of the legitimate theatre are cinematically convertible. The most significant changes in a literal adaptation are more likely to involve differences in time and space rather than language.

fundamental differences exist between the two mediums: the translator's problem in converting the word "road" to *"strada"* or *"strasse"* is not so acute as a filmmaker's problem in transforming the word into a picture (8-21). An example of this kind of adaptation is Richardson's *Tom Jones*. John Osborne's screenplay preserves much of the novel's plot structure, its major events, and most of the important characters. Even the witty omniscient narrator is retained. But the film is not merely an illustration of the novel. In the first place, Fielding's book is too packed with incident for a film adaptation. The many inn scenes, for example, are reduced to a central episode: the Upton Inn sequence. Two minor aspects of the novel are enlarged in the movie: the famous eating scene between Tom and Mrs. Waters, and the fox-hunting episode. These sequences are included because two of Fielding's favorite sources of metaphors throughout the novel are drawn from eating and hunting. In effect, Osborne uses these scattered metaphors as raw material or inspiration: his scenes are filmic "equivalents," in Bazin's sense.

Literal adaptations are pretty much restricted to plays. As we have seen, the two basic modes of drama—action and dialogue—are also found in films. The major problem with stage adaptations is in the handling of space and time rather than language. If the film adapter were to leave his camera at long shot, and restrict his editing to scene shifts only, the result would be similar to the original. But we've seen that few filmmakers would be willing merely to record a play, nor indeed should they, for in doing so, they would lose much of the excitement of the original, while taking no advantage of the adapting medium, particularly its greater freedom in treating space and time. Movies can add many dimensions to a play, especially through close-ups and edited juxtapositions. Since these techniques aren't found in the theatre, even "literal" adaptations are not rigidly so; they simply modify more subtly (8-22). Stage dialogue is often retained in film adaptations, but its effect on the audience is different. John Frankenheimer's *The Iceman Cometh* preserves most of Eugene O'Neill's dialogue, but in a stage production, the meaning of the language is determined by the fact that the characters are on the same stage at the same time, reacting to the same words. In the film, time and space are fragmented by the individual shots. Furthermore, since even a literary film is primarily visual and only secondarily verbal, nearly all the dialogue is modified by the images. The differences between loose, faithful, and literal adaptations, then, are essentially matters of degree. In each case, the cinematic form inevitably alters the content of the literary original.

FURTHER READING

BATTESTIN, MARTIN C. "Osborne's *Tom Jones:* Adapting a Classic," in *Man and the Movies,* ed. W. R. Robinson. Baltimore: Penguin Books, 1969. (Paper) A comparison between Henry Fielding's eighteenth century novel, and the 1963 British movie, directed by Tony Richardson and adapted by John Osborne.

BLUESTONE, GEORGE. *Novels into Film.* Baltimore: Johns Hopkins Press, 1957. (Paper) A discussion of film adaptations of such classic novels as

Pride and Prejudice and *The Grapes of Wrath,* with an introductory theoretical essay exploring the limitations and advantages of each medium.

CORLISS, RICHARD, ed. *The Hollywood Screenwriters.* New York: Avon Books, 1972. (Paper) A collection of articles and interviews with famous American screenwriters, including Furthman, Nichols, Hecht, Eleanor Perry, and others.

EISENSTEIN, SERGEI. "The Cinematographic Principle and the Ideogram," "Methods of Montage," and "Dickens, Griffith, and the Film Today," in *Film Form.* New York: Harcourt, Brace & Co., 1949. (Paper) Essays exploring the relationship between literature and film, with an emphasis on theoretical considerations.

GIANNETTI, LOUIS D. "Cinematic Metaphors" and "Godard's *Masculine-Feminine:* The Cinematic Essay," in *Godard and Others: Essays in Film Form.* Cranbury, N. J.: Fairleigh Dickinson University Press, 1975. Theoretical essays exploring the influences of literature on film, with particular emphasis on the works of Godard, Bergman, and Hitchcock.

LaVALLEY, ALBERT J., ed. *Focus on Hitchcock.* Englewood Cliffs: Prentice-Hall, Inc., 1972. (Paper) A compendium of articles about and interviews with Hitchcock, written by a variety of commentators.

RICHARDSON, ROBERT. *Literature and Film.* Bloomington: Indiana University Press, 1969. (Paper) A general study exploring a wide range of similarities and differences between the two mediums.

SARRIS, ANDREW. "The Rise and Fall of the Film Director," in *Interviews With Film Directors,* ed. Andrew Sarris. New York: Avon Books, 1967. (Paper) An exploration of why the director rather than the writer ought to be considered the primary artist in the collaborative enterprise of filmmaking.

SIMON, JOHN. *"Persona,"* in *Ingmar Bergman Directs.* New York: Harcourt Brace Jovanovich, Inc., 1972. A detailed analysis of four Bergman movies, including *Persona,* prefaced by a lengthy interview with the great Swedish director.

9 **avant-garde**

In the cinema, there are three broad classifications of film: fiction, documentary, and **avant-garde.** "Avant-garde" means in the front rank, in advance of the main body. (The "main body" in this case would primarily be feature length commercial fiction films.) The avant-garde cinema has been called many names, not all of them polite. In the thirties and forties, it was known as the "Experimental film" or the **"Poetic cinema."** In the fifties, these films were part of the "Independent cinema," and in America especially, they were also called **"Underground"** movies. Since the early sixties, most avant-garde films in the United States have been considered a part of the "New American Cinema."

THE AVANT-GARDE AESTHETIC

By definition, avant-garde movies tend to be produced by and for a minority. Because of their restricted appeal, they are seldom produced within a commercial framework, where by necessity a film is considered at least in part a profitable commodity (9-1). Nor are avant-garde films generally considered a part of the entertainment industry, as most fiction movies are. Experimental films can be exciting, witty, and provocative, but seldom are they relaxing or blandly entertaining. For the most part these works are technically complex and difficult to understand, at least on first viewing. To many, they are an acquired taste: one needs to be actively disciplined, sympathetic, and tolerant in order to enter the rather rarified world of the avant-garde cinema.

There are almost as many kinds of experimental films as there are filmmakers. In general, however, these movies are made on small budgets because of their limited profit-returning potential. Some of them run to six or eight hours in length, while others are merely a few seconds long. Most of them are under a half hour in duration. For the most part, these films are shot in 16 mm rather than the more expensive 35 mm, which is the standard gauge for fiction films. A few experimental filmmakers have even turned to Super 8 mm in order to cut expenses.

Many avant-garde film directors avoid courting public acceptance and will accept it—if it comes—only on their own terms. In many cases, these filmmakers reject the main body of film culture, dismissing it as glossy, false, and aesthetically dead. They are particularly in revolt against the "Big Lie of Culture," with its glib morality, its false cheer, and its refusal to explore the less "attractive" aspects of life. Many viewers are initially offended by the deliberate vulgarity and "bad taste" of avant-garde films. Shock techniques are common in these movies, for many of them are meant to jolt the audience out of its complacency and self-satisfied smugness. Viewers are commonly abused, ridiculed, and treated contemptuously—especially those who cling to conventional middle-class values, which these filmmakers consider sterile and life-denying.

Virtually all avant-garde films are **expressionist** (9-2). These directors use film as a means of exploring beneath the surface of the material world. They aren't concerned with recording actual life but with creating a totally imaginary universe. They prefer to invent rather than discover, to present rather than represent. Many of them are preoccupied with an interior psychological reality, or with a submerged mythical existence—spiritual realms which are not visually apparent in the literal world.

Independent films are generally conceived and executed by a single individual. Unlike most fiction filmmakers and many documentarists, the experimental director usually shoots and **edits** his own **footage.** To keep costs down, the collaborative aspect of the filmmaking process is kept to a minimum (9-3). Usually the "actors," if any, are the director's friends or family. But this necessary economy can also result in greater precision and more complete artistic control. The director is ultimately answerable only to himself. Hence, the avant-garde filmmaker believes that his work is more

9-1. *Metropolis.*
Directed by Fritz Lang.
Although most avant-garde films are not widely known nor produced within a conventional commercial framework, a few of them, like Lang's science fiction classic, have enjoyed considerable popularity and profit.

personal than the average commercial move, for *all* the major **artistic** decisions are made by him.

Autobiographical elements are commonplace in these movies. Many avant-garde artists are primarily concerned with conveying their "inner impulses," their personal and subjective involvements with people, ideas, and experiences. Emphasis is often placed on a *direct* expression of emotions, and not on an objectified presentation. For this reason, avant-garde movies are sometimes obscure and even incomprehensible, for the audience's engagement is not always as intense as the artist's expression. Like James Joyce in his novel *Finnegans Wake,* many of these filmmakers have evolved their own personal language and symbology. Unless the viewer is attuned to this essentially private world, these movies can seem wildly out of control. However, in the best of these films—the symbolic and mythological works of Jean Cocteau and Jordan Belson, for example—the necessary extra effort is richly rewarded.

The avant-garde cinema has excelled in treating taboo subjects—those "forbidden" topics which were ruled out to commercial filmmakers due to public censorship (9-4). Many of these movies were (and still are) considered

avant-garde **380**

9-2. *The Cabinet of Dr. Caligari.*
Directed by Robert Wiene.

The German Expressionist movement of the late teens and early twenties is regarded by some scholars as the first phase of the avant-garde cinema. Like many **Dadaist** and **Surrealist** movies of the twenties, this film is strongly indebted to the various experiments in distortion that were being conducted by painters, poets, and sculptors.

(Museum of Modern Art)

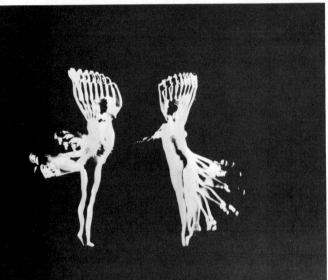

9-3. *Pas De Deux.*
Directed by Norman McLaren.

The avant-garde cinema is almost exclusively an expressionistic movement, concerned with subjective, personal, and sometimes intensely private ideas and emotions. Many of these movies are related to the more abstract arts like music, dance, and painting rather than literary and narrative arts such as drama and fiction.

(Museum of Modern Art)

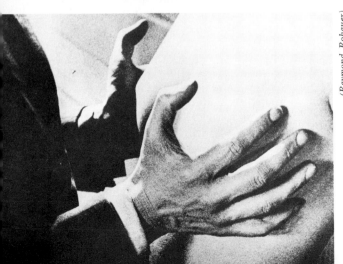

9-4. *Un Chien Andalou.*
Directed by Luis Buñuel and Salvador Dali.

Avant-garde movies often deal with socially taboo themes and subjects that are ignored by the commercial cinema because of the problems of public censorship. Human sexuality has been one of the most popular and enduring of these themes.

(Raymond Rohauer)

9-5. *Un Chien Andalou.*
Directed by Luis Buñuel and Salvador Dali.
Almost from its inception, the avant-garde cinema has excelled in exploring distortion as an artistic technique. These films are often visually flamboyant, profuse with special effects and distorting lenses and filters.

shocking, immoral, and outrageous. Political and sexual themes abound, especially the latter which have included overt homosexuality, lesbianism, voyeurism, fetishism, bestiality, masturbation, and sado-masochism, among others. Many avant-garde films have provoked outcries of public indignation. Some have been confiscated by the police. A few have even caused riots. Indeed, avant-garde artists are often delighted by such spectacles of moral outrage.

With a few notable exceptions, avant-garde films are generally unscripted. In part, this is because the filmmakers themselves shoot and edit their own footage, and are therefore able to control their material at these stages of the filmmaking process. These directors also value chance and spontaneity in their movies, and in order to exploit these elements, they avoid the inflexibility of a preordained script. Conventional narrative structures are rare in these films. They seldom tell a story, but tend to explore an idea, emotion, or experience in a nonlinear fashion. **Shots** are joined in associative clusters rather than in a logical sequence of consecutive actions. Sometimes these clusters are poetic analogies, other times they may seem totally irrational.

Indeed, the roots of the avant-garde can be traced to Dadaism, an artistic movement that placed a high premium on the values of irrationality and anarchy. Many present-day Underground filmmakers would justify the nihilistic and uncontrolled elements in their work as a perfect artistic reflection of contemporary social conditions. In a world without order, stability, or coherence, what could be more appropriate, they would argue, than an art which stresses disorder, instability, and incoherence?

Technically, the avant-garde cinema has gloried in the wide spectrum of expressionist methods at its disposal (9-5). The images of these films are densely saturated with detail. Like poetic language, the visuals of many experimental films are highly condensed, elliptical, and therefore often too complex to be absorbed at one sitting. Distorting **lenses** and **filters** are used with intoxicating abandon; **double** and **multiple exposures** are frequent; colors are employed non-naturalistically; lighting effects can be startling and flamboyant; and special effects are commonplace, especially in the American avant-garde.

With the exception of the Surrealists, who tended to edit rather conventionally, avant-garde films are generally cut in a furious, abrupt style. The lack of traditional story **continuity** in most of these movies offers maximum opportunity for juxtaposing every manner of shot, often with a minimum of logic. Sometimes the shots seem to machine-gun by at a breathless clip. Robert Breer's *Image by Images I,* for example, is composed totally of single-**frame** shots. That is, each shot is less than 1/24th of a second long! Many experimental filmmakers delight in throwing together shots of incongruous objects. In the political satires of Bruce Conner, for example, the juxtapositions can be hilarious. Two of his Underground classics, *A Movie* and *Cosmic Ray,* hurl headlong at a frenzied pace, the shots colliding wittily in a junk heap of newsreels, cartoon characters, nude figures, "found objects," and prominent politicians.

Time and space in these films are generally subjective and psychological rather than literal. Jean Cocteau's *Blood of a Poet,* for example, opens with a shot of a high tower collapsing. The fall is not completed until the end of the film, one hour later, when we see the tower hurtling to the ground. Similarly, space in these films is often magical and dreamlike. Objects seem to exist in a **symbolic** limbo of some kind. In Maya Deren's *A Study in Choreography for the Camera,* for example, a dancer leaps gracefully from a wooded setting to a living room to an art museum in one fluid movement (9-6).

Very few of these movies employ **synchronous sound.** In the first place, the equipment used by many experimental filmmakers is incapable of reproducing sound adequately, if at all. But there are also aesthetic reasons for the avoidance of synchronization. The rebellion of the avant-garde against the fiction feature is based in part on its "theatrical" use of sound —especially language. When sound derives from the image, an increased sense of **realism** is almost inevitable. But most of these filmmakers are revolting against realism in the cinema. To reinforce the unreality of their worlds, they prefer to create a disjunction between image and sound. Like the Soviet expressionists, then, avant-garde filmmakers tend to incorporate sound as part of their **montage** technique, as another source of juxtaposing different or even conflicting information.

A few avant-garde filmmakers have even made movies without a camera. These films are composed "cinegraphically"—that is, instead of *photographing* images on the raw **stock,** the stock is used as a translucent medium upon

9-6. *A Study in Choreography for the Camera.*
Directed by Maya Deren.
Time and space in many avant-garde movies are subjective and dreamlike, rather than literal. People glide through space with graceful fluid movements in Deren's film —movements that couldn't be duplicated in a literal space like a dance stage.

which the artist paints, draws, scratches, or etches the subject matter by hand. These techniques are particularly popular with painters and sculptors who have turned to filmmaking. The Canadian Norman McLaren has even created an artificial soundtrack by scratching directly on the sound portion of the film emulsion. In Stan Brakhage's *Mothlight,* bits of moth wings, flowers, seeds, etc. were glued between layers of editing tape, from which a master print was then struck. Some artists have punched holes in the film strip, glued sand to it, even grown mold on it.

Film historians generally subdivide the avant-garde cinema into three phases: 1) the **Dadaist** and **Surrealist** periods, roughly from 1920 to 1931, based primarily in Berlin and Paris; 2) the poetic and experimental period, roughly from 1940 to 1954, and centered mostly in the United States; and 3) the Underground period, from 1954 to the present, also centered primarily in America. Convenient as these subdivisions are, they can also be mis-leading. In many respects, the avant-garde cinema can be dated from the time of Georges Méliès at the turn of the century. Though there have been periods of relatively little activity (most notably during the Depression thirties), the avant-garde has never ceased to produce important new films. Furthermore, though the most famous films tended to be produced in

Paris, Berlin, New York, and San Francisco, the avant-garde is essentially international, and a great many important works were and still are being produced in London, Vienna, Toronto, Zagreb, Prague, and many other cities, not to speak of a multitude of communities in the United States and Canada.

Some avant-garde filmmakers were producing movies throughout this time spectrum. Jean Cocteau and Hans Richter, for example, began making films in the twenties and didn't stop until the sixties. Luis Buñuel is still producing excellent pictures, though not as radically avant-garde as those he made in the twenties and thirties. A number of the most significant American Underground filmmakers began their careers in the forties and fifties and are still prominent: Stan Brakhage, Jack Smith, Gregory Markopoulos, the Whitney brothers, Kenneth Anger, and Jordan Belson, to name only a few.

DADAISM

The teens and twenties represented the most exciting period of avant-garde experimentation in the arts. The impulse to discover new modes of artistic expression was particularly fervent in Paris, which was generally regarded as the avant-garde capital of the world. In the plastic arts especially, the so-called "Isms" flourished. Perhaps the most significant of these was Cubism, which developed the idea of fragmentation, not only in painting and sculpture but in literature and cinema as well. After World War I, a new tone permeated the avant-garde—one reflecting a spirit of cynicism, disillusionment, and in some cases, nihilism.

Dadaism developed out of this social and artistic milieu. Painters, writers, and intellectuals formed this movement as a violent protest against "civilization," which they believed had been responsible for bringing about the Great War. Using humor, irrationalism, and outlandishness as their chief weapons, these iconoclasts wanted to tear down the scaffolding of traditional values. In their place, the Dadaists glorified disorder, cynicism, and the spirit of anarchy. They were anti-intellectual, amoral, and anti-aesthetic. All social inhibitions—sexual, artistic, and personal—were dismissed with contempt. What the Dadaists valued most was an uncensored, child-like spontaneity.

The Dadaists believed that traditional culture, the "Fine Arts," were bankrupt. Essentially Romantic revolutionaries, this cheery band of lunatics fervently wanted to épater la bourgeoisie with their gleeful assault on the bastions of middle-class culture. Detesting the excessive refinement of "high art," the Dadaists constantly ridiculed the notion of "classical harmony" so venerated by the artistic Establishment. The new movement was steeped in a subversive aesthetic: a frontal attack was launched against "decency" and "good taste" in art. The Dadaists wanted to create a wholly new art, one that was free, improvisatory, vulgar, funny, and fun (9-7). Art, they felt, should be a revolution for the hell of it. Needless to say, a lot of people thought they were crazy.

It's not hard to see why so many of them turned to the cinema as a major mode of expression. Film, after all, was a new medium, with no real

9-7. Neighbours.
Directed by Norman McLaren.
Although McLaren is not regarded as a Dadaist, several of his films are characterized by the same sense of irreverence, absurdity, and whimsy. Like many Dadaist movies, *Neighbours* deals with a serious theme—war—in a hilarious manner.

aesthetic tradition behind it, and no official critical body of "rules" to confine its development. Furthermore, it was a popular medium, still decidedly *déclassé* with its predominantly working-class audiences. The Dadaists especially delighted in the crazy chase sequences in the films of Mack Sennett, which they thought were perfect reflections of the comic absurdity of life (9-8). The cinema was also eclectic, and the Dadaists, with their scorn for traditional techniques and artistic "purity," were excited by the experimental possibilities of the medium. Anything that could be photographed could be tossed into a movie, and where anything goes, nothing matters.

Few of the Dadaists used narrative structures in their films, for they believed that plots are based on some kind of logic and coherence. Furthermore, narratives are a carryover from literature and drama. In the movies, editing permits a filmmaker to present scenes that aren't "connected" in a sequential manner, in which there are no causes and effects. Hence, the director is able to create a world without "sense" or meaning. Indeed, the Dadaists rejected all organic conceptions of art. "There are no stories," Jean Epstein proudly proclaimed in 1921, "there are only situations without tail or head; without beginning, center, and end." This anti-organic attitude has persisted in the avant-garde to the present day. For example, one Underground filmmaker has accumulated thousands of feet of film so that when he wants to make a movie, he claims he simply "slices off" some footage "like a sausage."

Despite the gloomy philosophical implications of Dadaism, the films themselves can be joyous, even exhilarating. During the early twenties, the exhibitions of these movies were often more exciting than the films themselves. For example, in 1923, Man Ray, an American photographer working in Paris, was commissioned to produce a film for a Dadaist function. Ray concocted *The Return to Reason,* which was made by sprinkling objects (tacks, buttons, etc.) on film emulsion. He also included shots of a female nude bumping and grinding in front of a window, while sunlight and shadows made abstract patterns on her writhing torso. He hastily edited these shots together with some homemade glue. At the gathering itself, poets screamed their gibberish verses at the top of their voices, a "concert" of sirens and bells was performed, and Ray's film kept tearing off at the splices. The movie ultimately provoked a riot, and the members of the audience went berserk by ripping up the meeting hall. All in all, as film historian Arthur Knight has observed, "it was considered a very successful Dadaist evening."

Perhaps the most famous Dadaist films are René Clair's *Entr'acte* and Fernand Léger's *Ballet Mécanique,* both produced in 1924. Clair's film, scripted by the Dadaist poet and theorist Francis Picabia, was partly inspired by the chase films of Mack Sennett. A funeral procession is shown in **slow motion,** emphasizing the pomp and solemnity of the occasion. Suddenly the hearse breaks away, and there follows a very funny **fast motion** pursuit sequence with a group of dignified bourgeois gentlemen huffing and puffing after the runaway casket. Léger, one of the original Cubist painters, was more concerned with **abstraction** in film. *Ballet Mécanique* is a "visual dance" of ordinary objects (levers, gears, pots, pans, egg beaters) which take on abstract forms (9-9). The film consists essentially of a series of kinetic variations, though interspersed throughout the movie are twenty-three repetitions of the same shot of a washerwoman wearily climbing some stairs. The woman never does reach the top—which may or may not be symbolic.

In Berlin at about the same time, a number of artists were also experimenting with abstraction in film. Hans Richter, the best known of these, championed what he called the **"absolute film,"** which has no real content,

(Warner Brothers)

9-8. Blazing Saddles.
Directed by Mel Brooks.
The crazy chase sequences, epic pie battles, and other forms of inspired lunacy in the silent comedies of Mack Sennett are often said to have inspired the early Dadaists to even greater heights of absurdity. Film critics have noted the strong influence of these early pioneers on such later artistic anarchists as the Marx Brothers, Woody Allen, Robert Downey, and Mel Brooks.

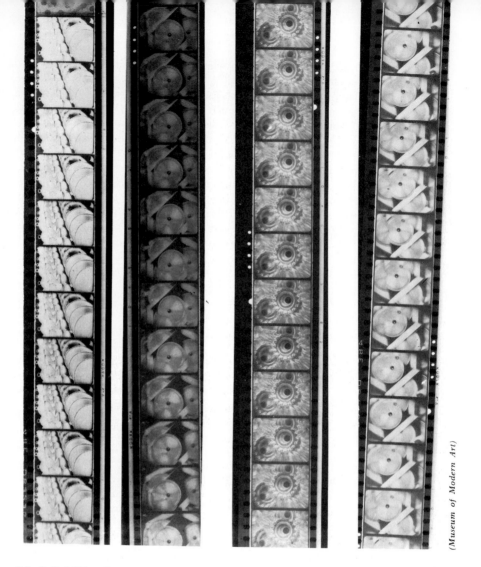

9-9. Ballet Mécanique.
Directed by Fernand Léger.
Best known for his cubist paintings, Léger was also one of the most famous Dadaist filmmakers. One of the first to explore abstraction in the cinema, he created many striking **kinetic** effects by "choreographing" perfectly ordinary objects like crockery, dishes, and machine gears.

but consists of "pure" forms. Along with his colleagues Viking Eggeling and Oskar Fischinger, Richter insisted that film's natural affinities were not with literature or drama, but with abstract art, music, and dance. Their films contained non-representational shapes, textures, and patterns, rhythmically choreographed into a kaleidoscope of shifting formal relationships. The titles of their films were often musical and deliberately neutral: Richter's *Rhythmus 21* (9-10) and Eggeling's *Symphonie Diagonale* were among the first of a long tradition of abstract movies within the avant-garde movement.

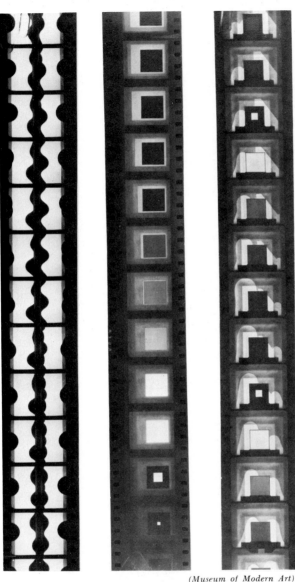

9-10. Rhythmus 21.
Directed by Hans Richter.
Along with a number of other German artists, Richter was a champion of the "absolute film," which consists solely of abstract shapes and designs. Insisting that movies should have nothing to do with acting, stories, or any kind of recognizable subject matter, Richter believed that film—like music and abstract painting—ought to be concerned with pure non-representational forms.

(Museum of Modern Art)

Other artists used music as the inspiration for their visuals. In *Disque 957,* for example, the Frenchwoman Germaine Dulac attempted to "translate" Chopin's "Prelude No. 6" into visual (and mostly abstract) patterns.

SURREALISM

Many of the original Dadaists were also prominent in the Surrealist movement, which developed in the mid-twenties, and flowered at the turn of the decade (9-11). They brought with them some of the same perverse

9-11. *Daydreams.*
Directed by Buster Keaton.
Just as many of the Dadaists looked to the films of Mack Sennett for inspiration, some of the early Surrealists were much impressed by the fantastic dreamlike quality in the works of Keaton. Although his movies are among the funniest ever made, a number of them reflect a vision of the melancholy absurdity of life, and suggest an underlying sense of anxiety.

iconoclasm that characterized the earlier movement: a love of irrationality, a rejection of conventional "civilized" values, and a contempt for restraint and "good taste." Like Dadaism, Surrealism encompassed painters and writers as well as filmmakers. Perhaps the central figure of the new movement was André Breton, a psychologist and poet, who issued the first "Manifesto of Surrealism" (i.e., super-realism) in 1924.

Surrealism differed from Dadaism in tone as well as content and technique. Surrealism was more self-consciously "artistic," with a new emphasis on mystery, anxiety, and paranoia. The humor was also different. Instead of the jolly rambunctiousness of Dadaism, with its sense of fun and irresponsibility, the comedy of Surrealism tended towards the grotesque and the macabre. Much of the wit in these films would now be described as "black comedy" because of its emphasis on sick jokes and cruelty. The Spaniards Luis Buñuel and Salvador Dali had particularly ghoulish senses of humor.

Influenced in part by **Marxism**, the Surrealists tended to be more serious and systematic in their rebellion. They viewed bourgeois values not only as silly, but as dangerous and repressive as well. The anarchy of Dadaism was somewhat displaced by a new leftist political orientation, resulting in a more

9-12. Stairway to Heaven.
Directed by Michael Powell.
Many conventional fiction films that contain dream and fantasy sequences are indebted to the experiments of the early Surrealists in exploring the subconscious. Some of the most famous Surrealistic dream sequences are found in Bergman's *Wild Strawberries*, Huston's *Freud*, Fellini's *8½*, and Hitchcock's *Spellbound*.

explicit attack on capitalism and all social institutions which they believed were reactionary, particularly the Catholic Church. In the thirties, this Marxist orientation became even more pronounced, especially in the works of Buñuel.

Perhaps the major influence on Surrealism was that of Freud, whose ideas were gaining wide currency in intellectual circles of the day. Freud's theory of the unconscious, his preoccupation with dreams as a mirror of existence with its own language, and his emphasis on sexual symbolism were to exert a profound effect on these filmmakers. By plumbing the wellsprings of the subconscious they believed they could reveal a truer reality, one that ultimately controls all conscious external behavior (9-12). Hence, the Surrealists preferred exploring pathological conditions rather than "normal" ones, dreams and nightmares rather than waking states. Many of these artists were obsessed with neurosis, hysteria, and madness.

Surrealists took a great interest in all spontaneous acts, whether they were found in primitive art, drunkenness, children's games, fantasies, or aberrant social behavior. They were particularly enthusiastic about auto-matism—any kind of "uncontrolled" artistic activity. The free association principle which was the foundation of the literary technique of stream-of-consciousness was incorporated in many Surrealist films. The cinema is the ideal medium for conveying the weird precision of dreams, the Surrealists believed, and most of them would agree with Dali that art is "concrete irrationality."

In general, the Surrealists were less technically oriented than the Dadaists. Surrealism is more realistic—though only in a relative sense. Less dependent upon flashy photographic distortions, the Surrealists emphasized a sense of disorientation in their **mise-en-scène.** Objects are dislocated from their ordinary contexts and placed in arbitrary, surprising locations. In *Un Chien Andalou,* for example, Buñuel and Dali placed dead donkeys on top of pianos (9-13). Nothing is explained or justified, and the viewer is left on his own to try and find "reasons" for the weird tableaux and events. The Surrealists delighted in this "strangeness" for its own sake, and they often sneered at critical explications of their work (9-14). "Nothing in this film symbolizes anything," Buñuel and Dali perversely "explained" of their film—which of course doesn't contain any dog, "Andalusian" or otherwise.

This hostility towards analysis and explication is characteristic of all Surrealists, who believed that most critics were too "literary," too anxious to explain away visual complexities with language—that most analytical and rational of all mediums of communication. Indeed, many avant-garde artists still retain this prejudice against words, and a good number of them tend to view the visual image as superior to language in terms of emotional impact. The medium of film criticism, of course, is non-visual, and for this reason, avant-garde artists believe that film critics are literally not speaking the same language that they are. At best, these filmmakers tend to believe that an art

9-13. *Un Chien Andalou.*
Directed by Luis Buñuel and Salvador Dali.
Most Surrealist movies feature a deliberate "strangeness" in the mise-en-scène. In-congruity is especially common: ordinary objects are found in totally inappropriate locations—dead donkeys lying on top of pianos, for example. Like dreams, art should portray "concrete irrationality," Dali once proclaimed.

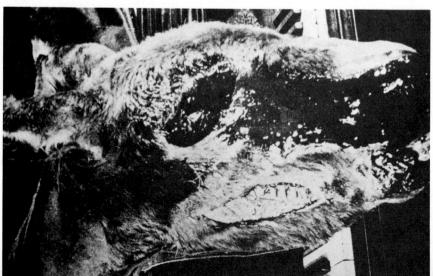

(Raymond Rohauer)

(a)

9-14a. *Gold Diggers of 1935.*
Directed by Busby Berkeley.
9-14b. *Limelight.*
Directed by Charles Chaplin.
9-14c. *The King of Marvin Gardens.*
Directed by Bob Raphelson.
The influence of Surrealism can be detected in the most unpredictable places, including many of the song and dance numbers in the musicals of Berkeley (a). Chaplin, like his spiritual disciple Fellini, suggests Surrealistic overtones in a scene depicting four absurdly comic musicians (b). Many fiction films exploit the Surrealist technique of dislocation to produce incongruity (c).

(Warner Brothers)

(b)

(rbc films)

(Columbia Pictures)

(c)

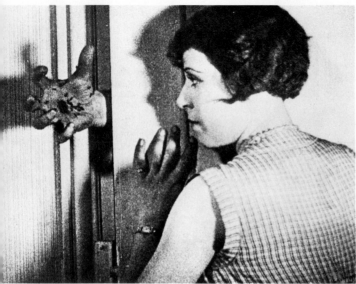

9-15. *Un Chien Andalou.*
Directed by Luis Buñuel and Salvador Dali.
Although most Surrealist films are densely saturated with symbols, often these symbols defy precise analysis. Many of them are deliberately disorienting and irrational—like a hand covered with crawling ants.

(Raymond Rohauer)

historian is likely to be more sensitive to their work than a film critic, whose orientation they claim is more literary and theatrical.

Actually, Surrealist films *are* rather densely symbolic, but a great many of the images simply defy precise analysis. Often the richness and ambiguity of these visuals would be reduced to some simpleminded "Freudian" set of explanations, and it was this reductionism that the Surrealists rightly regarded with scorn. Many of the scenes from these films were intended to jolt the viewer on an elementary visceral level (9-15). In *Un Chien Andalou,* for example, a woman's eyeball is slit by a straight razor wielded by Buñuel himself. The image functions on the level of primitive assault—it's an attack on the viewing audience as much as on the woman herself. A number of "explanations" have been offered for the scene, but they seem weak and inadequate when compared to the gut impact of the episode itself.

The Surrealists never forgot their Dadaist heritage, nor did they lose the capacity to stir up public indignation. *L'Age d'Or,* directed by Buñuel and partly scripted by Dali, created a riot when it was first exhibited. The film was subsequently banned, and most of the prints were destroyed. The movie is a bizarre blending of Marx and Freud, and it attacks both the Church and organized society. One of the most famous sequences features a sex orgy, inspired by the Marquis de Sade's *120 Days of Sodom.* Revelling in this sexual free-for-all, the master debauchee turns out to be none other than Jesus. The film is filled with other scenes of savage political and religious satire as well as sadism, masochism, and casual cruelty.

Perhaps the greatest of the Surrealist filmmakers was Jean Cocteau, who always maintained—apparently because of personal differences—that he was not a Surrealist director. An extraordinarily gifted man, Cocteau also distinguished himself as a painter, poet, critic, dramatist, and novelist. He didn't neatly compartmentalize his various activities: to him, all artists were "poets," whether they wrote with words, sounds, or images. Never one to disparage one art in favor of another, Cocteau felt that each form of poetic expression had its specialty. The film poet, for example, simply wrote with the "ink of light." He believed that the cinema was a first-rate vehicle for ideas, permitting the poet-director to take the viewer into realms that previously only sleep and dreams had led him to.

Cocteau was always deceptively matter-of-fact about his movies. Like the other Surrealists, he detested phony romanticism, and always claimed that he was a "realist." Indeed, he described his first film, *Blood of a Poet*, as "documentary scenes from another realm." Of course, to Cocteau as to the other Surrealists, "reality" in film is not the same as reality found on the average street corner. Cocteau was concerned with internal realities—the realms of the psyche and the soul, particularly of the artist. His monumental "Orpheus Trilogy," consisting of the features *Blood of a Poet* (1930), *Orpheus* (1950), and *Testament of Orpheus* (1960) is an exploration of the mysteries of poetic creation: what a poet is, how he creates, what he creates from, what his creations do to him.

"The more one touches mystery," Cocteau claimed, "the more important it becomes to be realistic." The aesthetic of film is based on photography, and what can be photographed *exists*, at least in some form. Thus, to take one of Cocteau's recurring film images, if the poet enters a mirror, we can't deny what we have *seen*. What is involved here of course is the literalizing of a **metaphor**. A verbal paraphrase of the scene might be: "poetic creation is like entering a mirror." Or, to convert the simile to a metaphor: "poetic creation is entering a mirror." In a whimsical dialogue exchange from *Blood of a Poet,* a statue tells the poet to walk through a mirror. "But one can't go into mirrors," he protests. "I congratulate you," the statue responds dryly, "you wrote that one could go into mirrors and you didn't believe it." The poet then walks through the mirror, into another world.

Many of Cocteau's most brilliant effects are literalized metaphors. Technically, they were achieved through trick photography. The mirror shot, for example, was accomplished by placing the camera on its side. The floor was then made to look like the wall, and the wall the floor. A vat of reflective liquid was placed on the floor; the edges of the vat suggested the frame of the mirror. Various props (chairs, etc.) were nailed on the wall above the vat. When the actor plunged into the reflective surface of the liquid from above, it looked as though he were entering a mirror once the shot was projected right side up. *Blood of a Poet* is a fascinating excursion into another world—yet it's always a "real" world, in Cocteau's sense of the term, never soft or fuzzy, never sentimental.

The first episode deals with "the scars of the poet," his solitude and loneliness. His isolation is so great that he lives out his own creations, which take on a life of their own. "The poet's work detests and devours him," Cocteau has stated. "There isn't room for both the poet and his work. The work profits from the poet." The poet wakes to discover a mouth on his hand; the mouth resembles a wound. At first he recoils from its freakishness, but gradually he grows fascinated with it. When he rubs his hand against a statue, the wound disappears and the statue comes to life. In revenge, it sends him through a mirror, into a world of terrible experiences, the world of artistic creation, which the poet fuses out of his childhood memories, his fantasies, and fears. Inside the mirror, he finds himself in a

9-16. The Testament of Orpheus.
Directed by Jean Cocteau.
The last film of the "Orpheus Trilogy" is filled with many dreamlike effects. Characters float in and out of the strange settings like phantoms. Cocteau himself (pictured, back to camera) wanders through his spiritual landscape like a bewildered alien.

long hotel corridor with many doors. He looks through a series of keyholes, where he sees, among other things, a girl floating on the ceiling of a room. After a number of painful and strange experiences, the poet shoots himself in the temple. The blood spurts profusely, and transforms into a toga. A laurel wreath appears on his head.

The scene shifts to a city square on a gray, wintry day. The poet is now a statue on a pedestal. Some callous schoolboys begin a snowball fight. The statue is now made of dirty snow, and the boys tear him apart while they use his snow to make their snowballs with. Later, an angel of death appears (in **negative image**), to the accompaniment of engine sounds. These merge with heartbeats, and we now see the poet's lapels throbbing with the wild beating of his heart. Again the poet shoots himself; this time he falls on a snow-covered table. As his blood gushes out, there is a cut to a theatre loge where fashionably dressed people are applauding: the poet's pain produces pleasure for others. And so the film continues in a series of striking images.

In *Orpheus*, the gates of hell are guarded by motorcycle toughs, the tribunals are bureaucrats in contemporary clothing. Orpheus receives coded messages from hell by radio. In *Testament of Orpheus,* Cocteau himself

avant-garde **396**

appears as "the author," thus splitting himself in two by having the author comment on the poet and vice versa (9-16). In this, his last movie, Cocteau pulls out all the stops: he employs written language, his own exquisite drawings, still photographs, slow motion sequences, double exposures, montage, reverse motion, and trick shots galore. His personal friends (including Pablo Picasso) appear in a kind of testimonial; Cocteau addresses the camera; other characters readily admit that they're performing in a movie. Weird man-horses walk about dreamily, and human statues with painted eyes on their eyelids seem both dead and alive. In a witty courtroom scene, Cocteau even satirizes himself by debunking the self-importance of "the author" and poets in general. To describe Cocteau's images is almost always to reduce them to banalities, to drain them of their ambiguity and charm. His greatest visuals simply elude description—much less explication—even after several viewings.

THE POETIC CINEMA

The second phase of the avant-garde movement was essentially a period of consolidation and modest expansion. A number of excellent films were produced during this period, but for the most part, they tended to develop the themes and techniques originally explored by the Dadaists and Surrealists. During the thirties, relatively few experimental movies were produced. Many of the filmmakers of the previous decade turned to making documentaries, which seemed a more appropriate artistic vehicle during the Depression. When the Nazis seized power during this period, many of the German experimentalists emigrated to other countries. By the conclusion of World War II, some of the most talented European avant-garde filmmakers had moved to the United States, which partly explains the emergence of New York and San Francisco as the new avant-garde capitals of the cinema.

Richter and Fischinger—who both moved to America—continued with their experiments in abstraction, though Richter's movies became more surrealistic as the years passed. Some of the boldest animated films were created by Norman McLaren and Mary Ellen Bute during the thirties. In *Camera Makes Whoopee* (1935), McLaren's "action painting," he developed new special effects techniques. *Colour Cocktail* (1935) was an exploration of symbolic color in animated films. *Allegro* (1939) was perhaps the first film in which sound was created by drawing directly on the film emulsion (9-17). Bute's films continued in the tradition of Germaine Dulac. *Rhythm in Light* (1936), *Synchrony No. 2* (1936), and *Parabola* (1938) were all "visual symphonies" of abstract shapes and ordinary objects made to look like abstractions, and cut rhythmically to classical musical compositions. Bute's career is one of the longest in the avant-garde cinema, ranging from this period to the mid-sixties, and culminating in her feature length adaptation of Joyce's *Finnegans Wake* (1965), which many regard as her masterpiece.

Throughout the forties, some of the best abstract films were being produced in San Francisco. Harry Smith, whose works weren't widely known at the time, made a number of striking non-representational movies. Jordan Belson began his career in 1947, though his greatest works were produced during the sixties. John and James Whitney also worked out of San Francisco, and made some of their most innovative films during this period. Not all avant-garde films made in this city were abstract, however. For example, the poet and playwright James Broughton, made several movies which were charming spoofs on Freudian concepts, many of which had degenerated into clichés by this time.

But the influence of Freud remained strong in the avant-garde, most notably in the films of Willard Maas, Sidney Peterson, and Maya Deren. Indeed, perhaps the main thrust of the poetic and experimental period was Freudian, though some of the psychological theories of Carl Jung were also gaining prominence, particularly his emphasis on myth and ritual. In many

(Museum of Modern Art)

9-17a. Rythmetic.
Directed by Norman McLaren.
9-17b. Pas De Deux.
Directed by Norman McLaren.
One of the most brilliant technicians of the avant-garde, McLaren has been engaged in experimental film-making for over four decades. *Rythmetic* (a) is in the tradition of kinetic abstraction pioneered by Richter and others. *Pas De Deux* (b) employs a technique called chronophotography, in which the movements of two dancers are staggered and overlayed by the **optical printer** to produce a stroboscopic effect: as the dancers move, they seem to leave ghostly imprints on the screen.

(a)

(b)

9-18. *Meshes of the Afternoon.*
Directed by Maya Deren.
Like many avant-garde works of the
forties, Deren's film is strongly
Freudian in emphasis, stressing the
psychopathology of everyday life.
The emotionally disturbed heroine,
enacted by Deren herself, is terrified
by a series of apparently insignificant
events which trigger off an increasing
sense of paranoia and persecution.

(Museum of Modern Art)

of the commercial films of the forties (Hitchcock's *Spellbound* is a good
example), a psychiatrist would "explain" even murderous behavior by trot-
ting out a string of facile Freudianisms, usually in the last few minutes of
the final reel. Such explanations generally involved a childhood "block" of
some kind, which, once removed by the omnipotent psychiatrist, rendered
the patient instantly "cured." Hitchcock even used this gimmick as late as
1964 in *Marnie.* (In *Psycho*, however, a psychiatrist's glib "explanation" is
wittily parodied.)

The avant-garde cinema tended to avoid this kind of slick over-simplifi-
cation. Freudian and Jungian ideas were used in a more complex manner,
to suggest possible motivations rather than to offer neat solutions. Explorations of the subconscious for the most part were not sensational in these
films, though sexual frustration still figured prominently. Unresolved anxieties, the search for identity, and the need to escape were popular themes in
the avant-garde cinema of the forties and early fifties, particularly in the
works of Maya Deren, who was perhaps the most influential and widely-
known experimental filmmaker of the period.

Deren's *Meshes of the Afternoon* (1943) was strongly surrealist in its
influence, and featured the director herself as the neurotic, terrified protagonist (9-18). There is a nightmare quality to the film, a sense of stark
terror and increasing paranoia as a young woman becomes progressively
more disoriented by a series of apparently trivial incidents. In her later
works, Deren explored the possibilities of dance and cinema, fusing the two
mediums with consummate artistry in such works as *A Study in Choreography
for the Camera* (1945), *Ritual in Transfigured Time* (1946), and *Meditation
on Violence* (1948). These later films were thematically more indebted to
Jung than to Freud, and were rather ritualistic in emphasis.

Deren was also an important theorist of the avant-garde cinema. She
wrote and spoke frequently of the advantages of the personal film over the
largely standardized products being produced in Hollywood. She differen-
tiated the poetic cinema from commercial films primarily in terms of struc-

ture. Like a lyric poem, personal films are "vertical" investigations of a theme or situation. That is, the filmmaker is not concerned so much with what's happening as with what a situation feels like, or what it means. The director is concerned with probing the depths and layers of meaning of a given moment. The poetic film then is not concerned with movement *per se,* but with the "metaphysical content of the movement."

Fiction movies, on the other hand, are like novels and plays—they're essentially "horizontal" in their development. The narrative filmmaker employs linear structures, and he must leap from situation to situation, from feeling to feeling. He doesn't have much time to explore the implications of a given idea or emotion, for he must keep his film "moving along." The poetic filmmaker ignores the strictures of time and space, whereas the narrative director (at least during this period) must be more careful in observing certain spatial and temporal **conventions,** which usurp much of his screen time.

Deren believed that in certain cases, it's possible—though very difficult —to combine these two types of structures. In the greatest plays of Shakespeare, for example, the actions move the drama along on a horizontal plane

(Museum of Modern Art)

9-19. Ritual in Transfigured Time.
Directed by Maya Deren.
Combining some of the ideas of Eisenstein and the Surrealists, Deren likened avant-garde films to lyric poems, in which the artist attempts to explore a theme "vertically" rather than in a linear sequence as in conventional fiction films. Images and sounds are clustered in layers of emotional associations—not all of them necessarily rational or decipherable.

of development. But occasionally, this forward action stops, thus permitting the dramatist to explore a given feeling within a kind of timeless void. The Shakespearean soliloquy is essentially a vertical exploration of an idea or emotion—rather like an aria in an opera, which temporarily suspends time, space, and movement. Deren believed that in film, such "arias" or set pieces are sometimes found in works that employ loose horizontal structures—the famous Odessa Steps sequence from Eisenstein's *Potemkin,* for example.

These soliloquies, arias, or vertical poems are what the avant-garde filmmaker tries to create without being encumbered by a horizontal narrative framework. Most poetic films are short precisely because they're emotionally condensed and narrower in scope. Since these films don't try to tell conventional stories, they're able to concentrate on the intensity of emotion, which is difficult to sustain for very long periods of time. The avant-garde cinema, then, is distilled, layered, and simultaneous, whereas the commercial film is distended, sequential, and (in most cases) characterized by a low symbolic density (9-19). Like poetry as opposed to prose, independent and commercial cinema have different aims—neither method is necessarily superior to the other.

Deren was also one of the key figures in publicizing the avant-garde cinema and in expanding its audiences. She spoke tirelessly to many groups across the country, urging them to form their own film societies in which personal films could be exhibited to new audiences. She booked her own works at a number of universities and art museums, and helped them to form private cinema groups where poetic films could be shown on a regular basis. Perhaps the most famous film society of this period, Cinema 16, was organized in 1947 by Amos Vogel in New York City. Throughout the fifties, this group exhibited virtually all the most important avant-garde movies produced in America. Two other famous film societies existed under the auspices of the Museum of Modern Art in New York, and the San Francisco Museum of Art.

After World War II, the so-called "art house" movement was also a boon to the avant-garde cinema in America. The number of small movie theatres which specialized in showing serious artistic films began to increase, and by the fifties they were proliferating rapidly. Located primarily in college towns and larger cities, these theatres not only showed important European features, but also some of the best domestic experimental films of the period. Instead of a conventional cartoon and newsreel art houses were likely to show a poetic or abstract film before the feature.

Towards the end of this phase of the avant-garde movement, a number of filmmakers were already beginning to explore themes and techniques that are more characteristic of the later Underground period. Sexual subjects particularly began to be treated more directly, less symbolically. A new uninhibited raunchiness could be discerned in such films as Brakhage's *Flesh of Morning,* which deals explicitly with masturbation. Kenneth Anger's *Fireworks* is a masochistic fantasy of a male homosexual, considerably less genteel and subtly allusive than the majority of poetic films of this period (9-20).

Indeed, a number of critics and publicists expressed alarm at this element of "perversity" which was fast becoming a dominant mode in the avant-garde film. Jonas Mekas, who was to become the most indefatigable

9-20. *Fireworks.*
Directed by Kenneth Anger.
In the mid-fifties, the avant-garde cinema was moving into a new phase characterized by a return to some of the shock techniques of the Dadaist and Surrealist periods. *Fireworks*, which is filled with images of violence and eroticism, deals rather explicitly with the sado-masochistic fantasies of a homosexual, played by Anger himself (pictured). These early Underground movies were characterized by a new tone of cynical mockery, and fused romantic elements with images taken from popular culture.

defender of such films less than a decade later, complained of a "homosexual conspiracy" in the experimental cinema. Amos Vogel was similarly dismayed by the obsession with crude sexuality for its own sake, which he felt characterized many of the works of the younger filmmakers. "The saleability of sex in a sexually repressed society is inevitable," Vogel observed, but he thought that most of these new films lacked artistry. They were exploiting the sexual hangups of American society, he believed, and functioned merely as an artistically pretentious kind of pornography. But the avant-garde was entering a new phase in the mid-fifties, one which repre-

sented a return in many respects to the Dadaist heritage of anarchy, iconoclasm, and total freedom of expression. The avant-garde had grown
somewhat genteel since the thirties, but now a new generation of crazies
took over—determined to rape the movement of its respectability.

THE UNDERGROUND PHASE

The Underground film represents the most prolific, stylistically varied, and
controversial phase of the avant-garde movement. Beginning in the mid-
fifties, when Underground filmmakers were loosely allied with the so-called
"Beat Generation," hundreds of young filmmakers sprang up across the
United States, though the main concentrations were still in San Francisco
and New York City. Despite harsh criticisms and persistent scorn from the
film establishment, these determined nonconformists continued to make
movies—some of them strident and shrill, others outrageously comic and
irreverent, a few of them profound and moving, and a great many of them
inept and incomprehensible. Critics either raved about or condemned these
films outright, as though they were all the same. Indeed, to this day, one
hears the same tiresome cliché that once you've seen one Underground film,
you've seen them all.

Perhaps one reason why these movies can seem unvaried has to do with
the way they're usually exhibited. Too often, a well-intended exhibitor will
schedule two or more hours worth of these movies, without regard to
similarities of style and theme. Since most of these films are brief, densely
saturated, and edited in an unpredictable, jumpy manner, they can begin
to merge in the viewer's consciousness after a while. Ideally, a program of
these films ought to be carefully selected, with an eye toward contrast and
variety. Perhaps the best method of exhibiting Underground films is to show
one before a feature length film, and another following the feature. After
all, a full evening of a similar diet of almost *anything* is likely to produce
fatigue and boredom.

The turning point between the era of poetic cinema and the Underground phase is not easy to pinpoint, since many of the same filmmakers
have been active in both periods. A number of historians and critics have
pointed to Stan Brakhage's *Desistfilm* as the watershed work. Made in 1954,
the movie has been called the first important "Beatnick film," reflecting a
new morality based on spontaneity, a preoccupation with youth, and an
emphasis on purely sensuous elements as opposed to the more literary and
psychological concerns of the previous phase of the avant-garde. The subject
of the film is a wild teenage party which builds to an hysterical climax.
Technically, *Desistfilm* established the main lines of what was to develop
into a new aesthetic in the avant-garde cinema, one emphasizing "roughness"
and a deliberate crudity of technique. Brakhage used a hand-held camera
which bobbed and weaved unsteadily in virtually every shot. The editing
style is frantic and rapid fire, with abrupt **close-ups** suddenly thrust upon
the audience. The framing seems clumsy and "unprofessional," and some
of the images are out of **focus.**

It was this technical crudity which seemed to arouse most of the
antagonism of the critics at the time. These young filmmakers were harshly

condemned for their lack of polish, and their unwillingness to discipline themselves, to learn the rules of their craft. And in fact, a great many of these new movies *were* (and still are) incompetent, self-indulgent, and boring. The lighting too often has a home-movie look, the cutting can be arbitrary and clumsy, the images out of focus, and the sound perfectly awful.

But in some cases, this crudity is intentional. Many of these filmmakers disdain the "costly look," which they associate with the empty gloss of most commercial movies—movies that they consider "beautiful but dead." The technical crudity of these films is at least in part a kind of anti-establishment gesture of contempt, then, a badge of sincerity and independence. Furthermore, like the **cinéma vérité** documentarists, these artists believe that a truly spontaneous movie will inevitably be crude in places, but the honesty and directness of the shots must take precedence over mere technical polish. Most of these filmmakers want to avoid (or in some case, free themselves from) what they view as technical over-kill. Their dislike of "discipline" is not necessarily a case of laziness, as many critics still maintain, but an unwillingness to sacrifice their spontaneity and freedom of self-expression at the sacred altar of Professionalism.

(Museum of Modern Art)

9-21. Thanatopsis.
Directed by Ed Emshwiller.
Rejecting the "costly look" of most conventional fiction movies, many Underground filmmakers wanted their works to look crude and unpolished. However, some of these artists, most notably Emshwiller, didn't share this contempt for traditional craftsmanship, and though his works can be wildly unconventional in other respects, most of them are photographed and edited with great skill.

A number of these artists are competent and even gifted technicians. Marie Menken, for example, was a special effects technician for several Signal Corp films; Stan Brakhage has done a good deal of "straight" filmmaking for various commercial organizations; and Ed Emshwiller has directed films for the rather conservative United States Information Agency. Emshwiller, generally acknowledged as one of the most gifted technicians of the Underground movement, is a self-conscious and precise craftsman. In such films as *Thanatopsis,* for example, his shots are painstakingly executed, and edited with great skill and subtlety (9-21).

In the mid-fifties, *Film Culture,* a journal devoted primarily to the avant-garde cinema, was established by Jonas Mekas. Mekas eventually became the principal publicist for the Underground movement, or "the New American Cinema," as he preferred to call it after the early sixties. Mekas championed these filmmakers tirelessly, devising public forums and new distribution channels in order to bring these works to a wider audience. When these movies were attacked for being self-indulgent and formless, Mekas responded with characteristic fervor:

> As long as the "lucidly minded" critics will stay out, with all their "form," "content," "art," "structure," "clarity," "importance"—everything will be all right, just keep them out. For the new soul is still a bud, still going through its most dangerous, most sensitive stage.

Eventually Mekas was condemned even more than the filmmakers themselves for his "ultra-permissiveness." The articles published in *Film Culture* were merely hysterical "appreciations," these critics charged, as cultish, shallow, and self-exhibitionistic as the films that were usually discussed. Amos Vogel and Parker Tyler, whose critical standards were considerably more stringent than those of Mekas, began to lose much of their enthusiasm for the avant-garde cinema. Out of the hundreds of filmmakers that seemed to be springing up each year, only a handful were worthy of serious consideration, they claimed. (Of course, a similar criticism could be made about the commercial cinema.)

In the sixties, the Underground movement flourished, and in many respects, surfaced. No longer isolated and alienated from the main cultural stream, these filmmakers now became a part of a new liberated and youth-oriented life style which burgeoned during this decade. The era of sexual permissiveness, political activism, rock and pop culture, and the drug scene coincided perfectly with the themes of the Underground cinema. Most important, perhaps, it was a time for youth—for child-like spontaneity and even for uninhibited infantilism. "If I were you," Robert Downey wrote to exhibitors about his film *Chafed Elbows,* "I wouldn't let anybody over forty years old in the theatre unless they're accompanied by a teenager."

The sixties was a decade of "doing your own thing," an extreme form of individualism that's profoundly American in spirit. All of the arts assumed a new sense of improvisation, fluidity, and freedom. Traditional "rules" and conventions were viewed with suspicion—even paranoia in some instances. Pop art, the Theatre of the Ridiculous, Happenings, mixed media —the new consciousness was to be found almost everywhere. Many artists were influenced by the communication theories of Marshall McLuhan,

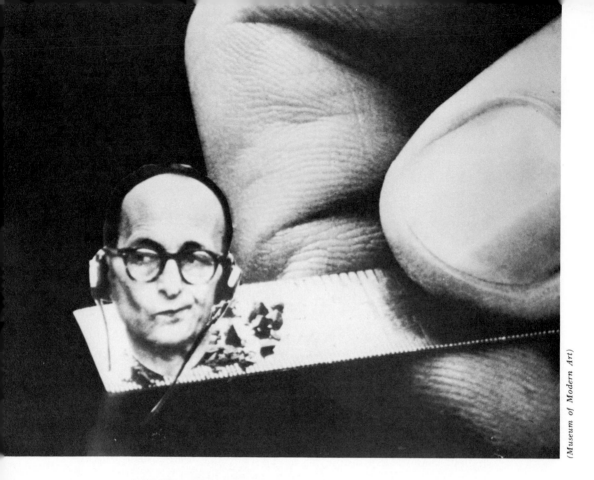

9-22. Skullduggery, Part I.
Directed by Stan Vanderbeek.
Among the most gifted political and social satirists of the Underground cinema, Vanderbeek exploits the Dadaist technique of incongruity with hilarious results. His witty "assemblages" move along at a breathless clip, juxtaposing pictures of public figures with ludicrous pop images of contemporary America.

Buckminster Fuller, and the composer, John Cage. The role of chance and the accidental became progressively more dominant in the arts.

In the cinema, these **aleatory** elements could be found not only in commercial movies, but also in cinéma vérité documentaries, and especially in Underground films. Brakhage was profoundly influenced by theories of chance structures, which had been explored originally by Cage. In *Third Eye Butterfly,* Storm De Hirsh used two simultaneous projectors in which pure chance determines the visual juxtapositions between the dual screens. Andy Warhol's *Chelsea Girls* also used two projectors, which project images that are totally aleatory. The projectionist is instructed to change reels when he "feels like it." Indeed, Warhol's lengthy work was originally intended for single projection, but he decided that the movie would be "shorter" if it were arbitrarily divided in half and shown simultaneously on two screens.

The sixties was a decade of political unrest and civil protest, and a number of Underground films reflected these anxieties, often in a satirical mode. Robert Nelson's *Oh Dem Watermelons* is a witty spoof on racist clichés about Negroes. Watermelons serve as a racist symbol of black people, and to the accompaniment of corny minstrel show songs, we see these melons kicked, crushed, splattered, and even seduced! Perhaps the most effective political satirist of this period was Stan Vanderbeek, whose "assemblages" are steeped in black humor and whimsical irreverence (9-22). Movies like *Skullduggery Part I* and *Part II* feature illustrations from magazines, film clips of politicians, and all kinds of incongruous photographs which emphasize the madness of American life. *Summit* is a satire of the Kennedy-Krushchev meeting, in which Vanderbeek **"animates"** the actors so that they look like calculating robots. *Breathdeath* is an anti-war film that features, among other things, a shot of Richard Nixon with a foot emerging from his mouth.

Sex has probably been the most popular theme of the Underground cinema. With the relaxation of public censorship during the sixties, however, many commercial film directors also began to explore the complexities of human sexuality, and the avant-garde was thereby co-opted of one of its traditional prerogatives (9-23). The Underground responded by concentrat-

(Rizzoli Films)

9-23. *Juliet of the Spirits.*
Directed by Federico Fellini.
With the relaxation of public censorship in the early and mid-sixties, the avant-garde was pre-empted of one of its most popular themes—sex. As commercial movies—like Fellini's rather surrealistic *Juliet of the Spirits*—began to explore human sexuality with more frankness, the Underground tended to move on to depict more unconventional sexual activities. Two of the most common of these were homosexuality and orgiastic sex.

ing on sexual aberrations—in other words, those areas of sexuality that have been considered abnormal by the middle-class majority. Homosexuality and orgiastic sex have been particularly popular subjects.

One of the classic examples of this type of film is Jack Smith's paean to pansexuality, *Flaming Creatures,* which is still banned in New York State. Smith's film is a glorification of the perverse, of the rapture of demonic lust. The camp-mythical universe of *Flaming Creatures* is hellish, suggesting Dante's *Inferno,* though without Dante's moral overview. Yet there's an undercurrent of despair in the film, reflecting perhaps the hopelessness of those who can never return to a world of normality. The movie features virtually every kind of sexuality: sado-masochism, transvestism, a gang-rape of an hermaphrodite, masturbation, oral sex, and even vampirism. Twisted arms and legs writhe like serpents in a steaming pit, and the top of the frame decapitates many of the pulsating, swirling figures. Much of the time we're unable to distinguish the sex of the people, until their full bodies stream into the frame and their genitals are visible. There's a ritualistic quality to these frenzied activities; it is a kind of Black Mass in which the celebrants abandon themselves totally to the ecstasy of violent sexual release. The soundtrack screeches and hisses with animal noises, mock-romantic Latin American music, rock-and-roll songs, and a cacophony of deliberately tasteless commercial tunes.

This concern with ritual and demonic sexuality is also characteristic of the works of Kenneth Anger, who considers his films invocations of black magic. His best known work, *Scorpio Rising,* is a mock heroic celebration of phallic narcissism (9-24). The film deals with a motorcycle gang and its essentially homosexual rituals. Anger satirizes the cyclists' preoccupation with "masculine" emblems—leather, chains, and shiny chrome phallic fixtures. With Dadaist perversity, he intercuts shots of the "super-stud" motorcycle leader and his gang with shots from a campy movie sequence portraying Jesus and his disciples and images of Hitler and his fanatical followers. Photographs of cult heroes like James Dean and Marlon Brando are juxtaposed with comic strip characters and Nazi emblems. A motorcycle race is intercut with a sequence showing Jesus entering Jerusalem on a donkey. Nazi hysteria over Hitler is portrayed as an unconscious death wish, which finds its parallels in the story of Jesus and his disciples, and in the erotic rituals associated with the motorcycle leader and his pack. *Scorpio Rising* is accompanied by a soundtrack of machismo-steeped rock-and-roll songs of the period.

Ritual and myth have always played a prominent role in the avant-garde cinema, and in the early and mid-sixties, these preoccupations became even more conspicuous in such films as Brakhage's *Dog Star Man,* Bruce Baillie's *Mass,* and the works of Gregory Markopoulos, who derived most of his subjects from classical Greek myths. Markopoulos' themes often revolve around homosexual love—masculine in the case of *The Illiac Passion,* and feminine in *Psyche.* As early as 1948, Markopoulos made a movie, *Lysis,* based on a Platonic dialogue on friendship. Like most of his works, the film is dazzlingly edited, flipping from past to future to present with casual audacity.

One of the greatest filmmakers to be influenced by myth is Jordan Belson, whose works are only superficially in the abstract tradition of the

9-24. *Scorpio Rising.*
Directed by Kenneth Anger.
One of the classics of the Underground cinema, Anger's film is a witty mock *epic,* spoofing the absurd super-masculine fetishes of a motorcycle pack. The soundtrack consists of banal rock-and-roll tunes of the period.

avant-garde cinema. Belson's films are profoundly mystical, inspired in large part by the philosophical literature of Zen Buddhism. His works have also been influenced by drug experiences, particularly with mescaline and peyote, which produce hallucinations akin to trance-like mystical states. Belson is a brilliant special effects technician, and his film *Allures* (1964) probably inspired the "Beyond Jupiter" section of Stanley Kubrick's *2001: A Space Odyssey.* Many observers agree that Belson's work not only predates that famous "trip" sequence but that it's artistically superior as well. The cosmic gaseous transformations that occur in Belson's film have a greater metaphysical impact and are more authentically mystical in their force, in part because they seem less mechanically produced than the Jupiter section of Kubrick's film.

Re-Entry is generally regarded as Belson's masterpiece. Originally inspired by John Glenn's historic penetration into space, the film is densely symbolic and mythical, though it can also be accepted as a purely abstract movie. Buddhist ideas of mystical reincarnation are likened to a spacecraft's re-entry into the earth's atmosphere. Belson used some of Jung's psychological theories to structure his film. The three stages of space travel—

launching, penetration of deep space, and re-entry—symbolize three mystical states: death, a limbo-like suspension in the cosmic void, and rebirth. The soundtrack for the most part is synthesized electronically, and consists of eerie sets of reverberations. Included on the soundtrack are some of Glenn's actual radio messages from space, though they're deliberately distorted and therefore incomprehensible to most audiences.

Before entering the world of the commercial cinema, Andy Warhol was the *enfant terrible* of the Underground movement. Critics either hailed him as one of the most audacious innovators of the avant-garde, or as one of its most outrageous frauds. Warhol's matter-of-fact disdain for all "professional" standards infuriated even other members of the avant-garde. His self-admitted indolence, his dead-pan manner of uttering the most outrageous statements, and his undeniable flair of gaining publicity alienated a good many devotees of the Underground cinema. Many of his films were only "produced" by Warhol at "The Factory," where he and his weird stable of flamboyant "Super-stars" did their thing. For the most part, Warhol was content to leave the acting, scripting, and directing to his "collaborators." There's a very strong element of the put-on in Warhol's movies, and humorless critics—including many of his staunchest admirers—often fail to discern it. Warhol himself didn't seem to take his films very seriously. When asked why he turned to the cinema after a successful career as a graphic artist, he laconically replied that movies were "easier."

Warhol made a number of films in the early and mid-sixties which have been given the rather solemn appellation of the "New Realism." Indeed, these movies out-Lumièred Lumière, for they consisted of lengthy unedited recordings of perfectly unspectacular events. *Eat* was a single-**take** forty-five minute film of a man eating a mushroom. *Sleep* was even more radically primitive, consisting of six hours worth of footage showing a man sleeping. Actually, the movie was composed of only three hours of footage, but each "segment" (reel) is repeated. Needless to say, the camera never moves, and the "editing" is confined to reel changes only. Perhaps the most spectacular example of Warhol's movies that don't move was *Empire,* in which the techniques are so **minimal** that the work is virtually a still photograph extended in time. Warhol set up his camera and photographed the Empire State Building in a single shot that lasts for eight hours. There's no sound to "distract" from the image, and real time is preserved more-or-less intact. The major "event" of the film takes place when the sun sets.

A number of critics have praised Warhol for his re-definition of the medium and for the purity of his minimal techniques. His cinema was a medium of time rather than space and movement, they claim, and by forcing us to concentrate on the minutest details, Warhol was able to create dramatic effects from the merest whisps of action. Hostile critics scoffed at such elaborate metaphysical explanations: these films are nothing but monstrous mountains giving birth to a mouse, they insisted. Most people would probably agree that Warhol's films of this period are more interesting to talk about than to watch, that his conceptions were more intriguing and provocative than his executions.

Stan Brakhage is perhaps the quintessential Underground filmmaker, and though he's still relatively young, he occupies a position of such prominence and prestige within the movement that many commentators consider him the leading contemporary avant-garde filmmaker. His thematic and technical range is extremely broad, extending from the almost documentary-like "home movie," *Window Water Baby Moving*, which shows the birth of his child, to films of pure abstraction (9-25). Like the documentarist Richard Leacock, Brakhage has experimented in Super 8 mm, and his lyrical *Songs*, which were photographed in this gauge, represented an important technical breakthrough for other avant-garde filmmakers.

Brakhage is an archetypal Romantic poet, an essentially mystical visionary who views the role of the artist as a kind of prophetic bard or seer. His greatest works are intensely personal and mythic. Like the works of the Romantic English poet William Blake, Brakhage's films are often obscure, saturated with private symbolism, and intensely egocentric. But Brakhage's

9-25. *La Chinoise.*
Directed by Jean-Luc Godard.
Although he is not generally regarded as an avant-garde filmmaker in the same sense as Brakhage and other Underground directors, the Frenchman Godard is perhaps the most radical innovator in the contemporary cinema. His stylistic range is incredibly broad, and includes—often within the same film—techniques of the documentary cinema as well as the most flamboyant audacities of the avant-garde. Here, for instance, he combines the flat pop-poster style of a Brechtian tableau with a live actress and a three dimensional toy airplane which zooms in and out of the frame.

(Leacock-Pennebaker, Inc.)

preoccupation with himself (and his children and wife Jane, who is virtually co-director of many of his films) is not a matter of mere vanity. Like most Romantics, Brakhage exploits himself as a universal symbol:

> I had the concept of everything radiating out of me, and that the more personal or egocentric I would become, the deeper I would reach and the more I could touch those universal concerns that would involve all men.

Dog Star Man is generally regarded as Brakhage's greatest work. The film is seventy-eight minutes long, and consists of a *Prelude* and four *Parts*. Like many of his works, this film employs a mythic structure. Though its treatment is rather abstract, the overt subject matter is relatively simple: a bearded woodsman (played by Brakhage) struggles to climb a steep mountain. Once he reaches the top, he chops down a white tree. But to paraphrase Brakhage's film in this manner is about as meaningful as describing *Moby Dick* as a story about a sea captain who pursues a white whale. Brakhage uses this action as a symbolic device to show Mankind's romantic striving to master the forces of Nature. The mountain climb itself seems to take place within the scope of a single day, yet the film also suggests a seasonal structure, which encompasses a full year.

The movie is richly symbolic, often totally abstract, and so fragmented and saturated with details that many audiences are confused by the work on first viewing. For example, the various forests that the Mountain Man passes on his upward climb seem to suggest several architectural and artistic periods. At one point, the snow resembles stained glass windows, and trees look like Gothic cathedrals. The white tree that the Mountain Man chops down seems to be a symbol of all religious monuments, or perhaps an image of Mankind's superstitious shibboleths.

Brakhage's technical range in this movie alone is very broad. The cutting is rhythmically sensuous, and there are expressionistic distortions in profusion. Multiple exposures, negative images, and a variety of lenses and filters are used to convey the emotional values of various stages of the journey. Brakhage sometimes inserts strips of black or white leader to convey metaphorically the terrifying blankness of certain experiences. **Point-of-view shots** are frequent, and in one sequence, Brakhage gives us a point-of-view shot of a scene, then cuts to shots of internal organs, cell tissues, and the blood stream, to convey the visceral impact of the original scene.

In his book *Expanded Cinema,* Gene Youngblood explores some of the directions that the avant-garde is already embarked upon and will inevitably expand. These developments include, for example, computer films, videotronics, multiple projection environments, and screenless holographic cinema in three dimensions. Indeed, the spectacular developments that await us in the future are likely to make all previous avant-garde movements look charmingly antiquated in comparison.

FURTHER READING

BATTCOCK, GREGORY, ed. *The New American Cinema: A Critical Anthology.* New York: E. P. Dutton, 1967. (Paper) An anthology of articles and interviews on and by independent American filmmakers, with an emphasis on the Underground phase.

CURTIS, DAVID. *Experimental Cinema*. New York: Universe Books, 1971. (Paper) A critical history of the avant-garde cinema, especially useful for its inclusion of many European filmmakers.

GILSON, RENÉ, ed. *Jean Cocteau*. New York: Crown Publishers, Inc., 1969. (Paper) A collection of articles on Cocteau, with excerpts from some of his film scripts.

MATTHEWS, J. H. *Surrealism and Film*. Ann Arbor: University of Michigan Press, 1971. An analysis of surrealism in film and the other arts, with background material on the intellectual and social milieu of the period.

RENAN, SHELDON. *Introduction to the American Underground Film*. New York: E. P. Dutton, 1967. (Paper) An historical analysis of the American avant-garde cinema, with emphasis on the works and artists of the fifties and sixties.

SITNEY, P. ADAMS, ed. *Film Culture Reader*. New York: Praeger, 1970. (Paper) A collection of articles and interviews taken from the journal that has been the main critical outlet for the American independent cinema.

————. *Visionary Film: The American Avant-Garde*. New York: Oxford University Press, 1974. An attempt to relate the American avant-garde cinema to the ideals and philosophical assumptions of the Romantic movement.

TYLER, PARKER. *Underground Film: A Critical History*. New York: Grove Press, 1969 (Paper) A critical analysis of the triumphs and failures of the avant-garde, with particular emphasis on the psychological and sexual.

VOGEL, AMOS. *Film as a Subversive Art*. New York: Random House, 1975. A critical history of the avant-garde, with particular emphasis on the forbidden, rebellious, and "blasphemous" aspects of these films.

YOUNGBLOOD, GENE. *Expanded Cinema*. New York: E. P. Dutton, 1970. (Paper) An exploration of the most recent technological and aesthetic experiments of the avant-garde cinema, with predictions for the future.

10 theory

Just as Louis Lumière and Georges Méliès might be regarded as the founders of the **realist** and **expressionist** traditions of cinema, these filmmakers also indirectly inspired the two major schools of film theory. Realist film theory tends to emphasize the documentary aspects of film art. Movies are evaluated primarily in terms of how accurately they reflect external reality. Stylistically, realists prefer films with "invisible" techniques, with an emphasis on **open forms** and subdued artistic effects. Most realists would stress the cinema's affinities with photography, and in some respects, with literature and drama.

Expressionist theories tend to emphasize the formal aspects of the

414

cinema. External reality is not necessarily—and certainly not primarily—the norm by which the "world" of the film is evaluated. Whereas realist theories emphasize *what's* being communicated, expressionist theories tend to stress *how* ideas and emotions are conveyed. In other words, realists are more likely to stress subject matter, expressionists technique. Expressionist theorists tend to prefer films in **closed forms,** in which the manipulations of the artist are rather apparent. Some of them would emphasize film's affinities with the more abstract, non-narrative arts—painting, dance, and music.

But these are general *tendencies,* not eternal verities. Indeed, at their best, both kinds of critics and theorists realize that these distinctions can become embarrassingly artificial. A realist like André Bazin and a formal critic like Robin Wood never entirely separate form from content, for they realize that ultimately the two terms are the same. Furthermore, in actual practice, intelligent film critics will use whatever theory seems to explain a movie most effectively. "Ideological" discussions of specific films usually seem forced, propagandistic, and often even irrelevant. In short, a film theory is only as good as it is useful. When it ceases to be so, it ought to be discarded in favor of an approach that *works.*

SIEGFRIED KRACAUER AND THE REALIST AESTHETIC

Perhaps no other theorist has been so influential as Siegfried Kracauer, whose book *Theory of Film: The Redemption of Physical Reality* puts forth some of the basic tenets of realist film theory. Kracauer doesn't ignore expressionist movies in his book. Indeed, he acknowledges a "formative tendency" (expressionism) which he traces back to the early experiments of Méliès. In general, however, he considers expressionist movies as aberrations of the central aesthetic of film. The basic postulate of Kracauer's aesthetic is that film is essentially an extension of photography and shares with it a "marked affinity" for recording the visible world around us.

Unlike other art forms, photography and cinema tend to leave the raw materials of actuality more or less intact. There is a minimum of "interference" on the artist's part. Kracauer would agree with Aristotle's precept that art is an "imitation" of nature, but the film theorist would insist that artists in other mediums imitate nature only in a general way. The novelist, for example, recreates experiences with words, but the meanings we derive from the medium of language are different from the meanings we would derive from the actual experience. Language produces a mental reality which is fundamentally different from the physical world of palpable reality. The camera, however, gravitates toward a more literal kind of imitation. A photographic image of a face, for instance, is virtually a copy of the original. Kracauer's fundamental principle, then, rests upon the literal quality of the camera's imitation of nature. Movies which stress artifice run the risk of violating the "basic properties" of the medium.

According to Kracauer, the cinema is characterized by a number of natural affinities. First of all, film tends to favor "unstaged reality"—that is, the most appropriate subject matter gives the illusion of having been found

10-1. *Picnic on the Grass.*
Directed by Jean Renoir.
According to Kracauer, movies are most faithful to the medium when they leave the raw materials of reality essentially intact, when the images suggest something discovered rather than arranged. This random and fortuitous quality is "inherently cinematic" because photography records the natural world objectively, with less distortion than is found in the other arts.

rather than arranged. Second, film tends to stress the random, the fortuitous. Kracauer is fond of the phrase, "nature caught in the act." That is, film is best suited to recording events and objects which might be overlooked in life—the stirring of a leaf, for example, or the rippling of a brook. Last, the best films suggest endlessness, they seem to be slices-of-life, fragments of actuality, rather than unified, enclosed wholes. By emphasizing open forms, the cinema can suggest the open-ended limitlessness of life itself (10-1).

Kracauer is hostile toward movies which demonstrate a "formative tendency"—that is, films which work against these natural affinities. Historical films and fantasies he regards as tending to move away from the basic concerns of the medium. Thus, he approves of certain elements in the early semi-documentary films of Eisenstein, which use nonprofessional actors, authentic locations, and natural lighting, but he condemns Eisenstein's **editing** practices, which distort the time-space continuum of reality. Furthermore, he disapproves of films that are propagandistic, for they impose an ideology, a single doctrine, over the neutral copiousness of reality. Kracauer condemns outright the works of Eisenstein's later career—the "operatic" *Alexander Nevsky* and *Ivan the Terrible.* The images and events of these movies are "uncinematic": they aren't fortuitous, but arranged, synthetic, and "theatrical," he says (10-2).

Kracauer also dismisses most literary and dramatic adaptations because he believes that literature is ultimately concerned with "internal realities," not external physical ones. For example, he thinks that if Shakespearean adaptations are performed on stylized sets, the result is mere filmed theatre, for the documentary realism of the medium is violated. If the plays are performed in natural settings (real castles, forests, and battlefields), the stylized language, the artificial costumes, and the "enclosed" world all clash with the open-ended authenticity of the locales (10-3). Adaptations from novels are permissible only when the narrative elements aren't too contrived, when the events seem totally realistic and unmanipulated. The fiction of Emile Zola, with its emphasis on objectivity and slice-of-life occurrences would be admissible in the cinema, but the novels of Jane Austen, with their neatly articulated plots, would not.

Kracauer tends to regard all self-conscious elements as "uncinematic." The camera ought to record what *is.* When the subject matter is not close to physical reality, we become conscious of the artifice, and hence, our

(Audio-Brandon Films)

10-2. *Ivan the Terrible,* **Part I.**
Directed by Sergei Eisenstein.
Kracauer has harsh criticism for the later works of Eisenstein, which the theorist believes are "operatic" and stagey. Unlike the director's early semi-documentaries, these later movies violate all the natural affinities for authenticity and objectivity which Kracauer believes are the essential characteristics of the photographic medium.

pleasure is diminished. For example, historical movies tend to be uncinematic because the viewer is aware of the "reconstruction." The world of the film is enclosed, for beyond the **frame** is not the "endlessness" of actual time and space, but the paraphernalia of the twentieth-century film studio (10-4). Similarly, in fantasy films we become too conscious of the contrivances: instead of concentrating on what's being shown, we become distracted by wondering how certain effects are achieved, for they have no literal counterparts in reality.

Kracauer underestimates the flexibility of an audience's response to nonrealistic movies. To be sure, it's easier for a filmmaker to create the illusion of reality if his story takes place in a contemporary setting, for the

(Columbia Pictures)

(a)

(b)

10-3a. *Hamlet.*
Directed by Tony Richardson.
10-3b. *Macbeth.*
Directed by Roman Polanski.
Kracauer believes that Shakespearean adaptations in the cinema are almost automatically doomed to failure, for theatrical productions stress the primacy of language, and employ closed forms, artificial settings, and stylized visual effects. If actual exteriors are used in Shakespearean adaptations, the authenticity and realism of the settings conflict with the stylization and artificiality of the language.

(a)

(New Line Cinema)

(b)

(United Artists)

10-4a. *Medea.*
Directed by Pier Paolo Pasolini.
10-4b. *The Wild Child.*
Directed by François Truffaut.
Kracauer believes that historical reconstructions run the risk of violating the basic properties of the medium. Films set in ancient Greece (a) or eighteenth-century France (b) are not open-ended, but "synthetic" and sealed off from the limitlessness of contemporary reality.

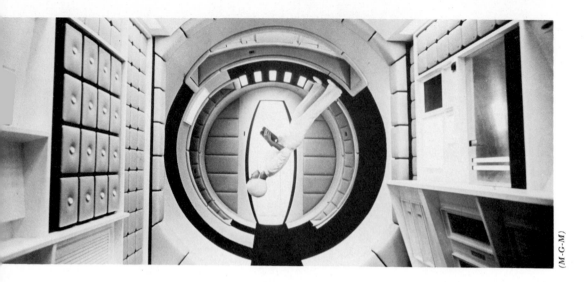

10-5. *2001: A Space Odyssey.*
Directed by Stanley Kubrick.
The "world" of a movie doesn't have to conform to the actual outside world in order to be *artistically* convincing. Viewers expect only that once the main characteristics of a screen reality are defined, the director does not violate this internal coherence with inappropriate references to outside reality.

world of the movie and the actual world are essentially the same. It's also true that we're often aware of the contrivances in historical movies and fantasies, but mainly when the cinematic techniques are heavy-handed and clumsy. On the other hand, there are hundreds of movies that seem saturated in the details of a remote period. Many scenes from *Birth of a Nation* appear as authentic as the Civil War photographs of Matthew Brady, for example. Kubrick's *2001: A Space Odyssey* was obviously not photographed in space, yet most viewers would agree that it's totally convincing in its *sense* of authenticity (10-5). Even an animated story film, like Disney's *Snow White and the Seven Dwarfs,* presents us with a self-contained "universe," which we are able to enter by temporarily forgetting the literal outside world of reality.

Other movies deliberately exploit the audience's double existence. As Dr. Johnson pointed out many years ago, audiences in a theatre don't literally believe that they're watching events of a remote period. Although viewers give a kind of voluntary credence to the events on stage, they're always aware of the fact that they are in a theatre, watching an artistic performance—not the real thing. The same principle of **aesthetic distance** applies to many movies (10-6). In *Tom Jones,* for example, the details of the period are authentic and believable, but Richardson deliberately breaks the illusion of reality by calling attention to the camera. In one scene, Tom is engaged in a furious quarrel with the mistress of the inn at Upton. Suddenly, in exasperation, he turns and addresses the camera—us. Richardson in effect reminds the audience that we're in a theatre, watching a movie.

The charm of this scene—and many others in the film—is precisely due to this technique of yanking the viewer in and out of the eighteenth-century world of the story proper.

Similar techniques are found in the historical plays of Bertolt Brecht, who endistanced his audiences from the world of the play in order to permit the viewer to draw certain political conclusions based on the contrasts between the two time periods. Actors step out of character to address the audience, commenting on the foibles of the characters they play. Techniques of this sort are common in the works of Brecht's cinematic disciple, Jean-Luc Godard. Godard insists that audiences should never forget that what they're

(Cinema Center Films)

10-6. *Little Big Man.*
Directed by Arthur Penn.
Some movies present us with a kind of double reality. Penn's film portrays events of the late nineteenth-century from the perspective of the present. Obvious anomalies, like present-day slangy expressions which are spoken by "period" characters, are deliberately meant to strike us with a comic sense of incongruity, to jolt us into a *contemporary* awareness of the significance of the past.

(M-G-M)

10-7. *The Band Wagon.*
Directed by Vincente Minnelli.
Despite its "fanciful scenery" and "stylized canvases," Kracauer admires Minnelli's musical and attempts to minimize its lack of "camera-realism" by defending the production numbers as "outgrowths of life's contingencies." Something of an aesthetic puritan, Kracauer seems unwilling to acknowledge that Minnelli's musical routines, like the brilliant "Triplets" number, are "cinematic" simply because they are so superbly staged and performed, not because they have anything to do with everyday reality.

watching is not reality but a manipulated *image* of reality. Indeed, in *Weekend,* Godard wittily spoofs naive realism in the cinema by having his characters comment on the "weirdness" of the movie they're appearing in. In *O Lucky Man!,* Lindsay Anderson prevents the audience from getting too emotionally involved in the story by interspersing the dramatic episodes with ironic musical commentaries, performed by the rock singer Alan Price.

Finally, as Pauline Kael has pointed out, audiences often enjoy the contrivances of a movie: it's part of the pleasure in watching a film. Musicals, for example, are generally appealing because they're *unlike* everyday reality (10-7). Similarly, in *The Exorcist,* the audience derives as much pleasure from wondering how William Friedkin achieved some of his extraordinary special effects as from the effects themselves. In short, film audiences are highly sophisticated in their responses to nonrealistic films: a viewer can almost totally suspend his disbelief, partially suspend it, or alternate between extremes.

Certainly Kracauer's book isn't of much value in explaining why expressionist films are effective. On the other hand, his theory is exceptionally sensitive in explaining the effectiveness of realist movies. The subtitle of Kracauer's book speaks not of the "imitation" or "recording" of physical reality, but of its "redemption." To redeem something is to recover it, to rescue it from oblivion. Even realistic movies, then, go beyond everyday life in some way: they show us things that we might not notice in the chaos and flux of everyday life. The camera preserves fortuitous fragments from this chaos, rescuing them from obscurity and decay.

An examination of virtually any good realistic movie demonstrates what Kracauer is getting at. In Bryan Forbes' *The Whisperers,* for instance, the **deep-focus** shots of the dingy apartment of the elderly heroine (Edith Evans) tell us much of her loneliness and neglect. Dozens of milk bottles clutter the table, yellowed photographs are crowded on the mantle. Only the sounds of the creaking walls and the dripping faucet seem to provide the old woman with active companionship—her "whisperers." Such desolate scenes are probably duplicated in millions of apartments everywhere. In real life, we often turn away to less disagreeable sights, but after witnessing these scenes, few people could remain indifferent to the solitude of the elderly and indigent.

The movies of Jean Renoir are filled with "commonplace" touches— details that are effective precisely because they are true to life as it can be observed. In *Grand Illusion,* for instance, the prisoners of war rummage through a trunkful of costumes in preparation for a theatrical show. Jokingly, a cynical prisoner instructs a delicate youth to put on one of the wigs and an evening gown. As a lark, the boy traipses off to get into costume. While the other men are engaged in excited preparations, the costumed youth enters the room. Suddenly a hush falls over the entire group. As the embarrassed boy wisecracks about his outfit, the camera slowly **pans,** revealing the sad, wistful expressions of the other men, as they are reminded how long it has been since they have seen their women. The scene is brilliantly effective, yet tactful and simple. As is the case with many situations in actual life, the scene captures the sudden shift in mood that can accompany the simplest event.

SOCIALIST REALISM

After the 1917 Revolution in Russia, the new society was characterized by an explosive proliferation of artistic as well as social experimentation. Influenced by the political and philosophical theories of **Marx**, Lenin, and Trotsky, such radical innovators as Pudovkin, Eisenstein, and Vertov reaped a rich cinematic harvest in this permissive cultural climate. In the early thirties, however, this radical experimentation came to a halt and was replaced by Stalin's monolithic theory of **Socialist Realism**, which became the official artistic style of the Soviet Union, and later of the Communist countries of Eastern Europe. But whether one is discussing the radical Marxist aesthetic of the early years of the Revolution, or the conservative aesthetic of Socialist Realism, these theories can be fully understood only within the wider context of the Marxist worldview.

Marxism is a political, social, and philosophical system of ideas that forms the foundation of such widely differing and often contradictory societies as the Soviet Union, the People's Republic of China, the disparate nations of Eastern Europe, and such isolated countries as Cuba. Furthermore, Marxism is a dynamic philosophy, altering significantly from year to year. Thousands of volumes have been written on the varying interpretations of the basic ideas of Marx and Lenin, not to speak of the modifications of such later figures as Stalin and Mao Tse-tung. Needless to say, only the barest outline of this worldview can be offered here.

Most Marxists would agree that the fundamental basis of all human societies is economic: those who control and consume the largest share of the material wealth are the ruling class. Marxists condemn capitalist and neocapitalist societies because the bulk of the material wealth is controlled by a relatively small ruling class, which insures its ever-increasing wealth and power by its control—either direct or indirect—over the basic means of production. The actual producers of this wealth—the workers—must be content with a disproportionately small percentage of the economic pie, which likewise produces a vastly diminished sense of power and self-determination (10-8). In capitalist societies, workers are "alienated" from their work, their peers, and their society because they are forced to compete economically against each other rather than cooperating in a joint effort to build a better society for all citizens. "Private property is public theft," Shaw once claimed, and most of his fellow Marxists would agree, which is why virtually all the means of production in Communist countries are publicly owned, and operated—in theory if not always in practice—in the public's best interests.

Marxists view history dialectically, and in objective materialist terms. Social structures and institutions are not mysteriously sanctioned and preserved by some cosmic outside force, but are built by *people*, who have selfish economic interests to preserve. Employing rigorously scientific and rational methods, the Marxist attempts to "demystify" various ruling-class subterfuges such as the concept of Divine Right, tradition, or social and religious ritual. Mysticism, religion, and all forms of philosophical idealism are dismissed as clever ruling-class strategies: they encourage ordinary work-

10-8. *The Grapes of Wrath.*
Directed by John Ford.
Based on John Steinbeck's Marxist novel of the same title, Ford's movie preserved the economic bias of the original, though its ideology was softened and humanized. Many Marxists would regard Ford's muted political theme as a betrayal of the novel, though some commentators have argued that Ford's film is more universal, and has stood the artistic test of time better than Steinbeck's book.

ers to think of their "riches" in the next world, rather than their poverty in this one. Marxists believe that an unsentimental examination of history reveals that the interests of a challenging class always conflict with those of the ruling class, producing a dialectic of constant redistribution of wealth and power.

Indeed, the optimism underlying Marxist theory is posited on the belief that history is evolving towards a classless society, in which wealth (and hence power) will be equally distributed. When genuine equality is established, individuals will be able to realize their maximum human potential, for they will feel totally integrated with their society, not alienated from it. Economic equality will allow individuals to behave humanly towards one another, for without the murderous competition encouraged by capitalist societies, citizens will enjoy a maximum of self-expression, freedom, and control over their own destinies.

Marxists analyze all human activity from this economic perspective. Even those areas of life that aren't generally regarded as particularly political

—like the arts—are evaluated in terms of material commodities, class, and power. Art is not politically neutral: it's produced by individuals for specific consumers. Implicit in all art, whether Marxist or not, is an acceptance or rejection of the political and social structure in which the art was produced. Marxist cultural critics never examine a work of art outside of its social and political context, for the value and degree of truth (as Marxists see it) of any artistic product will be determined by studying who produced it and for whom. Even "art-for-art's-sake," or the denial of all but purely formal and aesthetic meaning of a work of art, is viewed as political—as an implicit acceptance of the status quo.

Though Marxists differ over what methods and techniques are most effective in an artistic enterprise, they're in fundamental agreement that art must serve the revolution, that it must be relevant and useful in an understanding of the complexities of human nature and the nature of the material world. Some Marxists—especially the Socialist Realists—would also insist that art must be overtly ideological, that it must help to inculcate a revolutionary consciousness in its consumers. Since they are agreed about the subject, the major controversy among Marxist artists and theorists revolves not around *what* to portray, but *how* to portray it.

Interestingly enough, within the Marxist fold as in the non-Communist world, artists fall into two general types, the expressionists and the realists (10-9). Expressionists like Pudovkin, Eisenstein, and Vertov dominated the Soviet cinema in the earlier years of the Revolution, and in our own time, such radical Marxists as Bernardo Bertolucci and Jean-Luc Godard have pursued an expressionist course in western cinema. The essential argument of these expressionists is that a revolutionary purpose must have an art that is revolutionary in *style* as well as subject matter. Traditional (i.e., capitalist) art is decadent, pessimistic, cliché-ridden, and filled with stale bourgeois conventions. The techniques of the traditional cinema are bankrupt, and the truly revolutionary artist must forge a new language, one more relevant to a new society.

As Stalin solidified his position within the Soviet Communist Party, he put an end to many of these notions. Eisenstein and his more daring colleagues were criticized for their "formalism," their "effete" preoccupation with technique at the expense of subject matter. Many artists were condemned for their "elitism," for producing art accessible only to intellectuals and other artists, not to ordinary citizens. Furthermore, such artists were often chastised for their excessive "individualism," which was officially viewed as a bourgeois trait, totally out of keeping with the revolutionary ideals of collective action and collaboration between equals. In 1932, the democratically-controlled workers' organizations for the arts were dissolved, and with their dissolution, virtually all artistic experimentation came to a standstill.

In 1934, Stalin convened the First Congress of Soviet Writers, and though this gathering was primarily concerned with literary forms of expression, the same practical significance and theoretical implications applied to the Soviet cinema. "Guidelines" were established, in which priority was given to those artistic products that were judged to be most useful to the state. "Usefulness" was defined pretty much along ideological lines, the most overtly propagandistic art generally receiving the highest priorities.

10-9. The Conformist.
Directed by Bernardo Bertolucci.
As the works of Bertolucci testify, not all Marxists are realists, though most of them are agreed on certain basic principles: that the underlying basis of all social existence is economic, that history and social institutions must be demystified and explained in rational, scientific, and materialist terms; that no human activity is politically neutral; that art implicitly accepts or rejects the political status quo; and that art must serve the ultimate goals of the Revolution.

(Paramount Pictures)

All film production had to be authorized in detail by a special committee, to insure "ideological correctness" and to avoid wasteful, individualistic excesses. The task of all Soviet artists was to portray the benevolent power of the state as the greatest good, and to scorn the temporary sufferings of the individual. Furthermore, artists were sternly warned against excessive technical and formal experimentation. The Congress, in an official decree, established Socialist Realism as the only acceptable style in literature and film. This style "demands of the artist the truthful, historically concrete representation of reality in its revolutionary development. Moreover, the truthfulness and historical concreteness of the artistic representation of reality must be linked with the task of ideological transformation and education of workers in the spirit of socialism."

In plain language, what this definition involved was the portrayal of an objective, "scientifically verifiable" reality that is independent of the artist. Expressions of subjectivity and distortions were condemned as perverse, individualistic, and untruthful (10-10). Needless to say, if Socialist Realism produced only the flood of boy-loves-tractor stories that dominated

Soviet culture for so many years, we wouldn't take the theory very seriously. But particularly after the death of Stalin, the modifications introduced into the theory allowed for some artistically significant works, both in literature and the cinema. In Poland, Hungary, and especially Czechoslovakia, there were many excellent movies produced under the aegis of Socialist Realism—though in its modified, more sophisticated form.

Georg Lukács, the Hungarian aesthetician, was one of the most persuasive—and enduring—apologists for the modified theory of Socialist Realism. Although Lukács was concerned primarily with the novel, his observations could also be applied to the cinema. He expressed serious misgivings about Socialist art, particularly its psychological limitations. Unlike the hard-line Stalinists, Lukács rejected outright the simple-minded notion that all evil could be glibly explained away by a character's ignorance of or refusal to accept Marxist ideology. Reality is far more complex, he argued, and realistic art should likewise be more complex.

If a conflict arises over ideological correctness and objective reality, the artist's first allegiance is to reality, for otherwise how are ideological errors of judgment and fact to be corrected for future generations? Indeed, some of the finest Socialist films—like Milos Forman's amusing *Firemen's Ball*—are witty and emotionally touching precisely because of the conflict between what essentially decent people do in fact and how they ought to behave according to strict ideology. Although such candor as is found in the films of Forman and the Hungarian Miklós Jancsó was rare in the Socialist cinema before Stalin's death, it became more common after 1953.

Like most realists, Lukács disliked any form of extremism as an end in itself, especially stylistic eccentricity. He harshly condemned subjectivism and willful distortion of physical reality as self-indulgent and dangerously misleading. He believed that realism was the most comprehensive artistic style, the one closest to the copiousness of the observable physical world, and hence to the objective materialist approach of Marxism. All great art is essentially realistic, he claimed, even the "progressive bourgeois realism" of the nineteenth century, which included Balzac, Tolstoy, and Chekhov

(Museum of Modern Art)

10-10. *The Cabinet of Dr. Caligari.*
Directed by Robert Wiene.
Socialist Realism demands of the artist the portrayal of a "scientifically verifiable" reality in art. Gross distortions of the physical world that are found in such German Expressionist classics as *Caligari* were condemned as decadent, willfully individualistic, and without social value.

10-11. *The Emigrants.*
Directed by Jan Troell.
Although not characterized by a revolutionary consciousness or scientific rigor, artistic works produced by "progressive bourgeois" realists are often admired by more liberal theorists of Socialist Realism like Georg Lukács. Troell's film would probably be regarded as "bourgeois realism," but such works are valued in many Communist countries because they place characters in a concrete social (and by implication, political) milieu which is objectively and comprehensively portrayed.

(10-11). Lukács particularly admired the concrete social context in which these authors placed their characters. "It is a condition of great realism that the artist must honestly record, without fear or favor, everything he sees around him," Lukács wrote. To accomplish this goal, the artist must be objective, modest, and self-effacing—those same characteristics that are praised by such disparate theorists as André Bazin, Siegfried Kracauer, and the neorealists.

NEOREALISM

Kracauer often cites Italian **neorealist** films to illustrate his theories. Actually, neorealism is both a style of filmmaking and a specific cinematic movement which began in Italy during the last months of World War II.

10-12. *Open City.*
Directed by Roberto Rossellini.
This masterpiece of the Resistance movement established some of the basic characteristics of the neorealist cinema: the use of nonprofessional actors and authentic locales, an avoidance of theatrical lighting and special effects, a minimal use of editing, and a scrupulous fidelity to the look and feel of everyday reality. Episodic and loosely structured, Rossellini's movie is a good example of the open-ended cinema later advocated by Kracauer.

(Museum of Modern Art)

As a particularly Italian movement, neorealism was pretty much over by the mid-1950s, but as a style, it spread to many other countries. In India, for example, many of the films of Satyajit Ray are in the neorealistic style, and in America, Elia Kazan came under its influence. Beginning in the mid-1950s, neorealism became the dominant mode in England, and lasted for nearly a decade: the earliest movies of Tony Richardson, Karel Reisz, and Lindsay Anderson reflect both the political and stylistic biases of this movement.

Perhaps the quintessential neorealistic movie is Roberto Rossellini's *Open City,* which launched both the movement and the style. Scripted in part by Cesare Zavattini, one of the greatest screenwriters in the history of the cinema, *Open City* had an explosive effect on the film world (10-12). The film deals with the collaboration of Catholics and Communists in fighting the Nazi occupation of Rome. Reputedly, Rossellini shot some of the footage while the Nazis were actually evacuating the city. Technically, the film was rather crude. Since good quality film **stock** was impossible to obtain, Rossellini had to use inferior newsreel stock, but despite—indeed, because of—the technical flaws, the grainy images conveyed a sense of journalistic immediacy and authenticity. (Many neorealist directors began their careers as journalists, and Rossellini himself began as a documentarist.) Virtually the whole film was shot in actual locations, and there are many exterior shots in which no additional lights were used. With the exception of the principals the actors were nonprofessionals. The structure of the film was episodic—a series of vignettes showing the reactions of Roman citizens to the German occupation. Rossellini refused to idealize his characters, focusing not on heroes, but on ordinary people in heroic moments. Rossellini's peculiar blending of Marxism and Catholicism was founded on his humanistic compassion for all victims of war, including even those who betray their better instincts. The film is saturated with a sense of unrelenting honesty. "This is the way things are," Rossellini is said to have declared after the film was shown. The statement became the motto of the neorealist movement.

Within the next few years, there followed an astonishing series of films: Rossellini's *Paisàn* and *Germany: Year Zero*, Vittorio De Sica's *Shoeshine*, *Bicycle Thief*, and *Umberto D* (all scripted by Zavattini), and Visconti's *La Terra Trema*. The early works of Fellini and Antonioni, while not generally considered a part of the neorealist movement, were nonetheless heavily indebted to it. Some directors were influenced by Rossellini's Christian humanism, most notably De Sica and Fellini (10-13); others, particularly Visconti and Antonioni, were more influenced by the Marxist implications of *Open City*. Even as late as the sixties, neorealist influences could be seen in such low-keyed but brilliant films as Ermanno Olmi's *Il Posto* (also known as *The Sound of Trumpets*) and *The Fiancés*.

Although there are considerable differences among these directors, and even between their early and later works, the neorealist aesthetic provided a rallying point for most of the talented Italian filmmakers of the time. Their films tended to de-emphasize plots in favor of open-ended structures, suggesting a slice of life rather than clearly articulated beginnings, middles, and endings. A new honesty also characterized these movies: people were pictured more frankly, "warts and all." The films shared themes like war, the Resistance, and war's aftermath: poverty, unemployment, prostitution, the black market.

The films avoided phony idealism and sentimentality: complex problems weren't miraculously solved with slick solutions in the final reel. Characters as well as events were unextraordinary: most of the characters came from the working and lower classes—laborers, fishermen, peasants, and factory workers. Subsidiary themes included loneliness, solitude, and neglect —both personal and governmental. There was a strong emphasis on the social and political environment, which was either static and unresponsive, or thoroughly hostile to the needs of people. Many of these movies used

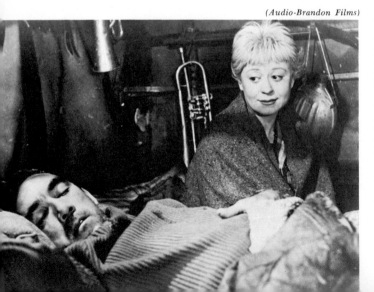

(Audio-Brandon Films)

10-13. La Strada.
Directed by Federico Fellini.
Although Fellini is not generally regarded as a neorealist, like most Italian directors, he came under its influence, particularly in his early movies. Films like *La Strada* are technically understated, with an emphasis on a direct recording of a subtly poeticized reality. Fellini was strongly influenced by Rossellini's Christian humanism, while other Italian movie makers, most notably Antonioni and Visconti, explored the Marxist implications of Rossellini's early films.

10-14. On the Waterfront.

Directed by Elia Kazan.

Although neorealism had a relatively small impact in the United States, a few American directors, most notably Kazan, came under its influence in the late forties and early fifties. Movies like *On the Waterfront, Panic in the Streets,* and *Boomerang* were shot in actual locations, and a number of minor roles were performed by nonprofessional actors.

authentic (and usually exterior) locales, **available lighting,** and nonprofessional actors even in principal roles. Following Rossellini's lead, these filmmakers de-emphasized editing and fancy camerawork in favor of **long shots,** lengthy **takes,** and open forms. Most of them strived to achieve a kind of "styleless" style, with an emphasis on subject matter, not technique (10-14).

Zavattini became the unofficial spokesman for the movement, though his strong Marxist leanings and fierce hostility to all technical artifice didn't always match up with the beliefs of his colleagues. His compassionate concern for the plight of the underprivileged and his anti-Fascist fervor, however, were shared by all these men. More than any single individual, Zavattini defined the ordinary and the everyday as the main business of the cinema. Spectacular events and extraordinary characters should be avoided at all costs, he believed. Anticipating some of the methods of **cinéma vérité,** Zavattini claimed that his ideal film would consist of 90 consecutive minutes from a person's actual life. Like the advocates of direct cinema, then, Zavattini believed that there should be no barriers between reality and the spectator. Ideally, neorealism should become a kind of heightened documentary: instead of *representing* reality, the neorealist film should *present* it directly.

Suspicious of conventional plot structures, Zavattini dismissed them as dead formulas. He insisted upon the dramatic superiority of things as they really *are,* the texture of life as it is experienced by ordinary people. Directors should be concerned with the "excavation" of reality: instead of plots, they should emphasize facts, and all the "echoes and reverberations" of facts. According to Zavattini, filmmaking is not a matter of "inventing fables," but of searching unrelentingly to uncover the implications of certain social facts. Thus, a whole film could be structured around the fact that a working couple wants to find an apartment. In a typical American movie, this fact might constitute only a minor scene, lasting some two or three minutes. But the neorealist explores the implications of this fact. Why do they want the apartment? Where did they live before? Why don't they stay there? How much does the apartment cost? Where will they get the money? How will their family react? And so on.

Anticipating Kracauer, the neorealists believed that the purpose of the cinema is to celebrate the "dailiness" of events. They wanted to reveal certain details that had always been there, but had never been noticed before. In Kracauer's term, they wanted to "redeem physical reality." Most of all, these directors insisted upon the innate dignity of the human spirit, which is revealed even in the most insignificant situation. These movies are generally so simple in terms of subject matter that they can seem banal when paraphrased verbally. Perhaps the greatest of them, De Sica's *Bicycle Thief,* deals with a poor man's attempts to recover his stolen bike, which he needs in order to keep his job. The man's search grows increasingly more frantic as he criss-crosses the city with his idolizing, urchin-like son. After a discouraging series of false leads, the two finally track down one of the thieves, but the protagonist is outwitted by him and humiliated in front of his boy. Realizing that he will lose his livelihood without a bike, the desperate man sneaks off and attempts to steal one himself after he sends his son away. But the boy observes from a distance as his frantic father peddles furiously to escape a pursuing mob. He is caught and again cruelly humiliated in front of a crowd—which includes his incredulous son. With all the bitterness of outraged innocence, the youngster suddenly recognizes that his father is not the super-heroic figure that he had formerly thought, but an ordinary man who in desperation has yielded to a degrading temptation. Like most neorealist films, the movie doesn't offer an overt solution. The final scene shows the boy walking alongside his father, both of them choking with shame and weeping silently. Almost imperceptibly, the boy's hand gropes for his father's, and they walk homeward—their only comfort a mutual compassion.

Bicycle Thief is an extraordinary achievement. Its two principals were amateurs who had never acted before. Its dialogue was not the standard literary dialect of Tuscany, but a slangy working-class speech that had the verisimilitude of a street-corner conversation. The techniques of the film are unobtrusive and direct: there are no fancy "memorable" shots, yet the very simplicity and directness of the images are what produce their overwhelming impact. In short, the movie embodies the highest ideals of the neorealist movement: a scrupulous fidelity to everyday life, and a compassionate humanism, stressing the indestructibility and grandeur of the human spirit.

RUDOLF ARNHEIM AND THE EXPRESSIONIST AESTHETIC

Rudolf Arnheim occupies a prominence among expressionist film theorists which is comparable to Kracauer's among realists. Arnheim's *Film as Art* was originally published in 1933, when film sound and color were still in their developing stages, but the book contains most of the basic tenets of expressionism as they are still espoused. His major premise is that film art is the direct result of the *differences* between physical reality and cinematic reality, that the movie director exploits the limitations of his medium—the *lack* of sound, color, depth, or space-time **continuity**, for example—to produce a world which resembles the real world only in a limited sense. Film art doesn't consist of a copy or reproduction of reality, but of a kind of "translation" of observed characteristics into the forms of the film medium.

As a gestalt psychologist, Arnheim is primarily concerned with the perception of experience, and his theory is based on the different modes of perception of the camera on the one hand, and the human eye on the other. Anticipating some of the theories of the communications specialist Marshall McLuhan, Arnheim insists that the camera's image of a bowl of fruit, for instance, is fundamentally different from our perception of the fruit bowl in actual life. Or, in McLuhan's terms, that the "information" we receive in each instance is determined by the "form" of the "content." Expressionist theorists celebrate these differences, for they believe that the very properties that make photography fall short of perfect reproduction determine the artistic forms of the film medium (10-15).

Technological advancements like sound, color, and **widescreen** were originally viewed with suspicion if not outright hostility by most expressionists. Like Arnheim, they believed that the resultant increase in realism brought on by these technical innovations actually worked against the expressive characteristics of the cinema. Virtually all the expressionists share Arnheim's belief that art begins where mechanical reproduction leaves off—that he who vies with nature deserves to lose (10-16). This is the main thesis of *The Cinema as Art,* for example, an influential and widely read book by Ralph Stephenson and Jean Debrix.

Arnheim discusses a number of examples in which significant divergences exist between the image that the camera makes of reality and that which the human eye sees. For example, the film director must choose which viewpoint to photograph an object from. He doesn't necessarily choose the clearest view, for often this does not emphasize the major characteristic of the object. For instance, to emphasize a man's power and authority, the camera would probably be placed at a **low angle.** To photograph him face-on (the clearest view) would not capture his essence (10-17). Sometimes the director wishes to attract the spectator's attention by viewing an object from an unusual position—by photographing an event from a helicopter, for instance.

In life, we perceive objects in depth, and can penetrate the space which

(a)

(Museum of Modern Art)

10-15a. *Metropolis.*
Directed by Fritz Lang.
10-15b. *Day of Wrath.*
Directed by Carl Dreyer.
10-15c. *Citizen Kane.*
Directed by Orson Welles.
Expressionist theorists like Arnheim tend to de-emphasize the relevance of reality in judging the effectiveness of a movie. Such theorists are more likely to value striking visual compositions (a), deliberately stylized groupings (b), and theatrical lighting effects (c) as artistic ends in themselves, regardless of whether such visual effects are accurate reflections of the real world.

(b)

(Janus Films)

(Janus Films)

(c)

surrounds most things. In movies, "space" is an illusion, for the screen has only two dimensions—a fact which permits the director to manipulate objects and perspective in an artistically effective manner. For instance, important objects can be placed where they are most likely to be noticed first. Unimportant objects can be relegated to inferior positions, at the edges or "back" of the screen, for example. Surprise effects can be achieved by suddenly revealing (through a **pull-back dolly**) what has been excluded by the frame. The frame itself is a delimiting device that has no real counterpart in one's perception of the natural world.

In movies, two objects can be photographed in such a way that one blocks out the other. In *Citizen Kane,* for instance, Kane threateningly tells his second wife that she will do precisely what he tells her to do: as he speaks, he moves closer to her, his shadow suddenly plunging her pale face into darkness. Because the **lens** doesn't make psychological adjustments for size and distance, the director can manipulate these elements to achieve symbolic relationships. A man can be "decreased" in stature by photographing him at a distance, while another subject—a whiskey bottle, say—can seem larger than the man because it is closer to the camera. The metaphorical dominance of the bottle is suggested by the distortion of the photographic process.

Lighting in movies, Arnheim would claim, is more than merely utilitarian. Lights can suggest symbolic ideas, they can bring out an object's essential characteristics, they can reveal or cover certain details, and they can shift a viewer's interest from one point on the screen to another. Sound

10-16. *The Blue Angel.*
Directed by Josef von Sternberg.
Expressionists believe that the film artist doesn't select his techniques on the basis of how clearly or realistically they present an action, but on how expressively they convey its *essence.* A scene can be photographed in literally hundreds of different ways, but the filmmaker selects that method of presentation which best captures its spiritual, psychological, or **symbolic** implications.

(Museum of Modern Art)

and color, if they're used, should not be employed merely to enhance the realism of an image, but to convey essential characteristics. The basic distortion involved in recording natural sounds and colors can be exploited to emphasize symbolic rather than literal characteristics—characteristics that have no counterpart in the natural world (10-18).

In real life, space and time are experienced as continuous phenomena, but through editing, the filmmaker chops up space and time and rearranges them in a more meaningful manner. Like other artists, the film director selects certain expressive details from the chaotic plenitude of physical reality. By juxtaposing these space and time "fragments," he creates a continuity that doesn't exist in raw nature. This, of course, is the basic position of the Soviet montage theorists.

Arnheim points out that there are many mechanical modes of "per-

10-17. Yojimbo.
Directed by Akira Kurosawa.
In choosing his camera **set-ups,** the director doesn't necessarily photograph a scene with the idea of giving the spectator an objective presentation of events. Often the viewer is startled by the unusual camera angles and the unconventional **mise-en-scène** a director employs.

10-18. Performance.
Directed by Nicolas Roeg and Donald Cammell.
Some movies employ harshly distorting special effects which have no counterparts in reality except within the human psyche. *Performance,* for example, deals with weird hallucinatory experiences that are induced by drugs, violence, sex, and "magic mushrooms." Such films are concerned with mental realities which, according to such realists as Kracauer, are not suitable subjects for the cinema because they are not found in the observable physical world.

ception" in the cinema that have no human counterpart. We can't manipulate our eyes the way that a camera can be adjusted to produce **slow motion, fast motion, reverse motion,** and **freeze frames.** Certainly our eyes have no real equivalents to **dissolves, multiple exposures, negative images,** distorting lenses and **filters, focus** manipulations, and all the other special effects that can be achieved through the use of the **optical printer.**

In short, Arnheim and most other expressionists would claim that film art is possible precisely because of the "limitations" and peculiarities of the medium. The very act of photographing an object involves profound distortions of that object as it's perceived in reality. In attempting to imitate nature, then, the film director doesn't merely record the physical world: he interprets it through his camera. In thus transforming his raw materials, he doesn't destroy physical reality so much as he transcends it by distilling, rearranging, and strengthening certain essential characteristics, according to the expressionists.

The problem with most expressionist theories is the same as with most realist theories: there are too many exceptions. Arnheim's analysis is certainly useful in an appreciation of Griffith's movies, for example, or Eisenstein's. But how helpful is the theory in explaining the films of Renoir or De Sica? It's virtually useless in helping us to appreciate the *oeuvre* of Chaplin, Flaherty, or Leacock. Even if we conceded Arnheim's basic premise —that the photographic process distorts reality—we still tend to respond to realistic movies primarily because of their *similarity* with physical reality, not their divergence from it. Ultimately, of course, these are matters of emphasis, for films are too pluralistic and eclectic to be pigeonholed into one tidy theory. Indeed, some movies—*Citizen Kane,* for example—have been "claimed" by theorists of both camps!

THE AUTEUR THEORY

In the mid-1950s, *Cahiers du Cinéma* revolutionized film criticism with its concept of *la politique des auteurs* (literally, "the policy of authors"), which was put forth by its pugnacious young critic, François Truffaut. This polemical stance became the focal point of a critical controversy which eventually spread to England and America. Before long, the **auteur theory** became a kind of militant rallying cry, particularly among younger critics, dominating such lively journals as *Movie* in England, *Film Culture* in America, and both French and English language editions of *Cahiers du Cinéma.* Indeed, though there were some fine writers of the next decade who disdained the theory, auteurism dominated most of the best film criticism of the sixties, and even its most passionate antagonists were eventually influenced by the theory. Auteurism was a defiant gesture of contempt towards the entire film establishment of the time. Indeed, because of the strident, often shrill tone of many of its practitioners, the theory managed to offend virtually all of the older and more traditional critics. Even Bazin, the founder and editor of *Cahiers du Cinéma,* wrote an essay warning of the excesses of the theory as it was practiced by some of his youthful disciples.

Actually, the main lines of the theory aren't particularly outrageous, at least not in retrospect. Truffaut, Godard, Chabrol and their critical col-

(20th Century-Fox)

(Universal Pictures)

(a)

10-19a. *Sounder.*
Directed by Martin Ritt.
10-19b. *American Graffiti.*
Directed by George Lucas.
Taking their cue from Claude Chabrol's seminal essay, "Little Themes,"
many auteurist critics are suspicious
if not openly contemptuous of films
with ambitious themes like brotherhood, injustice, and the nobility of
the human spirit—topics that can
easily slip into pretentiousness and
pomposity. In judging a movie's
worth, it's the treatment that counts,
not the extrinsic "importance" of its
theme, auteurists argue. A modest
subject like that found in *American
Graffiti* makes no grand pronouncements about the "human condition"
yet most auteurists would consider
it far superior to the thematically
more ambitious *Sounder.* Chabrol believes that the smaller the theme, the
more a director can give it a "big
treatment," that modest subjects, like
those traditionally found in **genre**
films, are the richest in terms of
artistic potential.

(b)

leagues were dismayed by the sad state of affairs in the French film industry
of the time. Movies were controlled by businessmen, not artists. Furthermore, those films that were often praised for their aesthetic value were
dominated by writers, who were generally regarded as the main creators of
the best films. Too often, "artistic films" were merely thematically pretentious, these critics scoffed, written by bland, if sincere, liberals. These movies
dealt with "Big Themes," which were often praised for their "seriousness"
and "maturity," but as *movies* they were dull, plodding, and visually
unimaginative. The director was viewed as a kind of executive assistant, a
metteur-en-scène whose job was essentially interpretive, and who merely

staged the production, much like a theatrical director stages a dramatist's play.

The auteur theorists proposed that the greatest films were dominated by the personal vision of the director, and this dominance could be perceived through an examination of a director's total output, which is characterized by a unity of theme and style. The writer's contribution—the subject matter —is artistically neutral: it can be treated with brilliance or with bare competence. Movies ought to be judged on the basis of "how" not "what." Like most expressionist theorists, then, the auteur critics claimed that what makes a good movie is not the subject matter per se, but the *treatment* of the subject matter, and it's the director who controls the treatment, provided he's a strong director, an "auteur."

As a standard of excellence, these critics turned to American movies, including thrillers, westerns, gangster films, and musicals. What they particularly admired about American films was their narrative vitality, their stylistic verve, and technical brilliance (10-19). Most of these writers would have agreed with Erwin Panofsky who observed that while commercial movies are always in danger of ending up as prostitutes, the so-called "art film" was equally in danger of ending up as an old maid.

Most of the American auteurs that these critics praised had worked within the studio system, a system which had broken the artistic dreams of many lesser filmmakers. What the auteurists particularly admired was how a cunning director could circumvent studio interference and even hackneyed scripts by his technical expertise. The subject matter of Hitchcock's thrillers and Ford's westerns varied considerably in terms of artistic potential. Yet both of these auteurs managed to produce great films, precisely because the *real* content was conveyed through the mise-en-scène, the editing, and all the other formal devices at the director's disposal. By analyzing these stylistic and thematic threads that run throughout a director's total output, the auteurists thought, we are able to arrive at a determination of his personal artistic vision. Before long, personality cults developed around the most popular of these directors. On the whole, these were filmmakers who had been virtually ignored by "serious" critics: Alfred Hitchcock, John Ford, Howard Hawks, Nicholas Ray, Samuel Fuller, for example (10-20).

The sheer breadth of their knowledge of film history permitted these critics to re-evaluate most of the major films of a wide variety of directors. In many instances, they completely reversed previous critical judgments. John Ford, for example, had been admired by highbrow critics for his "artistic" productions like *The Informer* and *The Fugitive,* which were dominated by rather literary scripts. But the auteur critics rightly insisted that such classic westerns as *Stagecoach, She Wore a Yellow Ribbon, Two Rode Together,* and *The Searchers* are artistically superior to Ford's rather pretentious films of social consciousness. They pointed out what is a commonplace in art and literary criticism: that the subject matter of an artistic work is not always a reliable index of its worth.

The French auteurists viewed the field of film criticism as a prelude to making their own movies, which most of them did beginning in the late fifties. In England and America, however, most auteurist critics remained in the field of criticism. Unlike their French counterparts, they were less knowledgeable about the problems and techniques of film direction, and

10-20. Public Enemy.
Directed by William Wellman.
One of the greatest strengths of the auteur theory is its proper appreciation of the liberating effects of vulgarity, high spirits, and panache—what actor James Cagney poetically referred to as "a touch of the gutter."

concentrated more on thematic and stylistic qualities of the films themselves. What to the French was a necessary evil—the studio system—now became almost a virtue, or at least a challenge. American auteurists like Andrew Sarris were interested in the "tension" between an artist's personal vision and the often routine genre assignments that these directors were given by their Hollywood bosses. The American and English auteurists placed major emphasis on how the director makes a silk purse of a sow's ear: how he performs under pressure. Quite correctly, these critics insisted that total artistic freedom isn't always a virtue. After all, Michelangelo, Dickens, and Rembrandt, among others, accepted commissioned subjects (10-21).

Though this principle of tension is a sound one—in the other arts as well as the cinema—some auteurists carried it to ridiculous extremes. In the first place, there is the problem of degree. *Hamlet* and *Crime and Punishment* are both "about" murder, deception, and detection, and as such, they share certain affinities with an Agatha Christie thriller. Given this kind of subject matter—unexplained deaths, narrative suspense, gradual revelations, etc.—a director could make a masterpiece out of it or a bomb, depending upon his artistic gifts. But it's doubtful that even a genius like Bergman or Welles could do much with the script and stars of *Abbott and Costello Meet the Mummy*. In other words, a director's got to have a fighting chance. When the subject matter sinks beneath a certain basic potential, the result is not "tension" but artistic annihilation. Too often, auteur critics devoted themselves to praising the "little touches" of style in otherwise banal movies. When one is reduced to dealing with only "a spare

(a)

10-21a. *Two Rode Together.*
Directed by John Ford.
10-21b. *The Birds.*
Directed by Alfred Hitchcock.
10-21c. *Red River.*
Directed by Howard Hawks.
The French auteurists were the first to praise such American filmmakers as Ford, Hitchcock, and Hawks as serious *artists,* not merely as entertainers. Undaunted by the traditionally *déclassé* artistic status of such genres as the thriller and the western, these critics pointed out that a great director, an *auteur,* can express his genius even when certain **conventions** and subjects are externally imposed.

(b)

(c)

shot or two" from such films, why bother? Especially when there are some neglected movies that are good throughout.

Furthermore, there are some very fine films—like Joseph H. Lewis' *Gun Crazy*—that seem untypical of a director's total output, both thematically and stylistically. Thematic unity per se is no gauge of worth, for it can characterize bad art as well as good—the Three Stooges films as well as the *oeuvre* of Fellini. Some excellent directors have explored a variety of themes and done so in many different styles and genres: Fred Zinnemann, Carol Reed, even the darlings of most auteurists, Roberto Rossellini and Howard Hawks.

Bazin expressed alarm at the injudicious negativism of some auteur critics. To praise a bad film, he felt, was unfortunate, but to condemn a good one was a serious failing. Bazin especially disliked the tendency to hero worship of many auteurists, which led to a priori judgments. Movies by cult directors were indiscriminately praised while films by directors out of current favor were automatically condemned. Auteur critics were par-

(*Warner Brothers*)

10-22. *The Maltese Falcon*.
Directed by John Huston.
Like all cinematic theories, auteurism suffers some serious drawbacks. Capricious arbitrariness and a predictable conformity of judgment are especially acute among auteur critics. Despite the fact that Huston has directed some of the greatest films of the American repertory, for example, most auteurists continue to denigrate his *oeuvre* or damn it with faint praise by acknowledging the director's "competent craftsmanship" in classics like *The Maltese Falcon*.

ticularly given to ranking directors, and their hierarchies could be bizarre: such competent technicians as Nicholas Ray, Jerry Lewis, Douglas Sirk, and Otto Preminger were elevated above major artists like John Huston, Elia Kazan, Billy Wilder, and Fred Zinnemann (10-22).

But despite these excesses, the auteur theory had a liberating effect on film criticism. Most importantly, it cleared away the literary prejudices of previous generations and established the director as the major creative force in the cinema. Though the emphasis on history and a director's total output tends to favor older directors at the expense of newcomers, this historical perspective also had a beneficial effect on film criticism, for it reduced the tendency to evaluate a movie only in internal terms—that is, outside of its cultural and historical context.

By the late sixties, the major battle had been won. Virtually all serious discussions of film were at least partly couched in terms of the director's personal vision. The tendency after this period was to expand the concept of auteurism, to explore the individual contributions of writers, actors, and **cinematographers.** A number of critics attempted to show how a director's vision was substantially effected by the influence of a writer, a producing studio, or a prestigious **star.** The concept of directorial dominance, however, remained firmly established, at least with those films of high artistic merit.

STRUCTURALISM AND SEMIOTIC THEORIES

In the late sixties and early seventies, two interrelated cinematic theories began to develop partly in response to the inadequacies and subjective vagueness of the auteur theory. **Structuralism** and **semiology** were attempts to introduce a new scientific rigor to film criticism, to allow for more *systematic* and detailed analyses of movies. Borrowing their methodology from such diverse disciplines as linguistics, anthropology, psychology, and philosophy, these two theories represented an attempt to supplant such sweepingly vague auteurist phrases as "the mystique of mise-en-scène" with a more precise analytical terminology.

There are a number of different semiological theories, most of them still in tentative, exploratory stages. The French theorist Christian Metz has been in the forefront in developing semiology as a technique of film analysis. Using many of the concepts and much of the terminology of structural linguistics, Metz and others have developed a theory of cinematic communication founded on the concept of signs or codes. Semiology is a study of *how* movies signify. The manner in which information is signified is indissolubly linked with *what*'s being signified. The "language" of cinema, like all types of discourse, verbal and nonverbal, is primarily symbolic: it consists of a complex code of signs which we either instinctively or consciously decipher while experiencing a film. Metz and his colleagues recognize that cinema is not all signs and symbols. There are other important dimensions to film as well.

In most discussions of film, the shot is generally accepted as the basic unit of construction (10-23). Semiological theorists reject this unit as too vague and inclusive. They insist that a more precise unit must underlie the systematic analysis of films, and accordingly have suggested that the "sign" be adopted as the minimal unit of signification. A single brief shot from a movie generally contains dozens of signs, forming an intricate hierarchy of counterpoised meanings. In a sense, this book—especially the first five chapters—can be viewed as a classification of signs, though necessarily more limited in scope than the intricate system envisioned by Metz and other semiologists. For example, each of the first five chapters is concerned with a kind of master code, which can be broken down into code subdivisions, which themselves can be reduced to even more minimal signs. Thus, Chapter One might be called an outline of the "Photography" master code. The subdivisions of the code then include: Shots, **Angles**, Lights, Colors, Lenses, **Filters**, Optical Effects, and so on. Each of these, in turn can be subdivided again. Shots, for example, can be broken down to **Extreme Long, Long, Medium, Close-up, Extreme Close-up,** Deep focus. Even these relatively precise designations could be broken down further: the various types of medium shots, for example. This same principle could be applied to other master codes: spatial codes (mise-en-scène), kinetic codes (movement), and

(Paramount Pictures)

so on. Language codes would be as complex as the entire discipline of linguistics, and histrionic codes would involve a precise breakdown of all the various techniques of signification actors use. What Metz and other semiologists envisage is an encyclopedic task of stupefying proportions.

There's no question that semiological techniques can be tremendously valuable in aiding film critics and scholars to analyze movies with more precision. But the theory is still in its infancy and already suffers some serious defects. For one thing, these are descriptive classifications only, not normative. In other words, semiology will permit a critic to discern a sign with more precision, but it's still up to the critic to *evaluate* how artistically effective any given sign is within an aesthetic context. Expressionist movies seem to lend themselves to easier classification than realist films: it's much simpler to describe the use of a **wide-angle lens** in Welles's expressionist *Touch of Evil* than it is to discern the meanings of Dietrich's ambiguous half-smiles in von Sternberg's *The Blue Angel.* These signs, in many respects, aren't comparable: one lends itself to quantification more readily than the other. Since expressionist signs seem more quantifiable, there might be a tendency to value films with a greater number of signs (or at least a greater number of *classifiable* signs) as more complex, and hence aesthetically richer, than films with a lesser density of signs (10-24). Conceivably, this could lead to the conclusion that the James Bond movies are superior to Chaplin's films because the Bond films contain more signs.

Another serious problem with semiological theories is their barbarous jargon, which often verges on self-parody. Indeed, after reading much of the literature of semiology, one is tempted to conclude that what's needed is not only a study of how movies signify, but another on how semiological theorists signify. Of course all specialized disciplines—including the cinema —have a certain number of necessary technical terms, but semiology seems to be choking on its own "scientific" terminology. Indeed, even within the

10-23. Blonde Venus.
Directed by Josef von Sternberg.
Semiologists believe that the shot—the traditional unit of construction in film—is too general and inclusive to be of much use in a systematic analysis of a movie. The symbolic sign, they argue, is a more precise unit of signification. Every cinematic shot consists of dozens of signifying codes which are hierarchically structured. Employing what they call the "principle of pertinence," semiologists de-code cinematic "discourse" by first establishing what the dominant signs are, then analyzing the subsidiary codes. This methodology is similar to a detailed analysis of mise-en-scène, only in addition to spatial, textural, and photographic codes, semiologists would also explore other relevant signs—**kinetic,** linguistic, musical, rhythmic, etc. In this shot, for instance, a semiologist would explore the symbolic significance of such major signs as Dietrich's white suit. Why a masculine suit? Why white? What does the papier-mâché dragon signify? The distorted perspective lines of the set? The "shady ladies" behind the archways? The symbolism of stage and audience? The **tight framing** and closed form of the image? The protagonist's worldly song? Within the dramatic context, semiologists would also explore the rhythms of the editing and camera movements, the symbolism of the kinetic motions of the performer, and so on. Traditionally, critics have likened the cinematic shot to a word, and a series of edited shots to a sequence of words in a sentence. A semiologist would dismiss such analogies as patently simple-minded. Perhaps an individual *sign* might be likened to a word, but the equivalent to a shot—even a banal one—would require many paragraphs if not pages of words. A complex shot can contain a hundred separate signs, each with its own precise symbolic significance.

(Warner Brothers)

(a)

(b)

(Museum of Modern Art)

10-24a. McQ.
Directed by John Sturges.
10-24b. The Bank.
Directed by Charles Chaplin.
Semiology is a descriptive rather than normative methodology. It helps critics to isolate and identify signs in a movie, but not necessarily to evaluate how skillfully they function within a work of art. Since semiology stresses quantification, the theory seems to be more effective in analyzing expressionistic films, whch tend to contain more classifiable signs. But different classes of signs or codes are not comparable, and hence, qualitative judgments are difficult to make on strictly quantitative evidence. For example, the shot from *McQ* contains many different signs which are structured into an image of great visual complexity. Chaplin's shot, on the other hand, is relatively simple, and contains few classifiable signs other than the expressions on the faces of the characters. While Sturges is a director of considerable skill, he's certainly not in Chaplin's class, yet a semiological analysis of these two works might lead some critics to the conclusion that Sturges is the better director because he uses more signs in his films.

field, one commentator justly pointed out that referring to a perfectly ordinary phenomenon as "signifier" or "signified," "syntagm," or "paradigm" doesn't in itself advance social knowledge to any particular degree.

The difference between semiology and structuralism are primarily differences in emphasis. Structuralism tends to center around practical criticism, while semiology is more theoretical in its emphasis. As Metz has pointed out, semiology is concerned with the systematic classification of single codes in a variety of different structures, while structuralism is the study of how various codes function within a single structure, within one movie. Structuralists liken the analysis of a film to the "reading" of a "text," and their methods are similar to the traditional *explication de texte* used by French literary critics. This technique involves a detailed examination and analysis of a given work in all of its technical complexity, accompanied by a synthesizing exposition of how these specific techniques work to produce a unified aesthetic effect.

Structuralism is one of the most eclectic forms of film analysis, and is often combined with other methods. The best known structuralists are British, and they often combine the techniques of semiology with those of the auteur theory. For example, Geoffrey Nowell-Smith's book, *Luchino Visconti,* is the study of a single auteur's work, in which certain basic thematic and stylistic motifs are analyzed. Other structural studies combine two or more approaches. In a 1972 issue of the British journal, *Screen,* for example, the editors of *Cahiers du Cinéma* (which by this time was Marxist in its editorial stance) presented a "collective text" of a "reading" of John Ford's movie, *Young Mr. Lincoln.* The analysis combined the methods of Marxist criticism with those of structuralism and the auteur theory (10-25). Like many structuralist analyses, this one linked the internal codes and signs of the movie with pertinent external (i.e., political, social, and commercial) codes that also form part of the film's total meaning.

Other structuralist critics use semiological methods to explore certain genres. Jim Kitses' *Horizons West,* for example, is an exploration of characteristic themes, structures, and formal elements in the westerns of Anthony Mann, Budd Boetticher, and Sam Peckinpah (10-26). Similarly, Colin McArthur's *Underworld USA* is a structuralist analysis of gangster movies

10-25. Young Mr. Lincoln.
Directed by John Ford.
Structuralism is the study of how various signs and codes are fused vis-à-vis a single work. Some structuralists concern themselves with only internal signs—that is, with purely aesthetic codes found within the "world" of the movie. Other critics use semiological methods to explore the significance of certain signs in relation to the external world. Such analyses are likely to combine the methodologies of a number of different theories. A celebrated "collective" reading of *Young Mr. Lincoln* combined the techniques of the auteur theory (the thematic and stylistic relationship of the film to Ford's *oeuvre*), with semiology (the various signs and codes found within this particular movie) and Marxist theory (the political reasons for making the film, and the significance of its ideas in relation to the producer, studio, and external culture that produced it).

(Twentieth Century-Fox)

and the *film noir* genre. McArthur explores the "iconography" of these genres by analyzing semiological classifications in the works of Lang, Huston, Fuller, Kazan, and others.

Many of these critics have been influenced by the theories of the French structural anthropologist, Claude Lévi-Strauss. Indeed, to distinguish themselves from structuralists in other disciplines, these English critics often refer to their field as cine-structuralism. The methods of Lévi-Strauss are based upon an examination of regional myths which he believes express certain underlying structures of thought in codified form. These myths exist in variant forms, and usually contain the same or similar binary structures, or pairs of opposites. These polarities are usually found in dialectical conflicts: they're in a constant state of dynamic flux. Depending upon the culture analyzed, these polarities can be agricultural (e.g., water versus drought), sexual (male versus female), generational (youth versus age), and so on. Because these myths are expressed in signs or codes, often their full meaning is hidden from their creators, and Lévi-Strauss believes that once the full implications of a myth are understood, it's discarded as a cliché.

Cine-structuralists use these dialectical methods to explore not only the internal "culture" of a movie, but also how these signs express certain underlying patterns of thought in the external culture that forms the movie's social context. For example, in his essay, "The Semiology of the Cinema," which is included in *Signs and Meaning in the Cinema*, Peter Wollen examines John Ford's western, *My Darling Clementine* in terms of its various binary structures. He sees "Garden versus Wilderness" as the "master antinomy" and shows how Ford instinctively varies dozens of other binary pairs into a complex aesthetic structure (10-27). Ostensibly, the film deals with the Wyatt Earp story, but Ford uses this narrative structure primarily

(Columbia Pictures)

10-26. Major Dundee.
Directed by Sam Peckinpah.
Some structuralists use the methodology of semiology to explore the way signs and codes are used in a given genre. Jim Kitses' *Horizons West* analyzes the stylistic characteristics, themes, and structures of the westerns of Peckinpah in comparison with other American directors of this genre.

as a framing device to explore the founding of a frontier community. Some of the polarities in the film are iconographic: the refined "Eastern lady" versus the sensual "saloon girl," the educated Boston-born gunfighter (Doc Holliday) versus the gentle but unlettered Westerner (Wyatt Earp), and so on. According to Wollen, Ford views the growth of Tombstone in mythic terms, as a Wilderness about to be transformed into a Garden. (In Christian terms, the Wilderness becomes the Promised Land.) Into America's frontier stream many divergent cultural traditions, sometimes conflicting, other times fusing: East and West; Indian, Spanish, Anglo-Saxon; male and female; young and old; secular and religious; civilized and primitive; individualistic and communal; traditional and experimental. Despite the occasional lapses into sentimentality, and the defects of some of the dialogue, Ford manages to manipulate these binary themes with astonishing sophistication, Wollen concludes. The church dance scene is the focal point of the movie, containing a number of symbolic ideas. The foundation and floor of the church building have finally been built in this frontier community, and most of the townspeople attend the celebration. When the fiddles begin to squawk their lively tunes, the townspeople choose partners and joyously

10-27. *The Grapes of Wrath.*
Directed by John Ford.
Influenced by the theories of the French structural anthropologist Claude Lévi-Strauss, cine-structuralists believe that movies, like cultures, employ symbolic myths which can be decoded. These myths can reveal the values and unconscious fears of a given culture, or in the case of cinema, of a given director. Most mythic structures are bipolar, and gain their artistic effects from the way in which opposites are held in some kind of tension, conflict, and resolution. For example, like many of Ford's films, *The Grapes of Wrath* is structured around a "master antimony" involving the Garden versus the Desert. The Oklahoma Dust Bowl symbolizes a failed dream, the destruction of a culture, and the disintegration of the family. California represents a Promised Land of reconciliation and reintegration. Within the movie, Ford characterizes the state in Biblical and mythic terms, as a "Land of Milk and Honey," and a New Eden.

dance beneath the blazing western sun, the American flag streaming in the wind high over head. Leading the dance are Wyatt Earp (Herry Fonda) and the gentle Boston-bred Clementine Carter (Cathy Downs), the characters embodying the moral center of Ford's universe. The dance itself is a perfect symbolic embodiment of the reconciliation of opposites, which Ford feels represents the genius and vitality of America.

Some structuralists insist that the only valid film criticism is that which sticks to the work itself—that is, to those aesthetic units found within a single movie. All external and historical considerations, while perhaps interesting, are ultimately irrelevant, these critics would claim: a movie either works *as* a movie or it doesn't, no matter what the director's intentions might have been, or the traditions of the genre, or the political and social context which produced the work. V. F. Perkins' *Film as Film* takes this position, arguing that a movie can only be judged in terms of how richly and complexly its *internal* aesthetic units are fused. Perkins believes that the best films "synthesize" thousands of constituent separate codes and signs into a coherent, complex, and emotionally rich artistic structure.

The cine-structuralists have been criticized on a number of counts. In the first place, one person's "myth" can be another person's cliché. An argument could be made, for example, that Ford's *Stagecoach,* for all its visual brilliance, consists of narrative and thematic commonplaces that had been exhausted in other mediums by the turn of the last century. In Lévi-Strauss' terms, the myth had lost its resonance and had degenerated into a compendium of clichés. In this respect, Perkins's tendency to analyze films out of historical context is particularly vulnerable to attack, for there are some bad movies that are "synthesized" with surprising sophistication, yet deal only with tired ideas and stale conventions. Many genre films fall into this category, like the westerns of Budd Boetticher, the "weepies" of Douglas Sirk, and the horror films of Terence Fisher. Technically, many of the movies of these directors are well-crafted and even brilliant in some of their effects, but the materials are simply too lifeless to be resuscitated.

In the end, as Pauline Kael has pointed out, it all depends on how it's done. Robin Wood, who himself uses certain structuralist techniques, has criticized the cine-structuralists for their excessively mechanical methods and their persistent tendency to equate quantity with quality. Structuralism and semiological techniques are merely convenient *tools* of analysis, Wood has pointed out, but in and by themselves, these tools can tell us nothing of the *value* of signs and codes within a film. Like every other cinematic theory, then, structuralism is only as good as its practitioners. Intelligence, taste, passion, knowledge, and sensitivity are what determine the value of a good piece of criticism, not necessarily the theoretical methodology that's employed.

FURTHER READING

ARMES, ROY. *Patterns of Realism.* New York: A. S. Barnes, 1971. An analysis of Italian neorealism, from its wartime beginnings to De Sica's *Umberto D* in 1951.

ARNHEIM, RUDOLF. *Film as Art.* Berkeley: University of California Press, 1957. (Paper) The standard text on expressionism in the cinema, or how film art results from the differences between reality and its artistic illusion.

Cinema Semiotics and the Work of Christian Metz, ed. Sam Rohdie. Special Double Issue, *Screen* (Spring/Summer, 1973). An exploration of the theories of Christian Metz and the discipline of cinema semiology.

ECKERT, CHARLES W. "The English Cine-Structuralists"; and Charles Harpole and John Hanhardt, "Linguistics, Structuralism, Semiology," in *Film Comment* (May-June, 1973). An exploration of semiology and structuralism in the cinema, with particular emphasis on the British cine-structuralists.

Film Theory and Criticism. eds. Gerald Mast and Marshall Cohen. New York: Oxford University Press, 1974. (Paper) An anthology of articles by many major film critics and theorists.

KAEL, PAULINE. "Is There a Cure for Film Criticism?" and "Circles and Squares" in *I Lost It at the Movies.* New York: Bantam Books, 1966. (Paper) Two scathing critiques, of Kracauer and auterism respectively, pointing out the limitations but not the strengths of each theory.

KRACAUER, SIEGFRIED. *Theory of Film: The Redemption of Physical Reality.* New York: Oxford University Press, 1960. (Paper) The standard text on realism in the cinema, or how film art results from a faithful reproduction of reality.

METZ, CHRISTIAN. *Film Language: A Semiotics of the Cinema.* New York: Oxford University Press, 1974, trans. Michael Taylor. An attempt to define the language of the cinema by exploring how signs and codes function within films.

Radical Perspective in the Arts, ed. Lee Baxandall. Baltimore: Penguin Books, 1972. (Paper) A collection of essays on Marxist aesthetics, including a wide variety of different approaches.

SARRIS, ANDREW. "Toward a Theory of Film History" in *The American Cinema.* New York: E. P. Dutton, 1968. (Paper) One of the basic documents of the auteur theory, written by America's most prominent auteurist critic.

WOLLEN, PETER. *Signs and Meaning in the Cinema.* Bloomington: Indiana University Press, 1972. (Paper) A collection of essays exploring some of the basic tenets of the auteur theory and the theory of semiology.

ZAVATTINI, CESARE. "Some Ideas on the Cinema" in *Film: A Montage of Theories,* ed. Richard Dyer MacCann. New York: E. P. Dutton, 1966. (Paper) One of the basic texts on neorealism, though not always a reliable guide to what other Italian filmmakers of this loose group were attempting to do in their movies.

glossary

Absolute film, Abstract film. A non-representational film in which pure forms—e.g. lines, shapes, colors—constitute the only content. Absolute or abstract films are often likened to music pieces, which similarly are "about" nothing but pure form.

Aerial shot. Essentially a variation of the **crane shot,** though restricted to exterior locations. Usually taken from a helicopter.

Aesthetic distance. Viewers' ability to distinguish between an artistic "reality" and external reality—their realization that the events of an artistic representation are simulated.

Aleatory techniques. Techniques of filmmaking which depend on the element of chance. Images are not planned out in advance, but must be composed on the spot by a director who usually acts as his own cameraman. Usually employed in documentary or improvisatory situations.

Allegory. A symbolic technique in which stylized characters and situations represent rather obvious ideas. The characters and situations of *O Lucky Man!* for example, are allegorical, representing Religion, Science, Commerce, and so on.

Allusion. A reference to an event, person, or work of art, which is usually well known.

Animation. A form of filmmaking characterized by photographing inanimate objects or individual drawings **frame** by frame, with each frame differing minutely from its predecessor. When such images are projected at the standard speed of 24 frames per second, the result is that the subjects of the images appear to move, and hence, seem "animated."

Anticipatory camera, Anticipatory set-up. The placement of the camera in such a manner as to anticipate the movements of a dramatic action before it occurs. An anticipatory camera often seems to suggest fatality or predestination.

Aspect ratio. The ratio between the horizontal and vertical dimensions of the **frame.**

Auteur theory. A theory of film popularized by the critics of the French periodical *Cahiers du Cinéma* in the 1950s. The theory emphasizes the director as the major creator of film art. A strong director (an auteur) stamps his material with his personal vision, often in spite of an externally imposed script.

Available lighting. The use of only that illumination which actually exists on a location, either natural (the sun) or artificial (house lamps). When available lighting is used in interior locations, generally a sensitive **fast film stock** must also be used.

Avant-garde. From the French, meaning "in the front ranks." Those minority artists and their works characterized by an unconventional daring, and usually associated with obscure, controversial, or highly complex artistic and social ideas.

Bird's eye view. A **shot** in which the camera photographs a scene from directly overhead.

Blimp. A sound-proof camera housing which muffles the noise of the camera's motor so that sound can be clearly recorded on the set.

Boom, mike boom. An overhead telescoping pole which carries a microphone, permitting the **synchronous** recording of sound without restricting the movements of the actors.

Cels. Transparent plastic sheets which are superimposed in layers by **animators** to give the illusion of depth and volume to their drawings.

Cinematographer, also **director of photography, lighting cameraman.** The film technician responsible for the lighting of a shot, and often for the actual photography of a scene.

Cinéma vérité, also **direct cinema.** A method of documentary filming, using

aleatory, direct methods which do not interfere with the way events take place in reality. Such films are made with a minimum of equipment, usually a hand-held camera and portable sound apparatus.

Cine-structuralism. See **structuralism.**

Classical cutting, *Découpage classique.* A style of **editing** in which the sequence of **shots** is determined by considerations of dramatic and emotional emphasis rather than for physical reasons alone. See **cutting to continuity, thematic montage.**

Closed forms. Used primarily by **expressionist** film directors, this style is likely to be rather self-conscious and conspicuous, with an emphasis on formal designs and carefully harmonized compositions. The **frame** is generally exploited to suggest a limited, self-sufficient universe which encloses all the necessary visual information. See **open forms.**

Close-up, Close shot. A detailed view of a person or object, usually without much context provided. A close-up of an actor generally includes only his head.

Content curve. The amount of time necessary for the average viewer to assimilate most of the major information of **a shot.**

Continuity. The kind of logic implied in the association of ideas between **edited shots.** "Cutting to continuity" emphasizes smooth transitions between shots, in which space and time are unobtrusively condensed. "**Classical cutting**" emphasizes dramatic or emotional logic between shots rather than one based strictly on considerations of time and space. In "**thematic montage**" the continuity is based entirely on ideas, irrespective of literal time and space. In some instances, "continuity" refers to the space-time continuum of reality before it is photographed.

Convention. A tacit agreement between the viewer and artist to accept certain necessary artificialities as real in a work of art. In film, **editing** —or the juxtaposition of **shots**—is accepted as "logical," even though a viewer's perception of reality is continuous and unfragmented.

Cover shots. General **shots** of an event photographed to be used **in editing** to insure a smooth **continuity** in the event that the anticipated continuity will not cut as planned.

Crane shot. A shot taken from a special device called a **crane,** which resembles a huge mechanical arm. The crane carries the camera and cameraman, and can move in virtually any direction.

Cross cutting. The alternating of **shots** from two **sequences,** often in different locales, to suggest the sequences are taking place simultaneously.

Cutting. See **Editing.**

Cutting to continuity. A type of **editing** in which the **shots** are arranged in such a manner as to preserve the fluidity of an action without showing all of it. An unobtrusive condensation of a continuous action. See **continuity, classical cutting, thematic montage.**

Dadaism. An **avant-garde** movement in the arts stressing unconscious elements, irrationalism, irreverent wit, and spontaneity. Dadaist films were produced mostly from the later teens to the mid-twenties.

Découpage. From the French, "to cut up." The breakdown of a dramatic action into its constituent **shots.** See **Editing.**

Découpage classique. See **Classical cutting.**

Deep focus. A technique of photography which permits all distance planes to remain clearly in **focus,** from close-up range to infinity.

Direct cinema. See **cinéma vérité.**

Dissolve, lap dissolve. These terms refer to the slow **fading** out of one **shot** and the gradual fading in of its successor, with a superimposition of images, usually at the midpoint.

Dolly shot, tracking shot, trucking shot. A **shot** taken from a moving vehicle. Originally tracks were laid on the set to permit a smoother movement of the camera. Today even a smooth hand-held traveling shot is considered a variation of the dolly shot.

Dominant contrast. That area of the film image which, because of a prominent visual contrast, compels the viewer's most immediate attention. Occasionally the dominant contrast can be aural, in which case the image serves as a temporary **subsidiary contrast.**

Double exposure. The superimposition of two literally unrelated images on film. See **multiple exposure.**

Dubbing. The addition of sound after the visuals have been photographed. Dubbing can be either **synchronous** or **non-synchronous.** Foreign language films are often dubbed in English for release in this country.

Editing. The joining of one **shot** (strip of film) with another. The shots can picture events and objects in different places at different times. Editing is also called **montage.**

Epic. A film **genre** characterized by bold and sweeping themes, usually in heroic proportions. The protagonist is generally an ideal representative of a culture—either national, religious, or regional. The tone of most epics is dignified and the treatment is larger than life.

Establishing shot. Usually an **extreme long** or **long shot** offered at the beginning of a **scene** or **sequence** providing the viewer with the context of the subsequent closer shots.

Experimental cinema. See **poetic cinema.**

Expressionism. A style of filmmaking which distorts time and space as they are ordinarily perceived in reality. Emphasis is placed on the essential characteristics of objects and people, not necessarily on their superficial appearance. Typical expressionist techniques include fragmentary **editing,** a wide variety of **shots** (especially **close-ups**), extreme angles, lighting effects, and distorting **lenses.** See **realism.**

Extreme close-up. A minutely detailed view of an object or a person. An extreme close-up of an actor generally includes only his eyes, or his mouth.

Extreme long shot. A panoramic view of an exterior location, photographed from a great distance, often as far as a quarter-mile away.

Eye-level shot. The placement of the camera approximately 5 to 6 feet from the ground corresponding to the height of an observer on the scene.

Fade. The fade-out is the slow fade of the picture from normal brightness to a black screen. A fade-in is the slow brightening of the picture from a black screen to normal brightness.

Faithful adaptation. A film based on another medium (usually a work of literature) which reflects the original in its essentials, and in which cinematic equivalents are offered for specific literary techniques. Jack Clayton's *The Great Gatsby* is a faithful adaptation of Fitzgerald's novel, for example. See **literal adaptation, loose adaptation.**

Fast motion, accelerated motion. If a subject is photographed at a slower rate than 24 frames per second, when it is projected at the standard rate of 24 fps, it will appear to be moving at a faster rate than normal. The movements will often seem jerky. See **slow motion.**

Fast stock, fast film. Film **stock** that is highly sensitive to light and generally produces a grainy image. Used often by documentarists who wish to shoot only with **available lighting.** See **slow stock.**

Filters. Pieces of glass or plastic placed in front of the **lens** which change the quality of the light entering the camera.

Final cut. The sequence of **shots** in a movie as it will be released to the public. See **rough cut.**

First cut. The initial sequence of **shots** in a movie, often constructed by the director. Also called "rough cut."

First person point of view. See **point-of-view shot.**

Fish-eye lens. An extreme **wide angle lens,** which distorts the image so radically that the edges seem wrapped into a sphere.

Flashback. An **editing** technique that suggests the interruption of the present by a shot or series of shots representing the past.

Flash-editing, flash-cutting. **Editing** sequences so that the durations of the shots are very brief.

Flash-forward. An **editing** technique that suggests the interruption of the present by a shot or series of shots representing the future.

Flash pan. See **Swish pan.**

Focus. The degree of acceptable sharpness and clarity in a film image. "Out of focus" means the images are blurred and lack acceptable linear definition.

Footage. Exposed film **stock.**

Frame. The dividing line between the edges of the screen image and the enclosing darkness of the theatre. "Frame" can also refer to a single photograph from the filmstrip.

Freeze frame, freeze shot. A shot composed of a single **frame** that is reprinted a number of times on the filmstrip which when projected gives the illusion of a still photograph.

Full shot. A type of **long shot** which includes the human body in full, with the head near the top of the frame and the feet near the bottom.

Genre. A recognizable *type* of film which depends on certain established **conventions.** The most common American genres are westerns, thrillers, musicals, and historical spectaculars.

High angle shot. A **shot** in which the subject is photographed from above.

High contrast. A style of lighting emphasizing harsh shafts and dramatic streaks of lights and darks. Often used in tragedies and melodramas. See **high key.**

High key. A style of lighting emphasizing bright, even illumination, with few conspicuous shadows. Used generally in comedies, musicals, and light entertainment films. See **high contrast, low key.**

Homage. A direct or indirect reference within a movie to another movie, filmmaker, or cinematic style. A respectful and affectionate tribute.

Independent cinema. See **underground films.**

Intrinsic interest. An unobtrusive area of the film image which nonetheless compels the viewer's most immediate attention because of its dramatic or contextual importance. An object of intrinsic interest will take precedence over the formal **dominant contrast.** See also **subsidiary contrast.**

Iris. A **masking** device that blacks out a portion of the screen permitting only a part of the image to be seen. Usually the iris is circular or oval shaped, and can be expanded and contracted.

Jump cut. An abrupt transition between **shots,** sometimes deliberate, which is disorienting in terms of the **continuity** of time and space.

Kinetic. Pertaining to motion and movement.

Leftist. A political term used to describe the acceptance, at least, in part, of the economic, social and philosophical ideas of Karl **Marx.**

Lens. A ground or molded piece of glass, plastic, or other transparent material through which light rays are refracted so that they converge or diverge to form the photographic image within the camera.

Literal adaptation. A film usually based on a stage play, in which the dialogue and actions are preserved more or less intact, though subtly altered by the film director's uniquely cinematic techniques, like **editing** and **mise-en-scène.** Mike Nichols' *Who's Afraid of Virginia Woolf* is a "literal adaptation" of Albee's play. See **Faithful adaptation, loose adaptation.**

Long lens. See **telephoto lens.**

Long shot. Includes an amout of picture within the **frame** which roughly corresponds to the audience's view of the area within the proscenium arch of the legitimate theatre.

Long take. A **shot** of lengthy duration.

Loose adaptation. A film based on another medium (usually a work of literature) in which only a vague general resemblance exists between the two versions of the subject. For example, Akira Kurosawa's *Throne of Blood* is an independent reworking of some of the characters and situations found in Shakespeare's *Macbeth.* See **Faithful adaptation, literal adaptation.**

Loose framing. Usually in longer **shots.** The **mise-en-scène** is so spaciously distributed that the subject photographed has considerable latitude of movement. See **tight framing, open forms.**

Low angle shot. A **shot** in which the subject is photographed from below.

Low key. A style of lighting emphasizing diffused shadows and atmospheric pools of light. Often used in mysteries, thrillers, and *films noir*. See **high key.**

Marxist. Any person who subscribes to the economic, social, political, and philosophical theories of Karl Marx. Any artistic work which reflects these same biases.

Master shot. A single uninterrupted **shot,** usually taken from a **long** or **full shot** range, which contains an entire scene. Later, the closer **shots** are photographed, and an **edited** sequence, composed of a variety of different shots, is subsequently constructed on the editor's bench.

Masking. A technique whereby a portion of the movie image is blocked out, thus temporarily altering the dimensions of the screen's **aspect ratio.**

Medium shot. A relatively **close shot,** revealing a moderate amount of detail. A medium shot of a figure generally includes the body from the knees or waist up.

Metaphor. A technique involving a comparison between two otherwise unlike elements, meaningful in a **figurative** rather than literal sense. See **symbol.**

Metteur-en-scène. The artist or technician who creates the **mise-en-scène—** that is, the director. Used pejoratively, this term can refer to a timid director who does not impose his personal vision on his materials, but merely stages the action, not bothering with anything else.

Mickeymousing. A type of film music which is purely descriptive and attempts to reproduce the visual action with musical equivalents.

Minimalism. A style of filmmaking characterized by austerity and restraint in which all cinematic elements are reduced to the barest minimum of information.

Mise-en-scène. The arrangement of volumes and movements within a given space. In the cinema, the space is defined by the **frame;** in the legitimate theatre, usually by the proscenium arch.

Montage. Transitional sequences of rapidly **edited** images, used to suggest the lapse of time or the passing of events. Often employs **dissolves** and **multiple exposures.** In Europe "montage" means **editing.** See also **thematic montage.**

Motif. Any unobtrusive technique, object, or thematic idea that is systematically repeated throughout a film.

Multiple exposure. A special effect, generally produced by the **optical printer,** which permits the superimposition of many images simultaneously. See **double exposure.**

Negative image. The reversal of lights and darks of the subject photographed: blacks are white and whites are black.

Neorealism. An Italian film movement which produced its best works between 1945 and 1955. Strongly **realistic** in its technical biases, neorealism emphasized the **documentary** aspects of film art, stressing loose episodic plots, unextraordinary events and characters, natural lighting, actual location settings, nonprofessional actors, a preoccupation with poverty and social problems, and an emphasis on humanistic and democratic ideals. The term has also been used to describe other films which reflect the technical and stylistic biases of Italian neorealism.

New American cinema. See **underground film.**

New wave, *nouvelle vague.* A group of young French movie directors who came to prominence during the late 1950s. The most widely known are Jean-Luc Godard, François Truffaut, Claude Chabrol, and Alain Resnais.

Non-synchronous sound. Sound and image are not recorded simultaneously, or the sound is detached from its source in the film image. Music, for example, is usually non-synchronous in a movie.

Oblique angle. A **shot** which is photographed by a tilted camera. When the image is projected on the screen, the subject itself seems to be tilted on its side.

Omniscient point of view. In literature, this refers to an all-knowing narrator, who provides the reader with all the necessary information. Most movies are omnisciently narrated by a camera.

Open forms. Used primarily by **realist** film directors, these techniques are likely to be subtle and unobtrusive, with an emphasis on informal compositions and apparently haphazard designs. The **frame** generally is exploited to suggest a temporary masking which arbitrarily cuts off part of the action. See **closed forms, loose framing.**

Optical printer. An elaborate mechanical device used to create special effects in a film print. For example, **fades, dissolves, multiple exposures.**

Overexposure. Too much light enters the aperture of a camera **lens,** blanching the image. Useful for fantasy and nightmare scenes.

Over-the-shoulder shot. A **medium shot,** useful in dialogue scenes, in which one actor is photographed head-on from over the shoulder of another actor.

Pan, panning shot. Short for "panorama," this is a revolving horizontal movement of the camera from left to right or vice versa.

Parallel editing. See **cross cutting.**

Pixillation. Also called "stop motion photography," this is an **animation** technique involving the photographing of live actors **frame** by frame. When the sequence is projected at the standard speed of 24 fps, the actors move abruptly and jerkily, suggesting primitive cartoon figures.

Poetic cinema. A term used to describe **avant-garde** movies, especially those produced in the 1940s and early 1950s in the United States. See **underground film.**

Point-of-view shot. Any shot which is taken from the vantage point of a character in the film. Also known as the first person camera.

Proxemic patterns. The spatial relationships between organisms within a given area. In film, the phrase can refer to the spatial relationships among characters within the mise-en-scène, or to the apparent distance of the camera from the subject photographed.

Psychological film. An approach to filmmaking emphasizing internal personal conflicts rather than sweeping social events. Frequent use is made of **close shots** which exploit the human face as a barometer of subtle emotions and ideas.

Pull-back dolly. A technique used to surprise the viewer by withdrawing from a scene to reveal an object or character that was previously out of the **frame.** See **dolly shot.**

Rack focusing, selective focusing. The blurring of focal planes in sequence, forcing the viewer's eye to "travel" with those areas of an image that remain in sharp **focus.**

Reaction pan. Similar to a **reaction shot,** only instead of cutting, the director pans to a character's response.

Reaction shot. A cut to a **shot** of a character's reaction to the contents of the preceding shot.

Realism. A style of filmmaking which attempts to preserve the space-time continuum by emphasizing **long shots,** lengthy takes, eye-level camera placement, and a minimum of **editing** and special effects photography. See **expressionism.**

Re-establishing shot. A return to an initial **establishing** shot within a scene, acting as a reminder to the viewer of the physical context of the closer shots.

Reverse angle shot. A shot taken from an angle 180° opposed to the previous shot—that is, the camera is placed opposite its previous position.

Reverse motion. A series of images are photographed with the film reversed. When projected normally, the effect is to suggest backward movement—an egg "returning" to its shell, for example.

Rough cut. The crudely **edited** total footage of a film before the editor has tightened up the slackness between shots. A kind of rough draft of the finished "final cut" print. See **final cut.**

Scene. A unit of film composed of a number of interrelated **shots,** unified usually by a central concern—a location, an incident, or a minor dramatic climax. See **sequence, shot.**

Selective focusing. See **rack focusing.**

Semiology, semiotics. A theory of cinematic communication which studies signs or **symbolic** codes as the minimal units of signification. Influenced by the methodology and theory of structural linguistics, semiological theories are descriptive rather than normative, and are concerned with the systematic identification and classification of cinematic signs.

Sequence. A unit of film generally composed of a number of interrelated **scenes,** and leading to a major climax. See **scene, shot.**

Set-up. The positioning of the camera and lights for a specific **shot.**

Short lens. See **Wide angle lens.**

Shot. Those images which are recorded continuously from the time the camera starts to the time it stops. That is, an unedited, uncut strip of film. See **scene, sequence.**

Slow motion. Shots of a subject photographed at a faster rate than 24 fps, which when projected at the standard rate produce a dreamy, graceful, dance-like slowness of action. See **fast motion.**

Slow stock, slow film. Film stocks that are relatively insensitive to light and produce images of great crispness and sharpness of detail. Used in interior settings these stocks generally require considerable artificial illumination. See **fast stock**.

Socialist realism. A **Marxist** theory of art, strongly propagandistic in its emphasis, stressing the need for the artist to portray a scientifically verifiable picture of reality which exists independently of the artist. Also known as the "Stalin School" of art, Socialist Realism was the official artistic style of the Soviet Union and the Communist Eastern European nations from the early 1930s to the mid-1950s.

Soft focus. The blurring out of **focus** of all except one desired distance range. Can also refer to a glamorizing technique which softens the sharpness of linear definition so that facial wrinkles can be smoothed over and even eliminated.

Star. A film actor or actress of great popularity who tends to play only those roles that fit a preconceived public image, as opposed to a straight actor who plays roles of great variety. John Wayne is a star, Dustin Hoffman is a straight actor. The term "star" can also refer more generally to any performer who enjoys great popularity and prestige within the industry.

Stock. The raw unexposed **footage** of a film. There are many types of movie stocks, including those highly sensitive to light ("**fast**"), and those relatively insensitive to light ("**slow**").

Structuralism, cine-structuralism. Cinematic theories employing various **semiological** methods to determine how complexly and artistically certain codes and signs are synthesized in a single film, a **genre**, or the *oeuvre* of a filmmaker.

Subjective camera. See **point-of-view shot**.

Subsidiary contrast. A subordinated element of the film image, complementing or contrasting with the **dominant contrast**.

Sub-text. A term used in drama and film to signify the dramatic implications beneath the language of a play or movie. Often the sub-text concerns ideas and emotions that are totally independent of the language of a text.

Surrealism. An **avant-garde** movement in the arts stressing Freudian and Marxist ideas, unconscious elements, irrationalism, and a **symbolic** association of ideas. Surrealist movies were produced roughly from 1924 to 1931, though there are still surrealist elements in the works of many directors, most notably Fellini, Buñuel, and Godard.

Swish pan. Also known as a flash or zip pan, a swish pan is a horizontal movement of the camera around its axis at such a rapid rate that the subject photographed blurs on the screen.

Synchronous sound. The agreement or correspondence between image and sound, which are recorded simultaneously, or seem so in the finished print. Synchronous sounds appear to derive from an obvious source in the visuals. See **non-synchronous sound**.

Symbol. A figurative device in which an object, event, or cinematic technique has a significance in addition to its literal meaning. Symbolism is always determined by the dramatic context: a raging fire between two lovers, for example, can symbolize sexual passion. Otherwise a fire is just a fire, unless the context suggests other symbolic ideas.

Take. A variation of a specific **shot.** The final shot is often selected from a number of possible takes.

Telephoto lens, long lens. A **lens** which acts as a telescope, magnifying the size of objects at a great distance. A significant side effect is its tendency to flatten perspective.

Thematic montage. A style of **editing** in which the connections between shots are determined on the basis of their intellectual associations, irrespective of literal time and space. Popularized by the Soviet directors, most notably Sergei Eisenstein. See **classical cutting, cutting to continuity.**

Third person point of view. In literature, a non-participating narrator who provides the reader with all the emotions and ideas of one central character. In movies, a loose equivalent of this form of narration is a **shot** or series of shots of the protagonist.

Three-shot. A **medium shot,** featuring three actors.

Tight framing. Usually in **close shots.** The **mise-en-scène** is so carefully balanced and harmonized that the subject photographed has little or no freedom of movement. See **loose framing.**

Tracking shot, trucking shot. See **dolly shot.**

Two-shot. A **medium shot,** featuring two actors.

Underground films. An **avant-garde** movement which began in the United States around 1954, emphasizing film as pure form, and the filmmaker's self-expression over considerations of subject matter alone. Mostly short, non-narrative movies.

Vignetting. A technique used to round off the corner edges of a movie image with a soft blurring effect, sometimes by using **masking** devices.

Wide angle lens, short lens. A **lens** which permits the camera to photograph a wider area than a normal lens. A significant side effect is its tendency to exaggerate perspective. Also used for **deep-focus** photography.

Widescreen, also **CinemaScope** and **scope.** A movie image which has an **aspect ratio** of approximately 5 by 3, though some widescreens possess horizontal dimensions that extend as wide as 2.5 times the vertical dimensions.

Wipe. An **editing** device, usually a line which travels across the screen, "pushing off" one image and revealing another.

Zip pan. See **swish pan.**

Zoom lens. A lens of variable focal length which permits the cameraman to change from **wide angle** to **telephoto shots** (and vice versa) in one continuous movement.

Zoom shot. A shot taken with the aid of a **zoom lens.** The lens changes focal length during the shot so that a **dolly** or **crane** shot is suggested.

index